DATE DUE

The Therapeutic Community

George De Leon, Ph.D., is an internationally recognized expert in the treatment of substance abuse and is acknowledged as the leading authority on research in therapeutic communities. He is the director of the *Center for Therapeutic Community Research,* funded by the *National Institute on Drug Abuse (NIDA),* and Clinical Professor of Psychiatry at *New York University.* In addition to numerous research publications, Dr. De Leon has made notable contributions in the area of clinical practice and professional education. He provides training in therapeutic community practice to psychiatric fellows, psychologists, nurses, social workers, and other health care professionals in treatment programs. He is also project coordinator for *Therapeutic Communities of America* in developing national standards for accreditation of therapeutic community programs in correctional settings. He is on the advisory board of the *American Academy of Health Care Providers in the Addictive Disorders* and a member of the *Expert Advisory Committee on Chemical Dependency of the American Psychological Association College of Professional Psychology.* He is a founding member of the *New York State Psychological Association's Division on Addictions,* as well as a founding member and past president of the *American Psychological Association's Division 50 on Addictions.*

Dr. De Leon is a recipient of several awards. The most notable are the Therapeutic Communities of America award for Distinguished Service (1978); the Eugenia Maria De Hostos and Jose Marti award for dedication and contribution to the field of psychology presented by the New York Society of Clinical Psychologists (1984); the award for Distinguished Service to Psychology (1990) presented by the Society of Psychologists in Addictive Behaviors (SPAB), and the 1993 NIDA Pacesetter Award for Outstanding Leadership in Pioneering Research on the Therapeutic Community Approach to Drug Abuse Treatment. He has maintained a private clinical practice in New York City for over 30 years.

The Therapeutic Community

Theory, Model, and Method

George De Leon, PhD

 Springer Publishing Company

Springer Publishing Company, Inc.
536 Broadway
New York, NY 10012-3955

Acquisitions Editor: Bill Tucker
Production Editor: Barbara Beard Trocco
Cover design by James Scotto-Lavino

00 01 02 03 04 / 5 4 3 2 1

Library of Congress Cataloging-in-Publication Data

De Leon, George
    The therapeutic community: theory, model, and method / George De Leon.
      p. cm.
    Includes bibliographical references and index.
    ISBN 0-8261-1349-4 (hardcover)
      1. Therapeutic communities. 2. Substance abuse--Treatment. I. Title.

RC489.T67 D42 2000
362.29'186--dc21

99-089660
CIP

Printed in the United States of America

For Nancy, Joshua, Giovanna, Ariel, and Alexa

Contents

PART I   *Introduction*

PART II   *The Perspective and Approach*

PART III   *The Model*

PART V   *The Process of Change*

Tables and Figures

Figures

Tables

Acknowledgments

This book reflects my intimate involvement with therapeutic communities for more than thirty years primarily as researcher but also as trainer, teacher, and program developer. Although it represents my own attempt to formulate the therapeutic community in terms of theory and method, the influences on my thinking are many. My earliest conversations about the curative elements of the therapeutic community were with a lifelong friend, Zev Putterman, who invited me to participate in a Synanon encounter group in New York in 1962. This led me to weekly Integrity Therapy groups during 1963/1964, facilitated by O. H. Mowrer at Daytop Village on Staten Island, N.Y., a therapeutic community program then under the creative directorship of David Deitch.

Throughout my long affiliation as director of research with one of the earliest and distinguished therapeutic community agencies, Phoenix House, theoretical and clinical discussions were continually ongoing in seminars, rap sessions, workshops, and almost daily conversations. My colleagues in these exchanges were the residents, the clinical staff, facility directors, and agency heads, some of whom are especially notable: David Deitch (later at Phoenix House), Rae Dibble, Tony Endre, Gary Guttierre, Jack Hurst, Howie Josepher, Julio Martinez, Kevin McEneaney, Frank Natale, Mitchell Rosenthal, and Ron Williams. These dialogues informed the first curriculum of therapeutic community essential elements, which I outlined for staff training at Phoenix House in the period 1979–1984.

In subsequent years, the essential elements were further elaborated into theory and method through research findings, staff training sessions, and in discussions with those in the field throughout the world. Some individuals who were particularly helpful in this stage of the process were

Arne Andresen, Naya Arbiter, Eric Broekaert, Charles Devlin, Bob Galea, Maxwell Jones, David Kerr, Martien Kooyman, David Mactas, Robert Millman, Rod Mullen, Msg. William O'Brien, Donald Ottenberg, Martha Ottenberg, Richard Pruss, Dwayne Simpson, Anthony Slater, Peter Vamos, and Charles Winick.

A number of others have directly helped this book project. Donna Boundy, Barry Brown, Patrick Flynn, Herb Reich, and Joan Zweben provided valuable critiques of the manuscript. My coworkers at the Center for Therapeutic Community Research (CTCR) served as audience, reactors, and readers of drafts; they include Elaine Abraham, Robert Hilton, David Kressel, Doug Lipton, Gerald Melnick, Stanley Sacks, Fred Streit, Fred Tent, Harry Wexler, and my executive assistants, Sally Howard and particularly, Hulya Sakarya, who has been responsible for the preparation of the manuscript.

Special gratitude is owed to my friend and colleague, Allan Bernhardt, whose clinical thinking contributed to this work. Nancy Jainchill, my colleague and spouse, has been a continual source of intellectual and emotional support, as well as a tireless reviewer of materials.

I wish also to recognize three organizations, Therapeutic Communities of America (TCA), which is the national association of North American programs, the National Institute on Drug Abuse (NIDA), and the National Development and Research Institutes (NDRI). As a member of TCA, as well as serving as its director of research and training for two years, I had welcome access to the wide diversity of programs and residents. NIDA's commitment to therapeutic community research helped to establish the scientific credibility of the modality as a bona fide social and psychological treatment approach. NIDA's funding of my own studies over twenty-five years provided me with an uninterrupted opportunity to acquire the experiences and information needed for this project. Some key people formerly and currently associated with NIDA who deserve special mention are George Beschner, Barry Brown, Eleanor Carroll, Robert Dupont, Arthur M. Horton, Jerome Jaffe, Alan Leshner, Richard Millstein, Charles Schuster, and Frank Tims. For the past eleven years, NDRI has been the congenial home for my research on therapeutic communities.

Lastly, I must extend my respect to the numerous un-named, but not unremembered, residents in therapeutic communities whose recovery and personal change are the prima facie evidence for the validity of the therapeutic community method and an inspiration for writing this book.

George De Leon, Ph.D.
Center for Therapeutic Community Research at *NDRI, Inc.*, New York City

PART I

Introduction

The therapeutic community (TC) for addictions descends from historical prototypes found in all forms of communal healing. Inevitably, however, such alternative communities disappear; they dissolve through irrelevancy, mutate through cooption, or become diluted by assimilation. The thesis of this book is that the contemporary TC challenges the fate of its historical prototypes. As a hybrid, spawned from the union of self-help and public support, the TC is an experiment in progress, reconfiguring the vital healing and teaching ingredients of self-help communities into a systematic methodology for transforming lives.

The background for this thesis is the subject of the introductory material in part I. The initial chapter outlines the current issues in the evolution of the TC that compel the need for a comprehensive formulation of its perspective and approach. Chapter 2 explores the sources of this formulation. It traces the essential elements of the TC and organizes these into the social and psychological framework, detailed throughout the volume as theory, model, and method.

Chapter 1

Therapeutic Communities: Evolution and the Need for Theory

The therapeutic community (TC) has proven to be a powerful treatment approach for substance abuse and related problems in living. The TC is fundamentally a self-help approach, evolved primarily outside of mainstream psychiatry, psychology, and medicine. Today, however, the TC is a sophisticated human services modality, as evident in the range of its services, the diversity of the population served, and the developing body of TC-related research.

Currently, TC agencies in the United States serve thousands of individuals and families yearly (The 1996-97 TCA Membership Report, 1997). TC clients are a diverse group: individuals whose drug histories consist of an ever-expanding menu of drugs and who, in addition to chemical abuse, often present complex social and psychological problems.

The TC's basic approach of treating the whole person through the use of the peer community, which was initially developed to address substance abuse, has been amplified with a variety of additional services related to family, education, vocational training, and medical and mental health. Staff compositions have been altered to include an increasing proportion of traditional mental health, medical, and educational professionals serving alongside the recovered paraprofessionals (Carroll & Sobel, 1986; Winick, 1990-1991).

The traditional TC stay of 12–18 months has evolved from planned durations of stay of 2–3 years (Cole & James, 1975). Recent changes in client population, clinical realities, and funding requirements have encouraged the development of modified residential TCs with shorter durations of stay (3, 6, and 12 months), as well as TC-oriented day treatment models (e.g., Karson & Gesumaria, 1997; Lewis, McCusker, Hindin, Frost, & Garfield, 1993). In addition, correctional facilities and

3

community residences and shelters, overwhelmed with alcohol and drug abuse problems among clients, have implemented modified TC programs within their institutional boundaries (De Leon, 1997a; Jainchill, 1997; Wexler & Williams, 1986). Some educational programs have incorporated basic elements of the TC's drug-free philosophy and view of "right living" into their programs (e.g., Bratter, Bratter, Bratter, Maxym, & Steiner, 1997; Moberg & Thaler, 1995).

Research into the TC has also increased significantly since 1976 when the National Institute on Drug Abuse (NIDA) organized the first Therapeutic Communities of America (TCA) planning conference, including a panel of only six researchers (De Leon & Beschner, 1977). In contrast, the 1992 TCA planning conference included some 20 researchers and a program with a considerable number of scientific papers and symposia (Proceedings of the TCA Conference, 1994).

Although not quantitatively analysed, the increase in TC-related research is evident in several indicators: (a) the number of published studies in American journals collated in bibliographies and reviews of TC research (e.g., De Leon, 1985; De Leon & Ziegenfuss, 1986; Tims, De Leon, & Jainchill, 1994); (b) the number of federally funded TC-related grants and contracts and TC agencies themselves that receive grants; and (c) perhaps the most convincing indicator of the developing status of TC research, the existence of the NIDA-funded Center for Therapeutic Community Research (CTCR) at National Development and Research Institutes (NDRI), the first such center exclusively devoted to studies of a specific treatment modality (Millstein, 1994).[1]

ISSUES OF EVOLUTION

The evolution of the TC reveals the vigor, resourcefulness, and flexibility of the TC modality to expand and adapt to change. However, the evolution of the TC also contains a number of issues that provide the fundamental rationale for the present volume.

The Wide Diversity of TCs

The adaptation of the TC to different settings and different populations has resulted in a proliferation of programs with unique treatment protocols

---

[1] For example, activities relevant to the present volume are supported in part by NIDA center grant 5P50 07700.

and varied durations of stay. Even the long-term traditional model is variously implemented. The range and extent to which these adapted programs retain the basic elements of the TC model is not known. Moreover, this wide diversity of programs makes it difficult to evaluate the general effectiveness of the TC modality and underscores the need for defining the essential elements of the TC model and method.

The TC Treatment Process is Not Understood

Although much is known about *whether* TCs work in terms of successful outcomes, less is understood as to why and *how* TCs work. The link between treatment elements, treatment experiences, and treatment outcomes must be established to firmly substantiate the specific contribution of the TC to long-term recoveries. Moreover, illuminating the treatment process is essential for improving the TC treatment itself. Thus, wise modification of the approach must be guided by an understanding of the active "ingredients" in the treatment model, the course of recovery, and the complexity of individual change.

The TC Approach has been Conveyed Orally

Teaching the TC approach has been primarily accomplished in the oral tradition. The model and method of the TC emerged from the trial and error experience of its first participants creating and managing their own self-help communities. Since then, three generations of participant workers, or "paraprofessionals," have learned the TC approach, primarily through personal experience and apprenticeship. This oral tradition, while an essential and intimate mode of communication in the TC, has limited the broader application of the TC approach.

The Limits of Personal Experience

In the course of the last 30 years, many of the daily activities of the treatment programs have hardened into habits and routines. This reflects the fact that the fundamental therapeutic and educational reasons underlying these activities are often unclear to the participants. Why the TC does what it does is often understood only from personal experience: "It worked for me," or "That's how it was when I came through," or simply, "That's the way things are done."

The knowledge gained exclusively from the experience of personal recovery and program ritual tends to remain static, unresponsive to individual differences or circumstantial change. A conceptual or theoretical understanding of the TC approach is therefore essential to adapt its principles and practices for the greater diversity of clients entering treatment today.

Call for a Return to TC Basics

Successive generations of staff who have recovered in TCs have become quite removed from the original roots of the approach. This has contributed to a progressive weakening in the application of clinical methods and tools of the TC and laxity in maintaining the structure of the traditional program. In response to these negative developments, there has been a call for training in the "basics" of the TC (Blieland, Geralamino, & Smock, 1990). In this regard, an explicit theoretical framework is needed which defines, conceptualizes, and illustrates the basics of the TC. Indeed, such a framework could facilitate the development of a consensus in the field as to the basic principles and methods of the TC.

Increasing Numbers of Professional Staff

There are increasing numbers of conventional professional staff (social workers, nurses, psychologists, etc.) working in TCs. Based on their education and professional training, they introduce various concepts, language, and methods that often counter or subvert the fundamental self-help features of the TC. An explicit theoretical framework can provide a common perspective for training *both* professional and paraprofessional staff so that they can be united in their approach to treatment.

Counselor Certification

The sophistication of the TC is evident in the fact that Therapeutic Communities of America (TCA) has established criteria and procedures for evaluating counselors and certifying their competency (Kerr, 1986). However, a theoretical framework organizing the knowledge base of TCs is needed to strengthen the professionalism of TC staff. Clear theory and methods can help define the wide range of skills, competencies, and information that workers must possess to be effective within the TC.[2]

---

[2] Specifically, material in the present volume has facilitated the development of curricula and procedures for staff training and education in the TC model and methods. Requests for further information should be forwarded to the author at the Center for Therapeutic

Program Accreditation and Quality Assurance

Many drug treatment programs label themselves TCs. Whether these are valid TC models is often unclear. Thus, there are pragmatic reasons for developing standards for TC programs: to maintain quality assurance and best practices, to guide staff training, and to evaluate the effectiveness and cost benefit of TC treatment. A theoretical framework of the essential elements of the TC is needed to facilitate the development of program standards for formal accreditation and licensure efforts.

Misperceptions

The traditional TC has been perceived by those on the outside in many ways, both positively and negatively, often without sufficient information. Given its history as an unconventional, "alternative" treatment approach dating back to the early 1960s, there is a particular need to accurately portray the contemporary TC as effective, safe, and credible. An explicit account of the perspective, rationales, principles, and methods underlying the TC approach could help correct some of these misperceptions and provide a more balanced picture of the TC's place in a spectrum of human services.

The above issues of evolution have defined the general purpose of this volume—the delineation of the TC approach as a theory, model, and method. The volume's aims, however, are several: to communicate the essentials of the approach to those within and outside of the TC, to facilitate staff training based upon a codification of TC, to serve as a catalyst for the continued refinement of the TC method and model, and to stimulate research into the TC process.

THEORY AND TCS

Contrary to the myth that TCs are anti-intellectual, most contemporary programs are intellectually open-minded and receptive to new information and ideas. Indeed, good programs thrive on information, viewing intellectual expansion as essential to personal growth and recovery. It is not new information but *abstract* formulations that TCs have questioned

Community Research (CTCR) at NDRI, Inc., 2 World Trade Center, 16th Floor, New York, NY 10048.

or rejected, often seen by staff as irrelevant to real life inside and outside of the TC.

The present volume presents the author's formulation of the TC as theory, model, and method. It evolved from clinical and research experience obtained primarily in the traditional long-term residential TC. This model still serves as the prototype for the current diversity of TCs, and its effectiveness has been documented (Anglin & Hser, 1990b; Condelli & Hubbard, 1994; De Leon, 1985; Gerstein & Harwood, 1990; Hubbard et al., 1989; Hubbard, Craddock, Flynn, Anderson, & Etheridge, 1997; National Treatment Improvement Evaluation Study [NTIES], 1996; Simpson, Joe, & Brown, 1997; Simpson & Sells, 1982).

The TC is presented in a social and psychological framework. Though not in the jargon of TC participants, the vernacular of this framework has been accepted over the years by TC workers, in my writings and those of others, and to a considerable extent in general TC practice. The concepts, language, and techniques from different schools of psychology and therapy are both present and past influences in the TC. These include psychoanalysis, gestalt therapy, regression therapy, role therapy, conditioning and behavior modification, social learning theory, relapse prevention, and cognitive-emotional therapy, among others. Many of these were discovered or rediscovered in TCs independently of their original sources, while some were, and continue to be, directly introduced to the TC by outside "experts" as TCs widen their scope.

This social and psychological framework formulates the concepts and principles that the TC uses to understand and explain itself. It is broad enough to communicate the extraordinary work of the TC to mainstream education, mental health, and human services professionals, to students, and to the lay reader as well. This is in accordance with the general purpose and specific aims of this volume.[3]

SOME CAVEATS AND LIMITS

Theories and codification of elements and methods seem to inherently contradict the dynamic nature of community life. Some of the more problematical examples of this caveat are briefly noted along with other limits concerning the framework presented.

---

[3] Sugarman makes the distinction between "native theory," the TC as understood by the residents themselves, and formal theory as developed by academic workers (Sugarman, 1974). The present framework reflects both academic and native theoretical properties.

Rigidity

Codification could lead to rigidity in practice. Not infrequently, the flexibility required to accommodate changing problems and individual differences can be hampered by the specifics of the written word. Spontaneous innovative strategies are often inhibited by writings that appear to be doctrinaire or to mandate selected procedures. Thus, codification contains some risk of fostering orthodoxy and rigidity.

Artificiality

TCs do not conceive of themselves analytically nor did they devise their methods from a theoretical plan. In their perspective, individual change results from the global impact of community life. Thus, dismantling the approach into simple elements presents a somewhat artificial picture of TCs. Moreover, the therapeutic and educational features, which are common to most TCs, are implemented in each new setting as a vital process of *re-creating* communities that can heal and teach.

Variability

No two TCs are alike. As separate, self-contained communities, their cultures evolve uniquely. In addition to more obvious differences in client composition, staff experience, program age, size, and resources, differences in beliefs and leadership style may evolve as well. Although traditional TCs are more alike than different, a single theoretical framework cannot actually capture these important nuances in culture, practice, philosophy, and psychological grounding.

Lack of Consensus

The framework presented does not represent a consensus position in the field. Rather, it aims to facilitate such consensus by assisting workers in defining the TC as a model and method for the treatment of substance abuse and related problems in living. The validity of this—or any theoretical framework—lies in how closely it represents clinical and research experience. Its real utility will be measured in how much it stimulates the field to understand and improve itself.

Utilization

Written texts are not substitutes for training and experience. Thus, the present volume should be viewed not as doctrine, but as one *resource* to facilitate staff training and treatment planning and to provide a conceptual balance to experiential learning.

Literature Cited

There are limits as to the literature cited. The explicit aim of the present work is to provide a comprehensive framework of the addiction TC, based upon the clinical and research experience in TC programs. Neither the TC, itself, nor the present framework *derives* from mainstream addiction treatment, social science, psychology, or psychiatry. Although principles and practices from social learning, group process, and psychotherapy are recognizable in the TC, they are not the a priori basis for the present theoretical framework. Thus, reference to the general sociological, psychological, and addiction treatment literature outside of the TC would be distracting to the reader.

The relevant literature is mainly discussed in the initial chapters. These selected citations illustrate general clinical and research support for factual assertions about substance abusers being treated both in and outside TCs. Subsequent chapters undertake an exposition of the present framework that requires relatively few references to literature. These illustrate clinical research and observational support for some of the theoretical assertions in the framework.

Finally, the resident statements in the text that are in quotation or block quoted are for purposes of illustration. They are the author's representations of actual clinical examples recalled through paraphrase, reconstruction, and construction over the years.

CONCLUSION

The successful evolution of the TC for addictions defines the basic rationale for the present volume. An explicit theoretical formulation of the TC is needed to assure the fidelity of its broad application and to retain the distinctive identity of its approach. The proposed theoretical formulation represents a convergence of *the real* and *the ideal* features of TC by clarifying the essential elements of the approach. The sources for these elements are explored in the following chapter.

Chapter 2

In Search of an Essential Therapeutic Community

The *idea* of the therapeutic community (TC) recurs throughout history implemented in different incarnations. Communities that teach, heal, and support appear in religious sects and utopian communes, as well as in spiritual, temperance, and mental health reform movements. Limited expressions of community as "therapy" are also present in various forms of group process and in the self-help groups emerging from the human potential movement.

In its contemporary form, two major variants of the TC have emerged. One, in social psychiatry, consists of innovative units and wards designed for the psychological treatment and management of socially deviant psychiatric patients within (and outside of) mental hospital settings. The other form TCs have taken are as community-based residential treatment programs for addicts and alcoholics. It is the latter with which this chapter and book are concerned.[4]

The addiction treatment TCs, while serving diverse populations of addicts for varied durations of stay, all have similar designs, subscribe to shared assumptions, concepts, and beliefs, and engage in similar practices. These commonalties may be viewed as the *essential elements* of the TC.

Some of these essential elements reflect self-help beliefs, truths, and practices, present in all varieties of social communities that function therapeutically. Others reflect influences directly transmitted from one program to another as the TCs evolved.

---

[4] Kennard (1983) outlines the origins and common attributes of four variants of the TC: the institutional or mental hospital (e.g., Northfield Hospital, England), the democratic-psychoanalytic (e.g., Jones TC, Henderson), the concept-based (e.g., addiction TCs), and the antipsychiatry (e.g., Kingsley Hall).

11

This chapter briefly explores the sources and evolution of these communities to illustrate how they contribute to the theoretical framework of the TC as presented in this volume. In this review, emphasis is on the direct and indirect influences shaping the essential elements of the modern TC.

HISTORICAL SOURCES

Although the addiction TC draws on various sources, both recent and ancient, the term "therapeutic community" is modern. It was first used to describe the psychiatric TCs that emerged in Great Britain during the 1940's. Other than the name, whether or how the British psychiatric TCs influenced the addiction TCs of North America is unclear. However, a brief review of the TC's use in social psychiatry reveals some features generic to all TCs.

The TC in Social Psychiatry

TCs in psychiatric hospitals, pioneered by Jones (1953) and others in the United Kingdom, appeared about 15 years earlier than TCs for addictions in North America. The emergence of the psychiatric TC is often viewed as part of the "third revolution in psychiatry," a shift from the use of individual therapists to a social psychiatric approach stressing multiperson involvement, the use of group methods, milieu therapy, and administrative psychiatry (Kennard, 1983; Main, 1946, 1976; Rapaport, 1960). The name *therapeutic community* evolved in these hospital settings to describe a place "organized as a community in which all are expected to contribute to the shared goals of creating a social organization with healing properties" (Rapaport, 1960, p.10).

The prototypical psychiatric TC was first developed in the social rehabilitation unit at Belmont Hospital (later called Henderson) in England during the mid-1940's. This was a hundred-bed unit geared to treat psychiatric inpatients with long-standing personality disorders. Maxwell Jones and his colleagues have outlined in depth the various features of the psychiatric TC (e.g., Jones, 1953; Rapaport, 1960; Salasnek & Amini, 1971). These features are summarized in Table 2-1.

The general thrust of the Jones TC—the therapeutic nature of the total environment—foreshadows the fundamental concept of community as method in the later addiction TC. The Jones TC has remained a viable model for treating psychiatric patients in hospital settings in Great Britain, other parts of Europe (e.g., Scandinavia and Finland), and to a lesser extent, in the USA (e.g., Gralnick, 1969; Wilmer, 1958). However, its specific adaptation for substance abusers in Europe was implemented with only mixed results (Kooyman, 1993). In the USA, modified versions of the psychiatric TC have been adapted for chemical abusers primarily in Veterans Administration hospital wards (Seidel, Guzman, & Abueg, 1994), although there is little data as to its efficacy for these populations.[5]

TABLE 2-1. Characteristics of the Psychiatric (Jones) Therapeutic Community

- The total organization is seen as affecting therapeutic outcome.
- The social organization is useful for creating a milieu that will maximize therapeutic effects and is not simply the background administration for treatment.
- A core element is democratization: the social environment provides opportunities for patients to take an active part in the affairs of the institution.
- All relationships are potentially therapeutic.
- The qualitative atmosphere of the social environment is therapeutic in that it is balanced between acceptance, control, and tolerance for disruptive activities.
- High value is placed on communication.
- The orientation of the group is toward productive work and a quick return to society.
- Educational techniques and group pressure are used for constructive purposes.
- There is a diffusion of authority from staff to patients.

Source. Adapted from Kennard (1983).

Precursors to the TC for Addictions

To date, there is no comprehensive or in-depth history of addiction TCs, although there is some literature that contains limited surveys of their evolution (Bratter, Bratter, & Heimberg, 1986; Broekaert, Wanderplasschen, Temmerman, Ottenberg, & Kaplan, 1998; Brook & Whitehead, 1980; De Leon, 1985; De Leon & Rosenthal, 1979; De Leon & Ziegenfuss, 1986; Deitch, 1973; Glaser, 1974; Kennard, 1983; Kooyman, 1993; Mowrer, 1977; Slater, 1984). In these writings, TC concepts, beliefs, and practices are traced to indirect influences found in religion, philosophy, psychiatry, and the social and behavioral sciences.[6]

Some suggest that the TC prototype is ancient, present in all forms of communal healing and support (Mowrer, 1977; Slater, 1984). For example, the Dead Sea scrolls at Qumron detail the communal practices

---

[5] There are other successful examples of patient–community models for the mentally ill outside of institutional settings (see, for example, Fairweather, Sanders, Maynard, & Cressler, 1969 and Jansen, 1980).

[6] I am indebted to Michael Slater for providing material on historical sources (Slater, 1984).

of an ascetic religious sect of perhaps Essenes, including a section on the "Rule of the Community." Decrying "the ways of the spirit of falsehood," this Essene code addressed the problems of greed, lying, cruelty, brazen insolence, lust, and "walking in the ways of darkness and guile" (Slater, 1984). Adherence to the rules and teachings of the community was the exhortation in order to live righteously and healthily.

The Essene code of sanctions bears remarkable resemblance to the modern TC. For specific transgressions such as lying, bearing a grudge, foolish speech or laughter, sleeping during a community meeting, or leaving a community meeting, sanctions usually consisted of periods of banishment from the community or restricted rations and privileges. Although considerably harsher than those found in modern TCs, these sanctions are functionally similar in addressing the relationship between the individual and the community.

Reference to the idea of diseases of the soul is also contained in the writings of Philo Judeaus (BC 25 to AD 45) in his description of a group living in Alexandria Egypt. This was a community of healers (*therapeutrides*) of the "incurable" diseases of the soul. They "profess an art of medicine for (excessive) pleasures and appetites...the immeasurable multitude of passions and vices" (Slater, 1984).

Histories of medicine and mental health offer other examples of illnesses of the body or mind that are commonly attributed to disorders of the soul and are approached through spiritual ministrations. Notable in the above references to ancient versions in western literature, however, are two elements that have their parallels in the modern TC for addictions: (a) The disease of the soul is manifested as a disorder of the whole person, characterized particularly by problems in behavioral and emotional self-control; and (b) healing the disease of the soul occurs through some form of community involvement. Similar ideas are contained in the vast literature—both ancient and modern—on eastern philosophy, religion, and medicine.

A GENEALOGY OF THE MODERN ADDICTION TC PROGRAM

The immediate precursors of the modern addiction TCs (also termed "concept" or drug-free TCs) are readily traced through the genealogy of programs that proliferated during the 1960s and 1970s in North America and later in Europe (Brook & Whitehead, 1980; De Leon & Ziegenfuss, 1986; Glaser, 1974; Guydish, Werdegar, Chan, Nebelkopf, & Acampora,

1994; Kooyman, 1993). To a considerable extent the basic elements of contemporary TCs were honed in these programs.

Glaser (1974) traces a conceptual and organizational lineage of the modern TC programs beginning with the Oxford group circa 1921 (also named the Buchmanites, First Century Christian Fellowship, or Moral Rearmament [MRA], the final name) to Alcoholics Anonymous (AA) (circa 1935), Synanon (1958), and Daytop Village (1963).

In the period 1964–1971, TC programs were rapidly spawned directly and indirectly from Synanon and Daytop Village (including Gateway House, Gaudenzia, Marathon House, Odyssey House, and Phoenix House). These and other first generation American TCs were literally seeded or designed by members of one of the "parent" programs, directly transmitting common elements of the philosophy, social organization, and practices from the original programs to the contemporary TCs. However, the direct *sources* of many of the essential elements are attributable to three notable precursors: the Oxford group, AA, and Synanon. The contribution of each is outlined below.

The Oxford Group

The Oxford group (sometimes labeled a movement) was a religious organization founded in the second decade of this century by Frank Buchman, a Lutheran evangelical minister. Its initial name, First Century Christian Fellowship, conveyed its basic message—a return to the purity and innocence of the early church. The Oxford mission for the spiritual rebirth of Christians broadly accommodated all forms of human suffering. Although not a primary focus, mental illness and alcoholism as signs of spiritual erosion were within the purview of the movement.

Frank Buchman and Dr. Samuel Shoemaker, an Episcopal clergyman at the Calvary Episcopal Church in New York (headquarters of the Oxford world movement), were influenced by the Quakers and Anabaptists, who were also precursors to the Mennonites and Amish. These early religious influences on the Oxford group and AA reappear as elements of the modern TC. Some of the commonly held ideas and practices include the work ethic, mutual concern, sharing guidance, and evangelical values of honesty, purity, unselfishness and love, self-examination, acknowledgement of character defects, making restitution for harm done, and working with others (Ray, 1999; Wilson, 1957).[7]

---

[7] Today the influence of the Oxford movement on recovering individuals persists through a self-run and self-supported housing initiative begun in Silver Spring, Maryland in 1975.

Alcoholics Anonymous (AA)

AA was founded in 1935 in Akron, Ohio by two recovering alcoholics, Bill Wilson (Bill W.), a New York stockbroker, and Dr. Bob Smith (Bob S.), an Akron physician. The history of AA and full expositions of the 12-step principles and traditions are well-described in the literature, most notably in *Alcoholics Anonymous Comes of Age: A Brief History of AA*, written by Bill Wilson in 1957.[8]

The influence of the Oxford group on AA is associated with particular individuals. Rowland H., an alcoholic whose recovery was sustained by religious conversion in the Oxford group (housed at the Episcopal church of Rev. Dr. Sam Shoemaker in New York), made it his personal mission to save other alcoholics. One of his converts was Ebby T., who attempted to help Bill W., an old drinking compatriot in late 1934, by speaking of religion and the Oxford ideas. However, it was during a subsequent hospitalization for drying out that Bill W. experienced a spiritual awakening grounded in maintaining sobriety, reportedly influenced by William James's volume *Varieties of Religious Experiences* (Slater, 1984).

During a subsequent business trip to Akron, Bill W. experienced a compulsive craving for a drink. Henrietta Sieberling, associated with the Oxford group in Akron, offered Bill W. the name of Bob S., another alcoholic. The conversation between the two men was a founding moment for AA. The experience of mutual sharing launched their own mission to help other alcoholics.

The 12 steps and 12 traditions of AA are the principles that guide the individual in the recovery process (Emrick, 1999). These emphasize admission of one's loss of control over the substance and a surrender to one's "higher power," self-examination, seeking help from one's higher power in changing one's self, making amends to others, praying in the personal struggle, and helping others to engage in a similar process.

Those principles of AA that stem directly from the Oxford group movement include the notion of confessing to others, making amends, and the conviction that individual change involves conversion to the belief of

---

Members of the initial Oxford House chose to name their group after the Oxford Movement (see Malloy, 1992).

[8] A nineteenth century antecedent to AA was a group called the Washingtonians, founded by several recovering drinkers. Although this movement eventually died out, it contained some elements that later appeared in TCs, including a pledge of abstinence, proselytizing its message to others, and the practice of self-appraisal during group meetings (see Deitch, 1973).

the group. However, AA departs from Oxford's orientation toward a religious god as the spiritual source of higher power. The individual member of AA could relate privately to his or her *own* concept of a higher power, while the Oxford group member related specifically to a Christian god. Both orientations, however, stress a power greater than the self as the ultimate spiritual source of personal change. The nonsectarian AA orientation is further contrasted in Synanon and later TC teachings, which rely even less on a concept of an external power and more on the self and group process as the source of the individual change.[9]

Synanon

The essential elements of contemporary TCs for addictions—the concepts, program model, and basic practices—first evolved in Synanon, founded in 1958 in Santa Monica, California. A considerable literature documents the history and features of that remarkable program (Casriel, 1966; Endore, 1968; Yablonsky, 1965, 1989*)*.

The founding force of Synanon was Charles ("Chuck") Dederich, a recovering alcoholic, who integrated his AA experiences with other philosophical, pragmatic, and psychological influences to launch and develop the Synanon program. The beginnings were humble and classically self-help. Dederich, along with several AA companions, initiated weekly "free association" groups in his apartment. These evolved into a unique encounter group process ("the game"), which resulted in distinct psychological changes in the participants, including Dederich himself. Participants viewed the groups as a new form of therapy. Within a year the weekly meetings expanded to become a residential community, and in August 1959 the organization was officially founded to treat any substance abuser, regardless of the chemical of choice.[10]

For some 15 years Synanon thrived as an entrepreneurial organization and an innovative treatment program. Although viewed as the prototypical addiction TC, it followed its own evolutionary path outside the national and international TC movement. Its gradual involution, troubled internal organization, and diminishing role in the addictions field over the last

---

[9] Separation of religion and therapy is explicit in North American and western European TCs. Among some TCs in other regions and cultures such as Latin America, religious practice and teachings have been integrated into the daily regimen of TC life.

[10] The name *Synanon* purportedly was adapted from the ramblings of an intoxicated addict who—upon seeking admission to one of the weekly groups—mispronounced the word *seminar.*

three decades are well-described in the literature (Deitch & Zweben, 1980; Yablonsky, 1989).

Synanon and AA

The influences of AA on Synanon are fundamental, although some of the key similarities and differences between the two underscore the evolution of the TC as a distinct approach. Both shared the premise of self-help recovery, a belief that the capacity to heal and change lies in the individual, and that healing occurs primarily through therapeutic relationships with similar others (Anglin, Nugent, & Ng, 1976). The importance of individual and organizational self-reliance and the regular assembly of groups and meetings were direct extensions of AA traditions and program activities.

Although Synanon did not prescribe an explicit 12-step protocol, it did view change in terms of phases having parallels to the AA steps (Anglin, Nugent, & Ng, 1976). For example, early phase recovery in the TC involves breaking through denial and engaging in the change process, which is similar to moving from denial to making the decision to change in AA (Steps 1–3). The intense period of self-examination and socialization that marks the middle phases of the TC process reflects AA's Steps 4–9—which involve taking personal inventory, sharing confession with another person, and making amends. The maturational and increased autonomy expected of individuals in the re-entry phases of the TC reflect to a degree the later steps of AA (Steps 10–12), which insist on continued personal honesty, humbly asking for help to sustain recovery, and actively helping others.

There were also critical *differences* in the Synanon TC, distinguishing it from AA and to a considerable extent defining the addiction TC as a new recovery modality. These concerned the residential setting of the program, its organizational structure, profile of participants, and its goals, philosophy, and ideological orientation.

Setting and organization

The most notable change was the shift from AA's nonresidential setting of regular meetings and groups to the TCs intensive 24-hour residential community, including all the activities of daily living, work, relationships, and recreation, as well as therapeutic groups and community meetings. This was accompanied by a change from a relatively unstructured fellowship to a highly structured hierarchical organization operating residential TCs. Although Synanon retained the AA tradition of fiscal independence, it was entrepreneurially oriented. It developed profit-making businesses and pursued funding from both the public and private sectors. The social organization of the Synanon TC treatment program itself was managed through a hierarchical structure. Although any member of the program could rise to higher levels, all decision making was autocratic, resting in the hands of a few.

Client profiles

The socio-demographic and drug use profile of the membership in Synanon differed from AA. This reflected a change from serving alcoholics exclusively to inclusion of opioid addicts and substance abusers of all kinds. Although statistics are not available, the proportion of non-White minority and female members in Synanon appears to have been markedly higher than in the AA of those times.

The change in client profile and drug use patterns seen in Synanon was particularly significant in the evolution of TCs. It established self-help TCs as a viable treatment option for narcotic addicts and other users of illicit drugs and for socially disenfranchised substance abusers in general. These individuals typically did not find their way to AA. Most were unserved by the conventional medical and mental health systems. Their addictions were either temporarily interrupted in detoxification clinics, on medical wards, through incarceration in jails or prisons, or they ended in death.

Goals

The explicit goal of regular participation in AA meetings was maintaining sobriety. In Synanon and later TCs the explicit goals were psychological and lifestyle change—a process which only *begins* with sobriety. The residential community represented a total social learning environment essentially designed to achieve these goals.

Synanon institutionalized a drug-free prerequisite for participation in the program. Thus, unlike AA meetings, which would include active drinkers, Synanon residents were required to remain chemical free as a condition of participation in the program. Contemporary TCs maintain this cardinal rule of no drug use, although over years their response to violations has become more flexible.

Orientation

A core change in Synanon from AA was its *psychological orientation* to the addiction problem and the personality of the addict, one grounded in the direct experiences of the participants in early group encounters. As elaborated below this psychological emphasis shaped the key elements of the perspective and social organization of early Synanon and later TCs.

Although the basic AA concepts of self-examination and mutual self-help were incorporated in Synanon, the AA emphasis on a spiritual "higher power" was replaced by a secular ideology grounded in existential assumptions about self-determination and individual responsibility. As in AA, the recovering individual was viewed as primarily responsible for self-change through personal commitment and adherence to recovery teachings. For the TC, however, the power of change primarily resides within the individual and is activated through his or her full participation in the peer community.[11]

In TC programs, there is tacit acceptance of a spiritual element in recovery. Respect for cultural differences, religious beliefs, and the affiliations of its members is stressed, although religious dogma, rituals, and practices are generally discouraged while individuals are in the treatment program. Notable is the shift from private confession, where psychologically sensitive issues are divulged to a special "other" (e.g., the AA sponsor, the Oxford group's god, or the Christian priest), to that of public disclosure and personal sharing with the entire peer community—a practice closer to the ancient confessional rites.

Group process

A significant example of a change in practice from AA to the TC is the form of group process used. In Synanon there developed *the game* or encounter group (a term apparently borrowed from the existential vernacular extant in the human potential movement of that period). These weekly "free association" groups reflected some of the psychoanalytic influences on Dederich and the first TC participants. These groups rapidly evolved a distinctive format marked by intense mutual confrontation designed to expose and weaken defenses against personal honesty and to encourage the disclosure and expression of authentic feelings. Free association, monologue, and controlled dyadic dialogue alternated with

---

[11] It should be noted that AA accepts atheists, suggesting that they view the group as their higher power—a view similar to that of TCs.

collective verbal reaction, all of which were directed to and about individual members.

Thus, in Synanon (and in later TCs) the aim of group process, as signified by the encounter group, was to help the individual uncover and change the characteristic behaviors and attitudes associated with addiction. Group interaction was used to raise individuals' self-awareness of those negative personality features through their impact on others, and group persuasion was used to elicit absolute personal honesty, self-disclosure, and commitment for self-change.

In the AA groups, the process was considerably less intense in terms of interaction or challenge. Emphasis was on sharing one's personal story, understanding the issues of staying sober, and using the group for support in maintaining sobriety. Thus, the AA group or meeting was primarily sobriety-oriented. Voluntary self-disclosure of "deeper" psychological matters, though accepted, was not the primary goal of the group.

Curative factors in the AA groups are primarily healing and supportive properties that are also present in TC groups (Emrick, 1989; Yalom, 1975). However, the significant psychological emphasis of group process in the TC, e.g., dissolving defenses, personal exploration, teaching, and training, is less apparent in the AA groups.

A second important change from AA with respect to group process was the introduction of varieties of groups in addition to the encounters. These groups shared the general aim of strengthening peer cohesion. However, they differed in focus, format, composition, and leadership to address the wide range of therapeutic and educational themes and issues related to individual recovery and everyday living.

In summary, the Synanon TC creatively reconfigured a variety of influences into the prototypical addiction TC. It inherited moral and spiritual elements from the Oxford group and AA and some of the 12 principles and traditions of AA. It integrated these elements with other social, psychological, and philosophical influences of the times (e.g., existentialism and psychoanalysis), all with a goal not only of maintaining sobriety but of changing personalities and lifestyles. Most significantly, in a 24-hour residential setting, individuals were removed from the social, circumstantial, and interpersonal elements in the larger community that could influence their substance use. In these settings, TCs evolved a social learning technology using the totality of community life to achieve complex goals. Thus, the Synanon TC represented an evolutionary step from its precursors, but it was also revolutionary in that it innovated a basically new approach to the treatment of addictions.

BROADER (NONSPECIFIC) INFLUENCES ON THE ADDICTION TC

Thus far, the historical sources of TC elements represent a confluence of moral (or spiritual), social, and psychological influences, mediated by various pioneers and leaders, programs, and movements. However, there are other influences not specifically traceable to particular people, events, or lineage. These are broader social, cultural, and psychological factors that appear to have helped shape the activities and social organization of Synanon and the first generation of TCs. Three in particular reflect the interplay of the social climate of the early 1960s, certain personality features of Synanon's developers, and unique characteristics of American culture.

Social Background and Social Climate

For the addicts, alcoholics, and ex-offenders who began Synanon, the only frame of reference they could have had for organizational structures was that of jails, hospitals, and their own (often dysfunctional and abusive) families. Thus, it is not surprising that the social organization they used for Synanon was an autocratic, hierarchical family surrogate model. Moreover, the stigma of addiction and the constant fiscal pressures on these still marginalized community-based programs often reinforced their familial cohesiveness.

Personality Influences

The social organization of the addiction TC could not be sustained without an emphasis on self-control and an acceptance of authoritative leadership. The early leadership and participants characteristically revealed lifetime problems with authority, impulse control, and low self-esteem associated with impeded social performance. The original participants knew their own personality features and understood that without firm self- and communal control, these could lead to personal as well as social disorder. In psychodynamic idiom, the social organization of the addiction TC itself reflected elements of reaction formation and sublimation. It redirected negative energy and rebellious impulses toward constructive social involvement, which participants themselves called a "turnaround."

This general interpretation also illustrates a psychological essential underlying the coexistence of both self-help and authority elements within the addiction TC. Participants could not listen to or "behave" for others (parents, teachers, or mental health professionals), but they could listen to and influence each other. Acceptance of autocratic (often charismatic) leadership revealed the positive side of participants' ambivalence toward authority or parental figures. However, the significant requirement for acceptance of authority was credibility, which was most unambiguously symbolized in recovering staff.

Cultural Influences

The influence of American culture on some of the teachings and social organization of the North American TC cannot be ignored. In TCs, emphasis is on vertical mobility within the social organization and aggressive pursuit of the tangible social rewards of status and privilege. These elements reflect qualities of the American national character—entrepreneurial, pragmatic, and acquisitive. Paradoxically, though the first generation of the TC was separated from the establishment as a distinctly self-help phenomenon of the disaffiliated, the TC concept of health and personal success embraced mainstream conformity and the conservative, traditional values of family, social responsibility, self-reliance, and the work ethic.

Thus, culture, social climate, and psychology all provided a context for early development of TCs for addictions. Though briefly characterized here, these broad influences offer a rounded view of the sources from which the essential elements of the TC evolved and particularly, how it is distinguished from its precursors.

CONTEMPORARY TCS

Most if not all of the programs that followed after Synanon were developed with the help and involvement of civic leaders, the clergy, politicians, and health and human service professionals. Thus, although the TC for addictions was pioneered by recovering addicts and alcoholics, its recent evolution has also been significantly influenced by the traditional fields of education, medicine, psychiatry, law, religion, and the social sciences.

The nonrecovering professionals who became involved in the TC movement were committed to the self-help concept and to maintaining the "purity" of the TC program model. Their contributions were usually practical and political, concerned with agency survival and development (e.g. fund-raising, research, and dissemination of the work of TCs).

Today, TC agencies and programs vary in their psychiatric, psychological, educational, vocational, and human services resources. Social and psychological perspectives (e.g., Freud, Rogers, Erikson) are standard curricula in TCs depending on their leadership. Programs differ with respect to vernacular (e.g., psychological terms), special services (e.g., family groups), and varieties of therapeutic and social themes addressed (e.g., sexual abuse, gender, cultural issues).

Although subsequent generations of TCs retained many of the elements of the Synanon prototype, various intervening influences led to some profound differences in organization, philosophy, and practices. Some of these were immediately evident; others were more gradual developments (see Table 2-2). These changes have not altered the basic or essential elements of the TC approach, but they signal the evolution of the TC from an alternative, esoteric self-help approach to a mainstream human services modality.

Of special interest concerning the evolution of the addiction TC—particularly its relationship to the psychiatric TC—is the label *therapeutic community*. Although Tom Main, a noted British psychiatrist, coined the term for the psychiatric model, there is no clear-cut evidence that these earlier psychiatric TCs had any direct influence on the origin of addiction TCs. Thus, the origin of the *therapeutic community* label for addiction TCs of North America is not precisely known.[12]

References to *therapeutic community* appear in relation to chemical dependency in early publications dealing with particular programs, such as Synanon, Daytop Village, and residential programs developing in Illinois in the mid-1960's (Casriel, 1966; Jaffe, 1969; Yablonsky, 1965). However, these represented the use of the term by specific individuals rather than reference to a widely accepted label.[13]

[12] The phrase *therapeutic education* has been utlized in various ways since the beginning of the 20th century to describe special schools for maladjusted children; see for example, Bridgeland (1971) and Broekaert et al. (1998).

[13] Although Synanon explored various ways to describe itself, it never endorsed the label *therapeutic community*. Rather than viewing itself as an agency for treating addictions, Synanon considered itself more broadly as an alternative community for teaching and living (Z. Putterman, 1995, N. Arbiter, 1985, R. Mullen, 1985, R. Hilton, 1990, personal communications). Synanon and Delancey Street, a first generation derivative of Synanon, have not participated in the national or international TC conferences (see Silbert, 1986).

TABLE 2-2. Key Developments in Contemporary TCs for Addictions

- A shift from being an alternative community for deviant addicts who presumably could not function in mainstream society to a human services agency preparing individuals for reintegration into the larger society
- A shift from indefinite tenure in the same residential community to a planned duration of residential stay guided by a treatment plan and protocol
- A shift from complete or partial private and entrepreneurial sources of support to virtually sole reliance on public funding for operational budgets, necessitating compliance with requirements for accountability and oversight by external boards of directors
- A de-emphasis on charismatic leaders and increased importance of peer leadership, staff as role models, and multiple decision makers
- Inclusion of increasing proportions of nonrecovered staff in primary clinical and administrative roles from varied professional disciplines
- Development of aftercare programs for those who complete the residential phase of treatment
- Reintegration of AA 12-step principles and traditions into the treatment protocol of many residential TCs
- Gradual rapprochement between psychiatric and addiction TC models and methods
- Adaptation of the TC for special populations and in special settings such as mental health facilities and correctional institutions
- Development of a research and evaluation knowledge base by independent and program-based investigative teams
- Codification of competency requirements for staff training, staff credentialing, and program accreditation
- Development of regional, national, and international TC organizations
- Promulgation and dissemination of the TC for addictions worldwide through training, program development, technical assistance, and research

It is generally agreed among the first generation of TC agencies that the popularization of the term occurred first in New York City. One version holds that some of the people (e.g., Alexander Bassin, Daniel Casriel, David Deitch, Joseph Shelley) who were involved in developing programs, such as Daytop Village and Phoenix House, were knowledgeable about the work of Maxwell Jones and labeled the new programs *therapeutic communities* after the Jones model.

A related version attributes the official dissemination of the term specifically to Dr. Efren Ramirez, a psychiatrist who developed drug rehabilitation residential programs in Puerto Rico and who was also familiar with the work of Jones and others. As commissioner of the Addiction Services Agency under Mayor John Lindsay, Ramirez and Deputy Commissioner Dr. Mitchell Rosenthal, a child psychiatrist and the developer of Phoenix House, oversaw the rapid implementation of drug-free residential programs during the mid-1960's in the New York City area.

Thereafter, the interaction with local and federal funding-agencies appears to have encouraged unofficial use of the term *therapeutic communities* for treating addictions. Contracts, grants, and verbal negotiations included references to a treatment modality called *therapeutic communities.* Official endorsement of the term by programs themselves occurred when Therapeutic Communities of America (TCA), the national organization of North American TC programs, was launched during a federally funded annual conference on drug abuse in New Orleans in 1975.

DEFINITIONS, CONCEPTIONS, AND THEORIES OF THE ADDICTION TC

TC participants in the first generation of programs tended to *resist* formal definitions of the TC. To them, such a term would imply fixed categorization and a certain superficiality. Definitions also triggered intuitive, but genuine, concerns about the TC's identity and a fear that the essence and uniqueness of the TC as a personal and communal experience would be oversimplified, diminished, or simply lost in the process of codification.

Nevertheless, contemporary TCs have largely evolved toward mainstream health agencies and now fully recognize the need for a characterization or definition that validly describes what the TC is, as well as how and why it works. This recognition has encouraged continuing efforts to define and conceptualize the TC within the modality. However, not unlike attempts to define families, communities, or villages, capturing the essence of the TC has eluded simple definition and description.

Self-Definitions

Throughout the past three decades TC workers and participants have continually grappled with the task of self-definition. Talmudic-like discussions mark these efforts in individual programs, regional meetings, institutes, and national and international conferences. A notable example was a 1989 world institute on the TC convened in New York City, where over 300 registrants were directed to devote more than three full days addressing the theme "Back to Basics" (Blieland et al., 1990).

Thirteen years prior to the above meeting, however, the National Institute on Drug Abuse (NIDA) funded the first TC planning conference in Crystal City, Virginia. There, TC workers assembled for the first time to deliberate and clarify the nature, purpose, and agenda of TCs as a treatment for substance abuse (the wide range of definitions, conceptions, and characterizations offered by the deliverants are summarized in Table 2-3).

TABLE 2-3. Some Definitions of the TC Explored at the TCA Planning Conference, 1976

Essential definitions for TC
Identification of the most generic nature and principles of the TC:
> The TC is a group of persons who, by following certain salient interpersonal principles, have largely overcome the pain and pain-inducing maladaptive behaviors produced by isolation, and who have a high skill and willingness to help other previously alienated persons achieve a clear sense of community fellowship; it is a community that includes people who have been out of community and know how to help other people get back in.

Functional or methodological definitions
Identification of how TCs characteristically operate to achieve their goals:
> The TC provides moral and ethical boundaries and expectations for personal development; it employs potential banishment, positive reinforcement, shame, punishment, guilt, example and role modeling to coerce personal change and development.

Purposive definitions
Definition of the TC by its goals for individual members and for the group:
> The TC aims at the development of a new social self and self-definition; it aims at self-improvement and re-entry from the sub-culture to the larger society; it aims at the reconstruction of a lifestyle.

Normative definitions
Focus on the norms and values intrinsic to the TC:
> Trust, concern, responsibility, honesty, optimum self-disclosure, nurturance.

Historical definitions
Focus on the derivative, evolutionary forms, and processes that have resulted in contemporary TCs:
> TCs, thus, have been characterized as emerging from ancient forms of apostolic movements, the moral temperance movement, and AA.

Structural definitions
Focus on both static and dynamic organizational features of the communities:
> Egalitarian or hierarchical, residential or nonresidential, status differentiation, size, membership, open or closed system, upward mobility.

Source. De Leon & Beschner, 1977

This initial TC planning conference provided official federal recognition of the newly formed national organization of North American TCs, Therapeutic Communities of America (TCA), but more importantly it marked an important step in the evolution of the TC from an alternative treatment to a major human service modality. The written proceedings of this landmark conference reflect the growing complexity and diversity of the TC modality (De Leon & Beschner 1977).

To some workers TC programs are more like schools rather than treatment centers. In these *learning communities,* the activities of everyday life in the community provide the entire curriculum for learning about self, relating to others, and *right living.* Learning unfolds in stages, with realizeable goals leading to an ultimate graduation. Participants in TCs lean toward this conception because it merges the ideas of therapy and teaching, capturing the reality of what they actually do and experience in programs.

TC programs also view themselves as *families*, or rather surrogate families that correct historical injuries from the dysfunctional families of the clients they serve. Thus, the TC strives to sustain the main characteristics of the "good" family: structure to provide order in daily living; nurturance through physical and psychological safety; individual acceptance and encouragement, conditional only upon honest participation in the struggle to change; and the transmission of values through a daily regimen of activities for social learning.

Family-related terms are prominently used among participants for each other—such as family, brother, and sister. Less frequently ascribed is the surrogate *mother* and *father* references for particular staff. The treatment experience itself is viewed in maturational terms. Former residents of TCs for example, often refer to their program as the place where they "grew up" rather than where they recovered from addiction. During the course of treatment, members gradually extend their family orientation beyond their immediate peers to the larger social group in residence, referring to the entire program as family. Thus, the terms "family" and "community" become interchangeable in the TC.

To many of its participants (as well as observers) the TC has been likened to a *microsociety.* With the critical deletion of drug use and antisocial behavior, the TC contains many of the elements of the larger macrosociety—a daily regimen of work and education, social relationships, and especially, an occupational structure. Individual progression up the hierarchy of job functions is much like the movement up the occupational ladder in the "real world."

A key difference, however, is that the TC fosters trial-and-error learning, providing an environment in which one can fail safely. This is in contrast to the outside world where there is greater risk of loss, humiliation, or punishment from performance failure. Thus, the TC is viewed as a microsociety that prepares the individual to live successfully in the macrosociety of the real world.

Theoretical Formulations of the Addiction TC

The wide variety of existing definitions and conceptions of the addiction TC among participants makes the point that no single characterization captures or explains what a TC is, or how and why it works. Although all make reference to certain essential elements of the TC, they largely illustrate how participants perceive and label particular programs. Understandably, these are not objective formulations, and subjective perspectives alone cannot provide a complete account of the essential elements of the TC. Thus, the search for these must be sought in the theoretical–conceptual literature on the addiction TC.

Compared to theoretical writings on the psychiatric TC, whose traditional origins are in science and medicine, the theoretical literature on the addiction TCs is modest, reflecting its nontraditional origins in self-help recovery. Theoretically oriented themes are discussed largely in conference papers and articles. The relatively small number of books on the addiction TC are largely devoted to narrative exposition of particular programs, though basic elements are often revealed in these. Only a few books and articles have actually outlined theoretical–conceptual formulations of the TC.

Noteworthy among the theoretically oriented writings are Bratter, Bratter, and Radda (1986); Brook and Whitehead (1980); Casriel (1966); De Leon and Ziegenfuss, (1986); Deissler (1970); Deitch (1973); Deitch and Solit, (1993b); Densen-Gerber (1973); Frankel (1989); Furuholmen and Andresen (1998); Goti (1990); Holland (1986a); Kennard (1983), Kooyman (1993); Ottenberg (1984); Ramirez (1984); Sugarman (1974, 1986); Volkman and Cressey (1963); Yablonsky (1986); and Zarcone (1975).

These writings contain similarities in their conceptualization of the addiction TC, in part underscoring the dissemination of literature throughout the rather small universe of TC writers and scholars. Also, however, similarities reflect uniformities that have been transmitted through the diffusion of addiction TCs worldwide. New programs in any culture are generally "seeded" or launched by former residents and staff of older parent programs, who implement their experiential understanding of the concepts and components of the model. The first generation of addiction TCs in North America emerged from this natural "pollination" and has since served as the primary colonizers of many subsequent programs.

The convergence in the literature on the elements of the addiction TC is illustrated in Table 2-4, which summarizes the key concepts, assumptions, and program activities from several formulations.

Differences in these and other formulations reflect the academic proclivities and perspectives of the writer–observers. For example, Sugarman, a sociologist, attempts to relate how the processes of individual change are fostered by social structure (Sugarman, 1986). Holland, a research psychologist, emphasizes measurable elements of treatment process in the TC (Holland, 1986a). Kooyman, a psychiatrist, grounds the TC in contemporary psychodynamic theory (Kooyman, 1993). Ramirez, an existentially oriented psychiatrist, provides a formulation of the TC adapted from Erikson's developmental framework (Ramirez, 1984). Frankel (not shown in the table), an anthropologist, presents a cultural anthropological study of one TC in terms of power and context (Frankel, 1989).

Across these formulations, consensus is evident on some of the essential elements of the contemporary addiction TC. Similarities are most apparent on the components of the program model and treatment philosophy. However, in these formulations and in the theoretical writings in general, there is little agreement as to classification of TC principles, program components, or assumptions concerning treatment process, nor in distinctions of terms such as concepts, tools, and techniques. In part, this reflects the fact that various theoretical conceptions are mainly based upon observations of single TC programs.

A Theoretical Framework for the Essential Elements of the TC

Notably missing in the literature in general and in theoretical writings in particular is a single theoretical framework that presents the TC for addictions and related problems as a uniform approach accessible to mainstream public health, science, and education. The formulation presented in this volume was conceived to fill this gap. It selects and organizes the essential elements of the TC into a theoretical framework that can guide clinical practice, research, and program development. It broadly extends the boundaries of other theoretical–conceptual efforts in several distinctive ways.

TABLE 2-4. Elements of Addiction TCs—Various Formulations

Holland	Kooyman	Ramirez	Sugarman
• Treatment activities: - individual /group/family counseling • Functional activities: - work assignments - departmental meeting • Productive activities: - outside employment - educational programs • Re-entry activities: - vocational /rehabilitational - job seeking skills - financial skills - job counseling • Interpersonal Activities -recreation -social skills • Hierarchical job structure • Rewards and sanctions • Role models • Scripted performances: -pull-ups -confrontations -personal narratives • Interaction: frequency, intensity, and context	• Substitute family • Consistent philosophy • Therapeutic structure • Balance between democracy, therapy and autonomy • Social learning through social interaction • Learning through crisis • Therapeutic impact of all activities in the community • Responsibility of the resident for his/her behavior • Internalization of a positive value system • Confrontation • Positive peer pressure • Learning to understand and express emotions • Changing negative attitudes to life into positive ones • Improvement of the relationship with the family of origin	• Commitment to participate • Safe facility • Trained staff (exaddicts, professional supervision • Steering Committee (responsible members of residents' families) • Human Resource Bank (other volunteers) • Alumna Committee (ex-addicts' help) • Faith • Group therapy • Work therapy • Educational therapy • Urbanism • Existential confrontation and marathon groups • Family and managerial therapy • Spiritual therapy	• Behavioral limits • Positive peer pressure • Helping each other • Confrontation • Structure to facilitate expression • Modeling • Constructive activities and achievements • Living in a self-sufficient group • Open system of communica-tion • Insulation from outside world • Pressure to recruit and hold clients • Counseling • Education and formal skills training • Supervised community contact • Organized recreation • Preaching and public confession • Ritual participation • Concept of a higher power

Source. See Holland, 1986a; Kooyman, 1993; Ramirez, 1984; and Sugarman, 1986

First, the framework defines the TC as a unique *self-help approach*—albeit a bona fide *social and psychological one*—to the treatment of chemical addiction and related problems. The term "therapeutic" denotes the social and psychological goals of TCs, namely changing the individual's lifestyle and identity. The term "community" denotes the primary method or approach employed to achieve the goal of individual change. The community is used to heal individuals emotionally and to train them in the behaviors, attitudes, and values of healthy living.

Second, the framework identifies the essential elements of the TC approach as the collection of concepts, beliefs, assumptions, clinical and educational practices, and program components common to TC programs. The "essentiality" of these elements is derived from multiple sources: the author's own observations and research of TC programs over some 30 years, the manuals of many contemporary TC programs, and the conceptual and historical literature of both addiction and psychiatric TCs.

Third, the essential elements organized into a single framework consist of three components: the perspective, model, and method. The perspective depicts how the TC views the substance abuse disorder, the individual substance abuser, the recovery process, and right living. The model presents what the TC is as a treatment program, its structure, social organization, and daily regimen of activities, all of which are grounded in the perspective. It distinguishes the unique, self-help element of its approach—*community as method*—in which individuals are taught to use the peer community to learn about themselves.

Fourth, the present formulation relates the three main components—perspective, model, and method—to the process of change. All the elements of the TC are intended to facilitate individual changes in lifestyle and identity. How these changes unfold reflects the individual's interaction with community and the internalization of its teachings.

CONCLUSION

The search for an "essential TC" reveals a universal idea recurring in various forms throughout history: that of healing, teaching, support, and guidance through community. In its contemporary form, the TC for addictions evolved from Synanon, although essential elements can be traced to AA and the earlier Oxford movement. The organization of these elements into a theoretical framework presenting the TC as a unique social and psychological approach is a further step in the evolution. The detailed exposition of this framework is the task of the remainder of this volume.

Part II

The Perspective and Approach

The therapeutic community (TC) treatment approach is grounded in an explicit perspective that consists of four interrelated views: the drug use disorder, the person, recovery, and right living. In chapters 3 and 4 drug abuse is presented as a disorder of the whole person. The problem is the person, not the drug. Regardless of individual differences, substance abusers share important similarities. Substance abusers reveal problems in socialization, cognitive and emotional skills, and overall psychological development. Chapter 5 details the TC view of recovery as a global change in lifestyle and identity that occurs in the social learning context of the TC. The view of right living emphasizes explicit beliefs and values essential to recovery. These guide how individuals relate to themselves, peers, significant others, and the larger society. Chapter 6 outlines the fundamental components of the TC treatment approach summarized in the phrase community as method.

Chapter 3

View of the Disorder

In the therapeutic community (TC) perspective, the substance abuse disorder is not distinct from the substance abuser. A picture of dysfunction and disturbance of individuals entering treatment reflects a more fundamental disorder of the whole person. This chapter presents the TC view of the disorder in the context of current biomedical, social, and psychological understanding of chemical dependency. Chapter 4 details the social and psychological characteristics of the person that comprise the disorder.

THE PRESENTING DISORDER

Those seeking admission to long-term residential TCs present a picture of disorder that extends beyond their misuse of substances. Despite their diversity in social background, demographics, and drug preferences, a typical clinical profile of this disorder can be outlined in four main areas (Table 3-1).

Overall, the picture that individuals present when entering the TC is one of health risk and social crises. Drug use is currently or recently out of control; individuals reveal little or no capacity to maintain abstinence on their own; social and interpersonal function is diminished; and their drug use is either embedded in, or has eroded to, a socially deviant lifestyle. Although individuals differ in the severity, extent, or duration of their problems in each area, all require the residential TC to interrupt a self-destructive or self-defeating lifestyle, to stabilize psychological and social functioning, and to initiate a long-term process of personal and lifestyle change.

TABLE 3-1. TC Admission: Areas and Indicators of the Presenting Disorder

A life in crisis
- Individuals reveal out of control behavior with respect to drug use, criminality, and often sexuality
- Suicidal potential through overdose
- Threat of injury or death through other drug-related means
- A high degree of anxiety and fear concerning violence, jail, illness, or death
- A history of profound personal losses (financial, relationships, employment)

Inability to maintain abstinence
- An inability to maintain any significant period of drug abstinence or sobriety on their own; multiple substance use although often having a primary drug of choice
- Some previous treatment experiences, self-initiated attempts at abstinence, or cycles of short-term medical detoxification

Social and interpersonal dysfunction
- A diminished capability to function responsibly in any social or interpersonal setting.
- Involved in the drug lifestyle (friends, places, activities), a poor record of maintaining employment or school responsibilities, and minimal or dysfunctional social relations with parents, spouse, and friends outside the drug lifestyle
- TC needed which focuses on the broad socialization or habilitation of the individual, building these basic skills and fostering the individual's progress through developmental stages that were missed previously

Antisocial lifestyle
- Past criminal histories including illegal activities, incarceration, and court proceedings; some were involved with the criminal justice system as juveniles; a considerable number are legally referred to treatment (De Leon, 1988; Hiller, Knight, Broome, & Simpson, 1998; Hubbard et al., 1989; Simpson, 1986; Simpson & Friend, 1988)
- Other characteristics highly correlated with drug use include exploitation, abuse, and violence, attitudes of disaffiliation with mainstream society, and the rejection or absence of prosocial values

A DISORDER OF THE WHOLE PERSON

In the TC perspective, drug abuse is a disorder of the *whole person,* affecting some or all areas of functioning. Cognitive and behavioral problems are typically involved, as are mood disturbances. Thinking may be unrealistic or disorganized; values are confused, nonexistent, or antisocial. Frequently there are deficits in verbal, reading, writing, and marketable skills. Moral and spiritual "bankruptcy" is evident, whether described in psychological or existential terms.

The Person Not the Drug

New admissions to the TC will commonly be asked by others, "What is your problem?" Their usual reply "Dope, I shoot dope" is invariably countered with "That is your symptom, not your problem" (Levy, Faltico, & Bratter, 1977, p. 44).

This typical exchange aptly illustrates the TC view of the disorder. It is a view that remains essentially the same regardless of an individual's drugs of choice or patterns of use. What is more relevant than either of these are the behavior, attitudes, values, and lifestyle of the abuser. Destructive behaviors to self and others are associated with regular substance use. Typically, these include domestic violence, unsafe sexual practices, criminality, suicide attempts, violence toward others, involvement in vehicular and other accidents, child neglect and abuse, and neglect of health.

Other self-defeating signs evident in the person involve social functioning. Substance abusers in TCs tend to have troubled family relations, drop out of school, be withdrawn from mainstream socialization, and display a variety of work problems (absenteeism, declining job performance, loss of jobs, multiple job changes, etc.). Even among the substance abusers who appear to maintain their functioning in work or school, their quality of life eventually erodes, leading to the appearance of some of the above problems. Thus, regardless of differences in drug preferences and patterns, the behavioral–attitudinal and emotional characteristics that define the disorder are evident in all residents.

The above picture of multiple dysfunction is not unique to TC admissions. A considerable clinical and research literature attests to the wide range of medical, social, and psychological problems in those with severe alcohol and other drug problems (Galanter & Kleber, 1999; Margolis & Zweben, 1998; McLellan, Luborsky, Woody, & O'Brien, 1980; Platt, 1995; Rounsaville, Weissman, Kleber, & Wilber, 1982). However, in the TC view multiple dysfunction defines the disorder—it is not the drug but the whole person that is the problem to be treated.

Sources of the Disorder

In the TC view, social and psychological factors are recognized as the primary sources of the addiction disorder. Although forged primarily from clinical experience, this view is consistent with extensive research on social and psychological risk factors in the etiology, initiation, and maintenance of chemical dependency disorders (Hawkins, Arthur, & Catalano, 1995; Hird, Khuri, Dusenbury, & Millman, 1997; Joe, Chastain, & Simpson, 1990; Nurco, Hanlon, O'Grady, & Kinlock, 1997).

Typical antecedents include socio-economic disadvantage, family dysfunction, ineffective parenting (e.g., Aron, 1975; Cancrini, Constantini, Mazzoni, Cingolani, & Compagnoni, 1985; Loeber & Stouthamer-Loeber, 1986; Nurco et al., 1997; Vaillant, 1973; Wright & Wright, 1994), negative role models and deviant social learning (e.g., Agnew, 1991; Elliot, Huizinga, & Ageton, 1985; Nurco et al., 1997; Oetting & Donnermeyer, 1998), and early oppositional personality traits (e.g., Hawkins et al., 1995).

Substance abusers themselves cite a variety of reasons and circumstances as causes of their drug use (e.g., De Leon, 1976, Simpson, 1986). The most common reasons suggest an attempt to self-medicate physical and psychological pain, heighten or lower stimulation and arousal (e.g., Khantzian, 1997; Kooyman, 1993; Lettieri, 1989; Zuckerman, 1986, 1994), celebrate good times or commiserate bad times, escape or better face reality (Hawkins & Wacker, 1986; Washburne, 1977), belong to or withdraw from social groups (Zackon, McAuliffe, & Ch'ien, 1985), avoid interpersonal demands, or mask or unmask personal feelings (Khantzian, Halliday, & McAuliffe, 1990). Matching these subjective reasons are the countless objective situations that residents see as precipitants of their use. These range from the ordinary stresses and strains of daily life to the extraordinary or catastrophic events that mark the lives of many users: violence and abuse, crime, financial insecurity, and homelessness.

In the TC view, however, addicts characteristically *use* both fact and fiction in their life history and circumstances to explain, excuse, defend, or otherwise rationalize their continued use of substances (Levy, 1987; Vaillant, 1981). Underneath the manifold feelings and reasons, however, is a person whose life is controlled by drug seeking and drug use and whose capacity to live a sober, orderly life is undeveloped or eroded. In their many and varied reasons for using drugs, substance abusers deny or do not accept their own contribution to their problems, nor do they fully recognize their own potential for the solutions. In the mind of addicts, what causes their drug use is the implacability of their external reality, the tyranny of the drugs, or even admitted problems in their personalities. However, underlying these attributions is an individual whose self-view is characterized by disempowerment in regards to changing circumstances, lifestyle, or self.

Taking Responsibility for the Disorder

Although valuable for illuminating who the individual is, the social and psychological history or biological factors of the individual are not considered sufficient causes or reasons for current behavior. The emphasis is on the individual's *own* contribution to his or her problems in the past and to the solutions in the present and future. Thus, an essential element of the disorder is the failure of individuals to take responsibility for their decisions and actions. Individuals may not be responsible for their physical predisposition to drug use or social and psychological influences beyond their control, such as their child rearing and the early, or in some cases, current social and family environments of their lives. However, they are responsible for their actions and for the choices they make, particularly with respect to drug use.

When substance abusers are actively using drugs, they have diminished capacity for making responsible decisions and much less commitment to sobriety or lifestyle changes. In effect, they do not have any realistic choice except to interrupt their out of control behavior. Indeed, it is usually only when individuals admit having lost control of their drug use and decision making that they come to TCs. The very act of seeking treatment is usually a call for help in interrupting their self-defeating behavior.

Although active drug abuse itself impairs one's capacity to make decisions, the initial choice to use drugs remains the responsibility of the individual. When the corrosive effects of drug use on decision making abates during treatment, it is again the responsibility of the individual to *choose* to remain drug free. Residents in TCs, therefore, only "discover" that they have choices in life after they have lived clean and sober for a period of time.

Assuming responsibility means that the individual makes a voluntary decision to cease drug use as a prerequisite for recovery. How and when individuals arrive at this decision varies widely. Some people only make that "voluntary" choice when health, legal, or family pressures have reached an extreme crisis point. For others, the decision evolves slowly, without apparent external threats. Irrespective of the forces that contribute to these decisions, individuals must voluntarily assume responsibility for their recovery for it to occur and be sustained.

Thus, in the TC view, recovery is always the responsibility of the individual, regardless of the etiology of substance abuse. Paradoxically, overemphasis on historical influences could weaken the individual's ability to take responsibility for his or her recovery. Indeed, for workers and residents in TCs, the process of recovery begins when individuals *accept* responsibility for their actions and are accountable for their behavior.

Patients, Clients, Members, and Participants

The assumptions concerning responsibility and accountability are fundamental in the TC's self-help view of recovery. Although the disorder reflects social and psychological dysfunction, TCs are "reluctant to label any resident as emotionally ill since this implies a legitimization of irresponsible behavior" (Bratter, Bratter, & Radda, 1986, p. 483). Thus, rather than patients, residents in TCs are described as participants or members to emphasize their active involvement in a community to change themselves. They are clients when they receive specific services, e.g., legal, vocational, educational, family, or mental health.[14]

BIOMEDICAL CONCEPTS AND THE TC PERSPECTIVE

The TC view of the disorder emerged primarily from the clinical and personal experiences of its participants. Nevertheless, this view can integrate familiar biomedical concepts of disease, illness, and physical dependency with personal responsibility for self-change.

Physical dependency, withdrawal, detoxification, and craving, though acknowledged elements of the disorder, are seen in the wider social and psychological context of the individual's life and recovery. Physical addiction, reflected in escalating tolerance for the drug of choice and characteristic withdrawal symptoms, is a transient physical crisis for the individual. Withdrawal effects are temporary physiological and psychological upsets and can be usually managed through self- or medically supervised detoxification. In the TC view, then, dependency describes the continuous behavioral, cognitive, and emotional preoccupation with drug use. Daily life is dominated by drug seeking, as well as thoughts, feelings, and social contacts related to drug use.

---

[14] In the addiction treatment field and for convenience in this volume, the terms *resident, participant, client,* and *individual* are used interchangeably to refer to substance abusers in TC-oriented programs.

Detoxification

The issues of withdrawal and detoxification for the substance abusers who enter TCs must be understood from its recovery-oriented perspective. The immediate goals of detoxification are to reduce the physical and psychological discomfort associated with escalating dependency and to interrupt a period of loss of control. Seeking detoxification does not necessarily indicate individuals' readiness to change themselves or their lifestyles.

For some, detoxification is the initial step in a more intensive treatment involvement such as the TC. For others, it is a circumscribed attempt to interrupt a temporary period of loss of control, after which, the drug-related lifestyle will be resumed. For still others, detoxification is a genuine attempt at long-term abstinence, although the individual may still reject any significant treatment involvement to this end.

The pain and pressure of recurrent cycles of use, detoxification, and withdrawal may provide the experiential incentive for individuals to eventually seek treatment in a TC. Conversely, however, this discomfort-induced incentive may also dissolve soon after transient relief is obtained. Rapid and reliable relief from detoxification, whether self- or medically managed, effectively interrupts the painful psychophysiological cycles, but this can also inadvertently sustain the addiction pattern. Thus, in the TC perspective, life crises involving physical and psychological pain and the episodes of withdrawal and detoxification present opportunities for initiating attempts at long-term change.

Cravings

During their tenure in TCs, residents frequently experience drug cravings. Drug cravings are viewed as thoughts, images, and associated sensations about drug taking, which may or may not lead to actual drug-taking behavior. Cravings are triggered primarily by material (e.g., drug paraphernalia), social, emotional, and physiological cues. In the early stages of chemical detoxification, the physiological cues for craving have relatively more impact than social and emotional cues. As the time since the last drug-taking episode lengthens, however, cravings are more directly triggered by social and emotional cues. For example, residents in TCs may experience cravings months after living drug free, these usually related to social cues (interpersonal stress or conversations about drugs), emotional cues (disappointment, hurt, or frustration), or circumstantial and material cues (return to old neighborhoods or engaging with active users, witnessing drug use paraphernalia).

Stabilized recovery requires tolerance for cravings. TC staff studiously avoids providing direct relief from the physical discomforts associated with drug abuse withdrawal so as not to inadvertently strengthen a poor tolerance for discomfort. There is no succor provided for the physical complaints associated with withdrawal or for craving reactions, beyond that of peer understanding and encouraging tolerance of these transient states.

Specific Drug Effects

Although the TC perspective emerged primarily from treating opioid, polydrug, and alcohol abusers, its views regarding the physical effects of drug use are the same regardless of the drug of choice. For example, the persistent mood- and mind-altering effects of cocaine, crack, marijuana, hallucinogens, and other drugs common to recent generations of TC residents are still seen as having both physical and psychological effects. These are managed with special peer and staff counseling strategies in the TC (De Leon, 1993a). However, the focus remains on drug use as a social and psychological disorder.

Pharmacotherapy

The use of medically prescribed drugs for substance abuse withdrawal or psychotropic medications for psychological symptoms is inconsistent with the TC perspective of the disorder and recovery. The strategic need for such medications is recognized and accepted by TCs, as in cases of medically managed drug detoxifications and pharmacological interventions for psychiatric emergencies. As a rule, however, these cases are managed in referred settings. The only medications that are dispensed in TC programs are those required for routine health care and for residents with chronic health conditions, such as diabetes, hypertension, the HIV virus, and AIDS.

A key assumption in the TC view of the disorder is that drugs are used and abused to avoid the challenge of ordinary living. Sobriety is a requirement for learning to manage feelings and behaviors needed to meet this challenge, and continued abstinence is essential to maintain recovery and sustain right living. Thus, in the TC perspective, medications that alter emotional, physical, or mental states could reinforce the disorder and impede the recovery process.

TC policy on the use of pharmacotherapy is currently undergoing modifications. Some TC agencies allow the use of psychotropic medication for selected cases, reflecting the greater influx of admissions with serious psychological symptoms, drug and non-drug-related. Increasingly, programs recognize the special psychopharmacological properties of cocaine/crack dependency (e.g., craving, severe mood alterations, violence, energy shifts) and how these affect the course of recovery in residential treatment as well as relapse rates in posttreatment. Thus they accept the limited use of psychopharmacological adjuncts to help ameliorate the depression and anxiety associated with the after effects of these drugs. Some agencies also manage methadone detoxification in outpatient clinics. Others have special residential methadone to abstinence programs for methadone clients. These facilitate involvement into the drug-free regimen of the TC through a gradual (3–6 months) detoxification from methadone. More recently, an adaptation of the TC as a day treatment model has been demonstrated for methadone-maintained clients (e.g., De Leon, Staines, Sacks, Brady, & Melchionda, 1997). This and other examples of the integration of pharmacotherapy with TC methods are discussed elsewhere (Carroll & McGinley, 1998; Sacks, De Leon, Bernhardt, & Sacks, 1997; Silberstein, Metzger, & Galanter, 1997).

Psychological Predisposition to Drug Abuse

The overdetermined or conditioned features of addiction are well-documented in the research literature (e.g., Childress, Ehrman, Rohsenow, Robbins, & O' Brien, 1992; Marlatt & Gordon, 1985). In the process of becoming addicted, any event—internal or external—can trigger cravings. Any stress produces discomfort, and drugs may be used to relieve all forms of discomfort.

TCs acknowledge the conditioned features of addiction. Residents indicate that a wide range of physical, social, emotional, and interpersonal factors are cues for their drug use behavior. In the TC view, however, physiological cues and physical addiction may be important factors for some substance abusers. For most, these factors are minor compared to the general social and psychological deficits that accumulate with continued substance abuse, and which contribute to the cycle of chronic use.

Notably, the conditioning features in chemical addiction can be usefully incorporated into the TC view of the disorder, particularly its understanding of the individual's vulnerability to drug abuse. TCs view chemical abusers as having a psychological proneness to substance use, which may precede or stem from their substance abuse. For example, residents characteristically use substances to "alter their states," "feel good," or stop "feeling bad." Eventually a myriad of social and emotional situations become cues for both their feeling states and their use of chemicals to change these states. Indeed, continued drug use itself lowers tolerance for any discomfort.

Thus, in the TC view, psychological proneness may be related to personality factors or biological substrates. However, it is also *acquired* through the repeated association of feeling and cognitive states with drug use. Central to the TC approach is helping residents recognize, accept, and manage their psychological proneness to using substances. This involves teaching them alternate ways to deal with triggers and cope with emotions, particularly how to tolerate discomfort.

Disease, Disorder, and Sickness

In the current medical convention, addiction is defined as a disease that parallels other physical diseases. It has a biological basis, characteristic signs and symptoms, a predictable course and outcome, and lack of "intentional" causation (Lewis, 1991).

The TC places less emphasis upon a biological basis of drug use. It stresses the importance of "intentional" factors, particularly motivation and responsibility, in the recovery process. Rather than disease, its view of treating the whole person justifies the more general concept of substance abuse as a "disorder."

As used in the TC, the terms disease, disorder, and sickness are not rigorous scientific concepts. Notwithstanding the understanding of the health correlates and consequences of substance abuse, TCs do not see addiction as a primary medical disease or sickness. Nor do they accept the conclusion that addiction is necessarily a chronic disorder requiring unlimited episodes of treatment, despite the fact that relapse is inherent in the recovery process (see Brown, 1998)

It is true that a variety of serious medical and psychiatric illnesses is associated with chemical addiction, particularly among opioid and alcohol abusers. There is a higher than average rate of cardiac, liver, and kidney conditions; TB; Hepatitis C; HIV; sexually transmitted diseases; and psychological symptoms (Platt, 1986, pp. 80-112). But rather than being seen as underlying causes of substance abuse, medical problems are viewed as either correlates or consequences of sustained drug use. They illustrate a basic element of addiction disorder, which is that substance abusers characteristically display poor self-care in terms of diet, hygiene, regular medical checkups, and other health habits (Brehm & Khantzian, 1992; Khantzian, 1997; Krystal, 1988; Stevens & Glider, 1994).

Physical complaints and illness are common among substance abusers in TCs. These are often related to drug withdrawal or neglected health status. Other than for bona fide medical and mental illness conditions, however, the word "sick" is used to characterize ways of thinking and acting that are self-defeating and destructive. For example, terms like "stupid," "off the wall," "crazy," or "sick" are not uncommon in the heat of peer exchanges and confrontations to heighten awareness of negative thinking or behaving. Recovered TC graduates may humorously refer to themselves as having been crazy or sick during their pretreatment days of active use to describe their dysfunctional behaviors and patterns of thinking. Such retrospective descriptions are expressions of the essential social and psychological disorder rather than of some biological or mental disease state.

Most admissions to TCs are dually disordered—they have a psychiatric diagnosis in addition to their substance abuse. Most prominent are depression, anxiety, post-traumatic diagnoses, and antisocial and other personality disorders (De Leon, 1989, 1993b; Jainchill, 1994). In the TC view, however, dual disorder underscores the validity of treating the whole person. This view is supported in research documenting the effectiveness of the TC approach in improving psychological function as well as reducing substance abuse (Biase, Sullivan, & Wheeler, 1986; De Leon, 1984b, 1985; De Leon & Jainchill, 1981-82; Ravndal, 1994; Ravndal & Vaglum, 1998).

However, standard TCs exclude the seriously mentally ill chemical abusers (MICAs), as well as those who are mentally retarded (although increasing numbers of admissions display learning disabilities, low intelligence, and frank, cognitive deficits). Successful adaptations of the TC approach for mentally ill chemical abusers (and other special populations) are described elsewhere (De Leon, 1993b, 1997a; Tims, De Leon, & Jainchill 1994). In these adaptations the TC view of the disorder remains fundamentally unchanged in its focus upon the whole person, although modifications in the treatment approach are guided by the special needs of these clients.

Genes, the Brain, and Addiction

In the decades since the inception and development of TCs for chemical dependency, research has mounted considerable evidence for the contribution of biological factors in chemical dependency problems. Brain mechanisms of drug action are being sketched based on the identification of receptor sites, neurotransmitters in cocaine abuse, and endorphins in opiate abuse (e.g., Leshner, 1997). Research on T cells, HIV/AIDS, and a variety of other health conditions implicate immune factors as causes, consequences, and correlates of substance abuse. Genetic factors are firmly implicated in the biological basis for chemical addictions (e.g., National Institute on Alcohol Abuse and Alcoholism [NIAAA], 1993). For example, heritability hypotheses for certain types of alcoholism are supported in studies on family substance abuse patterns and identical twins. Concise reviews of the genetic literature on substance abuse can be found in Margolis and Zweben (1998), and several reports on familial transmission of substance use disorders are contained in the *Archives of General Psychiatry* (Vol. 55, Nov. 1998).

The TC maintains a respectful distance from these biomedical developments, which fundamentally do not alter its basic view of the substance abuse disorder. TC workers acknowledge the importance of biological factors in understanding substance abuse: as predispositions to use chemicals that alter mental and emotional states, as physical elements of craving, as influences in detoxification, as triggers to relapse, and as health consequences of drug use. However, attributing the drug abuse disorder to specific biological, genetic, social, or psychopathological factors provides only a limited understanding of the disorder and inadequate guidance in the recovery process. Recovery always involves change in the behaviors, attitudes, emotions, and values that comprise the disordered person; it is the person who assumes responsibility for their own recovery.

CONCLUSION

The TC views substance abuse as a complex disorder of the whole person. Self-defeating or destructive patterns of behaviors and thinking reveal disturbance in both lifestyle and individual functioning. Although genetic, physiological, and chemical influences are recognized, the individual is seen as primarily responsible for his or her disorder and recovery. Thus, in the TC view, addiction is a symptom, not the essence of the disorder. The problem is the person, not the drug. In the following chapter, the specific social and psychological characteristics of substance abusers will be discussed, detailing the disorder of the person.

Chapter 4

View of the Person

In the therapeutic community (TC) perspective, the core of addiction disorder is the "person as a social and psychological being"—how individuals behave, think, manage emotions, interact, and communicate with others, and how they perceive and experience themselves and the world. Although individuals in the TC differ in demography, social, and psychological background, they all share these features of the disordered person.

This chapter details the TC view of the person in terms of typical cognitive, behavioral, emotional, social, and interpersonal characteristics. Although this view emerged from the recovery experiences of residents over the years, it is consistent with the considerable research on the personality and psychological characteristics of substance abusers in general (see for example a review of psychopathology and personality research in Platt, 1986, chap. 8; see also Hendriks, 1990 and Ravndal, 1994).

COGNITIVE AND BEHAVIORAL CHARACTERISTICS

Residents in TCs display a variety of cognitive characteristics associated with their substance abuse and lifestyle problems. Typically these include poor awareness, difficulties in decision making, poor judgment, and lack of problem solving skills. Additionally, many lack educational, vocational, social, and interpersonal skills, and increasing numbers reveal frank learning disabilities (see Table 4-1).

TABLE 4-1. Typical Cognitive Characteristics of Substance Abusers in TCs

---

Lack of awareness

Residents are not conscious of, do not recognize, or fail to consider how their actions affect others or how the behavior of others affects them. They either lack the skills to think of the consequences or they choose not to exercise them, often erasing such considerations through blocking, distraction, and impulsive behavior.

Faulty judgment

Residents exercise faulty judgment, particularly in terms of problem solving, decision making, and assessment of consequences. These difficulties appear to relate to poor impulse control and an inability to delay gratification, all of which impair development of judgment skills (means/ends problem solving) or impede the exercise of them.

Lack of insight

Residents do not see or understand the connections between what they experience (feelings, self-perceptions, and actions) and the reasons, influences, or determinants of their experience. A specific insight difficulty is their lack of awareness of the relationship between their drug thoughts or actions and the various emotions and circumstances that serve as cues or triggers for these.

Poor reality testing

Residents do not see themselves, others, or circumstances as they actually are. They are unwilling to confront the everyday issues of their lives and tend to avoid or escape these in their thinking and behavior. They have difficulty making distinctions between their feelings and facts, and between wants and needs. Most lacking in realistic assessment is their self-appraisal, as they typically have difficulty distinguishing the actual level of their personal resources from their aspired level.

Habilitation

Residents often do not possess the cognitive, educational, and work skills to earn incomes or effectively negotiate the social system. They also lack the basic behavioral habits and attitudes associated with employability or work readiness. For others with vocational and educational skills, overall social potency to pursue material goals is seriously impeded by drug involvement.

Two points should be stressed with respect to cognitive features of the resident in treatment. First, their cognitive characteristics are interrelated. For example, assessment of the positive and negative aspects of situations (judgment) depends on facing reality and having some degree of understanding (insight) as to the connections involved in negative, self-defeating consequences. Awareness is the basic prerequisite for judgment, reality, and insight. Thus, training people to be aware of themselves, others, and their environment is central to the TC approach.

Second, a number of substance abusers display effective cognitive and behavioral skills but primarily in the pursuit of their drug abuse lifestyle. Elements of planning, reality testing, and judgment are evident in securing the resources to obtain, use, or sell drugs (e.g., Casey & Preble, 1969;

Johnson et al., 1985). Eventually however, these skills erode with the fatigue and fears associated with drug use. In the TC these individuals must undergo a socialization that redirects their skills toward socially acceptable goals.

PERCEPTUAL CHARACTERISTICS

Almost universally, substance abusers have negative perceptions of themselves (Platt, 1995, chapter 8). Residents in TCs have problems in how they see themselves as individuals in terms of personal worth and as members of society (e.g., Biase & Sullivan, 1984; Biase, Sullivan, & Wheeler, 1986; Carroll & McGinley, 1998; Carroll & Sobel, 1986; De Leon, 1974, 1984b; De Leon & Jainchill, 1981-82; Frankel, 1989; Holland, 1986b; Preston & Viney, 1984).

Low Self-Esteem

Residents in TC display little self-respect and characteristically reveal poor self-perceptions as to their moral or ethical behavior and their relations to family. Their poor self-esteem is inextricably associated with their antisocial or amoral behavior, and frequently it is associated with their drug use and chronic inability to develop a productive lifestyle or prevent the gradual erosion of that lifestyle. Residents find it difficult to like or value themselves because of who they have been to others and their perceived poor self-control. However, for many, low self-esteem preceded their serious drug involvement, stemming from childhood and adolescent experiences, such as physical, sexual, and emotional abuse; neglect; school difficulties; social anxieties; and guilt concerning their failures to meet expectations of themselves and others (Chi'en, Gerard, Lee, & Rosenfeld, 1964; Stevens & Glider, 1994).

Negative Identity

Most substance abusers in TCs display negative social identities and unformed personal identities (Bassin, 1975; Biernacki, 1986; Casriel, 1981; De Leon, 1974, 1980, 1984b; Frankel, 1989; Jainchill, Battacharya, & Yagelka, 1995; Kaplan, 1980; Zackon, McAuliffe, & Chi'en, 1985). How residents label, perceive, and accept themselves stems from their histories of drug use and often their troubled childhoods. Their social identities may be the internalized, negative public images that others have of them. Typically, these images are of the *social deviant* (street tough, the addict, the criminal) and the *life victim,* who is injured either personally (i.e., the problem child or sick child due to catastrophe, circumstances, or abuse), or socially through the lack of social opportunity. Their personal identity, or concept of themselves as authentic people, is unstable or largely unformed. Many do not know who they are in terms of their real feelings, honest thoughts, goals, and values.

EMOTIONAL CHARACTERISTICS

Residents in TCs have difficulties experiencing, communicating, and coping with feelings. These difficulties appear to be common among serious substance abusers reflecting a general problem of maturity (e.g., Washburne, 1977) or more specifically, self-regulation (e.g., Brehm & Khantzian, 1992; Khantzian, 1997; Krystal, 1988; Wurmser, 1974). They often have low thresholds to emotional cues, a limited repertoire for emotional communication, and few behavioral boundaries in their emotional reactions. Their lack of emotional self-management is associated with much of their self-defeating social behavior.

Intolerance of Discomfort

A basic characteristic underlying the emotional difficulties of residents is poor tolerance for discomfort. Compared with non–substance abusers, they appear to have lower limits, or thresholds, for tolerating discomfort and shorter delays in their actions to reduce or escape the discomfort, these actions often being self-defeating, interpersonally disruptive, and socially deviant.

In the TC, the word "tolerance" relates to behaviors and emotions, rather than physiology. Tolerance is evident in behavioral self-management during periods of discomfort. For example, residents in TCs typically will have difficulty in restraining some forms of negative behavior when they feel denied, impatient, and emotionally aroused or provoked because they can't tolerate these feelings well.

Residents' difficulties with tolerance are associated with physical withdrawal from chemicals, common illnesses, mood disturbances, circumstantial frustration and anxiety, and with understimulation or boredom (Zuckerman, 1986). Tolerance is also a problem vis-à-vis the positive or neutral events in a residents' lives. For example, they reveal difficulty in tolerating the tension of anticipation, expectation, or the uncertainty associated with life's more ordinary stressors (e.g., being alone, interpersonal pressures, demands for social responsibility). To effectively avoid or reduce these discomforts, addicts have acquired a complex repertoire of behaviors—both socially acceptable and unacceptable—the most prominent of which is drug use. Thus, the TC views the inability to tolerate frustration and discomfort as the underlying problem in emotional management. Teaching tolerance is central to learning delay of gratification, impulse control, and effective emotional management.

Varieties of guilt

Contrary to the common view that antisocial or character-disordered addicts are those without guilt, most residents in TC treatment are plagued by various feelings of guilt and shame (e.g., Lecker, 1974). Indeed, of all their emotions, guilt is potentially the most destructive for substance abusers. The TC phrase *guilt kills* powerfully captures the escalating cycle of unmanaged guilt. Negative behavior or thinking initiates guilt feelings that drive more elaborate negative behaviors to escape these feelings. The latter give rise to more guilt, which ultimately can only be dulled by compulsive drug use.

The problem is not one of capacity for experiencing guilt, but of coping with the experience. Substance abusers' low tolerance for any emotional discomfort and poor training in self-discipline are an inadequate foundation for managing the special pain of guilt feelings. Their usual mode is (cognitively) to block out guilty thoughts or (behaviorally) engage in excessive use of rationalization or to use drugs in order to dull the discomfort of guilty feelings.

In the TC, self-management of guilt is essential to recovery. Residents learn how to manage ("deal with") guilt more effectively when they can identify and distinguish the various guilt feelings they have, the conditions under which they occur, and the particular actions that can ameliorate them.

Guilt arises from many different sources and reference points. During the course of treatment TC residents invariably disclose the secret guilts of their past and present, associated with various episodes and people, some known and not known. The main sources of guilt can be organized around four themes: guilt regarding the self, guilt regarding significant others, guilt regarding the TC community, and guilt regarding society at large (see Table 4-2).

TABLE 4-2.   Varieties of Guilt Problems for Residents in TCs

---

Guilt to the self

Arises from injuries to the self. Residents in the TC experience the special pain of having violated personal moral and social standards of behavior and failed in meeting their own aspirations and life goals. This pain is expressed in such phrases as "who I have been, should, and could be" and the frequent lament "how I have wasted or thrown away my life." A related guilt concerns their deceptions, lying, and manipulation of teachers, employers, and the system in general. This is a guilt that is specifically related to a violated social identity or self-concept, of "who I have been as a social person."

Guilt to significant others

Arises from the injuries to those known by the resident. Family members have often been directly hurt by residents' stealing, their physical, verbal, and sexual abuse, or from having been introduced to drug use by them; indirectly they have been hurt through the residents' legal and health problems. Peers have been betrayed; spouses or mates abused; parents disappointed. Residents with children often have histories of parenting problems, including physical and psychological neglect; physical, verbal, and sexual abuse; or custodial loss of their children. Guilt concerning their roles as parents appears to be most prominent among female addicts. However, it is not uncommon among males either. Many fathers have abandoned or have never seen their children and discover their guilt as parents for the first time during treatment.

Guilt to society

Arises through injury to anonymous others. Residents in treatment often confess personal secrets involving past actions that have hurt people unknown to them. Typically, these are crimes of violence resulting in bodily injury or death or other crimes, such as stealing, robbery, burglary, mugging, and drug dealing.

Guilt to the TC

Arises from personal secrets associated with violations of the rules, norms, and social expectations of the peer community. Residents also experience guilt specific to their role as members of the TC. These may include any infraction, such as borrowing a cigarette lighter without permission, sexual acting out, drug use, or the condoning of negative behaviors and attitudes of peers. Such infractions, which violate or strain the moral imperatives of the community itself and often lead to community guilt, must be identified and ameliorated to assure that the individual will remain in treatment.

The social and interpersonal context of community life in the TC provides a setting for the emergence of all varieties of guilt. For example, identification of guilt to the community often helps bring to the surface the individuals' deeply buried guilt to the self, significant others, and society. Teaching the individuals new ways of coping with guilt is essential for their recovery.

Hostility and Anger

Hostility and anger are common characteristics among substance abusers in general (e.g., Biase, 1971; Biase & De Leon, 1974; De Leon, Skodol, & Rosenthal, 1973; Holland, 1986b; Nurco et al., 1997; Pallone & Hennessy, 1996). Anger and hostility are related negative affect or feeling states. Although discussed together, anger reflects a more intense and specific emotional experience than hostility, which is revealed in attitudes and gestures that are negative and sometimes threatening to others.

For many residents anger and hostility have been the predominant emotions expressed, in their families and social networks and in institutional settings. Indeed, for them, hostility and anger have been the *only* form of affective expressions. These serve to protect the individual from confronting or experiencing other emotions that may be more upsetting or uncomfortable, such as fear, hurt, disappointment, sadness, or love. In the TC, hostility as defensive coping must be distinguished from anger as an authentic personal expression. The resident must learn to express both of these in socially effective ways.

Dysphoria and the Loss of Feelings

Dysphoria and the loss of feelings are general affective states that are common to serious substance abusers (e.g., Barr, 1986; Carroll & McGinley, 1998; De Leon, 1989; Jainchill, 1994; Lewis, Rice, & Hetzer, 1983; Powell, Penick, Othmer, Bingham, & Rice, 1982; Rounsaville, Rosenberger, & Wilber, 1980). In dysphoria (disturbed feelings), residents lack a sense of physical or emotional well being. This typically gets expressed through somatic complaints and vague but persistent moodiness or low-level depression. Relatively high rates of suicidal ideation and attempts among substance abusers are documented in the literature (De Leon, 1976; De Leon, 1993a; Hawke, Jainchill, & De Leon, 1999; National Center for Health Statistics, 1993; Watterson, Simpson, & Sells, 1975). These rates may be associated with dysphoria as well as depression.

Anhedonia is a loss of capacity to feel pleasures. Residents may assert that they no longer look forward to once pleasurable events; that they lack satisfaction in sexual or social activity, through eating meals, or even in their drug use, though they continue to engage in these various activities. Some residents claim not to have any feelings at all (*dis*-affected). As described in the literature they may display defensiveness or fighting (Khantzian, Halliday, & McAuliffe, 1990). Other residents displaying these affective problems may mournfully express statements such as "not having a right to exist at all" (e.g., Kooyman, 1993, pp. 45). This abject view is usually associated with lack of self-care and self-regard and can be altered when residents recover the full range of feelings.

Emotional Management

Substance abusers generally have difficulties in the management of their feeling states regardless of the conditions that produce these states. These include expressions from others whether negative (e.g., criticism, rejection) or positive (e.g., affection). Often "good feelings" will lead to self-defeating celebratory reactions such as drug use. Relatively neutral conditions such as boredom, understimulation, general arousal, or frustration can elicit problematic reactions, as will ordinary upsets such as uncertainty, disappointment, or sadness. Residents often do not have the skills for appropriately coping with their emotions in any of these conditions.

TCs focus on two characteristic problems of emotional self-management: *acting out* feelings and *acting off* feelings. The distinction between these problems can be briefly illustrated. Acting out describes behavioral reactions that are indirectly or symbolically related t o emotional events. For example, a resident's unexpressed guilt over condoning the drug behavior of a peer leads to cursing at a staff person, which in turn may result in a disciplinary action. Acting off feelings refers to difficulties in immediate self-control. They are impulsive overreactions to the interpersonal and social environment. For example, a resident is criticized by a staff member, feels angry, threatens the staff member, and leaves the program without sufficient consideration of the events or the consequences.[15]

Both these problems in emotional management reveal poor tolerance for feeling states and both may manifest in similar self-defeating behaviors, including rebellion, rule breaking, revenge, hostility, violence, sexuality, simply running away, or drug use.

---

[15] Acting out and acting off reactions can generally be contrasted with the emotional problems of those without character disorder who more often act *in,* displaying symptoms such as depression, anxiety, obsessions, suicidal thinking and actions, etc. In all cases, however, the issue is one of learning appropriate emotional management.

Abstinence and Emotions

A basic assumption in the TC perspective is that recovery is not stable until an individual understands his or her feelings in connection to drug use behavior and other problems, and learns how to express these feelings constructively. The first requirement in this new emotional learning is for the individual to actually experience all feelings while remaining abstinent, unaltered by drug use. A common effect of remaining drug free is that the individual may experience emotions and sensations including body pains in a new way. For the first time, the abstinent resident feels *a range of emotions,* not only joys and affections, but also anger, hurts, disappointments, sadness, and guilt. These new experiences are often disturbing for the individual and paradoxically can precipitate his or her dropping out of treatment and using drugs again.

Abstinence also raises diagnostic and management concerns because of the residents' characteristically poor tolerance for discomfort. Authentic physical conditions must be differentiated from minor ordinary discomforts and malingering—that is, the use of real or imagined complaints to avoid the demands of the daily regimen.

SOCIAL CHARACTERISTICS

Residents display problem behaviors and attitudes that disturb their social relationships with others and the world in general. Typical social characteristics addressed in the TC are residents' sense of entitlement, their irresponsibility, and their lack of trust.

Entitlement

The resident's persistent attitude (or sense) of entitlement refers to having unrealistic expectations concerning needs and wants. Commonly residents behave with indignation or withdrawal at perceived injustices concerning their unmet needs. Residents in TCs, for example, complain about what they don't have, should have, and deserve to have: "Why should I wait?" "Why can't I get promoted?" "Why do I have to start at the bottom?" "Why should he get something that I didn't get?" or, "The food stinks in this program," "There's no privacy...and not enough personal attention by the staff."

In the TC view, the sense of entitlement reflects the characteristic difficulties substance abusers have in distinguishing between their genuine needs vs. their immediate wants, in managing their impatience and frustration while waiting for satisfaction, and in their disinclination to work for or earn their own rewards. Thus, entitlement is dysfunctional, impeding self-reliance and limiting one's ability to cope with performance demands. Individuals who look to others to provide what they deserve are disempowered to provide for themselves. Valid entitlement means that individuals deserve the opportunity to change themselves—that is, that they receive the help required to improve their lives and pursue their needs and wants on their own, in legal and ethical ways.

Responsibility, Consistency, and Accountability

Residents in TCs almost universally view the triad responsibility, consistency, and accountability as the main problematic characteristic of their disorder. For example, those entering TCs most often claim that "being responsible or consistent" is what they need to learn or relearn to make it in life.

To be responsible means being appropriately responsive to one's obligations to self and others. To be consistent means being reliable or predictable in meeting those obligations. To be accountable means providing an honest record to oneself and others, of the activities related to meeting obligations and expectations. Though interrelated, responsibility, consistency, and accountability reveal specific differences among residents and are addressed in different ways (see Table 4-3).

As with other characteristics of the substance abuser, problems with responsibility, consistency, and accountability are both causes and results of drug use. For example, the activities of seeking illicit drugs, as well as the typical physiological and psychological effects of persistent substance use, interrupt routines, distract one from planned schedules, and cloud memories of obligations. For many residents, however, irresponsible patterns were evident prior to their regular drug use, often reflecting poor or inadequate early training in meeting obligations or histories of parental overindulgence. Such long-standing patterns of irresponsibility may be maintained by regular drug use.

Regardless of their sources, however, many of the cognitive, social, and emotional characteristics of substance abusers described earlier are reflected in their problems with responsibility, consistency, and accountability. Meeting obligations depends upon having a realistic understanding of the time, effort, and skills needed (reality testing); the ability to delay gratification and patience to carry out each needed step (tolerance); and the ability to manage impulses and disturbing feelings that could intrude on planned steps (emotional self-control).

TABLE 4-3. Responsibility, Consistency, and Accountability Problems among Substance Abusers in the TC

Responsibility

Many residents are initially responsible in their conventional jobs, but this diminishes or erodes with their continued substance abuse. Others, who do not hold conventional jobs, may be "responsible" with respect to their drug abuse, exercising all the skills required to obtain money for their drug use—licit and illicit. They can identify dealer connections or sources for their drugs and be consistent in organizing their efforts and time in order to secure drugs. Indeed, the compulsive element of their substance abuse illustrates their capability for responsibility. It is in their non-drug-related obligations that the responsibility erodes.

Consistency

Typically residents fail or are inconsistent in meeting their obligations to others and themselves. They have a long history of not finishing what they started, dating back to chores in the family, early school and work tasks, and constant breaking of promises to self and others. Many substance abusers can work episodically at acceptable standards but cannot sustain their efforts. Their pattern is to work only in binges and bursts, driven by immediate needs, a desire to please others, or fear of failure. Others never developed the ability for consistent performance, short or long term.

Accountability

Being accountable in meeting obligations underscores the personal and social honesty elements of responsibility. Substance abusers often find ways of getting around the needed steps in meeting obligations, failing to provide others a truthful account of the time or effort expended in these tasks. Thus, learning accountability, viewed as a prerequisite for recovery in a TC, means becoming absolutely honest about one's own behavior.

Moreover, the individual's *anticipated* problem with meeting responsibilities or being consistent produces anxiety or discomfort itself. This results in an avoidance of obligations, often through drug use, which further impedes their responsible behavior. Lying about or forgetting the details of obligations is often the substance abuser's main means of coping with the discomfort associated with his or her irresponsibility or inconsistency.

In the TC, learning responsibility, consistency, and accountability reflects complex personal growth. Assuming and fulfilling one's role or obligations involve acquiring the skills for completing tasks or fulfilling roles; acquiring or reclaiming values that support meeting obligations (e.g., a belief in the importance of doing a good job, helping peers.); acquiring a habit of honesty in accounting for oneself; and acquiring a willingness to conform (e.g., positive regard for the expectations of others). Finally, sticking to a task or routine requires tolerating and coping with all sorts of discomfort that can intrude upon task completion, from boredom with routines to anxiety about expectations and performance demands and fear of failure or success.

Trust

A lack, loss, or violation of trust is a distinctive marker of the substance abuser's personality and lifestyle (e.g., Bassin, 1975; Bratter, Bratter, & Radda, 1986; Chi'en et al., 1964; Kooyman, 1993; Salasnek & Amini, 1971). For some residents in TCs, trust problems can be discerned in their childhood history of general misconduct, patterns of lying, excuse making, or falsification. For most, the deceit, manipulation, and lying that are embedded in the drug abuse pattern itself undermine the development of any form of trust.

Although varied, the sources of the trust problems in TC residents typically reflect social and psychological influences. These include histories of unsafe and abusive families, poor parental models of trust, and negative peer socialization. Thus, for residents in TCs the problem of trust is multifaceted. They mistrust relationships, authorities, and systems, while trust in them by families, children, friends, and employers has eroded or never developed.

The problem, however, is not only of trusting others or the world outside, but of self-trust, being safely and reliably guided by one's own feelings, thoughts, decisions, and behaviors. For substance abusers, there are powerful intrinsic influences contributing to the absence or erosion of self-trust. These stem from the individual's chronic struggle with self-regulation and self-efficacy. Substance abusers cannot "trust" their feelings, thoughts, or behavior, as their impulses and poor judgment have repeatedly resulted in negative consequences. Furthermore, their feelings, thoughts, and behavior, having been constantly altered by drugs, are untrustworthy.

DEVIANT COPING STRATEGIES

Substance abusers reveal characteristic ways of coping with challenges or confrontations to their behavior and attitudes. Often, when confronted or questioned by family members, friends, legal authorities, or employers as to what they are doing, they resort to conscious and unconscious deception of others and themselves. They are deft at manipulating people, procedures, and systems in the service of their immediate wants.

Lying and Manipulation

The prominence of lying, manipulation, and deception may reflect long-standing features of a character or conduct disorder that has been significantly exaggerated by drug use. Wrongly or rightly, many residents have negative views of their families, believing them untrustworthy or abusive. Teachers, police, physicians, social workers, mental health professionals, and social service bureaucrats are often seen as hypocritical, naïve, or corrupt people. Characteristically, residents have learned to get around and exploit such systems (i.e., "beat the system") and to disrespect or manipulate (i.e., "get over on") the people who are part of such systems. They often defend their lies with arguments about victimization, entitlement, the necessities of survival, the need to "even the score," and other rationalizations, projections, and excuses. In TCs, residents and staff refer to these strategies pejoratively as "typical dope fiend thinking and behaving." They are seen as socially and interpersonally noxious features that are habitual ways of coping with others, avoiding perceived pressures, and obtaining relief.

Defenses

Substance abusers also display characteristic behavioral, gestural, and cognitive ways of shielding the truth about themselves from themselves and others. These are the familiar defense mechanisms referred to in psychology. Those most typically employed by substance abusers are denial and its common variants, such as rationalization, externalization, projection, and somatization. Although residents have elected to enter the TC, indicating some acceptance of their problems and their needs for help, defenses against changing the whole person persist.

Denial is the bedrock defense or coping strategy of substances abusers, at least in the early stages of their disorder. It consists of the many ways in which individuals reject or diminish the scope and severity of their drug use and related negative behavior and attitudes. Although most evident in substance abusers outside of treatment programs, engaging in denial is seen in residents even during their tenure in treatment. For example, residents may deny the severity of their drug use, convinced that a brief period of abstinence is all that is needed. They may also deny the severity and pain of the impact of their drug use on others (parents, children, friends) in order to avoid associated guilt. Even when they accept their drug use problems, they may deny their other social and psychological problems. Indeed, the extent to which individuals display problem acceptance often predicts whether they will stay in treatment (De Leon, Melnick, Kressel, & Jainchill, 1994; Joe, Simpson, & Broome, 1998). Table 4-4 summarizes other typical defenses of residents in TCs.

TABLE 4-4.   Typical Psychological Defenses used by Residents in TCs

Rationalization

Residents invoke an infinite variety of reasons, excuses, and logical accounts to explain, exonerate, or at least minimize their own contribution to their problems. Excuses and stories will identify stressful circumstances, residents' physical condition, difficult people, and lack of resources (e.g., money or assistance) as reasons for their drug use and various troubles. A complexity addressed by TCs is individuals' use of insight as rationalization to explain rather than change themselves—a defensive manipulation prominent among more verbal and educated drug users.

Externalization

Residents blame forces outside rather than inside themselves for their problems. For example, social disadvantage, racial–ethnic discrimination, drug-infested neighborhoods, abusive families, negative peers, psychological hardships, poor parenting, and trauma are implicated by many residents as insurmountable impediments to their ability to initiate or sustain a positive lifestyle. That these forces are contributors to their problems may be valid. However, the basic defensive element in these externalizations is the divesting of any personal responsibility for conduct or feelings. Individuals may not be denying drug use and related problems, but they are abdicating their role in changing these behaviors.

Projection

Residents ascribe their own feelings, thoughts, and perceptions to others. For example, residents may perceive hostility, lies, guilt, or seduction as emanating from other people, whereas these are actually their own experiences and emotions that they cannot tolerate.

Somatization

Residents employ physical complaints to avoid the demands of ordered daily living and of treatment in particular. Headaches, colds, gastrointestinal distress, fevers, weakness, fatigue, and dental pain are only some of the physical complaints common among residents in TCs. These discomforts may be authentic symptoms due to the generally poor health of substance abusers. Often, however, they are conscious or unconscious manipulations to evade social responsibilities or painful emotional experiences.

SOCIAL DEVIANCY

Most TC residents have a history of criminal activity or legal problems (e.g., Anglin & Hser, 1990a; Hiller et al., 1998; Hubbard et al., 1989;

Simpson & Sells, 1982). The range and severity of these problems reveal the extent to which the individual is embedded in an antisocial lifestyle vis-à-vis his or her conduct, values, and affiliations. Some residents were antisocial in behavior and outlook prior to serious drug involvement. This group may or may not possess a core repertoire of employment or educational skills. Their criminal activities are both drug and non-drug-related and include violence (e.g., murder, assault, armed robbery, rape) and negative peer (gang) associations. The attitudes found among this group are rebelliousness and cynicism; their coping skills for problem solving or seeking personal gain range from violence, threats, and intimidation (hardened criminal) to exploitation, manipulation, lying, and "getting over" ("dope fiend" behavior). Their social images (e.g., machismo, the criminal mask) convey invulnerability or indifference.

For other residents, illegal activities were engaged in only *after* regular involvement with drugs. Their crimes mainly centered upon sustaining their drug use by obtaining money for drugs and maintaining their relationships with peers or significant others who were drug involved. Although these individuals are generally less violent, their crimes range from crimes against property (burglary and shoplifting) and people (drug dealing, stealing, and mugging) to "victimless" crimes (prostitution and pimping).

A smaller proportion of residents are well socialized but have seriously damaged or lost a prosocial lifestyle through drug abuse. Typically, these residents were at one time well educated and employed, with family and community ties. Those whose main substances of abuse were licit, such as alcohol or prescription drugs, often have no history of criminality. For others, illegal activities were exclusively associated with substance abuse (e.g., forging checks or medical prescriptions, purchasing and possession of illegal substances). Typically, however, the continued drug use of these substance abusers eventually led to greater social losses, more serious crimes against others, and to victimless crimes

All of these groups reveal serious drug use problems. The relative primacy of criminality *or* drug abuse, however, differs. Residents themselves distinguish the subtypes as "those who commit crimes to use drugs" and "those who use drugs to commit crime."

AN "ADDICTIVE PERSONALITY"

Although the TC view of the person pictures a typical profile of characteristics and problems, it does not necessarily depict an addictive personality. Based upon clinical and research considerations in the TC, however, the concept of an addictive personality is not rejected out of hand. For example, the physical and psychological predisposition to use substances (discussed in the chapter on the disorder) suggests a set of core distinguishing factors for those at risk for drug abuse. Indeed, participants in TCs continually remind each other of their proneness to use substances and perhaps engage in other compulsive behaviors (e.g., gambling, sexuality). Also, TC research indicates that many adolescents display features of conduct disorder that later evolve into adult character disorder (Jainchill, De Leon, & Yagelka, 1997).

The issue of an addictive personality remains to be clarified. Whether antecedent or consequent to serious drug involvement, however, the characteristics comprised by the TC view of the person are correlated with substance abuse. More importantly, they reflect how residents see each other and what they must change to achieve a stable recovery.

CONCLUSION

This chapter has detailed the cognitive, behavioral, emotional, social, and interpersonal characteristics comprised by the TC view of the disordered person. Although separately described, these characteristics are interrelated; they arise from varied biopsychosocial sources, and they are shared by most of the residents in the TC. Individual differences in social and psychological profiles are recognized, modifying specific treatment plans. However, as described in the following chapter, these differences do not alter the goal of changing the whole person or the course of recovery.

Chapter 5

View of Recovery and Right Living

In the therapeutic community (TC), recovery is viewed as a change in lifestyle and identity. It is a view that can be contrasted with the conventional concept of recovery in medicine, mental health, and other substance abuse treatment approaches.

Recovery, as a medically oriented concept, denotes *regaining* lost or diminished capability, health, or previous level of functioning. More broadly, it connotes *returning* to a state of physical or mental health from a state of sickness or disease. However, not all treatment approaches to chemical dependency are oriented toward recovery. In the public health experience of treating opioid addiction and alcoholism, drug abuse is viewed as a chronic disease, which focuses treatment strategies and goals on improvement rather than recovery or cure. Since relapse is not unexpected, the goal becomes that of extending periods of abstinence or reducing the level of drug use and minimizing social and health consequences.

Recovery perspectives of substance abuse that are non–medically oriented were initially fashioned outside the mainstream health establishment. These were based on the numerous cases of alcoholics and heroin abusers who overcame their addictions in the self-help cultures of Alcoholics Anonymous (AA) and TCs (e.g., Anglin & Hser, 1990b; Emrick, 1985), and to the smaller numbers who spontaneously recovered or eventually "matured out" of their substance abuse without the apparent contributions of formal treatment (e.g., Biernacki, 1986; Winick, 1962). These perspectives converge on a developmental view of change that depicts the abuser as moving from a status of active use and denial of the problem to one of stabilized abstinence and commitment toward maintaining a drug-free status (see for example, De Leon, 1995; Gorski, 1989; Prochaska, DiClemente, & Norcross; 1992; Zackon, McAuliffe, & Chi'en, 1985; Zweben, 1993).

The TC view of recovery extends much beyond achieving or maintaining abstinence (i.e., refraining from the use of any non–medically prescribed drugs) to encompass lifestyle and identity change (e.g., Catalano, Hawkins, & Hall, 1983; Frankel, 1989; Kooyman, 1993). The present chapter outlines this expanded view of recovery. The initial section details the goals and assumptions of the recovery process. The second section presents the TC *view of right living,* which summarizes the community teachings guiding recovery during and after treatment.

VIEW OF RECOVERY

The terms "habilitation" and "rehabilitation" distinguish between building or rebuilding lifestyles for different groups of substance abusers in TCs. Both capture the TC goals of recovery and its orientation to changing the whole person. The assumptions underlying the process itself are grounded in the TC approach to changing lifestyles. Multidimensional change unfolds as a developmental process of social learning, which occurs through mutual self-help in a social context.

Recovery Goals

A number of TC residents have some history of social functioning, educational and vocational skills, and positive community and family ties, but their substance abuse has eroded this prosocial lifestyle. For them, recovery involves *rehabilitation,* relearning, or re-establishing their capacity to sustain positive living, as well as regaining physical and emotional health.

Many other TC residents have never acquired functional lifestyles. Their substance abuse is embedded in a larger picture of psychological dysfunction and social deficits in education, employment, and social skills. Often they are antisocial or lack the motivation or capacity to pursue the values of right living. For these residents, their tenure in the TC is usually their first exposure to orderly living. Recovery for them involves *habilitation*, or learning the behavioral skills, attitudes, and values associated with socialized living for the first time. Regardless of differences in social background, the goals of recovery remain the same for all residents: to learn or relearn how to live drug-free positive lifestyles.

Recovery also involves changing how individuals perceive themselves in the world, i.e., their identities. In the TC view, changes in lifestyle and identity are related. Those who acquire lifestyle changes and experience the healing and self-efficacy resulting from these changes eventually come to perceive themselves differently.

The goals of lifestyle and identity change for substance abusers are not unique to the TC but are acknowledged by other clinicians and researchers (e.g., Brown, 1985; Kellog, 1993). However, the TC approach is distinctive in the use of a peer community model to pursue these goals, particularly among those who are antisocial and nonhabilitated.

Self-Help and Mutual Self-Help

Self-help has been increasingly acknowledged as an important element in medicine, mental health, and education as well in the addictions (Brill & Lieberman, 1969; Gartner & Reissman, 1999; Margolis & Zweben, 1998; Trimpey, 1988). The concept is mainly reflected in varieties of 12-step groups, most of which derive from AA, the worldwide self-help system.

In the TC perspective (as well as AA and related approaches), self-help is both a philosophy and a requirement for recovery to occur. Consistent with its view of the disorder and the person, individuals assume primary responsibility for their recovery.

Self-help recovery means that individuals make the main contribution to the change process. In the TC, treatment is not provided to the residents so much as made available to them. The TC environment; the staff and peers; and the daily regimen of work, groups, meetings, seminars and specific clinical interventions are the treatment elements in the recovery process. However, the effectiveness of these elements as change-inducing agents is dependent upon the individual. The residents must fully participate in the daily regimen in order to benefit from it; they must use the program—its people, teachings, and activities—to learn and maintain recovery.

Mutual self-help means that individuals assume responsibility for the recovery of their peers in order to maintain their own recovery. Although recovery is the responsibility of the individual, other recovering people are essential in promoting change in the individual. The main messages of recovery, personal growth, and right living are delivered by recovering peers through confrontation and sharing in groups, serving as role models, and providing support as encouraging friends in daily interactions.

Thus, in the TC perspective, treatment works because individuals make it work using other people engaged in the common struggle of recovery. There is an axiom in the TC that captures the essential meaning of mutual self-help: "You alone can do it, but you cannot do it alone."[16]

Motivation, Readiness, and Commitment in Recovery

Self-help and mutual self-help underscore the point that recovery in treatment evolves out of an interaction between the influences of the program (e.g., the peers, the social learning environment) and the individuals themselves. Individual factors that are particularly salient to the recovery process are motivation, readiness, and commitment (e.g., De Leon, 1996a; De Leon et al., 1994; De Leon, Melnick, & Hawke, in press; Erickson, Stevens, McKnight, & Figuerdo, 1995; Joe et al., 1998; Miller & Rollnick, 1991; Prochaska et al., 1992; Simpson, Joe, Rowan-Szal, & Greener, 1997; Zimmer-Hofler & Meyer-Fuhr, 1986). In the TC it is a daily task of the peer community to maintain these motivational factors in individual members.

Though related, motivation, readiness and commitment differ in the recovery process. Recovery depends on positive and negative pressures to change. Some people seek help for their drug use driven only by *external* pressures from families, relationships or employers, court mandate or pending legal problems, fears of illness or violence (domestic or street), or homelessness. Others are moved by more *internal* factors—a profound emotional and physical fatigue with the drug-using lifestyle and an expressed desire to change their lives.

Motivation based mainly upon external pressures, while sufficient to prompt an individual to seek treatment in a TC, is not enough to sustain the recovery process long term. Relief from external pressure (family backs off, legal problems resolve, etc.) often leads to leaving treatment prematurely if more internal pressures haven't developed within the individual. Regardless of the initial source of motivation, however, continued engagement in recovery must be sustained by internal motivation: the individual's pain concerning the negative aspects of his or her life and the hopes and aspirations for a more positive future.

Most residents entering the TC indicate that they are motivated to change based on a mix of both external and internal pressures (e.g., Condelli, 1986; De Leon et al., 1994). But relatively few are actually ready to undertake the long, arduous, and often fear-inducing effort involved in personal change in the TC. Readiness, defined as the person's

---

[16] This enduring axiom, now part of TC teachings, is commonly attributed to O. H. Mowrer, who was an ardent advocate for community as healer and an energetic supporter of contemporary TCs in their early years (De Leon & Beschner, 1977).

willingness to actively engage in the change process, has been identified as critical in recovery among substance abusers in general. Individuals in the TC display readiness when they give up or reject all other options to change except long-term residence in the program.

Individuals make a commitment when they resolve or promise to take an action, meet an obligation, carry out a suggestion, complete a task, or reassert their acceptance of community teachings. In the TC, making a commitment usually reflects individuals' motivation and readiness to change and their acceptance of the community's expectations and approach to change. However, making a commitment is also a means of sustaining motivation.

Even among those who remain in treatment, there are various degrees of commitment. These range from a willingness to continue in the program, to a full commitment to the goals of the program, and finally to a sustained commitment to remain in the change process. The ability to make and keep commitments is a vital goal in the change process for these residents, who have notorious problems with commitments to self as well as to others. Typically, in the history of a substance abuser there is a pattern of breaking promises or meeting commitments. They have difficulty in adhering to the obligations in their roles as parents, offspring, siblings, workers, students, friends, lovers, and citizens. The making and keeping of commitments is constantly emphasized throughout the program. Completion of the program itself represents a profound step forward in learning how to keep a commitment.

Thus, much of the mutual self-help effort of peers is focused on sustaining individuals in the recovery process by reminding them of past losses, current gains, and future possibilities—as it is only by remaining cognizant of these that commitment can be sustained.

Recovery as Multidimensonal Learning

Consistent with the TC view of the whole person, recovery is seen as multidimensional learning. Behavioral, cognitive, and emotional changes must be integrated as the foundation of recovery. Behavioral learning refers to the elimination of asocial and antisocial behavior and the acquiring of positive social and interpersonal skills. Cognitive learning refers to gaining new ways of thinking, decision making, and problem solving skills. Emotional learning is acquiring the skills needed for managing and communicating feelings.

Additionally, recovery involves subjective changes that are experiential and perceptual. Individuals not only actively engage in the behaviors and attitudes to be changed, they must undergo essential experiences and perceptions associated with change in their behaviors, attitudes, and emotions.

The experiences that are considered essential for recovery revolve around themes of emotional healing, social relatedness, and self-efficacy. The perceptions that are essential for recovery center upon the themes of self- and identity change. These experiences and perceptions occur through the manifold daily social interactions in the intimacy of community life. As individuals learn to behave effectively, think constructively, manage their emotions, and have new social experiences with others, they come to see themselves and the world differently.

Multidimensional learning occurs through *trial and error*. The community encourages and reinforces residents who are attempting to engage in new behaviors and attitudes. In fact, the term failure is rarely used in association with an error, but is reserved for the act of not trying or giving up. Thus, trying is changing, and residents who see themselves as trying are often motivated to continue working at changing.

"Going through changes" is a familiar expression used by residents to describe how they experience the trial and error process. It refers to the struggle involved in personal change: the requirements of learning to cope with feelings, understand others, face and tolerate uncertainty, and solve problems in new ways. In the course of treatment, the individual is repeatedly "put through changes" by planned or spontaneous interventions of the program. This trial and error process in the TC has been likened to the Eriksonian concept of maturation by "learning through crisis" (Kooyman, 1993, p. 44; Ramirez, 1984).

Learning to change a lifestyle can only occur in a *social context*. A substance abuser's negative patterns, attitudes, and roles were not acquired in isolation, nor can they be altered in isolation. Recovery depends not only on what has been learned, but how, with whom, and where that learning occurs.

In TCs all learning occurs through social interactions, experiences, and roles (Jones, 1953). This assumption is the basis for using community itself as primary teacher in the TC. Learning is experiential occurring through participation and action; a socially responsible role is acquired by acting the role. New ways of coping with life learned in the TC are threatened by loss of this community after leaving the TC, increasing the potential for relapse. Thus, sustained recovery requires a positive social network of others within and beyond the TC, one that can continually affirm healthy perspectives on self, society, and life.

Recovery as a Developmental Process

Recovery in the TC unfolds as a developmental process, entailing sequential passage through stages of incremental learning. The learning that occurs at one stage facilitates change at the next. In an analogy from physical development, crawling precedes standing, which is required for walking; while running uses an accumulation of these skills. In the TC, each stage of learning draws on the maturity, socialization, and personal autonomy acquired at the previous one. Residents often characterize their recovery in the TC as one of "growing up," coming in as babies or adolescents and leaving as adults. Consistent with the TC view of the whole person, growing up involves change in both conduct and self-understanding.

Recovery begins with *behavioral* change. In the TC developmental view of recovery, behavioral and attitude changes precede insight about the self, and in fact may be a prerequisite for it. This is expressed in common TC axioms that instruct the resident to "Act as if" or "Do it right, then you'll understand why you've been doing it wrong." However, behavioral change is insufficient for lasting recovery without insight and relevant emotional experiences. Insight is a resident's understanding of the important relationship between his or her actions, attitudes, and feelings and the conditions of his or her life. These connections may involve both current conditions and past history. Although understanding and insight are not necessary to initiate changes in behaviors and attitudes, they are essential to maintaining them.[17]

Residents must become able to recognize the triggers or cues to their drug use, the people, places, and external influences that elicit in them cravings to "get high." However, they must also come to recognize the inner thoughts, perceptions, and feelings (internal influences) that trigger cravings, drug seeking, and other self-defeating and self-destructive behaviors. Recognition of the current influences on their behaviors facilitates learning control of these, which reinforces a sense of self-efficacy.

Self-understanding also involves becoming more aware of those memories and experiences associated with past relationships and circumstances that have shaped current feelings, attitudes, conduct, and self-perceptions. Understanding themselves in the context of past history provides residents with some rational order to their disordered lives and thinking and helps to mitigate some of the associated self-blame, guilt,

---

[17] Recent clinical writings have begun to underscore similar conclusions concerning the relationship between behavioral change and insight in other treatment strategies (see Margolis & Zweben, 1998).

and shame. A comprehensible view of their disorder and of themselves provides rational meaning to their recovery efforts.

Thus, in the TC view, the main purpose of understanding the past is to improve the present. Past history involves conditions over which the individual has no control. The individual can, however, change his or her present reactions to those conditions.

Relapse in Recovery

In the TC view of recovery, abstinence is a prerequisite for a more complete change in lifestyle and identity. However, TCs recognize the reality of relapse and its profound importance in the developmental process of recovery.

The use of any substances during treatment can impede the recovery process of the individual. Moreover, the use of drugs in the drug-free environment of the TC has potentially corrosive effects on community life. Thus any substance use during residential treatment is viewed both in terms of its implications for the individual's recovery and for the morale and integrity of the community. In practical terms this view guides clinical and management policy with respect to the incidents of drug use and the people who relapse

In TCs, there is virtually no drug use during the residential phase of treatment, with the exception of incidents that occur while a resident is on furlough. Thus, the issue of relapse is more relevant for residents who are in the re-entry phase of treatment or who leave the TC as dropouts or graduates. Their ability to avoid relapse, or manage it constructively, reflects what they have learned in treatment.

Relapse, i.e., re-use of drugs after a period of abstinence, assumes different patterns, each having different implications for treatment and recovery (De Leon, 1990-91). Relapse may refer to a single, discrete incident (i.e., "slip"), a temporary period of high frequency use (i.e., "binge"), or to a full-blown return to the pretreatment levels of use. Relapse may or may not be accompanied by a reappearance of all the behaviors and attitudes associated with the pretreatment drug lifestyle. Thus, relapse may not necessarily mean total regression in the recovery process.

Conversely, the absence of actual drug use does not necessarily indicate sobriety or stable abstinence. Residents may display attitudes, behaviors, and emotions that have been characteristically associated with initiating drug use (e.g.,"stinken thinken"). Both the individual and the peer community are taught to remain vigilant as to these warning signs to prevent a cycle of actual drug use.

Every incident of relapse provides opportunities for learning. The anatomy of a relapse event (an in-depth review of the circumstances surrounding it, triggers, antecedents, etc.) usually reveals where the individual is in their recovery, how much (or how little) they have internalized recovery teachings, and how they are applying these teachings. If viewed from this perspective of learning, relapse is an integral element of recovery.

Treatment as an Episode

Residency in the TC is a relatively brief period in an individual's life but its impact must compete with the years of negative influences before and after treatment. For this reason, unhealthy "outside" influences are minimized until the individual is better prepared to engage these on his or her own. Thus, the treatment regimen is designed to have a high impact. Life in the TC is necessarily intense, its daily regimen demanding, and its therapeutic confrontations unmoderated.

That residency in the TC is a (relatively) brief episode highlights the important distinction between a specific period of treatment and the more general *process* of recovery. Treatment and recovery are not necessarily the same. For example, non–treatment factors may contribute to the recovery process, such as social resources and psychological stability, relationships, family, health, personal and material losses or gains, etc. (Biernacki, 1986; Simpson, 1986).

Treatment is only one contributor to the recovery process—however central it may be. Individuals moving through treatment in the TC are preparing to positively engage life and continue in their recovery. Completion or graduation from a TC represents the end of treatment, but it is just a stage in the recovery process. Lifestyle changes that begin in the TC must be sustained once people leave. The community teachings, collectively termed "right living," that guide recovery during and after treatment in the TC are the subject of the remainder of this chapter.

VIEW OF RIGHT LIVING

The TC perspective includes certain shared assumptions, beliefs, and precepts that constitute an ideology or view of healthy personal and social living. These community teachings, summarized in the phrase right living, can be incorporated into the broader concept of *living right*, which describes why and how people change in the TC.[18]

Sobriety is the prerequisite for learning to live right but right living is required to maintain sobriety. Living right in the TC means abiding by community rules; remaining drug free; steadily participating in the daily regimen of groups, meetings, work, and educational functions; meeting obligations; maintaining a clean physical space and personal hygiene; acting responsibly to self, others, and the community; and displaying socialized behavior such as civility, manners, respect, and keeping agreements. Living right also involves role modeling the TC values of right living, e.g., honesty, self-reliance, responsible concern, and the work ethic. It is the daily practice of living right within the community that in time evolves toward a changed lifestyle and identity.

The teachings of right living relate to the views of the person and of recovery. The consistency of living right in the TC provides a stark contrast to the disordered lives most drug abusers have lived. In particular, living right provides daily evidence of and experience with self-control for those who have usually been out of control. These contrasts in living are positive experiences that reinforce the TC's view of right living as essential for recovery. The experiences of ordered living provide a prototype to be referred to after separation from the TC. This is important for both those who have lost their capacity for orderly living through their drug life and for those who never had or knew an orderly life.[19]

The sources of right living teachings vary. Several can be traced directly and indirectly to some of the ancient and modern sources noted in chapter 1 of this volume (e.g., AA, the Bible, existentialism, religions, and ethical writings).[20] Others have originated from the experiences of those recovering in TCs over the years. They are framed in slogans, idioms, concepts, and credos and expressed formally and informally in seminars, tutorials, program writings, daily conversations, on wall signs, and in recommended readings. The main teachings of right living are organized and discussed as separate themes.

[18] The term "unwritten philosophy" is often used to refer to the beliefs, assumptions, and precepts of the TC perspective. The written philosophy is usually the treatment creed of a particular program.

[19] The importance of establishing values and norms that contrast with the street, drug culture, and prisons has been underscored as an essential therapeutic element in the recovery and TC literature (e.g., Frankel, 1989; Waldorf 1971, 1973; Yablonsky, 1965, 1986).

[20] The phrase *view of right living* was independently coined by the author to summarize TC teachings. However, it is akin to concepts such as "right thinking" in philosophical and religious writings of the East (e.g., Deitch & Solit, 1993a; Nan Huat-Chin, 1997).

Moral Code

TCs hold unambiguous moral positions, these guiding personal and social conduct both within and outside of the residential community. They include proscriptions against antisocial behaviors and attitudes, the negative values of the street, and irresponsible or exploitative sexual conduct. This moral code is expressed in cardinal rules, house rules, community norms, and general ethical expectations.

The need for an explicit moral code stems from the TC views of the person and the disorder, as well as from the dynamics of TC life. The lack or loss of moral development is a distinctive feature among substance abusers in TCs and is consistently documented by research (e.g., Biase et al., 1986; De Leon, 1989) and evident in their shame and guilt as perpetrators and victims. Their life stories are marked by broken promises, lies, sexual exploitation, crimes, and physical violation of self and others. The psychological characteristics of emotional tolerance, restraint, judgment, and self-control, which are the underpinnings of moral living, were either never adequately developed or weakened by years of drug use.

Without a firmly established moral code, the individual's recovery and personal growth are threatened. Defining right and wrong behaviors and rules of conduct, then, is a necessary step in learning personal boundaries, and provides the behavioral infrastructure for decision making. Learning to make any decisions, moral, ethical, or otherwise, means that the individual has choices that are feasible behavioral alternatives. However, those who cannot manage their behaviors are controlled by their behaviors; they are not free to assess alternatives or make decisions.

The intimacy of living in a close community also underscores the need for strict injunctions against lying, stealing, manipulation, lending, borrowing, sexual acting out or condoning such behaviors in others. Thus, without an explicit moral code, the very safety of the TC community itself would be threatened.

A profound distinction of the TC approach is that the collective community teaches morals by example. Moral development, modeled by the peer community, challenges the code of the street, jails, and negative relationships. A peer community that behaves morally can teach its members what they could not or would not learn from schools, religion, or families.

The Self and Social Perspective

TC tenets focus upon how individuals see themselves as moral and social beings. A balanced perspective on the self is necessary for learning and sustaining recovery. This perspective is communicated through teaching three basic distinctions (see Table 5-1). These address residents' poor self-perceptions, the negative influences of the past, and the need to reinvest in themselves.

TABLE 5-1.   Self and Social Perspective: Three Basic Teachings

Self as fundamentally good
   While the conduct, attitudes, and thinking of an individual may be wrong or "bad," the inner person is fundamentally good. In the recovery process, when a person is nurtured, understood, and accepted by others, that inner person can emerge. Many substance abusers connect their inner person with their bad behavior. Teaching them the distinction between their behavior and inner self is essential for initiating a change in identity. Learning to distinguish how they have behaved and what they have done from who they really are and who they can be offers residents hope and the possibility of change. Thus, a changing perspective on self unfolds as individuals change their negative behaviors through right living.

"The here and now"
   Right living stresses the personal present (here and now) as opposed to the historical past (then and when). Past behavior and circumstances are explored only to the extent that this can help change current patterns of dysfunctional behavior, negative attitudes, and outlook. Individuals are encouraged and trained to assume personal responsibility for their present reality and their future destiny.

A stake in self and society
   TCs explicitly instruct individuals to use the community and its teachings to create or re-create their lives. For many of the disaffiliated in TCs this instruction is critical. Self-rejection, shame, and self-devaluation indicate their loss of a personal stake, that is, they make no claim for themselves in terms of who they want to be or what they want to achieve. Among the socially disadvantaged this loss compounds an also missing social stake. They do not see themselves as having access to achievement in the larger society. Individuals gain a stake in society when they invest in themselves; aspire to material, ideological, and psychological goals; and when they come to value life itself.

The Primary Values of Right Living

There are specific values and maxims that guide right living. These apply to all situations and all people and transcend the foibles of the particular individuals teaching them, as illustrated in the phrase "principles before personalities." These principles include truth and honesty (in word and deed), the work ethic, the necessity of earning rewards, the value of learning, personal accountability, economic self-reliance, responsible concern toward peers and family, community involvement, and good citizenry.

Honesty (in word and deed)

This principle encourages interaction with others (and the self) in ways that stress honest communication and the importance of directly expressing honest feelings and reactions. It also means self-confrontation and the persistent and courageous self-examination of one's own behavior, attitudes, thoughts and feelings, and motivations.

Dishonesty has been integral to the substance abusers' disorder and negative identity. Thus for residents in TCs, learning absolute honesty is fundamental to their recovery.

Honesty in the TC is viewed as the path of least error. Although dishonesty may be easier or have fewer consequences in the short run, in the long run it has much more severe consequences. An example is the spiraling lie, where the initial truth about a slip to drug use is covered up and then the guilt associated with the cover-up itself escalates leading to a full blown relapse. Dishonesty also leads to social and personal isolation in the peer community. Hidden feelings and thoughts that cannot be addressed shield the individual from being seen by others. Personal isolation occurs when others cannot know or accept the real person.

Finally, it is the honest thoughts, emotions, and perceptions about self and others that comprise personal identity, who the person *is*. To the extent that one's inner self is not seen by others or oneself, the person's true identity remains unformed, unknown.

Responsible concern

The concept of responsible concern instructs residents to assume some level of personal responsibility for the recovery of their peers. The concept is framed as being one's "brother's or sister's keeper," highlighting the TC's orientation to family and community. However, responsible concern is a broader concept still, embracing the idea that monitoring, challenging, and affirming others in their struggle to recover is caring about them (e.g., Ottenberg, 1978).

The rationale for responsible concern is profound in terms of the view of the person, disorder, and recovery. Caring for others through responsible concern directly modifies the characteristic self-involvement of substance abusers. The practice of responsible concern also reinforces altruism, a social value in right living. However, the implicit message of responsible concern is that "your recovery is my recovery." Individuals foster recovery in others in order to sustain it themselves. If negative behaviors and influences in the community are not interrupted, they could undermine the recovery of all. Thus, though responsible concern is explicitly altruistic it is implicitly concerned with self-help.

Responsible concern is displayed not only when peers encourage and support each other, but also when they confront, challenge, and criticize each other for behaviors and attitudes not in keeping with the goals of recovery. This often risks painful interactions and consequences for the relationship. However, responsible concern places the health and welfare of the individuals involved above the relationship itself. This is in contrast with the code of the street, jails, or dysfunctional and misguided. families, wherein individuals are bound to protect each other from the truth. Thus, responsible concern uses personal friendship as a potent tool in the recovery process.

In the TC, *irresponsible* concern is enabling or condoning any activity that deliberately or inadvertently encourages, facilitates, or permits the other person to continue his or her substance use or overall negative behavior. Usually enablers are peers in treatment, friends, family members, or other relations who attempt to reduce the pain of the other person—often to avoid their own discomfort in dealing with that person. Seeing themselves or being seen as caring spouses, parents, or friends remains more important to them than truly caring for the individual enough to realistically confront his or her behavior.[21]

Work ethic

TCs teach a classic work ethic, a set of related values emphasizing good habits, self-reliance and earned rewards, excellence in standards, pride in performance, and personal commitment in effort. Each of these values helps to counter characteristics of those TC residents who have poor or erratic work histories. As described in a later chapter, work is a critical therapeutic and educational activity in the TC. Teaching the work ethic embraces the entire TC perspective, particularly the view of the whole person.

---

[21] The concept of enabling can be extended to impersonal entities, such as schools, local communities, and government. TCs have long argued that social policy could be better informed by understanding how specific policies can inadvertently facilitate drug abuse and crime, or how mental health policies concerning clients' rights can impede self-help recovery. Some discussion of this issue is contained elsewhere (see De Leon, 1997b).

Learning as a value

Learning, both formal and informal, is a central value in the TC. Education is stressed as essential for social efficacy and world awareness. However, the deeper value of learning is its relevance for recovery. All experiences in recovery can and should be used to advance personal growth, that is, to learn about oneself, better understand and express feelings and thoughts, and to learn self-management The lessons of personal growth, when realistically faced and acknowledged, are inherent in every gain and setback in treatment (and in life).

This prescription is particularly relevant to substance abusers who have characteristically avoided and learned little from the reality outside and inside of themselves. Courage to explore and experience the pains, guilt, and disturbing truths of their lives is strengthened by the value placed upon learning from experience. The painful lessons of the past, therefore, have the potential to earn dividends in the present and future.

TC Recovery Maxims

These precepts center on the theme of maintaining personal balance in the daily effort to achieve recovery goals. They correctively counter typical psychological characteristics of the resident such as unrealistic goal setting, impatience, frustration, tolerance, and fears of success and failure. Several are inherited from AA, while others are indigenous to the TC. Overall, enduring values and guides for living are embedded in these pragmatic recovery teachings.

"One day at a time"

"Take care of today and tomorrow will take care of itself" and "one day at a time" are related maxims, which help residents break time down into more manageable units. Substance abusers in treatment characteristically "rush" their recovery; they think about all of their problems yet to be solved and all that remains yet to do. They underestimate the time it takes to change and overestimate the progress they have made. Their temporal miscalculations and future-oriented thinking invariably lead to feelings of frustration about the recovery process itself and precipitate relapse. For example resident impatience with planned duration of residential treatment often leads to premature dropout. As one can only live in the present anyway, these temporal maxims with their emphasis upon living right each hour, each day, reduce anxiety and facilitate goal attainment.

"Keep it simple"

Residents frequently become overwhelmed when they attempt to deal with too many problems at once. This characteristic difficulty in coping often reflects their unrealistic self-appraisal of resources and skills. "Keep it simple" encourages residents to focus on one thing at a time: changing an attitude, managing a feeling reaction, or being on time. Trying to do too much is a setup to fail at everything.

"Step by step"

Residents characteristically want things quickly, even their recovery. As a result, they miss important steps in their learning. The maxim "step by step" reminds residents that recovery is about learning, and learning is incremental. What is learned at one point becomes the foundation for the next piece of learning.

"What goes around, comes around"

"What goes around, comes around" captures the importance of learning patience. Its broader intent, however, is to provide individuals a way to cope with the uncertainty and seeming unfairness of things that are out of their control. Injustices and injuries abound, in life, in relationships, in efforts not recognized, achievements not acknowledged, or interpersonal affairs not yet resolved. These are everyday events that can destabilize and encourage self-defeating responses if substance abusers don't have some way of "letting go."

Regardless of which role a resident plays, victim or perpetrator, in incidents of reversals or injuries, this maxim's message is twofold. First, unfairness or injustice is the rule rather than the exception in life and requires patience and tolerance. Second, some form of closure, resolution, or equity will likely occur at some point in the future—but remains beyond our personal control.

"No gain without pain"

Authentic changes in long-held behaviors, attitudes, and self-images involve struggle and even suffering; hence, for the TC resident there is "no gain without pain." Becoming personally "fit" in the TC is analogous to becoming physically fit. Developing physical strength, stamina, and endurance requires focus, effort, discipline, sacrifice, tiring workouts, and boring practice. But mainly, it involves aches, pain, and sometimes fear associated with stretching beyond previous limits.

The acceptance of pain as a criterion for growth is particularly relevant for substance abusers, for they have characteristically avoided discomfort in its various forms. Invariably, residents testify that the process of recovery in the TC is "hard." It is a continual struggle to stay clean, delay gratification, deal with the social and interpersonal demands of living in close proximity with others, face the problems and obligations of living with sobriety, and most uncomfortably—to maintain the unremitting task of self-examination, feeling feelings, tolerating guilt, discarding old self-images, and accepting both who they have been and who they really are. Simply remaining in the treatment environment is seen as a personal victory. Yet, anything worth having, residents learn, is worth working for.

"You get back what you put in"

"You get back what you put in," as a teaching, stresses the importance of investing in recovery through total commitment to the change process. The extent of personal and lifestyle change depends upon the individual's adherence to the program of change. This maxim helps residents focus upon participating fully in every TC activity, each of which can pay a small dividend toward the larger goal of personal change.

"Act as if"

"Act as if" is a basic TC concept instructing residents and staff to behave as the persons they *should* be rather than the persons they have been. Despite resistances, perceptions, or feelings to the contrary, they should engage in the expected behaviors and consistently maintain the attitudes and values of the community. These include self-motivation, commitment to work and striving, positive regard for staff as authority, and an optimistic outlook toward the future. In the TC view, acting as if is not just an exercise in conformity but a powerful mechanism for making a more complete psychological change. Feelings, insights, and altered self-perceptions often follow rather than precede behavior change.

A variant on acting as if is the phrase "Do it right, then you will understand why you have been doing it wrong." It specifically addresses the issue of skepticism in the recovery process. In particular, it speaks to those individuals who resist acting as if, often by seeking intellectual understanding before they try to change. This instruction directs individuals to go ahead and change the behavior even before they understand why the change is good for them. More generally, by living right, one comes to understand why they have been living wrong.

"Remember who you are"

"Remember who you are" is an assertive reminder to the individual to remember the basic goodness and potential of one's inner self—particularly in times of despair, intimidation, and fear. It exhorts individuals to stand up for themselves, to reaffirm their real feelings, and to put forth an honest struggle to change rather than avoid reality.

"Remember where you came from to know where you're going"

By emphasizing the importance of maintaining perspective about oneself, the maxim "remember where you came from to know where you're going" facilitates the process of recovery. Remembering the problems, pains, and identity of the past helps one to stay committed to the struggle in the present and the goals of the future. This reminder also underscores the importance of personal humility and the danger of overconfidence. Change and progress can be misleading. One never "arrives" at the end point; rather, recovery is ongoing. Remembering this helps counter the sense of expansiveness, entitlement, and narcissism that are characteristic of substance abusers. It also strengthens identification with and compassion for others in the struggle—as well as for themselves.

"There's no free lunch"

"There's no free lunch" emphasizes the values of earning rewards and of becoming self-reliant. In its literal meaning, it asserts that nothing is given without cost, that individuals should not expect, nor are they entitled to, something for nothing. Indeed, provision without appropriate return of effort only enables an individual to remain dependent and exploitative. In the TC, the daily sustenance of meals, clothing, and medical care are provided so long as the resident is an active participant in the community and the recovery process.

"You can't keep it unless you give it away"

The prescription "you can't keep it unless you give it away" encourages the individual to be generous in supporting and fostering recovery in others, giving time and energy to that end whenever possible. Recovery is viewed as a *possession,* earned with difficulty through a learning process of painful self-change. Residents often refer to "my recovery" as something to covet and value. However, recovery is also a *gift* to be given. Recovery is learned and maintained through interaction with others. Helping and teaching others is continually helping oneself through practicing, rehearsing, and reinforcing recovery teachings.

TABLE 5-2. Additional Examples of Recovery Maxims

"It's better to understand than be understood"
One may learn more by listening to others than finding it important for others to listen to him or her.

"Do your thing and everything will follow"
Honesty in pursuing your own recovery and in relating to others is the path of least error.

"Trust in your environment"
The ability to trust others is very important to personal and emotional growth.

"Growth before status"
One must demonstrate a certain amount of maturity before being placed in a position of responsibility.

"Be careful what you ask for—you just might get it"
Make sure that you are capable of handling a certain responsibility before asking for it.

"When you are looking good, you're looking bad"
A false or "cool" impression will not help to make good relationships, for it does not indicate real feelings or attitudes and is not honest.

"Compensation is valid"
When recognition is earned, it is deserved.

"Hang loose"
Try to remain open and honest when relating to others, even if this is frightening.

"To be aware is to be alive"
Becoming aware of oneself and others allows an individual to lead a much more fulfilled life.

Variations on the theme of right living teachings are constantly being innovated in different programs (see for example Table 5-2). The moral codes, the recovery maxims, and social and personal values are the content of most communication in daily transactions. In formal seminars, meetings, and tutorials and in informal ordinary exchanges, the words, concepts, and ideas of right living give meaning to the process of recovery and provide the rationale for the methods in the TC.

CONCLUSION

In this chapter the TC view of recovery is defined as change in both lifestyle and personal identity. This change unfolds as a developmental process of multidimensional learning in the social context of the TC. The community teachings, which are collectively termed right living, consist of moral injunctions, values, beliefs, and recovery prescriptions. These integrate the ideological and psychological views of the TC perspective to achieve the goals of sustained recovery and lifestyle change. The four views of the TC perspective guide the community approach to treatment, which is the subject of the next chapter.

Chapter 6

The Community Approach

The quintessential element of the therapeutic community (TC) approach is *community*. Community is both the context and method in the change process. It is the element of community that distinguishes the TC from all other treatment or rehabilitative approaches to substance abuse and related disorders. It is the use of community as method that distinguishes the TC from other forms of community.

When characterized broadly in cultural anthropological terms, the TC has features that are similar to other communities such as religious and secular communes, villages, neighborhoods, prisons, hospitals, clinics, the military, schools, and even corporations. It has a general purpose, an organizational structure, formal rules and informally shared norms, culture-specific values, beliefs, and mores. Like other communities, TCs depend upon the affiliation, investment, and loyalty of their participants for their own continuance.[22]

However, TCs differ profoundly from other communities in their rationale and purpose. Their specific objective is to treat individual disorder, but their larger purpose is to transform lifestyles and personal identities. Toward this purpose the TC uses community as a method to help individuals *change themselves.* Its structure (social organization), its people (staff and residents), and its daily regimen of activities (groups, meetings, work, recreation) are designed to facilitate healing, learning, and change in the individual. Communities that are TCs exist to serve the individual.

---

[22] The key distinction is that the use of community as a method promotes the health, welfare, and growth of the individual. This should be contrasted with communities or groups that use individuals to promote the survival of the community. Cults, as an extreme case, illustrate this profound distinction (see Galanter, 1990 and Ottenberg, 1984).

The initial section of this chapter discusses the general characteristics of community as a treatment approach: its relationship to the TC perspective, its healing and learning properties, and its social and cultural features. The second section translates this approach into a specific *method*—the components of which are the "active ingredients" in the treatment process.

COMMUNITY AND THE TC PERSPECTIVE

Recovering people innovated the TC to learn an alternative lifestyle and as an alternative to conventional treatment approaches. Their intuitive understanding of the relevance of the community approach is implicit in the perspective on the disorder—the person, recovery, and right living.

Community and the Whole Person

It is difficult to conceive of changing the whole person separately from a community of others. Unlike the psychotherapy hour or group therapy session, which sample relatively little of the individual, the complexity of the "whole" individual is gradually revealed in the varied situations of community life, with its social performance demands, multiple participant roles, and constant social interactions. In the 24-hour community of the TC, individuals can be observed in all of their dimensions: how they work, relate to peers and staff, maintain their rooms and personal hygiene, and participate in groups and community meetings. These are the everyday behaviors and attitudes that provide the steady input of data to be addressed and modified. Individuals change their attitudes, values, and conduct through continuous interaction with a community of others. It is the teachings of the community and the daily examples of how these teachings work to change people that encourage and reinforce residents to participate in the social learning process.

Community and the disaffiliated

Many substance abusers treated in TCs are, in addition to their addictions, variously psychologically disturbed, socially deviant, homeless, poor, and disadvantaged; they also include the socially advantaged who are misfits or rejected and the unsocialized from any sector of society. Although these groups differ in various socio-demographic and psychological ways, to a greater or lesser degree they are disaffiliated (socially impotent, disenfranchised, and isolated); disillusioned (hurt and disappointed by significant others in the present and in early childhood); and despairing (hopeless regarding their ability to succeed based on past failure or impotency, loss of self-control, and lack of confidence).

The disaffiliated are unable or disinclined to live ordered lives or identify with mainstream values. They mistrust themselves, authorities, helping professionals, and particularly "the system," which they rebel against, reject, exploit, or ignore. Their loss or lack of a positive stake in conventional living further prevents them from pursuing positive personal or lifestyle change. Consequently they are unmotivated, psychologically unprepared, and often unskilled in the appropriate use of conventional social, medical, and mental health services.

In the TC view, helping residents become affiliated with a peer self-help community is an essential first step in preparing them to engage the outside world. Stabilized abstinence, socialization, and some level of personal responsibility must occur before individuals can use and benefit from various social, educational, and vocational services. Learning how to constructively use the resources of their peer community is preparation for efficient use of services outside of the community. Thus, in ways similar to healthy families the TC provides the psychological "home base" (a microsociety) from which residents can gradually re-enter the larger world.

Community, identity, and right living

Residents in TCs have been labeled as bad or rebellious kids, dangerous addicts or criminals, failures or losers, sick or crazy. These various social labels reflect the social stigma of the drug abuse disorder, often reinforced by characteristic behaviors of the individuals themselves. The negative social labels become embedded in self-perceptions regarding their social and personal identities.

The community approach fosters change in the social and personal elements of identity. With its focus on social participation, mutual responsibility, and relationships based on trust and the values of right living, TCs provide the opportunities and context for developing elements of a positive social identity. These include being a role model for others, advancing in the work structure, progressing through the stages of the program, and relating in new ways to peers and staff. These changes in social identity are supported in the community's vernacular, concepts, and peer network (e.g., Biernacki, 1986; Kellog, 1993; Nielsen & Scarpitti, 1995, 1997).

The TC's emphasis on absolute honesty in word and action, and the sharing of private feelings and experiences also helps strengthen elements of personal identity. Community elements such as encounter groups challenge false images and help foster self-objectification, which in terms of personal identity strengthens the individual's "inner witness." Of special relevance to the development of personal identity is that of community acceptance of the authentically revealed individual. Teaching and practicing the values of right living in community also help to define personal and social elements of identity. In the TC perspective, recovery means a change in lifestyle that can only be achieved by living *differently,* not only in behaviors and attitudes but also in values and beliefs. Regardless of differences in their social backgrounds, TC residents have either lost or never acquired values to guide healthy, productive lifestyles. Learning or relearning these values requires practice in a real community that explicitly reinforces how individuals can "live right" with themselves, others, and society.

For all residents in recovery, the valued life is associated with achieving conventional social expectations: being a consistent, reliable, responsible, and self-reliant person; being a good parent, spouse, or child; and having and pursuing goals of education, career, money, homes, and relationships. For some, the valued life extends further to include being of service to others. Their recoveries through living in community inspire them to serve similar others, further shaping personal identity in terms of individual purpose and meaning.

LEARNING, HEALING, AND THE CULTURE OF COMMUNITY

Community defies simple definition. In the last analysis, however, individuals must perceive themselves in community. This perception constellates around the theme of affiliation—the individual's sense of belonging, being home, and being part of others. In the TC, the culture of community fosters healing and learning experiences that reinforce the individual's perception of and affiliation with the community.

The Healing and Teaching Properties

The key healing experiences are evoked spontaneously and by design. Individuals feel psychologically safe to be seen, understood and accepted by others in groups, meetings, and quiet face-to-face conversations.

Residents connect with each other through shared experiences, words of affirmation, and explicit gestures of affection such as individual and group hugs, arms on shoulder, cradling, or simply smiling. Thus, long-standing pains, often originating in disordered relations between self and others require healing experiences that are intrinsically social, mediated by the mutual reactions of people who perceive themselves in community.

Learning about the self as well as social learning occurs in the daily interaction between the individual and the community. Embedded in the context of community life, however, are familiar teaching factors that strengthen the process of learning, e.g., continuous observation of behaviors, attitudes, and emotions; repetition of the messages of recovery and right living; community feedback; collective or team learning; as well as vicarious learning.

In the TC community, learning and healing are mutually interactive and enhancing. Healing experiences can be motivators and reinforcers in the social learning process. Good feelings sustain the individual in the trial and error learning process and reinforce the individual's affiliation with the community.

Conversely, the learning process in the TC can result in healing experiences. For example, new job performance skills increase self-efficacy, self-worth, and self-acceptance; being responsible to self and others provides corrective/redemptive social and interpersonal experiences. These mitigate the guilt and self-rejection associated with earlier interpersonal injuries to others. Communication skills directly facilitate the effective resolution of interpersonal conflict and provide new modes of personal expression—skills that also facilitate affiliation and lessen personal isolation.[23]

The Culture of Community

In the TC, affiliation, teaching, and healing are transmitted through familiar cultural elements inherent in kinship, fraternities, villages, etc. These elements define the distinctive *identity of the community*. Each TC evolves its own culture, but all TCs use their culture to foster right living and recovery. Through stories, legacies, rituals, and traditions the messages of change, recovery, right living, and transformation are reiterated and amplified by the intensity and intimacy of community life.

---

[23] The healing and learning properties of community resemble general curative factors in psychological and group therapies (e.g., Hollidge, 1980; Kennard, 1983; Kooyman, 1993; Yalom, 1975).

Philosophy and language

The program philosophy is a fundamental cultural ingredient in all TCs. Each program constructs its own prescribed credo that embodies the essentials of the TC perspective (see examples in Appendix B). The program philosophy is collectively recited each morning to enhance the sense of community and to initiate a positive start to the day. Its memorization is considered a concrete sign of affiliation.

More generally, the concepts, beliefs, values, and norms that guide recovery and right living are expressed in the unique language of the TC culture (see the glossary in Appendix A). Learning this TC vernacular represents the individual's integration into the peer community and mirrors their clinical progress. Thus the individual's use of the argot measures his or her affiliation with and socialization in the TC community and reflects a change in social identity.

Celebration, tradition, and ritual

There are many occasions marked for celebration in the TC. Such community events are used as positive symbols of individual and collective change. TCs generally celebrate ethnic, national, and local holidays (Thanksgiving, Christmas, Martin Luther King Day, etc.), individual markers (birthdays, anniversaries), recovery landmarks (treatment phase changes, program and school graduations), and specific program events (a new facility acquisition, fundraising or media event). Secular prayers and meditations for community members in health crises and memorials for those who have died are more spontaneous events, bringing the community together in common experience. A prime example of a universal ritual in TCs is the daily recitation of the program philosophy.

Celebrations, traditions, and rituals enhance community cohesiveness, but they also reinforce individual progress. As constant, predictable activities they strengthen the perception of a stable environment and orderly life. The various protocols reaffirm the TC teachings on right living and directly train new social behavior, particularly in the use of leisure time and acceptable forms of emotional expression. The tradition of celebrating recovery phase changes in particular marks the process of change in members.

Personal stories

In the living culture of the TC, members come to understand the meaning of community and its role in the change process primarily through *shared stories.* Over time, each resident tells his or her story and witnesses the changing stories of others. In groups, lounges, dormitories, and one-to-one exchanges, the story of each individual gradually emerges in all its farcical and tragic detail. These stories are inherently dramatic, arresting the attention even of those with characteristically little patience or belief. The story content is familiar, promoting identification with others and lessening a sense of isolation.

Each individual storyteller is an extremely effective transmitter of the messages of personal change, providing living illustrations of how one's story can change positively. Members continually alternate in their roles as audience and performer in these stories. Thus, the community fosters learning and heightens its participants' awareness by giving attention to and investing special meaning in each individual story.

Legacy

A distinct outgrowth of community, legacy teaches through connection with unseen and unknown similar others. Stories of and by former residents and staff are frequently recounted to encourage, illuminate, and motivate those currently struggling in the change process. These "legendary" role models have typically led ordinary lives, but because of their transformation, appear larger than life. Their stories become concrete evidence that change is possible and that recovering people can create their own destinies.

Personal logs and diaries, which are useful self-monitoring tools in the TC, also become concrete articles of legacy. Autobiographies, letters, and writings left to later generations of residents are gifts of encouragement from those who went before. Similarly, photos of current and former residents and staff are common on the walls of dorms and common spaces in TCs. These identify notable faces in the community and affirm current relationships, but they also signal connections with more distal others who have travelled the same path. In this way, legacy "passes it on" from one generation to the next. For those disconnected or estranged from positive social roots of their own, "inheriting" the legacy of the TC provides an anchor in recovery.

Passing it on is a basic recovery rule, expressed also as "You can't keep it unless you give it away." The act of giving information to others about oneself contributes to the change process both for the giver and the receiver. Thus, while legacy evolves spontaneously as part of community life in the TCs, it has pragmatic importance for teaching the change process.

Community as theater

It is more than analogue to note the community's *theatrical element* as an amplifier of its therapeutic and learning effects. This element of theatre is inherent in the public nature and unique characteristics of the TC's community life: the multiple participant roles, the unmasking of individuals in varied social situations and private moments, the game-like quality of encounter groups, the staging of community meetings and special groups, and the humor and pathos present in the unfolding individual stories.

These features of community life in the TC all reflect another basic facet of theater—a contained setting where experiences are evoked and intensified for purposes of producing change. In the 24-hour compressed living situation of the TC, members constantly learn and experience together. In this continual dialogue between individual and community, the process of transformation is the paramount story.

COMMUNITY AS METHOD: BASIC COMPONENTS

The term "therapeutic community" connotes a community that can remedy, restore, or cure. However, the profound distinction between the TC and other treatments and communities is the use of community as a *method* for changing the whole person.

A method refers to the activities, strategies, materials, procedures, and techniques that are employed to achieve a desired goal. In the TC the overarching goal of the community is to sustain the individual's full participation in the community so that he or she can achieve the social and psychological goals of lifestyle and identity change. Participation infers that the individual engages in and learns to use all of the elements of the community as the *tools* for self-change. Though indirect, participation is the most comprehensive measure of individual change. Thus, *community* as method means that the membership itself establishes expectations or standards of participation and use of community. It assesses how individuals are meeting these expectations and responds to them with strategies that promote continued participation.

In this section community as method is described in terms of four interrelated components: the community *context,* which consists of peer and staff relationships, social roles, and daily regimen of activities; community *expectations* for individual participation; community *assessment* of the individual's progress in meeting its expectations; and community *responses* to its assessment. Each of these components is separately outlined.

Community as Context

Community as method means teaching individuals to use the context of community life to learn about themselves. The context of community life is designed to produce therapeutic and educational changes in the individual participants; and all participants are the mediators of these changes. The context, its activities, people, and teachings, are organized into ten broad elements summarized in Table 6-1. These characterize how the community is used for individual change.

TABLE 6-1. Community as Context: Basic Elements

Member roles

Daily life in the TC provides learning opportunities through the various social roles individuals assume as participants in the community. Member roles vary in different job functions such as worker, manager, and staff person, as well as in interpersonal roles as friend, group member, peer leader, student, tutor, and counselor. These roles require members to change behaviors, attitudes, emotional management and values as they related to others.

Membership feedback

A primary source of instruction and support for individual change is the membership's observations and authentic reactions to the individual. Providing such continual feedback is the shared responsibility of all participants. Whether positive or negative membership feedback is expressed with responsible concern.

Membership as role models

Each participant strives to be a *role model* of the change process. Along with their responsibility to provide feedback to others as to what they must change, members must also provide examples of *how* they can change.

Relationships

Relationships in the TC are used to foster the recovery and personal growth in various ways. They can facilitate engagement, develop trust, encourage emotional risk-taking and self-learning, and teach interpersonal skills. Relationships developed in treatment often become the basis for the social network needed to sustain recovery beyond treatment.

Table continues

TABLE 6-1. Community as Context: Basic Elements

Table continued

Collective learning formats

The experiences essential to recovery and personal growth unfold through social interactions. Therefore, education, training, and therapeutic activities occur in groups, meetings, seminars, job functions, and recreation. The individual engages in the process of change primarily with other peers. These collective formats incorporate the empirically demonstrated power of cohorts, teams, and groups in enhancing learning and change.

Culture and language

The TC is a culture of change. Thus, celebrations, traditions, and rituals are used to enhance community cohesiveness and to reinforce individual progress. In particular, the concepts, beliefs, values, norms, and philosophy that guide recovery and right living are expressed in the unique language or argot of the TC. Thus, learning the TC vernacular reflects assimilation into the culture of the TC and a gradual process of identity change.

Structure and systems

Job functions, chores, and prescribed procedures maintain the daily operations of the facility. These activities strengthen self-help and are vehicles for teaching self-development. Learning and growth occurs through following procedures and systems and in behaving as a responsible member of the community upon whom others are dependent. The system of privileges and sanctions maintain the order and safety of the community and facilitate individual change through consequential learning.

Open communication

The public nature of shared experiences in the community is used for therapeutic purposes for the individual and for others. The private inner life of the individual is a matter of importance to the recovery and change process, not only for the individual but for other members. When and how private issues are publicly shared are always at the discretion of the individual participant. Especially sensitive private issues (child abuse, sexual preference, past crimes, health status) may be initially shared with a close peer or staff counselor who preserves confidentiality but encourages eventual disclosure in groups. However, private issues relevant to the cardinal and house rules of the community (current drug use, stealing, lending money, criminality, sexual acting out, arson, violence, etc.) *must* be publicly shared to sustain the safety, credibility, and health of the community.

Community and individual balance

The purpose of the community is to serve the individual, but the relationship between the individual and the community is *reciprocal*. The needs of the community and of the individual must be balanced to sustain the member's positive perceptions of the community as authentic and credible. This requires that the community has a capacity for self-criticism through continued self-examination of the behavior and attitudes of staff, as well as residents. The membership itself, staff and residents, has the responsibility to confront, affirm, and correct the community.

Community Expectations

Community expectations are the implicit and explicit *demands* placed on the individual by the membership concerning standards of behavior and participation. Community expectations however, extend much beyond adherence to rules of conduct. They define individuals' participation in the community and their involvement in the process of self-change.

Residents explicitly learn these expectations, vicariously by observing their role models, and directly from instruction continuously exchanged between members. The residents observe and monitor each other's participation in all the activities and roles of the community as well as how they use these activities and roles for self-change. Thus, as goals and demands, expectations are pervasive influences that collectively constitute an active ingredient of the method.[24]

TABLE 6-2.   Community Expectations: Four Areas

Performance

As members move through the program, community expectations increase with respect to the resident's performance and attitudes in all activities. Their focus and efforts are expected to be *maximal* and *consistent* in their various roles and obligations, in work, groups, meetings, seminars, and recreation.

Responsibility

As residents move through the program, the community expects them to increase the scope of their responsibility and to be increasingly accountable. Residents initially assume responsibility for self, which then extends to immediate peers, and finally widens to the entire community.

Self-examination

As members move through the program, the community expects increases in self-examination. This is evident in their self-awareness and self-disclosure with respect to issues of personal change Their focus shifts from peer (i.e., external) identification of their behavioral, attitudinal, and emotional problems to self-identification of issues, and then to actively working on them.

Autonomy

As members move through the program, the community expects changes in all of the above areas to unfold with lessening dependence on others. Autonomy is evident when individuals initiate changes in all areas without dependence on others. They require less prodding or criticism from peers to maximally perform in their roles and tasks, to seek and assume greater responsibility and obligations in the community, to freely engage in honest personal disclosures, and to be vigilantly self-aware and self-correcting.

---

[24] Discussions of the concept of expectations as a potent therapeutic ingredient can be found in Bratter (1974), Glasser (1969), Ratner (1973), and Rogers (1961, 1969).

Community expectations pertain to four general areas: performance, responsibility, self-examination, and autonomy (see Table 6-2). These summarize a wide range of behaviors and attitudes that indicate the member's participation in the community. The level of expectations in each area increases as residents progress in the program. Residents who meet community expectations in these areas also reflect changes in their social and psychological growth.

Community Assessments

Throughout treatment, peers and staff continually assess if and how members are meeting expectations of participation and use of the community. Although informal, peer assessment is ongoing and pervasive. Peers continually observe, monitor, and provide feedback to each other concerning their participation in and use of the community. Indeed, peer observation and feedback itself is an explicit community expectation. Thus, a reliable indicator of participation and use of the community is whether members provide, as well as use, peer observation and feedback.

Staff assessment also involves observation, but includes actions that manipulate the structure and procedures to evaluate residents. For example, a job promotion may be granted that introduces more responsibility, elevated community status, as well as heightened demands to perform. How the member approaches, adjusts to, and uses this change reveals where he or she is vis-à-vis personal growth. The individual can fixate on the satisfactions of the advancement or can view the promotion as an opportunity for self-examination and ego-management, as well as for learning to tolerate greater status and responsibility.

Whether residents are meeting expectations is assessed through three general strategies: exposure, testing, and challenge. These strategies are used throughout treatment, although testing and challenge are more frequently used in the later stages.

Exposure strategies assess whether members are amenable to learning and using the community as a resource. Generally they involve orienting the individual to community resources, instructing them on the expectations, and observing if individuals are attending all activities, listening to information, and carrying out instructions.

Testing strategies initially assess whether residents can use the community tools without instruction, prompts, or reminders. Later, testing assesses how consistent residents are in using these tools to meet expectations in performance, self-examination, responsibility, and autonomy.

Challenge strategies place residents in new or unfamiliar situations that are not directly related to their skills, previous experiences, or personal strengths. To effectively cope with these, residents are compelled to extend or generalize what they have learned; to solve problems and make decisions on their own; and to innovate and correct standard procedures.

Although continually exposed and tested to new learning situations, challenge "stretches" members beyond their ceiling of functioning in every area of community expectation. In performance, for example, this would be to work 150 percent, to monitor the house 36 consecutive hours, to get things done with few resources, etc; in self-examination, to explore, reveal, and express inner feelings and to relate past conditions with present behavior, etc.; in responsibility, to assume obligations for self, others, and the community in general; and in autonomy, to self-initiate in all of the areas: performance, responsibility, and self-examination.

Community Responses

The responses of the community to its assessment of individuals consist of various reactions, decisions, and strategies employed to promote continued participation and correct use of the community. Responses in words and actions may be supportive, affirmative, critical, corrective, or punitive. Thus, job changes, affirmations, privileges, and disciplinary correctives, all may be employed to facilitate the resident's meeting of community expectations.

Community responses change over time, in accordance with changing expectations vis-à-vis the resident's stage in treatment. In general, community responses in the early stages are more liberal and flexible for the newer resident. The community is supportive and instructive and the resident is "given more slack" as he or she initially learns to meet community expectations. Later the same behaviors may elicit more confrontative or punitive responses reflecting expectations concerning senior residents.

To summarize, community assessments and responses accord with community expectations for performance, responsibility, self-examination, and autonomy at each stage in treatment. Early in the program the resident is exposed to community resources, its people and activities, in order to learn how to use these for self-change. In subsequent stages, the activities and elements of the community may be employed as strategies to *test* or *challenge* the individual in each area of community expectations. Community responses also reflect its expectations and assessments throughout treatment. What is acceptable behavior early in the program may be unacceptable later on, eliciting a different response from the community. These responses are designed to promote self-change. Indeed, members indicate their personal growth when they use the community's responses, positive and negative, as learning opportunities for further self-change.

CONCLUSION

In this chapter, the community as a treatment approach is presented in terms of its teaching, healing, and cultural elements. These elements are reformulated into a method consisting of four components: the community context, expectations, assessments, and responses. The fundamental assumption underlying community as method is that individuals obtain maximum therapeutic and educational impact when they meet community expectations for participation in and use of the community context to change themselves. Community as method, guided by the perspective, provides the theoretical framework for understanding the program model and treatment process in TCs detailed in the subsequent parts of this volume.

PART III

The Model

The therapeutic community (TC) treatment model is its social and psychological environment. Each component of the environment reflects an understanding of the TC perspective and each is used to transmit community teachings, promote affiliation, and self-change. The seven chapters in this section present these components as the "nuts and bolts" of a generic TC model. Chapters 7–9 detail how the physical, social organizational, and work components foster a culture of therapeutic change. Chapters 10–12 describe how the varied social roles of peers and staff and interpersonal relationships mediate socialization and the therapeutic process. Chapter 13 outlines how the program stages convey the process of change in terms of individual movement within the organizational structure and planned activities of the model.

Chapter 7

The Physical Environment

Therapeutic communities (TCs) are designed, both physically and programmatically, to enhance the residents' experience of community within the residence. It is this experience of community—with all its features of safety, consistency, predictability, etc.—that gradually enables newcomers to lessen their identification with and ties to the old drug culture and replace them with ties and loyalties to the people, values, and lifestyle of the TC. This chapter explores how the physical environment of the TC, its setting, facilities, and inner environment, can contribute to this perception and affiliation with community.

SETTING, RESOURCES, AND THE TC PERSPECTIVE

TCs for the treatment of addiction are located in a variety of settings, which may be determined by funding sources and the external resistance to or acceptance of rehabilitation programs. Some are situated on the attractive grounds of former camps, resorts, and ranches in rural settings, or in conventional houses or mansions in suburban neighborhoods. The majority, however, are located in inner-city areas often near drug-affected urban neighborhoods. These TCs are usually operated in building spaces converted from tenement housing, hotels, schools, churches, or nursing homes with the work of renovation frequently done with the assistance of program residents themselves. Larger, well-financed agencies may occupy several facilities in different settings to meet various clinical and administrative needs.

Invisible Boundaries

TCs seek to maintain a *social and psychological separateness* from the settings in which they are located. In the TC perspective on recovery, it is essential to remove the addict from the physical, social, and psychological surroundings previously associated with his or her loss of control and dysfunctional, negative lifestyle.

A complete chemical and "behavioral detoxification" is a necessary initial step in recovery. Residents must not only withdraw from the psychopharmacological effects of drug use, but must also detach from the people, places, and things previously associated with their drug use. This behavioral detox can be undermined if a new resident is constantly exposed to the world outside the TC, as he or she doesn't yet have the skills to resist the myriad of cues and triggers there. Indeed, the inability to maintain abstinence while living in the "real world" is usually the new resident's main reason for having to enter a residential program in the first place.

Secondly, drug subcultures are strong competitors to the positive peer culture of the TC. Thus separation from the outside world is needed to facilitate a gradual affiliation of the new resident with the TC community—a process essential to the TC approach.

Physical and psychological separation from the surrounding social setting is best achieved when the TC facility itself is located in a completely different area, such as a rural setting or even a city neighborhood relatively clear of drugs. However, residents must also learn how to cope with the "culture shock" when they return to the real world outside of the TC. Thus programs must achieve balance between separation from and preparation for re-entry into the outside world.

Some TC agencies operate multiple facilities so that those early in recovery can be initially housed far from their former negative influences but later transferred to a re-entry facility located in their home city or area. This gives them both the chance to solidify early recovery away from temptations and triggers *and* the chance to learn gradually how to cope with real-world influences during re-entry, before they become independently launched.[25]

Regardless of where the program is located, physical and psychological separateness is necessary to counter the negative influences of the outside

---

[25] Separate re-entry facilities are usually similar in design and concept to the program's main, primary residence, but smaller in size and capacity because they are expected to house fewer residents. There is also typically more private sleeping quarters, reflecting the greater autonomy afforded those in re-entry.

world. Indeed, by assimilating residents into its own *inner* community, the program creates a new peer culture, new lifestyle, and new values to replace the old, destructive ones.

Relationship to the Larger Community

While striving to maintain their "invisible boundaries," TCs must, for both clinical and political reasons, simultaneously maintain good relations and a sense of being integrated with the larger community. Local communities often resist placement of TCs in their locale out of fear about having certain racial groups, criminals, and drug addicts in close proximity and the imagined effects on quality of life, real estate prices, etc. This "NIMBY" (not in my back yard) resistance can impede the implementation of new programs, often in areas where they are needed most. However, in actual experience, once programs are established, community perceptions usually reverse as people see and experience their new neighbors (the program) as responsible concerning upkeep, appearances, safety, and civic participation (Nash, 1974; Wexler, H., personal communication, July, 1999).

For example, TCs are vigilant in maintaining an impeccable physical and social image. They strive to have their facilities seen as exemplary homes by the larger community. Hence the physical condition of the facility and its external grounds are in constant attendance by residents. Even in inner-city settings, TCs are often perceived with pride by the local community, who may note that streets with TC facilities are the safest and cleanest in the neighborhood.

In terms of civic duty, teams of residents may be sent out to provide a variety of community services, such as cleaning local parks and assisting the elderly. Special presentations to schools, business groups, religious organizations, and civic groups may be provided by the facility at little or no cost. Other elements of TC life that often impress local residents are the exemplary behavior of residents in public places, the open house invitations, and the generally active and positive relations with various community boards. In fact, TCs usually have a community relations department dedicated specifically to promoting positive community perceptions concerning the health, safety, and social standards of the program.

Although maintaining good community relations is driven partly by political necessity, it also complements the TC's treatment goals. In a sense, the TC itself becomes a role model for good citizenry. Residents learn the value of maintaining good appearances and experience the positive regard that results. They learn to participate in the larger community in a responsible manner—something they've often never experienced before.

Resources

Most programs are primarily supported by public funding and must supplement their funding by seeking additional private and public donations. Thus, there is wide variation in the amount of resources—financial and material—which agencies have at their disposal. Some own the buildings in which they operate; others lease space. Some are furnished entirely with donations of used articles from the community; others are beautifully furnished with new gear.

Whatever their basic level of public support, however, TCs typically incorporate fund-raising into their self-help approach, involving residents in these efforts as much as possible. For example, TCs routinely operate a "procurement department," which seeks from individuals and businesses in the larger community donations of everything from furnishings and clothing to sports equipment and electronics. Even foodstuffs, staples, and housewares are sometimes obtained at discounts negotiated with suppliers.

Residents may be involved in these procurement efforts through a work assignment. The procurement department operates under staff guidance and utilizes residents to serve on crews for street fund-raising campaigns, pick-up and delivery of donated goods, operation of the supply house, telephone negotiations with prospective donors, etc. In these roles, residents are like family members whose personal efforts to sustain the community also strengthen their affiliation *with* the community.

In addition, all residents in a TC must assume some responsibility for paying their own way. The large majority of residents in the typical TC are indigent and therefore unable to pay a fee. However, if they receive public assistance or food stamps, these allowances are donated to the program. Meanwhile, though their numbers are small, some residents with access to income are asked to pay a fee for their drug treatment. In the initial orientation, all new residents are made aware of the practical needs of the program and are helped to ascertain how they will contribute.

In the TC perspective the physical condition and resources of a TC facility convey important psychological messages to its residents. A building in disrepair, shabbily furnished, or serving poor-quality food can signal to residents that they are second-class citizens and reinforce their characteristically low self-esteem. Conversely, TCs housed in well-maintained, cheerful facilities providing appealing, well-prepared food convey the message "We value you and we expect you to value yourself. You deserve to live in nice surroundings." Even when TCs are located in poor neighborhoods, have more modest material resources, lack sufficient space, or have older furnishings, residents still learn the value of living with dignity if these modest accommodations are well-maintained.

While TCs stress the importance of maintaining decent living quarters, they also place this responsibility with the residents, as well as the staff. Giving residents the job of maintaining and caring for the facility teaches them in a very concrete way. TCs are often the first attractive, orderly, and comfortable residence that many socially disadvantaged addicts have ever lived in. Living in such surroundings helps to reinforce a shift in identity and higher expectations for themselves. "I *can* live in someplace nice, and I can keep it up. I want to keep doing this in the future." Learning to care for the facility provides a corrective learning experience that often contrasts with early experiences of deprivation, low expectations, and disorder. Even residents from advantaged backgrounds, who are accustomed to material benefits, often have never experienced the sense of earning these.

Notwithstanding the differences in the socioeconomic status of its residents, the TC utilizes its setting and resources to teach residents distinctions between inner *psychological* and outer *physical* space. This involves learning attitudes and values that are consistent with recovery and right living. Residents are taught to care for their living space and its furnishings; but in addition, they learn to value personal growth more than material gain, to cope with rather than escape the limitations of the "real" world, and to make the best of their existing reality while actively working to change it.

THE FACILITY

The physical characteristics of a given TC—it's size, grounds, condition, and inner spaces—are adapted to the TC's aims and teachings in various ways. Although each TC is laid out differently, there are common physical features that can be identified and their rationale explored through the TC perspective.

Size and Capacity

The residential capacity of a TC program varies widely ranging from 30 in small agencies to 2000 in large agencies that administer separate programs housed in multiple residential facilities. Typically, however, a particular "house" in a community-based setting will accommodate 40–80 residents.

Some houses are surrounded by expansive grounds, such as the land around a former farm, ranch, or resort. Others have only the lot that accompanies a suburban home, or, in the case of an urban tenement building, a small rear courtyard. The external space has programmatic and management implications for the TC.

For example, large open spaces are alluring to residents prone to "wander off" physically or psychologically, particularly early in treatment when least committed to the long-term recovery process. Even for more stable residents, the hidden corners and remote areas of sprawling grounds invite behaviors that are proscribed by the community, such as drug use, sexual acting out, or social withdrawal. Although these security issues are present in all TCs, on large campuses, special procedures may be required to monitor residents.

For these reasons, modest-sized facilities and grounds are generally more easily managed and have other important benefits as well: The experience of family and community is more easily shaped and strengthened when people are living and working within close proximity to each other; and, the compression of limited space intensifies the 24-hour living and learning process, as it evokes a wide range of emotions and attitudes that cannot be easily masked nor escaped by physically isolating oneself.

The "static capacity" of a TC is the maximum number of residents it can house at any one time. For instance, a TC may be a "40-bed" facility, or maintain "40 slots." Clinical and managerial experience has shown that a static capacity of between 40 and 80 is optimal. A critical mass of residents (about 40) is necessary for shaping the stratified peer structure (e.g., junior, intermediate, and senior residents) and filling all the posts needed in the hierarchical division of labor. This allows for vertical mobility, variations in status, and defined role models—elements considered essential to the TC model. Also, with at least 40 residents, goods can be purchased with economy of scale. More than 80 becomes cumbersome in terms of supervision and can work against building a cohesive sense of community.[26]

The "dynamic capacity" is the *actual* number of admissions per year. This is usually about four times higher than the static capacity. Given client turnover—through completion or graduation, client dropout, administrative discharge, etc.—the program may service many more than the "40 beds" over the course of the year (for a full discussion of retention rates see De Leon, 1991; De Leon & Schwartz, 1984; Sells & Simpson, 1976).

Access

Residential TCs are not locked facilities but semi-closed environments with restricted access. Doors are generally locked only at night; however, while a resident is in primary treatment (approximately 12 months), the program imposes strict limitations on his or her comings and goings. A resident's whereabouts is monitored with sign-in and sign-out sheets and bulletin boards. Trips to the outside include legal or medical appointments or family obligations (funerals, organized recreational or other special events attended outside the facility, etc., all of which are usually escorted). Residents may also perform special job-related assignments for the agency such as purchasing or driving vehicles.

Increased access is a privilege granted to residents showing clinical improvement over time. As residents demonstrate greater personal responsibility and appear more prepared to safely engage the outside world, they will be given more frequent and wider access to it. These are provided through day and overnight passes and weekend furloughs. During the re-entry phase of treatment, residents may also be allowed to attend work or an educational/training program. The rationale for limiting resident access to the outside world is the same as that discussed earlier regarding TC settings. There is a need to separate residents from the outside world in order to strengthen their sense of community and affiliation and also to reduce the number of negative pulls from the

---

[26] In recent years, some larger agencies operate residential facilities with a static capacity of 200–300 in community-based settings and even larger numbers in prison settings. Formative evaluations suggest that these capacities are feasible if managed as smaller units of 50–100 residents (e.g., Corcoran prison in California). Conversely, modified TC programs in shelters and mental health settings are smaller "houses" of 30–50 residents (e.g., De Leon, 1997a; Liberty et al., 1998). Increasingly, issues such as resident capacity, staff to client ratios, and number of programming hours are under regulatory influences (e.g. California Department of Corrections, 1998).

outside world that could threaten recovery. However, because the doors of a TC are not literally locked, a resident technically *chooses* to stay in the program each day, and this sense of personal choice helps to reinforce affiliation with the community.

Security

Residents themselves, under staff supervision, manage security. The main security tasks are to restrict unauthorized entry into and exit from the facility and to monitor the movements of residents around the grounds. One work assignment involves operating the "front desk," typically located near the main entrance. There, residents maintain daily logs of all access events, greet and sign visitors in, and handle all phone calls. In large facilities, additional residents may be stationed at critical junctures, such as the entrance to floors, corridors, and rooms not authorized for general use, to record activity and report incidents.

Unlike institutions such as jails, hospitals, or schools, TCs do not generally hire any police or guards to oversee security, instead relying on the residents themselves with staff supervision. This is a striking fact considering the profile of residents and the nature of the substance abuse disorder. Significant numbers of residents and staff have histories of arrest and incarceration; they have typically engaged in crimes against property and sometimes people, while prominent features of their personalities are low frustration tolerance and poor impulse control. These characteristics would challenge the security of any setting.

Resident management of security is a central tenet of the TC perspective and approach. The physical safety of the community is maximized when residents are empowered to hold themselves accountable.

THE INNER ENVIRONMENT

Spaces, rooms, and areas characterize the features of the TC inner environment. These may be ordinary in every way, but are utilized to reinforce, again, the experience of community, the fostering of a sense of home and ownership, the assurance of physical and psychological safety, and a setting that is conducive to personal interaction. All of these goals are inherent in the TC perspectives on recovery and right living.

Space and Areas

The key spaces in a TC are where the operational, educational, and therapeutic activities of the program are held. A few TCs, such as those located on ranches and farms, consist of complexes of single-story buildings, some used for sleeping dorms, others for administration, etc., all organized around a main house in which all of the communal activities occur. Most often, though, the TC facility is a single, self-contained, multilevel building that consists of a kitchen, dining room, sleeping quarters, administrative offices, and group and recreational rooms.

Although TCs vary in physical layout, they all attempt to utilize their space to best facilitate communal functions. Because of their typically modest resources, limited space must be creatively converted to serve multiple purposes. For instance, an area might serve as a group room by day, a seminar room in the evening, and a living room for a party on the weekend. With some exceptions, most common areas are also available at various times for contemplation, social interaction, one-on-one conversations, and spontaneous rap groups. The dining room is the area most often converted for other activities such as parties, dances, general meetings, and large seminars.

The rooms of the TC can be organized into common, private, and specially designated areas. Common spaces consist of lounges, the dining room, sitting areas, classrooms, the library, recreational areas, and resident dormitories. Private spaces (out of bounds without permission) are the offices and conference room used by staff and the residents assigned there for work. Specially designated spaces include those used for specific purposes, such as the kitchen, bathrooms, laundry room, group rooms, relating booths (areas set aside for one-on-one conversations), and the "bench" (an area set aside for self-examination).

The *kitchen* in a TC is customarily large and equipped for institutional cooking. This is not common space, but space in which only authorized residents belong. One staff person supervises it with a senior resident and a changing work crew of other residents. Labor is divided to handle the ordering and purchasing of food, meal planning, food storage and preparation, cooking, maintenance of the area and equipment, and kitchen cleanup. The work activity in the kitchen and dining room is ongoing from early morning until after dinner. Smaller programs often have small eating areas adjacent to the kitchen for off-hour snacks and socializing. Larger programs have snacks served in the dining room or sold in commissaries operated by residents.

The *dining room* is usually one of the largest areas in the facility. Managed by a senior resident, a crew of residents is responsible for setting up the room for three meals a day and snacks. Tasks include arrangement of chairs and tables, table setting, meal service, and dining room cleanup. In the practical sense, residents learn to set place settings, wait on tables, serve meals, and bus tables. As in the kitchen, working in the dining room also gives residents the opportunity to provide hands-on service to the community.

Communal meals are a time when most staff and peer level groups—senior, junior, and new admissions—come together for 30–45 minutes, three times a day. This is a distinctive example of how the TC uses community as method. Communal meals provide an opportunity for learning the conventions of social manners, dining, conversation, and appropriate interpersonal behavior—all of which are typically modeled by senior residents. Residents learn how to say "please" and "thank you" respectfully, to speak in moderate tones, and to display respect for the food served and for those who prepared and served it.

It is not uncommon for intense personal and social discussions to transpire around the dining table as residents learn the art of conversation and social discourse. Various social anxieties may surface during mealtime. By having to relate to others in close physical proximity—like a "normal family"—residents learn to sit and talk with people they may not particularly like, to speak about ordinary subjects like the news or weather, and even discuss personal issues related to their experiences in the program. Were they not in this treatment situation, the same residents might characteristically react to such a communal situation with hostility, withdrawal, early departure, or by sitting alone or with cliques of familiar others for "social protection."

Dining room behaviors and attitudes may be the material for encounter groups but more often are addressed in informal peer conversation. Senior peers serve both as role models for healthy dining room behavior and as supporters and trainers. They may actively "pull-in" (orient and engage) new residents with invitations and suggestions, such as "Come, let's eat together and tell me how you're doing," or "Why don't you sit here with us and talk to the women," or "Make sure you sit with different people every day."

Lounges are separate areas set aside for informal interactions, individual relaxation and reading, TV watching, listening to music, or simply sitting quietly. TC lounges and day rooms are typically carpeted and furnished with sofas, a variety of upholstered and hard chairs, reading lamps and material, and wall hangings.

In many TCs, the evening news is played in the lounge after dinner, with residents required or encouraged to watch and become informed about the world around them. The newscast can stimulate discussion, comments, and controversy, usually initiated by a senior resident or staff member. Residents are encouraged to freely offer opinions, ideas, and suggestions about a variety of social issues. Thus, the evening newscast becomes another "family"-like ritual fostering communication, intellectual expression, and community interaction on issues outside the TC and beyond the usual focus on individual growth. For a staff member observing such a discussion, the level of participation and the quality of the exchanges can also be of clinical utility in gauging the level of affiliation or general progress of the residents involved.

Although largely informal and spontaneous, the activities in the lounge can reveal much about the social and psychological status of individuals—and indeed the house in general. The lounge is only available for use to residents during certain hours of the day, e.g., during personal time after dinner, before evening house meetings, after evening groups, and on weekends. Thus, a lounge with too many residents at any one point is a negative sign in a TC. In the lounge, where there are fewer program demands, the social manners, attitudes, and energy level of individuals are often revealed. Hence, all members of the community are expected to observe the behavior and tone of the lounge. Behaviors such as avoiding others, bullying, yelling, sleeping, or forming small exclusionary groups are indicators of socialization and affiliation problems.

In larger TCs, there may be adequate space to set aside permanent rooms for classes, seminars, and workshops. Classrooms will typically be furnished with desks, chairs, lecterns, blackboards, flipcharts, overhead and 35 mm. projectors and screens, and computers. Separate areas may be designated for vocational training in carpentry/woodworking, printing, auto repair, etc. In those TCs that are smaller and have fewer resources, however, there may be no permanent schoolroom and so other common space will be converted as needed.

Whatever the degree of furnishings, when a room is being used as a classroom, the residents there are expected to behave as students. Emphasis is upon proper sitting, paying attention, taking notes, speaking, listening, and observing the rules of the classroom. Sleeping, dozing, speaking out of turn, or displays of temper or disrespect are considered negative behaviors that will be noted by senior peers and staff.

There are special spaces in the facility dedicated to encourage social relating. For example, a table and chairs arranged in a corner or hallway may be designated as a *relating area* or *relating booth*. These special areas afford space for prescribed social interaction, where residents can practice and rehearse relating to each other, person to person. Residents are expected to use these areas for one-on-one conversations that focus on shared experiences and immediate problem solving, as distinguished from confrontation or instruction. For example, staff may suggest that two junior residents talk to each other about whatever feelings they have about adjusting to the program; or, a male and female resident may talk to each other about their perceptions of each other. Although removed enough to promote private conversations, the relating areas are in full view of the passing community, so that peers and staff can observe the activity and participants involved.

Another designated relating area is a chair or bench placed near the front door of the facility. Referred to as "the bench," it provides a place for an individual to sit alone and think about matters that may be disturbing or provocative. For residents experiencing great hostility or upset, the bench provides a place to go for "time out" in order to cool down. Often the bench is used for residents who are threatening to drop out of the program. It permits them the opportunity to emotionally settle down, review the circumstances precipitating their wanting to leave, and evaluate the "pros" and "cons" of doing so—all in close proximity of the exit door. Although alone on the bench, the resident observes the familiar faces of peers who remain in the daily struggle for recovery and, conversely, peers witness and silently encourage the individual in his or her crisis period or period of decision. Though not readily obvious, these social factors indirectly contribute to residents' assessments concerning their status and future.

The relating booth and bench are examples of how the TC physical environment is designed to foster certain behaviors, attitudes, and values. Spaces are designated and used variously to foster social and individual relating, interrupt impulsive behavior, and provide opportunities to reflect. In all of these uses of space, the community is indirectly utilized to help monitor, support, and encourage "right living." So while the designated areas are used for semiprivate activity, they are of public importance to the entire community.

Sleeping quarters

Sleeping quarters reflect the hierarchical structure of the program. Quarters are arranged by seniority status, ranging from 2–4 bed dormitories to semi-private and private rooms. The dorm rooms—however modestly furnished—are required to be kept clean and orderly. A standard TC teaching, "clean bed, clean head," highlights the psychological importance of maintaining an orderly and clean personal living space, regardless of the quarters.

All dorms are segregated by gender, often with female and male sleeping areas located on separate floors or wings of the facility to facilitate management and security. In the TC perspective, it is noted that residents characteristically have had past difficulties with sexual acting out, and many have histories of sexual abuse, street or exploitative sexuality, low tolerance for sexual restraint, and a tendency toward sexual impulsivity. Moreover, the physical and social intimacy of communal life in the TC can intensify even healthy sexuality.

Considerable effort is put into helping residents resolve such histories of sexual disturbance and teaching them healthy sexual attitudes, values, and practices. Central to this effort is a requirement that while in residential treatment, all residents restrain from all forms of sexual contact—with anyone in the program or outside. An exception to this is accorded some residents during the later stages of the program, when permission may be granted to engage in safe sex while on furlough (see chapters 12 and 14).

Resident dormitories may also be separated by age. In age-integrated TCs the adolescents (residents under 18 years of age) are housed on separate floors or in separate facilities. (In TCs that treat adolescents exclusively sleeping quarters remain gender-segregated). Though separated by gender and age group, roommates may nonetheless be of differing racial and ethnic backgrounds. Communal life is utilized to explore and resolve issues of race–ethnic diversity and cultural sensitivities (e.g., De Leon, Melnick, Schoket, & Jainchill, 1993).

Resident toilets and showers are also separated by gender. Separate bathrooms are generally provided for staff reflecting their distinction in the program hierarchy. A service crew is assigned to maintain bathrooms, including cleaning urinals and toilet bowls, replacing paper supplies, etc. In the hierarchy of jobs, these chores are generally assigned to new admissions. As with sleeping quarters, residents are instructed to spend only necessary time in toilets and bathrooms, and frequent room and floor-checks by staff and resident monitors assure that peers are not tarrying there. As active addicts, bathrooms and bedrooms were often places where residents went to use drugs or alcohol, avoid obligations, or socially withdraw; they are, therefore, associated with avoidance, negative, and unproductive thinking and behavior.

Privacy

Practically all individual and collective activities in the TC are convened in public spaces, reflecting the TC's perspective and method. Living and working in an open community helps to (a) discourage personal isolation and withdrawal into the self, (b) promote peer solidarity and affiliation through interpersonal relating, (c) foster cooperative "teamwork" through group management of communal and personal spaces, and (d) encourage accountability through the constant observation of the individual by the community.

Individual privacy is highly valued, but within the context of the TC perspective, privacy is considered an earned privilege based on the individual's social and psychological growth. Private time and space are gradually increased in direct proportion to a resident's successful self-management, acceptance of increasing responsibility, role model attributes, and proven accountability to the community. For example, residents afforded more privacy are those who have demonstrated the ability to constructively manage time alone, successfully counter negative thoughts, participate fully in work and program activities, exhibit appropriate social manners, and make good decisions on furlough when coping with potential relapse traps, triggers, and cues.

Residents move into a TC with only the necessities (change of clothing, toothbrush, underwear). The first tangible symbol of earned privacy is being assigned to a small dormitory or semiprivate room. At certain stages of the program, residents may furnish these with personal accessories, such as a radio or CD player purchased from their own earnings or savings or received as gifts. How these spaces are furnished and decorated also reflects the individual's development and growth. Photographs, quotes, posters, or slogans on the walls conveying positive messages about right living signify more maturity and responsibility than, for example, pinups or commercial posters of consumer products.

HALLMARK FEATURES OF THE TC

There are four physical features of the inner environment that instantly identify what is unique about a TC program: the front desk, the structure board, wall signs, and decorative artifacts. However mundane, these features sustain the perception of community in both functional and symbolic ways.

The Front Desk

All traffic in and out of the TC is monitored at a desk situated close to the main entrance of the facility. Residents who are alert, cordial, and neatly dressed answer the telephones, handle the mail, and greet, screen, and direct all visitors. Under staff supervision they maintain a 24-hour watch, recording on a daily sign-in log the names of all visitors, their times of arrival and departure, and their destinations within the facility.

Working at the front desk is a highly valued, earned position, which like other job functions has educational and therapeutic elements. It trains residents in useful skills that are relevant to almost any kind of future work. The requirements and responsibilities of the position inherently strengthen the resident's sense of ownership and affiliation with the program. Front desk residents are the first to be seen by outsiders as well as new client admissions, and hence are the front-line representatives of the program to the outside world. Maturity, responsibility, efficiency, and an appropriate business demeanor are all needed to work the front desk. To the visitor, the residents at the front desk convey self-management in action, a sense of order in the facility, and optimism about the potential of recovery.

Structure Boards and Other Charts

On the walls behind or near the front desk is typically a large rectangular corkboard or blackboard that displays the structure of the TC in terms of its staff, key operational activities, and current functioning. This organizational chart visually reflects the stratification of the entire facility's membership, their identities, community position or program phase status, and where they are on a daily basis. Typically, it lists the names and positions of staff, peer level of residents (junior, intermediate, and senior) or their program phase (induction/orientation, primary, early re-entry, live-out, etc.), and their job or work crew function (kitchen, maintenance, etc.).

Additional charts may display monthly, weekly, and daily schedules of planned activities; a daily update of the population, house counts, scheduled trips, and appointments (legal, medical, etc.); those on furlough; the names of new admissions; and recent dropouts. Still another chart may picture the personnel and positions within the entire TC agency similar to organizational charts in conventional business settings.

Structure boards are explicitly used as general visual aides for the daily management and operation of the facility. However, their implicit use is to strengthen residents' perception of community and their affiliation with the program. For example, the listing of names facilitates recognition of the people in the community; the daily schedule and activities charts disseminate up-to-the-hour information about community members; the daily schedule board helps the resident set boundaries and give direction to the day; and the stratification of status and location helps the resident place himself within the community.

The various structure boards and charts provide a snapshot of the facility at any one time. But over time, they also provide a visual picture of mobility within the program by showing who has moved up and to where they've moved (a new job, in or out of the facility), thereby illustrating clear paths of navigation through the program.

Wall Signs

Whereas structure boards display concrete data about the organization of the program and its inhabitants, signs posted throughout the facility reinforce the philosophical basis for the community. Signs—often simple in form but profound in meaning—hang on the walls in practically all spaces and areas of a TC and are another essential element of the therapeutic environment. In words, phrases, slogans, and occasionally in pictures, the messages of recovery and right living stand as ever-present visual reminders of the TC's teachings and provide silent, continuous reinforcement to the residents.

The general function of these signs is to raise and maintain awareness of the TC teachings. Some specific themes often expressed in signs are encouragement ("every day in every way"), caution ("guilt kills") and coping strategies ("one day at a time"), or hope and equanimity (the AA Serenity Prayer). Usually written in the casual, colloquial language reflecting the real world of the substance user, signs variously employ metaphor, concrete advice, and symbolism. They may be a simple drawing or painting on paper, or an artful wood engraving.

Generally, signs reiterate the basic and relevant themes running through treatment. The phrases on the signs are often the same words spoken in groups and in peer conversations. They provide something for the individual to reflect on as he or she moves about the facility. They are ever-present reminders of what is needed or useful for recovery and personal growth

Many of the same signs appearing in the variety of contemporary TCs were also in early programs, illustrating how the TC culture has been transmitted across the generations irrespective of geography. They also reflect the expression of common, if not universal, experiences associated with recovery in self-help communities.

Historically, TC residents initiated the use of signs themselves. Many TC signs are now considered traditional, developed by earlier generations of residents and bequeathed to the program. However, signs are continually being reinvented, designed by successive generations and added to the treasury. Indeed, the making of signs is viewed as an instructional and therapeutic activity in its own right; a resident may be asked, for example, to make a particular sign in order to reinforce that specific concept in himself or herself.

The program philosophy is usually the largest, most elaborate sign hanging in a TC. Typically, it was created and written by one or more of the initial founding cadre of residents. The philosophy distinguishes the unique character and culture of each TC. It instantly becomes traditional, signifying its powerful role in the recovery of past generations of residents and holding forth hope to future generations. Daily reciting of the philosophy in the morning keeps it alive in the community, while memorizing it is an explicit measure of program affiliation.

Decorative artifacts

All TCs purposely seek to transform their inner environments into home-like surroundings regardless of setting. The artwork, poetry, sculpture, and crafts often created by residents are typically displayed in suitable places. In fact, the cheerfulness of the TC inner environment may be in stark contrast to the impersonal treatment environments found in conventional clinic or residential settings, especially within institutions such as prisons or psychiatric hospitals.

The artifacts displayed not only help to define the culture of that specific TC, but promote self-expression, self-esteem, and affiliation. Common among decorations are photographs of staff, graduating classes, and founding residents or "pioneers." These smiling faces transmit optimism and the possibility of change, while promoting identification with similar—albeit unknown—others who have lived the same struggle to overcome addiction and change lifestyles. The artifacts mirror the people, perspective, and culture of the TC.

CONCLUSION

This chapter has described how the physical environment of a TC facility is designed to foster a culture of change. Its separateness from the outside community in addition to its living spaces, furnishings, and décor are all utilized to promote affiliation, a sense of order, safety, and right living. Within this inner environment is a social and psychological ecology—the structure, people, and activities that define the TC as a treatment model and the subject of the following chapters.

Chapter 8

The Social Organization

Upon entering a therapeutic community (TC), one does not see the trappings of an institution, clinic, hospital, or even a treatment program per se. Instead, elements of a home, school, and business are apparent and a variety of housekeeping, educational, vocational, and community activities are in progress. From an anthropological perspective, the social environment of the TC more largely resembles an energetic village than an institution or service setting.

From a social and psychological perspective the TC can be distinguished from other institutional or treatment settings in that its social environment *is* the treatment model. The main elements of this model, its social organization, and social relationships are utilized for a single purpose—the reintegration of the individual into the larger macrosociety.[27]

Recovering substance abusers, themselves, evolved the social organization of the TC. The participant-developers of the first generation of TCs defined the tasks, chores, and responsibilities of running the house. A prototypical social organization emerged with its hierarchical division of labor, its explicit systems and procedures, its autocracy in decision making, and a highly structured daily regimen. Thus, the TC model directly reveals what substance abusers understood about their personalities, their social disaffiliation, and most clearly, their goals of recovery and lifestyle change.

---

[27] The concept of social organization is complex and reserved for sociological discussion. In the present context, the terms "social system" and "social organization" are used interchangeably, and "social environment" encompasses all forms of social interaction within the system. The term "structure" is contrasted with that of "process" to distinguish the social environment from the individual changes in it.

The social organization of the TC model may be described in terms of four major components: program structure, systems, communication, and the daily regimen of schedule activities. These same components exist in other more conventional organizations. In the TC, however, each component is utilized to facilitate the socialization and psychological growth of the individual members. The present chapter provides an overview of these components and how they contribute to the TC treatment approach.

TC PROGRAM STRUCTURE

It is important to distinguish between the organizational structure of the TC as an agency or service provider and that of the TC treatment program. In smaller contemporary TCs (as was the case in earlier generations of TCs), the distinction between the treatment agency and the residential treatment program is blurred, often involving an overlap of key personnel in both agency and program management functions. Today, however, TC agencies are complex not-for-profit entities similar to small hospitals or corporations. Although the main agency divisions still consist of the TC treatment program and other components of the larger agency, the organizational structures and personnel of each differ. Nevertheless, the treatment program is the core of TC agencies, large and small. It is the social organization of this program that is most relevant to the theory and practice of the TC approach.

The organizational structure of the TC treatment program can be depicted as a pyramid representing a stratification of staff and residents. The program staff is confined to the upper level of the pyramid, while residents at different levels of community seniority and job function represent most of the area downward to the base.

In long-term residential TCs, the ratio of residents to clinical program staff ranges from 10:1 to 30:1 approximating an average of 15:1 (Holland, 1982; Winick, 1980). The smaller ratios are mainly found in TCs that serve higher proportions of adolescent and other special populations clients who, for clinical or legal reasons, require more counseling, supervision and educational staff. If clinical support and technical and administrative staff are included, these ratios are somewhat smaller.

The relatively high ratio of residents to staff primarily reflects the self-help orientation of the TC. The daily operation of the facility is the task of the residents, working together in a broad range of job assignments under staff supervision.

Staff and Residents in the Pyramid

Staff in the residential facility is comprised of program management (also termed clinical or treatment staff) and program support staff. Program management consists of the director, deputy director, house manager, and senior and junior counselors. These staff members are responsible for all of the clinical and daily operations of the facility. They are usually—but not necessarily—TC graduates or others with experience in recovery. The highest authority in the treatment program is the director. In agencies with several facilities the highest authority for all of the treatment programs is usually referred to as the program clinical director.

Program management staff have primary responsibility for the operation of the facility and for the clinical status of the residents. They monitor and evaluate client progress, supervise groups, assign and supervise resident job functions, and oversee house operations. Clinically, program staff conduct therapeutic groups (other than peer encounters), provide individual counseling, organize social and recreational projects, and confer with residents' family members and significant others.

Program support staff consists of two subgroups: clinical support and facility-operations personnel. Clinical support staff provide specific educational, vocational, medical, and mental health services to the individual and the community. These services are integrated into the residents' treatment plans, which are managed by the program management staff. Clinical support personnel are traditionally trained educational and health professionals. Depending upon the size of the program these include a physician, a nurse, teachers, vocational counselors, social workers, and psychologists. These personnel are usually without direct recovery experience.

Facility operations staff provide technical services in the daily nonclinical activities of the residential facility. These staff members generally include those skilled in food services (e.g., culinary, purchasing) and maintenance (e.g., electricians, carpenters, plumbers) and office personnel (e.g., administrative assistants, clerks). Operations support personnel are trained and (where appropriate) credentialed technicians, some of whom may have recovery experience.

In addition to their specific work functions, all staff members in the treatment program assume various other roles in the community. For example, program management staff serve as facilitators and guides, rational authorities, counselors, therapists, and community managers. While support staff members in the TC are considered members of the community *regardless* of their education, training, professional discipline, personal recovery history, or program (agency) position. Thus, in functional work roles, staff provide particular services. However, as part of the community, staff are expected to exemplify and foster the general teachings of community and right living. The various roles of staff are discussed more fully in a later chapter.

Residents represent the largest component of the organizational structure in the TC treatment program. Residents in the pyramid are stratified into levels defined specifically by work and broadly by community status. The residents' work positions are supervised by the program management staff. Residents also occupy informal hierarchical positions of community status in the social organization based on two criteria: the resident's temporal seniority (time in program) and clinical progress (stage in program). These criteria confer community status on the individual not only in symbolic ways, but tangibly in the form of more desirable and responsible job functions, more privileges, and greater personal autonomy. Although stage and time in program are highly related, they are not perfectly correlated because residents' clinical progress occurs at various paces. Some residents may have a lot of time in the program but still not have progressed to the later treatment stage of re-entry.[28]

The organizational boundaries with respect to staff positions are explicit, but they are also completely permeable by both staff and residents. For example, a staff member who is qualified and motivated may change jobs, moving from clinical counseling to administrative positions both within the facility and in the larger agency. Indeed, for those interested in TC careers, experience in different paid positions is highly desirable.

Similarly, residents at the appropriate stage in their tenure may rotate through different job functions anywhere in the agency as apprentices in stipend positions, as staff-in-training, and eventually (if qualified) full-time paid personnel. This critical feature of the social organization makes social mobility real not only to staff, but to every admission to the program who observes residents and former residents as apprentices or in paid staff positions throughout the agency.

---

[28] The number of levels can vary, depending upon the criteria invoked. For example, under the "time in program" criteria, the resident hierarchy is generally stratified into 3–4 levels: entry level (1–4 months), junior (3–8 months), intermediate (9–12 months; optional), and senior resident (13–24 months). The "stage/phase" criteria usually generate 4–6 levels, classifying the resident according to prescribed clinical expectations. Typically these are defined as initial stage (inductee), second stage, several phases of primary treatment, third stage, and usually two phases of re-entry. A detailed description of the program stages is provided in a later chapter.

Authority

Although the social organization of the TC is grounded in self-help concepts, it is managed as an autocracy. Authority is formally and explicitly defined by community position and job function and informally by community status. Staff members possess both formal and informal authority, while residents have little formal but considerable informal authority.

The clinical program staff are the primary decision makers in all matters of resident status, discipline, promotion; transfers, discharges, furloughs, and treatment planning. The unique requirement of staff as decision makers is that they are *rational* authorities. Rational authorities make decisions grounded in the TC perspective to protect the community and specifically to foster the goals of individual growth.

The authority of support staff—teachers, vocational counselors, and medical and mental health personnel—is explicit in the area of their expertise. For example, physicians and nurses make assessments concerning the health status of members and their recommendations to the clinical program staff are key. Similarly, teachers are expected to make decisions concerning the educational needs and concerns of residents, chief cooks decide about food and facility maintenance, supervisors decide about repairs and other matters under their purview.

Although they do not have designated clinical authority, support staff are influential in clinical and community management, serving as generic role models, observers, teachers, as well as being authorities in their areas of expertise. In regular staff meetings and in less formal settings, support staff are expected to provide observations and suggestions that address residents' clinical progress and any problems in the community. Thus, for residents, members of the support staff have *perceived* authority in the community because they offer input into the decision making process, they understand and can explain decisions made by clinical staff, and they role model the basic TC values of right living.

Residents (peers) have no formal authority for making dispositional decisions concerning themselves or other residents. However, in the stratified peer levels of work and community status, residents have considerable informal authority. For example, those in positions at the upper echelon of the work hierarchy are all expected to train, supervise, and manage other residents' work behavior; monitor and confront any negative resident behaviors and attitudes; correct and communicate problems; and report progress to the clinical staff.

Peers also possess considerable informal authority as community members and role models. The stratified peer levels establish relationships of *mutual responsibility* with those ahead and behind. Senior residents are looked up to as *sibling authorities*. Younger residents are taught by their peers to listen respectfully to older residents, and to accept criticism, feedback, and guidance from them. The credibility of older or senior residents derives from their community status as role models; they are examples of positive personal change.[29]

SYSTEMS IN THE TC

Practically all TC activities are systematized. Formal policies and procedural maps (i.e., formats) provide the ordered steps for executing every activity, from a formal job function (or requesting a job change) to facility operations (fire drills, garbage disposal) and individual activities (personal telephone calls, medical appointments, library use). There are several standard systems for most formal activities in the TC (e.g., the formal communication pathways, reporting systems, trip sheets, requests for furloughs or for stage changes). Other examples are contained in subsequent chapters that detail systems for implementing job changes, delivering privileges/sanctions, or maintaining house security.

Written manuals outline procedures for the TC systems for newer residents. Usually, however, veteran residents orient these members to procedures through verbal instruction as to typical steps, relevant participants, and specific management purposes.

Maintaining Systems

Systems are in a constant state of erosion or breakdown. Ordered procedures are continually destabilized by the influx of new admissions, the outflow of experienced residents, frequent resident job changes, resident behavioral problems, and staff problems such as turnover, burnout, understaffing, and morale. Systems erosion impedes program operations and affects clinical matters. Therefore, there are key follow-up and review activities for maintaining the integrity of TC systems (see Table 8-1).

---

[29] A thoughtful formulation of authority and power issues in the TC is offered by Frankel (1989).

TABLE 8-1. Strategies for Maintaining Systems in TCs

Follow-up and feedback

Monitoring all systems is the obligation of both staff and peers. Follow-up involves observing and assessing whether procedures are appropriately implemented. Staff and peer feedback of relevant information is provided daily throughout the hierarchy as to how procedures are working. Corrections in the form of suggestions, sanctions, personnel changes, and recommendations are continually made to assure adherence to procedures and to assess the effect of changes in the system.

Follow-through

Delivering what is promised is essential to maintaining the perceived integrity of a system. For example, a program-wide promise of a recreational event and promises made to residents about job changes, phase changes, privileges, or discipline to be given must be delivered in a timely fashion. Failure to follow through on obligations or promises weakens morale and undermines adherence to systems.

Review

Assessing system breakdowns with staff and residents is essential to encourage all participants to assume responsibility. In the TC, these problems may reflect clinical issues for both peers and staff. Thus, particular focus is upon the attitudinal and emotional issues that contribute to the behavioral incident.

The continual follow-up and review of system problems and the offering of solutions and corrections by staff and residents not only reveals concern for the health of the program, it also enlists the concern of the community in assisting the individual residents involved.

Thus, systems require continual vigilance to maintain operational order, detect clinical problems and to sustain positive perceptions of the social environment. This involves daily monitoring of procedures and transactions in staff meetings, reviews with residents, considerable record keeping, and confrontations in peer groups. Accountability is the central theme of these efforts. One person may be the primary source of a breakdown, but all staff members and residents are accountable for preserving the integrity of the system.

COMMUNICATION IN THE TC

Communication in the TC occurs in formal and informal ways and in different settings and contexts. Communication (formal) can be a prescribed procedure for reporting or it can be a spontaneous interchange (informal); it can occur in relatively public settings of community-wide assembly (open) or in relatively private places, such as offices, dorms, and resident rooms (closed).

Seminars in classrooms and community meetings in the dining room are examples of formal communication in open settings; mealtime conversations in the dining room and resident interactions in the lounge are examples of informal communication in open settings. Peer group sessions and departmental meetings are examples of formal communication in relatively closed settings. The peer rap sessions in the dorm and staff-resident interactions in offices or halls are examples of informal communication that occur in private settings.[30]

Within the structure, the *formal* communication pathway is vertical. Information is passed in a prescribed order, top down to the lowest level of the pyramid and bottom up from residents to the top staff. Although decisions can be made at specific staff levels, the ordered steps of transmission must be adhered to by all residents and staff members. All information must be reliable and authentic. This includes information passed downward regarding program status and conditions (e.g. staff changes, facility moves, policy changes, daily schedule modifications) and upward from peers to staff regarding their feedback on individual residents or the community.

In a TC, *informal* information rapidly circulates about peers, staff, and the program. Although confidentiality is the rule concerning personal disclosures, there is little privacy concerning the status of individual participants. What is seen and said about individuals, groups, and the entire community is eventually transmitted throughout the community, much like communication in a small village. Resident dropouts as well as staff problems and changes are rapidly disseminated among the peers.

Indeed, the community quickly learns about the status of former residents (and staff), usually transmitted by peers who have returned from furlough. Some news reported is positive, such as jobs, education, marriages, births, and material acquisitions (homes, cars). Other news is negative, such as relapse to drug use ("falls"), illness (AIDS), criminal acting out (dealing), incarcerations, or deaths. Informal communication is usually loosely systematized, transmitted through the proximity of peers and personal relationships, outward and upward, eventually reaching the entire community.

Although rumor is often mixed with fact, the content of informal reports has important clinical and community implications for staff and peers. Like news in the outside world, the events, circumstances, and stories concerning peers—present and former—provoke reactions in community members, both for others and their own recovery. Thoughts,

---

[30] This discussion of the mode and setting of communication is modified from Frankel's excellent formulation (see chapter 4, Frankel, 1989).

feelings, and questions must be openly shared, processed, and resolved in groups and meetings, rather than left unattended.

The pervasive quality of informal communication in the social organization of the TC is an essential element of the treatment model. The cues for and meaning of recovery and personal growth are communicated in the myriad of social events and interactions that occur in various contexts and settings. Thus, informal peer communication is central to the TC method. It is a primary means of peer teaching and it strengthens community cohesiveness.

THE DAILY REGIMEN

The daily regimen is full and varied. The typical TC day begins with a 7 a.m. wake-up and ends at 11 p.m. This 16-hour day consists of morning and evening house meetings, job functions, therapeutic groups, seminars, personal time, recreation, as well as individual counseling on an as-needed basis. Weekend schedules are somewhat less demanding. Wake-up time is later, the frequency of groups and seminars is reduced, and there is focus upon general cleanup of the facility and more organized recreational trips.

The daily regimen is both a structural and systems component of the treatment model. Structure and routine are inherent in the density, regularity, and rigidity of the daily regimen. The regimen is also a system of interrelated planned activities designed to achieve management and clinical goals. It includes activities that are directly designed to strengthen affiliation and the perception of community. All residents and most of the staff come together for shared meals three times a day and also to attend three meetings a day (morning meeting, seminars, and house meetings). Thus, the daily regimen *programs* the activities of the treatment model, and by enhancing community, it facilitates achieving the goals of the model.

SOCIAL ORGANIZATION AND THE TC PERSPECTIVE

The social organization of the TC can be understood as reflective of its perspective, particularly the view of the client and recovery. Its major components—*structure, communication, systems,* and *the daily regimen*—are utilized to address behavioral, attitudinal, and emotional characteristics of the resident.

Structure and Individual

The organizational structure presents a social system with prescribed roles, responsibilities, and varying authority for staff and peers, and a hierarchy of job functions, which provides an explicit step-by-step path for upward mobility, especially helpful for those with a history of performance problems and failures. The peer levels of community status present opportunities for achieving social status through positive activity, a new experience for many.

In order to negotiate their way through the TC, residents must be aware of who people are in the facility, where they are located, what their functional roles are, and how to relate to them. Residents are characteristically self-involved, unaware of, or indifferent to their social environments and particularly to the consequences of their behavior on others. The more residents know about and involve themselves in the TC structure and systems, the less preoccupied they are with inner (often self-defeating) thoughts or personal withdrawal. Awareness of social reality is essential for residents in order to learn how their behavior impacts others and how others impact them.

The social organizational structure exposes residents to various roles and role relations that can surface characteristic emotional, attitudinal, and behavioral problems. These problems are revealed through residents performing their social roles and interacting with others, particularly those in *authority* (staff, teachers, senior peers).

Many TC residents have had difficulties with authorities in the past. Their relations with authority figures (parents, teachers, employers, police) have been often hostile, exploitative, or oppositional. The autocratic structure helps residents address these difficulties through their interactions with staff authority figures and by assuming informal peer authority roles.

Systems and Socialization

Systems in the TC addresses socialization and psychological characteristics of the residents. Residents are generally mistrustful of most environments and cynical or fearful of social and institutional systems, which they often view as remote, insensitive, hypocritical, uncaring, corrupt, or abusive. Indeed, among the first generation of TC participants, their fundamental difficulties in fitting in with conventional systems were significant motivators in developing their own self-help communities.

Residents are also notorious for their poor accountability. Characteristically, they fabricate or fail to provide a coherent or honest record of their activities, obligations, or responsibilities. In adhering to procedures and reporting the details of what they have done, residents learn to provide explicit and honest accounts of their actions. Accountability across the levels of the hierarchy is also the most explicit evidence of program integrity, strengthening the credibility and positive perception of the community among residents.

Systems in the TC also have profound clinical utility in facilitating socialization into the program. For example, the degree of adherence to procedures directly reveals the individual's level of compliance and conformity to the expectations of the TC. These are measures of the individual's acceptance of the community's teachings.

TC systems also provide the everyday framework for developing the psychological characteristics residents need to complete the orderly steps of their own goal attainment. The mandate for following explicit procedures—regardless of what the individual thinks of them or wants to do instead—inherently trains tolerance in those who characteristically have low thresholds for tolerance. Adherence to procedure requires that residents control their impulses, delay gratification, handle frustration, and manage their emotions in general.

Communication: Program and Clinical Management

Formal communication and reporting procedures are essential to the overall smooth functioning of the social organization. A breakdown in formal communication, described below as an example, illustrates how the communication structure and systems are purposively used for clinical as well as program management.

> A resident assigned to the laundry crew is observed by a crewmate to be not working but listening to the radio. The resident ignores the peer's urges to "move it." The peer reports the incident to the crew manager, who in turn passes it on to the departmental head (DH) and he or she reports the observation to the coordinator. The latter, however, does *not* report the observation to the house manager (a staff member) and fails to provide feedback to the DH.

This example of a breakdown has implications throughout the hierarchy. The resident's negative behavior is reinforced by neglect; the DH is rendered impotent; the coordinator appears incompetent; and staff remains out of touch with resident status. All involved are tainted, with the system perceived as hypocritical or weak by residents and staff. If not corrected, breakdowns in communication can inadvertently reinforce the street or jail norms against snitching, condoning, or turning in someone. Thus, the incident is scrupulously reviewed in a departmental meeting consisting of all relevant staff and crew and facilitated by the deputy director or director.

In addition to the management issues, the clinical aspects of the breakdown are underscored for the resident as well as all those in the reporting chain. Even if the resident had responded and gotten back to work, the peer crewmate is expected to bring up the matter in peer encounter groups, to try and surface possible reasons for the resident's negative attitudes. Similarly, the personal reasons between the coordinator and the house manager that related to the breakdown may be explored in the context of the departmental meeting.

Thus, an entire reporting or communication system is resurveyed to assess the links involved in a breakdown, the focus of which is both managerial and clinical. The reasons for breakdown are scrutinized to determine whether these indicate lack of skills, inadequate instruction, unusual circumstantial distractions, or a relapse to negative thinking and behavior. If instructional gaps are identified, tutorial groups may be utilized for retraining procedures. If the breakdown is found to involve the coordinator's behavior and attitudes, these may be directly addressed in peer encounters. Emphasis is on raising the residents' awareness of their specific problems, but also upon the importance of individual *and* collective accountability in the hierarchy.

The Daily Regimen and Clinical Goals

The lifestyles of substance abusers typically lack structure. Goal setting, productive routines, chores, and time-management abilities are conspicuously absent or deficient. To a certain extent, the lack of structure in their external lives mirrors deficits in their internal structure (e.g., characteristics of self-control, irresponsibility, inconsistency).

"Give me a break" might be heard from a resident to a coordinator or staff person, who replies "If I did, you would be out on the street" (Levy, Faltico, & Bratter, 1977, pp. 45). This typical exchange in the TC illustrates the clinical relevance of the daily regimen in the recovery process. Routine, in particular, teaches residents that goal attainment occurs one step at a time. Residents characteristically cannot pursue long-term goals because these require tolerance for repetition and sameness, patience in delaying gratification, and consistency in performance. These characteristics are notably lacking in most residents. Some substance abusers have never developed *consistent performance* at anything other than drug seeking. Others can work at high levels of performance, but only in binges and bursts and driven by needs to please or fears of failure. The daily schedule helps residents to perform consistently through teaching them to tolerate the boredom of repetitive activity, moderate any extreme behavior, and regulate their affective states.

The full and varied regimen of the TC also provides *certainty* regarding what to expect and reduces anxiety associated with free time. Typically, in the residents' past, free time and a lack of planned events triggered drug thoughts and other negative thinking. Finally, learning to properly adhere to the schedule of activities teaches residents *time management* skills. These are illustrated in making constructive use the brief hour of personal time, arriving to each activity on time, planning for weekend events, scheduling contacts and correspondence with significant others outside the program.

Thus, the scope and schedule of the daily regimen reflect an understanding of the resident, the disorder, and the factors that influence recovery. The daily regimen provides an orderly environment for many who customarily have lived in chaotic or disruptive settings; it reduces boredom and understimulation; and distracts from negative preoccupations that have in the past been associated with drug abuse. It offers opportunity to achieve satisfaction from a busy schedule and the completion of daily chores. For TC residents, the small gains in completing a good day drug free result in large gains in self-esteem and outlook. Although the activities of the daily regimen are essentially the same over days, weeks, and months, the individual is on a progressive path of change.

CONCLUSION

This chapter has provided an overview of the main components of the social organization of the TC treatment model. Its structure consists of staff and peer roles with lines of authority or decision making, and stratified resident hierarchy levels defined by job function and community status. Formal communication or reporting systems are for conducting operational and management affairs; informal communication, however, disseminates relevant information throughout the community. The daily regimen component structures the schedule of program activities.

Each of these components of the social organization reflects an understanding of the TC perspective and each is used to convey community teachings and promote self-examination and self-change. Within the *static* picture drawn of the social organization are the *dynamic* elements of the treatment model in the change process. These are described in the subsequent chapters on work, staff and peer roles, relationships, and program stages.

Chapter 9

Work: Therapeutic and Educational Elements

Work is one of the most distinctive components of the therapeutic community (TC) treatment model. Indeed, the telling mark of the TC social environment is the vibrancy of its work activities. Dressed and alert, residents have places to go and things to do. They are busy in their job functions, displaying positive attitudes and good humor, seeking and assuming responsibility, and giving assistance.

Although not obviously resembling a conventional treatment environment, treatment is going on all the time in the TC, not only in groups and individual counseling, but in daily job functions. Work in the TC is a fundamental activity used to mediate socialization, self-help recovery, and right living.

In the first residential TCs, recovering addicts assumed complete responsibility for managing the daily life and business of their facilities. A division of labor naturally emerged to conduct all the activities needed to sustain a social community, including renovation and maintenance of the physical facility and grounds, housekeeping, security, food preparation and service, office and administrative tasks, acquisition of resources (e.g., furnishings, clothing, pharmaceuticals, and private fund-raising).

Today, government subsidy supplemented by private funds helps pay for rent, staff salaries, food costs, and minimal medical care. However, labor required to operate the TC facility physically, socially, and psychologically still remains in the hands of residents supervised by staff. Thus, as in the first generation, TCs still rely completely on their own resident resources for daily operations.

WORK IN THE TC PERSPECTIVE AND APPROACH

Although the elaborate peer work structure in the TC was, and to a certain extent is, still grounded in necessity, it has assumed profound social and psychological significance in the self-help recovery process. The distinctive meaning of work in the TC can be illuminated by comparing it to work in the other treatment approaches.

The premise of most other residential treatment approaches to substance abuse is that the individual is a "patient" who is at least temporarily disabled. Treatment is needed *before* the individual can return to or learn work, and treatment must remain distinct from the individual's work activities. In the TC, rather than separate from treatment, work is an essential element of it. The primary aim of job functions is to facilitate meaningful personal change in the behaviors, attitudes, and values of individual workers. The material outcome (services or products resulting from the work) and even skills developed in the process are secondary to the intended gains in personal growth. In the view of the whole person, how the individual works reveals who he or she is. Thus, work life and personal life are indivisible; impediments to job performance and production are important indicators of personal issues. Remediation of these occurs on the job, or more accurately through the job, and is assisted primarily by peer coworkers.

Work and the Socially Disadvantaged Substance Abuser

For disadvantaged, antisocial, or nonhabilitated substance abusers, many of whom have few work skills, social identity and self-esteem are first acquired through participation in the work structure of the TC. Their work experiences are essential for investing in recovery, that is, for developing a personal and social stake in mainstream life. More specifically, learning to work in the program changes their perceptions about the future, giving them hope and a sense of possibility as well as a social and personal identity.[31]

Many socially disadvantaged residents have never believed that they could have the "good things" in life. Achieving community status in their TC work roles is often their first experience with social potency and self-efficacy. They learn that they can realistically aspire to the material

---

[31] The poor and irregular employment histories of substance abusers in general are documented in the research literature (see for example, Platt, 1986, chapter 9). However, the attitudes, values, and personality characteristics associated with problematic work and study behavior in TC residents are drawn mainly from clinical experience.

benefits of the conventional mainstream: careers, homes, education, and bank accounts. Thus, for these residents, job success is their first experience of personal success. Their work in the TC provides a tangible, experiential basis for hope and possibility regarding their future in the world of work.

Work success in the TC also represents for many residents a concrete element of change in both social and personal identity. Job mobility associated with community status are powerful interventions that can rapidly produce manifest examples of personal change and foster some of the positive self-perceptions that constitute identity change.

Work and the Socially Advantaged Substance Abuser

Substance abusers from the socially advantaged sectors who have work histories are still not necessarily well socialized or psychologically healthy. In fact, previously employed substance abusers in the TC present some or all of the characteristics of the disorder. Although habilitated, in that they may be educated and demonstrate some capacity for work, they are still chronic drug users, maintain rebellious or deviant attitudes, engage in illegal activities while gainfully employed, display problems in emotional self-management, lack a work ethic, or fail to adhere to clear values of right living.

There are two general types of "working addicts" in the TC who illustrate the relationship between work and the disorder. In one group, overall socialization is poor, marked by illegal activities and negative or missing values. Although employable, substance abusers belonging to this group display erratic and inconsistent workplace behavior leading to frequent job changes. This problematic work profile is not only a consequence of active drug use but invariably becomes a contributor to continued drug use.

A smaller group reveals a more functional work life, which nonetheless periodically breaks down with continued drug use. Although individuals in this group may have occupational and professional skills, they often display problematic work habits. Indeed, drugs are often used to assist in coping with work-related pressures and difficulties by providing, through escape, sedation, or the enhancement of energy. Paradoxically, among some well-socialized addicts, a functional work pattern may have impeded recovery. They may have completed their education, gone on to earn a living, and even advanced in their occupations, all the while remaining active drug users. The relative absence of social and economic losses limits how much these users experience the severity of their drug problems. They fail to acknowledge that their work, social, and interpersonal functioning is largely dependent on drug use.

Many working addicts see their drug difficulties as encapsulated problems, separate from the rest of their lives, and view themselves as very different from other drug abusers. Often middle class, they may not identify with "other addicts" who are socially disadvantaged or unemployed. They may acknowledge that their drug use episodically leads to a breakdown in social and work functioning, but they view returning to outside employment as the main goal-and-measure-of recovery. For these substance abusers, working well is *being* well, regardless of their drug use.

Residents in the TC with well-developed work skills often manage to avoid the painful process of self-change in treatment just as they do in everyday life. With their education or special skills they can rapidly achieve community status by gaining highly valued job functions in the program. Their positive work performance can appear as therapeutic improvement to staff and peers, shielding them from needed confrontation and full exposure of their psychological problems. Because their work-derived community status appears as clinical success, these residents can miss needed therapeutic interventions. Even if they complete or graduate from the program, their "missed psychological steps" predispose them to relapse.

More often, however, apparent clinical success through work leads to premature dropout. Residents can confuse themselves, viewing their work success in the TC as evidence of more meaningful personal change. If they do not accept the need for a whole person change and use their time in the TC as an opportunity for addressing these issues, they remain at high risk for early dropout and continued relapse.

THE HIERARCHY OF RESIDENT JOB FUNCTIONS

Within the TC, the resident job hierarchy defines the division of labor in the peer community. It represents the work needed to sustain the daily operations of the program and is used for skills training and for strengthening the individual's affiliation with the peer community. Most importantly, however, job functions address the residents' social and psychological characteristics that must be learned or changed. Thus, in this section the division of labor within the job hierarchy is described in terms of the categories of job functions, the relationship between these categories with resident characteristics addressed, and the therapeutic goals of job functions.

Figure 9-1 is a schematic of a typical resident work hierarchy in the TC. The distinction must be made between the resident job functions in the residential facility's clinical program and job functions within the various management and administrative departments of the agency, e.g., the fiscal, legal, medical, personnel, or management information departments.

FIGURE 9-1. Resident Work Role Hierarchy

The operations of the residential facility and management of the peer community directly involve clinical program job functions. These range from service crew members upward to chief coordinator, which is the highest level of resident job function. Positions higher than coordinator are considered staff-in-training or paid staff lines, e.g., junior counselor, house manager, deputy director, and full facility or clinical program director. Residents in clinical program or facility job functions are in daily interaction with program staff. Thus the peer community itself directly mediates the socialization and therapeutic impact of the clinical program job.[32]

Job functions within the greater management and administrative portion of the TC agency range widely from those requiring simple entry-level skills such as filing to those requiring a special educational or vocational background, e.g., office management, paralegal, nursing assistant, food services, or facility maintenance. Residents may be assigned an agency job early in residency as part of their overall assessment and treatment planning. In the re-entry stage they may seek agency positions through implementation of a conventional job search involving resumes, interviews, and recommendations. They may maintain these jobs until they leave the program as graduates or be asked to stay on as permanent workers.

Residents in agency positions are generally not in daily interaction with the peer community. Their job functions usually do not involve a hands-on relationship with peers. Nevertheless, these positions make an important contribution to the socialization and therapeutic goals of the resident, offering an occupational transition toward re-entry into the macrosociety. They approximate the setting, ambience, and expectations of the conventional workplace, and they require a full-time workweek, full job competency, and supervision by personnel who generally are professionals or managers.

Work and Resident Characteristics

Work in the TC addresses characteristics of the person and the disorder. These may be the result of years of drug use or reflect pre-existing personality traits. These characteristics can be classified into related categories: *personal habits, work habits, work relations, self-management,* and *work values* (see Table 9-1). The typical indicators of each are briefly described.

---

[32] TCs differ as to the range and type of job functions depending on their size and setting. For example, small single facility programs have a narrower range of job functions. TCs in prisons, hospitals, and day treatment settings require fewer resident jobs and some are unique to the setting, such as the prominence of farm job functions in some rural TCs.

Table 9-1. Typical Client Characteristics Addressed by the Work Hierarchy

Personal habits
  Punctuality, dress, attendance
  Time and chore management
  Goal setting

Work habits
  Responsibility, consistency, accountability
  Poor problem solving skills
  Manipulation or exploitation of people and systems

Work relations
  Rebelliousness, problems with authority
  Cooperativeness and competition with coworkers
  Accepting and giving supervision, praise, and criticism
  Interpersonal and communication skills
  Assertiveness, aggressiveness, and passivity

Self-management
  Tolerance for and coping with disapproval, criticism, not being liked by subordinates
  Tolerance for frustration, delayed gratification, and immediate rewards
  Coping with job-related stress and demands: promotion, demotion, and lateral changes

Work values
  Learning work ethic
  Learning self-reliance, excellence, pride, and ownership of performance
  Work commitment: making a maximal effort

The characteristics listed under personal habits reflect client histories of unstructured lifestyles and immaturity. Many residents have a poor or non-existent work history, few work skills, little sense of competence, and low self-esteem with respect to performance. They have not acquired or stabilized the fundamental personal habits, e.g., punctuality, dress, and attendance, that are prerequisites for engaging in routine work, much less developed work skills. Typically, these fundamental behaviors include waking up at a set time in the morning, dressing appropriately, getting to work or school on time, and once there, managing time and chore obligations.

Clients' work habits reflect their typically poor reliability as workers in the areas of task completion, responsibility, consistency, and accountability. Although some residents have basic personal habits and job skills, they are unpredictable concerning their work performance.

The client characteristics addressed by work relations reflect the underdevelopment of clients' interpersonal and social skills on the job. Residents often reveal problems relating to coworkers, supervisors, and subordinates in the workplace. Interpersonal conflict is common, as are difficulties with being supervised, accepting and giving criticism and praise, and seeking and offering assistance

Characteristics in the area of self-management reflect clients' historical difficulty coping with the demands and stress of the work setting. Substance abusers, oriented towards immediate gratification, often display problems in tolerating frustration and managing their feelings. In work situations this may involve coping with performance expectations, disappointment, success, criticism from authority, increased responsibility, promotions, demotions, or lateral changes. To a considerable degree the problem of self-management is central to all other work issues.

Work values address the "work ethic" often lacking among TC residents. Characteristics such as self-reliance, a commitment to excellence, and pride in performance are generally not present. Many residents have been nonconformists or social deviants with negative attitudes about conventional work, viewing mainstream wage earners as "suckers" or "squares." These residents have mainly engaged in illegal or marginal work activities, manipulating systems and people to get money the "easy way."

Those residents who do have conventional employment histories or job skills often lack a work ethic also. They work strictly to make money to acquire drugs, material possessions, and a social image. They have never earnestly invested themselves in educational or work efforts and so lack the inherent satisfaction, rewards, and self-esteem thus derived.

Job Functions and Resident Characteristics

The job functions in Figure 9-1 can be grouped into levels. These describe the complexity of skills, the range of responsibility for tasks and for other people, the status or value of that job in the community, and the therapeutic focus. Different levels test and challenge the resident with respect to job performance, social behavior, and personal growth. Each job level reveals the individual's characteristics and problems in the areas of personal and work habits, values, and self-management, and each level tests the change made relative to the previous level. Two main levels of job functions are briefly characterized.

Initial level positions consist of kitchen crew (preparation of community meals), dining crew (delivery of all community meals and clean up), and service crews (maintain cleanliness inside and outside of the facility). They involve less complex skills (e.g., peeling potatoes; washing dishes, setting up tables, waiting on tables, mopping, polishing, washing windows). These facilitate relatively easy learning of the tasks and permit opportunities to assess the resident's overall work-related characteristics and performance uncompounded by the difficulty of the job functions.

The main responsibility of residents in an initial level job function is to themselves—to learn or strengthen personal work-related habits and to complete the single task such as sweeping the floor. Competency, which is readily acquired in these functions, provides opportunities for assessing, testing, and training basic personal habits and basic self-management. Specific emphasis is on improving emotional management skills such as coping with the need to take orders and directions from supervisors.

Second level positions include facility maintenance (assist in plumbing painting, carpentry) and entry level office work (assist in filing, typing, word processing, reception, and phone management). These positions assume that the resident has some degree of program affiliation, stable personal habits, and an adequate degree of emotional control. The primary focus is on the improvement of work habits, such as consistency and accountability, as well as on work relations. Self-management issues arise from more complex job skills, which assume greater responsibility for tasks and people and increased program expectations. Thus, skills and task complexity increase while responsibilities expand to immediate co-workers, all of which impose greater performance demands on the resident. Some of these job functions expose residents to the pressures of more conventional work settings.

The hierarchy of job functions is roughly associated with *time in program.* Generally, job levels and complexity of skill demands increase as residents remain longer in treatment. However certain positions such as crew leaders and expeditors may be available to residents early in treatment based upon clinical as well as program needs.

At the later stages of the program the residents have rotated through all or most of the clinical program job functions and selected agency job functions. Most are in school or working full-time on jobs that are out of the facility, although some may work full-time as paid apprentices or staff-in-training in the clinical program or other divisions of the TC agency. The latter positions involve complex office skills such as preparing files for residents court trips. But regardless of their regular job function, re-entry candidates remain community members. If they are still living in the TC, they may also assume informal job functions in the house as needed, such as night managers, security monitors, or special escorts.

Community Work Roles and Therapeutic Goals

The therapeutic goals of the work can be further illuminated by brief descriptions of four main work roles within the clinical program, crew leader, expediter, departmental head, and coordinator. Each respective role involves an increasing level of job skills, responsibility for tasks and people, authority, and community status. Additionally, each role may have stratified grades, such as a junior, senior, and chief expediter, which generally correlate with a resident's time in program.

Crew leaders/asst. department heads/ramrods have direct supervisory responsibilities for other members of a crew, although they have no authority beyond the work realm. Skills and tasks include monitoring the personal habits, work performance, and attitudes of crew members; providing specific directions for task completion; role modeling self-control; and motivating task initiation and completion. This "entry-level" authority exposes the resident to having responsibility for others and as such, informally introduces them to accountability, authority, and management. Thus, the crew leader has competency in the crew member's tasks, good personal habits, and emotional control so as to communicate constructively to the crew. In the role of crew leader, personal growth goals center on stabilizing work habits and improving self-management by dealing with any emotional reactions from crew members who are usually newer residents.

Expediters are the "eyes and ears" of the community—monitoring and directing resident activity. Expediters reinforce community rules directly by reminders ("pull ups," criticisms, and affirmations) and indirectly through their input to the decision makers in the hierarchy. Skills needed for this position include the ability to give directions, detect, and report behavioral and physical problems in the facility and communicate with peers and staff in all matters of program protocol. Expediters possess some degree of informal authority, as they are placed in a visible community position from which they must report everything about the house. Thus, the resident must be fully familiar with all aspects of the program, the personnel, daily regimen, the systems and structure, and physical facility.

Notably, the expediter must be sufficiently affiliated with the program to defy the street code against "snitching," as his or her position requires the reporting of rule infractions, attitude problems, etc. to those in authority. Thus, the expediter job provides basic (on-the-job) training in how to cope with disapproval and criticism from peers. The high visibility of the position increases residents' self-awareness and compels them to engage in the change process, usually through coping with peer reactions to them in the group encounters. The expediter role can be assigned specifically to help address a resident's grandiosity or timidity or to bring to the surface any reactions to increased status and responsibility.

Departmental head (DH) is the highest-ranking resident job function in terms of direct responsibility and supervision in a specific area of work. The DH is sometimes supervised by a member of the support staff with expertise in that departmental service, for example culinary, maintenance, or carpentry. Thus, this position is analogous to those in the macrosociety in terms of responsibility and management skills required.

The resident DH is tested in all work-related areas, from practical skills to relations with others and work values. Key elements of personal growth in the DH position involve accountability and authority and also maturity in accepting professional supervision and criticism. Additionally, however, the DH is expected to assess the residents they train and supervise, not only in terms of work performance but also clinical status. For some residents, particularly the socially disadvantaged, the DH position represents a landmark in personal growth. Other residents can function easily as DH based on prior real world work experience. However, the latter may be assigned to DH because they need to be challenged on the personal issues that have since surfaced, thus assuring progress in their recovery.

Coordinator is the highest-ranking management position in the resident work hierarchy, and the person in this position is usually viewed as a potential candidate for staff training. The house manager, usually a staff member, directly supervises coordinators, who have considerable informal authority in the facility. Coordinators assist treatment staff in managing the community and have wide-ranging responsibilities over all facility activities. They directly supervise expediters, run house meetings, review daily and weekly schedules and population changes, and oversee the staff directives concerning client sanctions, privileges, and disciplinary actions. Residents in this job function provide critical input to staff concerning client dispositions and community and facility conditions. They also assist in planning the composition of encounters and other groups, suggesting job changes, and recommending disciplinary actions. Thus, all communication lines in the facility are channeled through the coordinator, putting him or her closest to the pulse of the program. In larger programs there may be several junior coordinators who report to a chief coordinator.

Given its elevated position in the TC, the coordinator is the prototypical resident role model, demonstrating various aspects of clinical and personal growth. These include (a) the ability to handle being in a position of authority, including the use of power, judgment, and independent decision-making; and (b) personal growth features such as the ability to cope with success in terms of distinguishing between personal and vested status.

The Job Hierarchy and the Real World

The resident job hierarchy in the TC is designed to approximate work in the real world. For adult residents, work is the most prominent activity in the daily regimen (adolescents in TCs divide their time between school and work in the program). All job functions take approximately 20–30 hours per week. Progression up the hierarchy of job functions is much like the movement up the occupational ladder in the real world. The new resident begins at the bottom and advancement requires discipline, good work, and social skills. Thus, the entering client can navigate the occupational ladder, moving through the resident job functions to staff-in-training; eventually, some may obtain a clinical administrative or management paid job function anywhere in the agency.

Unlike the real world, however, the resident remains a member of the peer community and what occurs in his or her work life is integrated into the clinical program. In addition to the job, a resident participates in groups and all other activities of the daily regimen, although the level of participation in these activities diminishes in re-entry stages.

Unlike the real world, residents do not earn salaries until they assume positions of staff-in-training. In some programs small stipends are paid to residents as they move up the job ladder as token financial rewards but primarily for clinical purposes (e.g., to teach the resident how to manage and save money). In the TC the job function is considered a privilege. The resident has an opportunity to serve the community, to learn specific skills, and to use work for personal growth and therapeutic change. These valued rewards could be undermined by the payment of money for services rendered.

USES OF WORK IN THE TC

Work in the TC reflects its view of substance abuse as a disorder of the whole person and its reality orientation to recovery. Work has long been considered the hallmark of emotional health and a positive lifestyle. Being able to work consistently, responsibly, and effectively requires not only marketable skills, but a psychological level of maturity and adherence to values such as self-reliance and earned achievement (right living). Thus, in the TC, work is both a *goal* and a *means* of recovery. Job functions are utilized in three main ways: for skills training and education, for therapeutic change, and to enhance the peer community.

Work as Education and Training

Realistically, the TC cannot provide a comprehensive vocational training within its limited internal work component, although a considerable degree of skill proficiency is often achieved. Moreover, residents differ in their skill repertoires, education, and overall work histories. Thus, there are distinctions in the education and training goals specific to each individual's abilities and needs.

The initial goal of training is to prepare the individual for further vocational training and education. Focus is on the personal and interpersonal habits and skills needed to continue formal education or job training when a person leaves residential treatment. These include wake-up habits, appropriate dress, language, punctuality, ability to pay attention and follow instructions, and emotional management related to receiving criticism and compliments as well as giving and following orders.

When individuals are prepared to obtain entry-level positions in the job market the goal is to make them *employable*. Focus is on basic literacy and job-seeking skills such as preparing resumes, interviewing, and letter writing. Activities to meet the goal of employability may involve completing minimal high school education (the General Equivalency Diploma or GED) or remediation training. For those who are prepared and employable the training goal is *marketability,* making residents competitive in the job market. For example, resident job functions can later be used to meet formal job requirements for paid positions in a variety of areas, for example, culinary arts, computer programming, and substance abuse counseling. Training in these areas can also be obtained or augmented outside the TC while the individual is still in residency.

The various training goals emphasize how the TC job hierarchy addresses individual differences with respect to work histories. However, for all residents the fundamental goal of skills development is personal growth. Residents are challenged to learn more complex jobs not only because they are socially valued, but because their efforts represent the common goal of achieving maximal capacity, extending or reaching toward personal limits or personal best. For residents who have been unskilled or semiskilled, encouragement to become fully skilled in an area fosters not only social mobility but also personal growth. It symbolizes being more than they have been or thought they could be.

Ironically, for some skilled residents, drugs have been used to sustain work by reducing the anxiety associated with it. For others work has been compulsive, another escape or avoidance of personal growth. Thus, for skilled residents the focus is less on marketability and more on the stability of their commitment to excellence and the healthy use of work.

TC job functions teach *positive attitudes* and *values* concerning work itself. In all work activities residents are expected to be thorough, pursue excellence, and take pride in their work. So, for example, lower-level job functions such as cleaning toilets and scrubbing dishes, though they appear to be less socially valued, contain inherent psychological value for the recovering person. The lesson is that individual self-worth depends not on the social value of a job, but on one's personal investment in that job and it's contribution to the well-functioning of the community overall.

Work as Therapy

Although important, skills development and work values are not sufficient to advance recovery and right living. Beyond the training of practical and useful skills, job training is used primarily to further the individual's personal growth and socialization. Thus, the specific therapeutic uses of work in the TC are to identify behaviors, attitudes, and emotional problem areas of the resident; to test the stability of newly acquired changes in these areas; and to challenge individuals to change further by facing higher performance demands and expectations.

Ordinary stresses inherent in various job functions evoke residents' characteristic problems and deficits in social, interpersonal, and self-management skills. The job function is used as a *clinical intervention* to modify these problem areas. Residents are continually moved upward, downward, and laterally in their job functions in order to expose them to situations that reveal, test, and challenge them with respect to particular clinical problems.

When a resident is promoted to a higher job function, it inevitably puts new demands on his or her emotional skills in coping with the increased performance demands and expectations. Typically, TC residents have difficulty meeting these increased responsibilities, characteristically failing or avoiding them. Conversely, demotion to lower job functions typically results in profound feelings of disappointment, frustration, and perceived injustice. These reactions characteristically have been disruptive for residents, leading to breakdown in performance, dropping out of treatment, and relapse to drug use. The TC work regimen provides an opportunity to experience, address, and then change these patterns.

Therapeutic goals are not easily achieved if job functions are relatively routine, easy to perform, or even master. For example, a job change may be enlisted particularly to prevent residents from getting too comfortable in their job functions. Job functions requiring higher levels of individual responsibility and independent decision-making *challenge* the resident by placing further demands on his or her development. Paradoxically, therefore, a job change is indicated when the job function ceases to be a vehicle fostering personal growth in terms of skill levels and psychological change.

Job changes are also utilized for *disciplinary purposes*, not only to maintain community expectations in the program, but to teach residents specifics about their behaviors and attitudes. How a resident copes with the feelings resulting from such a temporary loss of job status and privileges in the community is telling. Demotion can initiate a process of self-examination concerning his or her contribution to the demotion. Such a disciplinary action also provides the resident with pragmatic experience in the real world consequences to his or her behaviors, reinforcing the resident's obligations and expectations in such situations.

Thus, *changing* the resident's job function is a continuously used clinical intervention. These changes may be vertical, in terms of promotion or demotion to another level of complexity, responsibility, and community status. A change may also be horizontal, essentially a lateral move involving no change in these features but a difference in activity. The criteria for job changes are based on the clinical needs of the individual, i.e., addressing specific social and psychological goals. Through multiple job changes, the resident is helped to generalize past learning and apply them to new situations, leading to higher levels of functioning.

Work and Community Needs

A basic assumption in the TC is that the hierarchy of job levels is the structural parallel to the developmental recovery process. As residents move up the hierarchy engaging in job functions of greater responsibility, complexity, and community status, they display a corresponding increase in their socialization and psychological growth. This parallel is limited by clinical and management considerations that also influence progression up the job ladder in the TC. In actuality, decisions concerning job mobility are complicated by the practical needs of the program.

Residents with specific competencies may be needed in facility operations such as maintenance or office administration. They may be moved to higher level administrative job functions, although their clinical progress may remain limited. Similarly, the peer division of labor in the pyramid may be unbalanced by a disproportionate number of junior residents. This creates a management need for more senior resident functions such as departmental heads, expediters, and coordinators to sustain the peer self-help community. Thus, residents may be promoted to these positions before they have met the basic clinical criteria for such a level change.

Regardless of program needs, however, work in the TC is a vehicle for achieving personal change rather than an end in itself. The focus is always on where individuals are in their recovery, what they need to advance their recovery, and how the job function can be used to further the process of recovery and personal growth.

Work and Community as Method

The work hierarchy in the TC is vital for the functioning of the program and for strengthening the peer community. On the most practical level, resident job functions carry out the basic tasks to sustain the community on a daily basis. Resident labor replaces the expenditure on professional labor. The latter can undermine the potency of self-help recovery as well as inflate the costs of treatment. However, work also provides the organizing infrastructure for the community itself and is integral to community as method.

Jobs are also viewed as a means of *transmitting community teachings* concerning recovery and right living. Every resident rotates through all nonspecialized job functions in the TC. In providing direct manual service to the general membership, these "lower-level" job functions move the individual away from self- to social-centeredness. Similarly, in their positions as crew leaders and department heads, senior peers transmit community teachings to junior peers who are working under them.

Residents are both providers and consumers, tenants and "owners" of the program, charged with the responsibility of keeping their house in order. This element of *ownership*, both real and symbolic, reinforces the residents' perceived value of the community itself. More specifically, peer job functions provide the vehicle for residents to make a direct contribution to the life and sometimes the survival of the community itself.

Active participation in the program through meaningful work as a needed member of the peer community is the critical facilitator of *affiliation*. Working in the community is a personal investment in the community, which reinforces affiliation.

An analogy can be drawn from a healthy family structure. Children are unconditionally loved for being who they are. However, children who are genuinely needed and relied upon as contributors to the health and welfare of the family are also valued participants. Their perception of being needed by others helps bond them to the family, strengthens their resistance to negative outside influences (from peers), and gives organization and purpose to their lives.

Overall, the work hierarchy contributes to the resident's perception of the TC as a community and as a culture of individual change. The successful and often dramatic personal changes in current staff or former residents are often illustrated through their job functions. Conversations with senior peers and staff may recount the trials and tribulations of their experiences in ascending the job ladder. In these stories lie the fundamental but positive messages of hope and the possibility of change.

CONCLUSION

This chapter has described how work mediates essential educational, therapeutic, and community goals. The resident job hierarchy is stratified by level of complexity and time in program to address individual problems in all areas of work: habits, skills, conduct, attitudes, values, and emotional growth. Work is also used to manage and enhance the community. In addition to the work component, therapeutic and educational change is mediated through various staff and peer roles in the social organization of the TC. These are the subjects of the subsequent two chapters.

Chapter 10

Staff in the Therapeutic Community

Contemporary TCs are complex organizations involving many different jobs or functions. Thus, personnel in these agencies consist of a mix of traditional and nontraditional professionals, serving in a variety of clinical, management, administrative, and supportive service positions. However, the TC treatment program remains the raison d'être of the agency, and the clinical management staff is viewed as the core treatment personnel.

The primary focus of this chapter is to describe the various roles and functions of the treatment program or clinical management staff in the residential facility. The roles of support staff and agency personnel are characterized more broadly and in less detail. Though vitally important, their contribution to the model and method is primarily through their specific work or service skills. Teachers, physicians, nurses, psychologists, social workers, lawyers, and accountants in the TC ply their professions in the usual way. These are conventionally understood and need no special description.

STAFF IN THE PERSPECTIVE

The peer hierarchy of work and community status defines the roles, functions, and relationships that mediate socialization and therapeutic change, while the peer culture, embodied in the norms, values, and beliefs of right living, guides the change process. However, it is the *staff* that remains responsible for the management and quality assurance of the program. The staff hierarchy supervises the daily activities of the peer community and makes the final decisions in all matters concerning resident status. Although the program staff hierarchy is a vertical extension of the peer hierarchy, the boundary between peers and staff is explicit. All members of the community—staff and residents—are expected to role model the community teachings concerning recovery and right living. Senior staff are role models for junior staff as well as for the peers. Junior staff are role models for senior and junior peers, and senior peers are role models for junior peers. However, since residents are learning how to manage themselves and their environment as well as how to interact with others, they are limited in their ability to guide each other in the change process.

The relationship between staff and peer roles is rooted in the evolution of the TC. The staff of the first generation of TCs emerged from the ranks of peers as residents who assumed leadership in launching and managing TC programs. Their main credential to be staff was their own experience in self-help recovery. As role models of lifestyle and identity change, they qualified as authorities and guides in the change process.[33]

Thus, recovered staff and residents are equal as people involved in personal change, but they are *unequal* in their location in the change process. This fact defines the explicit position of staff members in the structure of the social organization and their relations with residents. Staff members have the highest status in the community. They are also the ultimate authority in the clinical and community management of the facility.

TREATMENT STAFF: ROLES AND FUNCTIONS

In the TC approach, the role of staff is complex and can be contrasted with that of mental health and human service providers in other settings. For example, among case managers, counselors, and therapists outside of the TC, the relationship between client and staff is viewed as the primary therapeutic element. In the TC, the essential therapeutic element is the client's relationship to the peer community. To enhance this therapeutic alliance between individual and the community and to foster the process of mutual self-help recovery, staff must engage various functions and activities. These multiple role attributes may be summarized and separately described as *facilitator/guide, counselor, community manager,* and *rational authority.* Although they obviously overlap, each has distinct characteristics and emphasis, and each impacts the individual resident and community in different ways.

---

[33] In general, clinical staff today still emerges from peers although increasing numbers are traditional professionals without recovery experience.

Staff as Facilitator/Guide

To guide means to assist others in a journey, a voyage, or passage. Guides lead others because they have traversed the same path and terrain successfully themselves, and as facilitators, they use what they know about the path and terrain to assure safe passage. This characterization of the facilitator/guide is applicable to the clinical program staff in the TC.

In the TC, the journey is the individual process of recovery and personal growth. The path is the planned course of change outlined in the program phases and levels. The terrain is the social environment—the structure, people, and activities that challenge the individual to learn and change. As guides, staff members know the path, and as facilitators they know how to use the terrain of the social environment to create the opportunities for learning.

The goal of a facilitator is to guide the individual through a process of self-discovery and change, insuring that they receive the growth experiences necessary to derive and then incorporate the principles and values of right living. The general features of the facilitator/guide underscore the significance of the distinctive experiential nature of the process. Guides know the change process from their own recovery experiences and from their experience in observing the change process in many others. Thus, most often clinical program staff are those who have successfully recovered in the TC. Or, they may have been involved in self-help recovery outside of the TC, usually through a 12-step program.

A smaller number of clinical staff are those without histories of substance use problems. However, they have experienced recovery from other disorders—physical or psychological—or have undergone profound changes in personal growth related to other life crises. In any case, their eligibility as guides comes from their intimate knowledge of the change process through personal experience and in years of first-hand observation of substance abuse recoveries. Notably, they understand the TC perspective and the types of personal experiences needed to produce lasting change.

As guides, staff understand that authentic personal growth and recovery requires internalized learning and that this can occur only through direct personal experience. As facilitators, they arrange, design, or foster situations that can result in learning opportunities for residents, situations requiring problem solving, coping, and decision making. Staff can lead the individual to these learning situations but the individual must take the personal risks of engaging in the behaviors and private disclosures that lead to new skills, self-perceptions, and meaningful experiences of self-change.

Staff as Counselor

The use of the formal term "counselor" is a relatively recent development in the TC, reflecting the movement of the modality toward mainstream health and human services. In the earlier days of the "standard" TC, there was no designated counselor role, although peers and staff continually engaged in all varieties of counseling activities. Today, senior and junior counselor positions are part of the staffing pattern of the TC, although most counseling remains informal and ongoing, conducted by peers as well as staff.[34]

Still, the very existence of the counselor position in the TC stresses the staff's responsibility to attend to individuals' specific needs. In the complexity of community life, individual residents can become relatively invisible or "lost in the sauce" because they are either being overlooked or, through their own design, managing to avoid the demands of the program.

Thus, staff must assure that every resident in the community obtains relevant individual counseling. Staff may confer with support staff, resident supervisors, peers, and the resident himself or herself to assess a particular individual's issue and then oversee how counseling will be delivered. Most often, the staff person will encourage resident–peer conversations, both informally and formally through the use of the groups, reflecting the TC's emphasis on self-help and the use of community as method.

Staff as Community Manager

As community managers, members of the program staff oversee all the activities in the TC residence. Their varied functions and responsibilities include maintaining physical operations, supervising clinical programs, and sustaining the daily regimen of educational, therapeutic, and work activities. The role of community manager underscores the general responsibility of program staff to the community in *assuring* the physical

---

[34] In the course of a day, staff continually talk to residents in dining rooms, halls, offices, and lounges about their issues, progress, and plans in shorter conversations as well in longer scheduled office sessions. These informal and formal contacts accumulate into considerable amounts of staff counseling in the TC.

and psychological safety of the community and empowering peers to sustain the self-help process.

For TC residents, safety issues can jeopardize their remaining in the program—much less their engaging in the change process. Staff have the primary responsibility for insuring the physical and psychological safety of the community. Peer perception of safety in the community is created primarily by the peers themselves through mutual instruction, self-control, the role modeling of safe behavior and attitudes, and social influence. However, peers cannot enforce sanctions against infractions of rules and regulations. Therefore, staff—as manager—must rigorously implement all disciplinary actions for individuals (sanctions, loss of privileges) and the community (bans, general meetings). Thus, peer perceptions of a safe environment are based on their self-management reinforced by reliable staff actions.

As managers, program staff *maintain all the general systems* of reporting and communication. The key goal is to maintain the integrity of the peer–staff hierarchy and protect the "pecking order" or chain of command. This usually means assuring that communication is directed to the appropriate person in the staffing pattern and especially in the peer hierarchy. For example, resident inquiries or complaints are initiated at the appropriate peer level and work their way up to the highest level of management for decision or disposition. This management function preserves order in the structure, which is essential for teaching the residents to behave in an orderly fashion, respect authority, and use systems appropriately.

In their role as managers, program staff are constantly surveying and reviewing procedures to detect any problems in these and improve them. Changes in systems may involve the deployment of staff to modify unusually high early-dropout from the program, implementing special tutorials to correct breakdowns in communication procedures, increasing the frequency of house surveillance by senior residents and staff to assess the tone of the facility, implementing step-by-step guidelines for initiating contacts with the resident's family, or inventing new systems of reporting to speed the accuracy of communication and feedback.

As managers, staff *assure the fidelity* of implementing interventions. The effectiveness of any therapeutic, educational, or disciplinary intervention for an individual, group, or the entire peer community depends upon the fidelity of its implementation. This means any intervention with the individual or community must be followed up for a prescribed period of time to assess its impact and side effects. For example, if one resident is assigned to escort another to the medical office, staff will check with the medical office to confirm that both arrived there. If a staff member counsels a resident to discuss a particular problem in group, that staff member will later confer with the group facilitator or senior peers concerning the outcome of the group's discussion.

In their role as managers, program staff *maintain accountability* in the social organization by monitoring the follow-up process throughout the peer and staff hierarchy. In the organizational structure the path of follow-up moves up and down the peer and staff hierarchy in accordance with the communication chain. Directors follow up with house management, who checks in with counseling staff, who follows up with resident coordinators, who initiate follow-up in the peer hierarchy among expediters, department heads, crew leaders, and work crews. Additionally, follow-up may involve clinical and technical support staff in the TC.

In all their managerial functions, program staff foster, enhance, and promote self-help as a concept and activity. Their general approach is to use the relationships with individual residents and *manipulate* the social environment in order to maximize peer influences. For example, staff avoid directly instructing residents but encourage them to seek information, guidance, and instruction in conversations with peers. Peer transmission of the community teachings on recovery and personal growth is in itself a self-help activity.

In more direct manipulations of the social environment, staff may change a resident's job or roommate in order to introduce him or her to people and situations that initiate or sustain mutual self-help. For example, it may be arranged for a new female admission to room with a junior and senior female resident, peers at two different levels of the program and recovery process. This configuration provides the new admittee with some degree of identification with a proximal peer and guidance from the more advanced peer.

Staff encourage the use of positive role models within the community whenever possible. As managers, they place residents who display role model characteristics in situations with high community visibility. This not only reinforces the resident's role modeling behavior but provides examples to others. Finally, staff minimize their direct involvement in any peer-led activities such as seminars, morning meetings, and certain encounter groups. In these activities staff may be used as resources, planners, or facilitators in order to encourage resident leadership and to promote the general concept of self-help.

Staff as Rational Authorities: Concept and Features

As rational authorities, staff make all decisions concerning the status and welfare of individuals and the community, and their decisions are expected to be respected and unchallenged by residents and other staff. Thus, of all staff roles, rational authority most explicitly reflects the actual and perceived power of staff and the social boundaries between staff and residents in the TC. As in all their roles, however, staff as rational authority fosters the self-help developmental learning process. By exercising their power to teach, guide, facilitate, and correct residents rather than punish, control, or exploit them, staff role model a "good" and trustworthy authority. This serves as a corrective experience for residents, most of whom have had, or at least perceive themselves as having had, negative experiences with authority figures.[35]

In the TC perspective, autocracy and self-help are integrated concepts. TC residents have often had difficulties with authorities, who have not been trusted or perceived as guides and teachers. They need a successful experience with an authority figure, one whom they can view as credible (recovered), supportive, corrective, and protective, in order to gain authority over themselves (personal autonomy). This involves practice in listening to authority and responding in a manner respectful of authority yet also permitting self-respect and effective action.

In accordance with the TC approach, the decisions made by staff in their role as rational authorities are used to expose and correct the residents' characteristic problems with authority. Changing how residents cope with the feelings, thoughts, and attitudes resulting from staff decisions and how they perceive the decision maker are key clinical objectives of staff as rational authorities.

The defining element of the term rational authority is contained in the word "rational." Authorities who are rational provide explicit *reasons* for their clinical and dispositional actions. Staff decisions concerning the disposition of the entire community or a single resident (disciplinary actions, job changes, privileges, etc.) must be grounded—and explained—in terms of the TC perspective of the disorder, the person, recovery, or right living.

Thus, in the TC, all staff decisions are rational when made for the welfare of the individual and the community. Conversely, staff members whose decisions and actions reflect reasons that are personal, arbitrary, or

---

[35] Excellent discussions of the potential for abuse of power by staff and peers in TCs and how these are minimized can be found in Frankel (1989); see also Bratter, Bratter, and Heimburg (1986).

otherwise unrelated to the TC perspective, vis-à-vis the welfare of the community or the individual, are not behaving as rational authorities.

How a staff member delivers a decision is as important as the decision itself. The integrity of the relationship between residents and staff in the TC is grounded in reality and honesty. Therefore, the resident should experience authority figures as real people with feelings and moods. For example, a staff member may express honest feelings of disappointment, frustration, or anger, providing realistic feedback as to the resident's impact on others.

> I am angry with you; you continue to ignore my suggestions and have hurt other peers. I don't want to deal with you now. You need to think things over in the pots (demotion to the kitchen crew); maybe we'll talk in two weeks.

However, expression of feelings with loss of control on the part of staff member would indicate his or her poor self-management. The manner or style itself must also reflect the rational purpose of helping the resident. Whether harsh, supportive, distant, intimate, or nurturant, the manner should be flexible to facilitate a positive change in the resident.

As rational authorities, staff must be guided by considerations concerning the individual as well as the general community when making decisions. Some examples of these considerations underscore the residents' characteristically "allergic" reactions to authority figures. Others illustrate the relationship between staff as authority and the peer community (see Table 10-1).

Most importantly, staff *follow up* their decisions to determine whether the resident understands and accepts them and how the individual received information from the peer community, e.g., from specific peer interactions, direct conversations with other staff, or from insight developed from the disciplinary experience itself. Thus, staff decisions concerning individuals are utilized to empower the peer community as teacher and reinforce the community teachings themselves.

TABLE 10-1. Some Guidelines for Staff as Rational Authorities

---

Address resident characteristics

Residents often display an extreme sense of entitlement and exaggerated reactions to perceived unfairness, a need for immediate gratification in the form of instant answers, resistance through arguments, and a tendency to manipulate authority figures. Thus, when making decisions and explanations, staff should consider the following:

- Avoid providing immediate gratification to residents in terms of full explanations of disciplinary actions or verbal correctives
- Teach residents to tolerate injustice, ambiguity, and uncertainty
- Teach residents to tolerate normal temperament shifts in authority without their becoming destabilized, rebellious, or cynical

Promote use of the community

Staff decisions should maximize the strength of the peer community and minimize any authoritarian features of the staff member involved. Thus, staff explanations concerning a decision may be withheld from the resident to achieve certain ends:

- Teach residents to seek information in the peer community—the teaching impact of a staff decision is enhanced when peers explain its meaning to the individual; moreover, peer explanations reinforce the message for the peers themselves as well as enhancing the general perception of the community as teacher
- Foster development of blind faith as a basis for learning trust—if a resident obtains information from the peer community that eventually helps him or her understand the reasons for a staff sanction or corrective, this strengthens trust in the community process and in the rational authority; this concept is analogous to the typical delayed appreciation for parental wisdom illustrated in the expression "My father was right"

Interrelated roles

The four roles and functions of the treatment staff are interrelated. Indeed, in all their roles, when staff test or challenge residents they are serving as guides and facilitators. For example, in changing the resident job functions, the staff (as managers) are creating opportunities for individuals to learn new ways of coping with the demands of higher levels of performance and expectations. In granting furloughs and dating privileges, staff as managers expose residents to situations where they will have to cope with the triggers, temptations, and circumstances of drug use on their own, unprotected by the peer community. In suggesting that a resident end a negative relationship, staff (as counselors) ask residents to confront and deal with loss and aloneness. In delivering disciplinary actions, staff (as rational authorities) precipitate frustration and anger, which the residents must learn to tolerate and self-manage. Finally, although there is no explicit attempt to create parental roles in the TC, features of these roles emerge spontaneously. Staff may assume parental attitudes toward residents, particularly young adults or adolescents whom they view as "kids." Former residents often remember certain staff members as father or mother substitutes despite the chronological ages of each. These resident perceptions of staff as parental figures may reflect a convergent effect from all of the staff roles. Staff who are effective as guides, counselors, managers, and rational authorities may be viewed as positive parents. Indeed, these convergent role features characterize the "good parent" in general. Not infrequently TC graduates cite particular staff members as the good parents who never stopped believing in them, their struggle, and their recovery (Bratter, Bratter, & Radda, 1986).

STAFF MEETINGS AND GROUPS

The various roles of staff do not completely capture the full picture of staff activities in the TC. Staff members are not simply employees, but—like the peer residents—members of the community. Their investment of time and energy in TC work typically goes far beyond conventional expectations. The intensity of community life, their multiple roles, and the special characteristics of the residents combine to make enormous personal demands on TC staff, while material compensation in money and career status are minimal. The primary rewards lie in the work itself and—for a number of staff members—work reinforces their own recoveries and continued personal growth.

An array of staff activities underscores the distinctively humanistic focus of the TC. As in any organization, staff are engaged in a variety of meetings and groups that focus on management and administrative issues. Regularly scheduled *business meetings* for all house staff are conducted by the program or facility director. The agenda includes record keeping, client admission and dropout rates, program changes, and special work problems such as understaffing, shift coverage, and communication pathways. Regularly scheduled *case conferences* include all members of the clinical and support staff and focus specifically on the clinical and management issues of specific residents.[36]

Notably, certain *staff groups* meet as needed to address issues of individual adjustment, job adjustment, personality, life crises and circumstances, and interpersonal conflict among staff. The format of staff groups utilizes certain elements of resident encounters and probes (described in later chapters). In contrast with staff meetings, the issues

[36] Typical issues that are addressed are client progress, discipline, strategies for clinical impasses, special social and psychological difficulties, resident "significant others," and stage and phase plans.

addressed in staff groups are always personal and interpersonal, including emotional reactions to others, situations, and the job itself. The goals are conflict resolution, emotional relief, personal support, and guidance.

These groups are facilitated by senior management staff, usually the director. "Hats off" is the rule, however, meaning that the hierarchical status differential across junior and senior staff is ignored. Group members are permitted (and indeed expected) to speak to each other as equals on all matters without concern for work reprisal. Less common are hats off groups in which staff participate as equal members with residents in resolving issues. These quintessentially democratic groups provide an important immunity to abuses of power by staff or peers.

Staff retreats are special groups consisting of designated staff or all staff which are assembled as needed. The agenda of a retreat is usually mixed, consisting of some personal, some management issues. However, the major aim of a retreat is broader renewal, staff cohesion, and rededication. A staff retreat usually takes place over two or three days and is held away from the facility. It is planned and conducted by the director and senior staff. The format consists of intensive groups, recreation, and communal meals.

Some programs view staff groups and retreats as essential to the health of the program, reflecting its capacity to address its own problems and issues. The need for these groups is unique to the TC, which is a culture of self-examination and in which staff "burnout" problems are potentiated by the intense demands of the peer community (e.g., Freudenberger, 1980).

In addition to serving individual staff members, there is a community function to staff groups. The number and variety of staff groups role model self-management for the residents. Residents view staff as a group of people who, like themselves, are continually in self-examination and personal growth. Staff groups sustain the perception of an open community with a collective process for problem solving.

SUPPORT STAFF ROLES AND FUNCTIONS

As noted, in the first generation of residential TCs clinical staff members were those with recovery experiences in TCs and AA. Many of these former residents also assumed administrative positions as needed to sustain their agencies, often under the tutelage of nonrecovered specialists. The clinical and nonclinical division of labor became more pronounced as TCs expanded in scope and evolved in complexity. Today, support staff members are primarily those without recovery experiences and serve in a number of distinct roles and functions, briefly summarized in Table 10-2.

TABLE 10-2.   Support Staff Roles and Functions

Agency support staff

Responsible for the agency's administrative infrastructure, providing support services in legal, fiscal, public relations, research, clerical, and administrative areas. Usually skilled personnel from outside the TC, program, some program graduates, or others with recovery experiences and appropriate skills. Although involvement with the community is mainly peripheral, they may serve as supervisors or trainers for specific residents who work in the agency's administrative or business infrastructure.

Clinical support staff

Provide direct services to the residents in areas such as medicine and mental health, education, legal services, and vocational and family counseling. Outside of their special purview, clinical support staff have no formal custodial, clinical, or managerial functions in the TC. They may participate in certain resident and staff groups, case conferences, and community events.

Facility support staff

Manage the operations of maintenance, food services, security, and administration. Also serve as supervisors, mentors, and trainers for residents who assume job functions in these units as crew members, crew leaders, and departmental heads.

Residents usually have job functions in the units of support personnel. They are *learning* how to perform in these conventional work roles not only in terms of a competency, but also acceptable personal and work habits, positive work relations, and a work ethic. Thus as trainers and supervisors, support staff must maintain a fine balance between meeting the clinical needs of the resident and the operational needs of program.

STAFF AS COMMUNITY MEMBERS

Central to understanding the meaning and effectiveness of staff in the TC approach is the distinction between staff's generic role as community member and its specific function by skill specialty. All staff, treatment, supportive, and administrative, have special job functions in the community that define their work roles in the TC. Like residents, however, each staff person is also a community member, a *generic* role characterized by several attributes (see Table 10-3). Indeed, it is the community member role that integrates all staff in the perspective and approach of the TC, regardless of their differences in recovery histories, professional discipline, education, and training.

TABLE 10-3. Staff as Community Members in the TC

- All staff are role models who set examples vis-à-vis behavioral expectations of dress, daily work habits, interpersonal communication, positive attitudes, temperament, emotional self-management, adherence to facility rules, and living the values of right living (sobriety, honesty, openness, self-disclosure, responsible concern, work ethics, etc).

- All staff are observers of the social, physical, and psychological environment of the TC, noting any incidents, resident attitudes, or behavioral infractions, as well as the cleanliness and order of the house and the general morale. Their concerned feedback contributes to maintaining the authenticity and health of the self-help community.

- All staff are expected to serve as teachers, seminarians, mentors, and tutors, training both residents and other staff. Formally, they teach based on their special expertise. Informally, they teach authenticity and right living by their personal example of optimism, humility, enthusiasm, vulnerability, intellectual curiosity, and self-examination.

- All staff are part of a *rational authority system*. Each member is expected to offer information concerning individual residents and the community through team meetings or by direct feedback to clinical management. These contributions enhance the validity of the decision-making process by utilizing input or data from multiple observers. Each staff member understands the TC perspective and community as method. Staff can explain and defend dispositional decisions to the residents. All staff, therefore, are perceived by residents as members of a consistent, rational authority system. This is a critical perception as it presents the entire staff as a unified family concerning authority decisions.

- All support staff have a unique *clinical function* in the TC. As community members, they understand that the entire milieu of the TC is therapeutic, that the implicit goal of every activity in the facility is designed to advance the personal growth of individuals. For example, resident performance on the job, in the classroom, or at the nursing station must be considered from a clinical perspective. Support staff are expected to observe and identify behavioral, attitudinal, or emotional problems, to hear complaints or comments from residents, to encourage and support residents in the process, and to use the communication pathways to transmit clinical observations to primary treatment staff.

CONCLUSION

This chapter has described how primary clinical staff in the treatment program supervise the daily activities of the peer community through their interrelated roles of facilitator, counselor, community manager, and rational authority. Other staff provide educational, vocational, legal, medical, and facility support services. Regardless of education, training, professional discipline, recovery history, or agency position, all staff members in the TC are members of the community. In their specific job functions, they provide the special services needed by the community. In the generic role of community member, staff exemplifies and fosters the community expectations and teachings based upon the TC perspective and method. The effectiveness of staff in sustaining a community environment that enhances self-help recovery is most evident in the resident peer roles described in the following chapter.

Chapter 11

Peers in the Therapeutic Community

In the therapeutic community (TC), peers are the primary change agents. In their varied social roles and interpersonal relationships, residents are the mediators of the socialization and therapeutic process. Peers constitute the main membership of the community, and the peer hierarchy is the principle component of the social organization. Indeed, all residents are peers, equals in the struggle to change their lives. In the peer hierarchy, however, equality is indicated by the resident's community status and personal progress. Thus the program exists and is designed to empower peers to assume responsibility for its operational, therapeutic, and educational activities.

More generally, all peer relations are designed to reinforce the norms and values summarized in the TC view of right living. Learning to live successfully in the program is learning how to live effectively in the world outside of the program. Thus, a single set of norms, values, and beliefs defines life in and outside of the TC. Transmitted by peers, these norms, values, and beliefs are continuous with those of the conventional mainstream. This and the following chapter detail how peer roles and relationships are utilized by the community to facilitate the goals of socialization and psychological change.

PEERS IN THE TC PERSPECTIVE AND APPROACH

The socialization history of serious substance abusers is marked by negative peer influences (e.g., Hawke, Jainchill, & De Leon, in press; Hawkins, Lishner, Catalano, & Howard, 1986; Jainchill, Yagelka, Hawke, & De Leon, in press; Kandel & Logan, 1984; Oetting & Donnermeyer, 1998). Typically, residents in TCs have been particularly susceptible to negative peer influences, and most trace their initiation into drug use to peers (De Leon, 1976; Simpson, 1986). Usually, other drug users were their main peer relationships during the years of active drug use. In addition to drug use behavior, other aspects of their socialization have been influenced by peer relationships. For example, early street images acquired in a peer context usually foreshadow the more fully defined adult "masks" or social identities of "dope fiend," criminal, or social deviant.

Generally, the criminal history of substance abusers is also related to peer influences (Agnew, 1991). For most residents in TCs, their illegal activities commenced with regular drug use, usually in conjunction with or initiated by peers, such as pimping, prostitution, drug dealing, stealing from family members, and forging checks. With continued abuse or addiction, these criminal patterns persist and may worsen in severity, escalating to burglary and mugging, robbery, and crimes of violence.

Among a smaller proportion of residents, criminal activities preceded their regular use of drugs (Jainchill, Hawke, Yagelka, & De Leon, in press; De Leon, 1976). This group typically displayed early conduct problems at home, in school, and on the street, including stealing, truancy, and fighting. Peer influences were also evident in later problems for this group. For example, peers usually introduce them to drug use and, often in juvenile correctional settings, to more serious crime involving weapons and violence.

In the TC perspective a positive peer culture must be maintained within a context of a rational authority system to counter negative past and current peer influences. Old peer attachments must be replaced by new peer relations that *reverse* the historically negative peer influences. Often these new peers have similar profiles to those of the resident; or in some cases, they may even be old peers who have changed. New residents are redirected toward positive thinking, conduct, and values by peers who—though similar to their associates of the past—are different in the present.

In the TC approach, peers influence each other through their participation in various social and interpersonal roles. Roles are collections of related behaviors and attitudes that are socially labeled. For example, a facility coordinator, peer tutor, or parent each describes a complex array of skills and attitudes. Collectively these can often be learned more rapidly than by training the discrete behavioral or attitudinal elements separately. In the TC, then, the continual exchanging of roles provides ample opportunities for mutual learning among residents and is an efficient means of changing the whole person.

THE MAIN PEER ROLES

During their tenure in the TC, residents assume a variety of social roles, which can be organized into two broad related categories, functional and community member roles. These roles have common goals for the individual: to learn about others, to learn about the self, and to practice social roles for application in the real world.[37]

Functional Roles

Functional roles in the TC are those involving performance demands, prescribed skills and attitudes, and defined relationships with others. These include the various, work, teaching, student, and peer counseling roles of resident.

Peer conversation is a powerful recovery tool in the TC. An informal tool, *peer counseling* affirms positive changes and (more importantly) interrupts any negative changes in others. Thus, residents are constantly engaged in conversations about themselves and others. The themes of these conversations usually center upon the program, the people, and the change process itself. Specifically, residents talk to each other to validate personal growth or avoid personal isolation, check reality, ventilate feelings that unexpressed could trigger negative patterns, confess past wrong doings, complain, and sometimes threaten dropping out of treatment. In these exchanges peers continually reverse the roles of *counselor and counselee* and benefit from the mutual self help process. Both seeking and giving advice and support are ways of helping oneself.

Work roles are generally defined by specific job functions, which change continually and are more fully detailed in the chapter on work. Although residents have no ultimate formal authority over other residents (vis-à-vis treatment dispositions), they are trained to handle increasing amounts of authority through their job functions and under staff supervision. Service crew leaders, expediters, department heads, and coordinators are expected to supervise and manage the work of residents, confronting negative behaviors and attitudes and reporting these to staff. Additionally, peers model other work-related characteristics that

---

[37] Although similar to the familiar social-therapeutic method of *role-playing,* the use of roles in the TC is better understood as *role training*. In both role-playing and training, individuals can learn about themselves and others by assuming certain roles. However, role training has the larger purpose of facilitating role rehearsal for the outside world. Thus, the use of roles in the TC change process is therapeutic, educational, and social—to better prepare the individual to assume similar roles in the larger society.

transcend the particular job such as motivation, personal best standards, cooperativeness, competition, attitudes toward subordinates and superiors, and adherence to a work ethic. Thus, peers in their work roles mediate broad educational and therapeutic change in other residents.

As *peer tutors,* all residents are expected to provide specific assistance to others in areas that they have special expertise in and that further the goals of the program. For example, all residents are tutors in that they continually assist each other in daily adjustment. Those with skills and experience in particular vocations or professions may voluntarily provide seminars and workshops to their peers, and those with academic proficiency may offer regular tutoring to individuals in areas such as language, typing, mathematics, reading, and writing.

All residents are *students* and *apprentices* in that they are continually engaged in learning. However, residents are expected to exhibit the proper habits and attitudes of a student, including adhering to dress codes where indicated; behaving appropriately in teaching settings in terms of attention and quietness; reading, writing, and studying; keeping personal logs; and displaying respect for the tutor, mentor, or teacher. The peer tutor and student are related roles that are continually reversing among residents.

The roles of *mentor, teacher,* and *leader* amplify the basic elements of tutor and student roles described above. However, these roles connote the increased responsibility for peers and for the community as residents move up the peer hierarchy and move through the stages of the program. For example, senior residents are expected to be teachers as well as leaders in taking initiatives to improve the community.

Peers as Community Members

Community member is defined by the expectations concerning peer responsibilities to each other and to the community. Three prominent community member roles are peers as managers, as siblings (big brother or sister), and as role models.

Peers as community managers

In the role of community manager, peers display accountability to each other and the community as communicators and monitors. As *communicators,* peers are expected to provide feedback and share information to facilitate the process of change in each member. Peer feedback consists of authentic reactions concerning the observed behavior and attitudes of the individual. The information given may be in the form of sharing feelings, affirmations, suggestions, or criticisms about how they see or experience the individual. Peer disclosure consists of private truths provided by peers about themselves to facilitate change in others. All information about problems, solutions, and change is based on the individual's own struggle and experience in the change process. There are specific forms of peer communication that must be learned by the membership in its management role (see Table 11-1).

TABLE 11-1. Specific Forms of Peer Communication

Pull-ups

Peers are expected to speak to (remind) members of lapses in expected behaviors or attitudes, including any drop in motivation, lack of energy, withdrawal, daydreaming, sluggish work performance, negative talk, disrespect to staff and peers, lack of responsible concern, uncooperativeness, tardiness, or wandering attention in meetings, and groups. The explicit intent of a pull-up is to raise the member's awareness of behaviors or attitudes that should change; however, pull-ups reinforce changes in those who deliver them (see note below).

Push-ups

Residents are expected to provide positive feedback to each other at every appropriate opportunity. The explicit intent of the push-up is to encourage the flagging resident or to affirm any sign of progress in a peer. Implicitly push-ups balance pull-ups and other verbal correctives. As with all peer feedback, push-ups serve as self-reinforcers.

Pulling-in others

Residents are also expected to reach out to others and "pull them in," particularly newcomers, to help them affiliate with the community. Pulling-in others is the conscious effort to observe and detect signs of *non*-affiliation (personal withdrawal, isolation, or lack of participation) or dis-affiliation (negative talk and attitudes about the program). Alone or with other peers, a resident is expected to try and reverse these problems of affiliation with varied strategies: words and actions that encourage residents to remain in the program and participate in the process.

Note. An excellent analysis of the functional elements of pull-ups is contained in Hawkins & Wacker, 1986).

As *monitors,* peers are expected to observe the behavior and attitudes of residents for signs of negativity and confront these directly through conversations, pull-ups, or criticisms. If these corrections are not heeded or are received disrespectfully, peers are responsible for reporting the incident ("booking it") to those directly above in the peer hierarchy, e.g., expediters, coordinators, or staff.

Peer accountability also extends beyond the individual to the condition of the facility and the welfare of the general community. As monitors, each member is expected to remain alert to the signs of facility neglect, as well as individual and collective problems that may be potential threats to the community itself. To this end, a peer would be expected to deliver a pull-up to the entire membership and to report to others their observations.

Although they have no formal authority over the disposition of other residents, peers have considerable informal authority in their community management role. This is further illustrated in the concept of *condoning*. Failure to confront or report negative behavior or rule infractions is considered condoning, and those who do it are considered equally responsible for the consequences. Condoning, itself, therefore is viewed as a serious negative behavior that must be confronted and reported when observed in others.

Thus, the intent of peer monitoring is profound when viewed from the TC perspective. It maintains the community culture by challenging the number one street code—"don't snitch or tell on a peer"—and counters the potentially subversive effects of negative alliances and cliques.

Condoning negative behavior in others not only undermines the integrity of the community but can destabilize the recovery of the individual who condones. Most residents in TCs have historical patterns of secrecy and lying, which are related to their characteristic difficulties in trusting, being trusted, and in managing guilt. For these residents, condoning reinforces this pattern and invariably contributes to guilt felt toward themselves and the community.

In summary, the community management role can be described in terms of peer responsibilities to other peers and peer accountability to the community. Residents are expected to observe individual peers and the community, provide feedback to others, or explain to peers and staff why they haven't been observing or acting. Ignoring signs of difficulty in individuals is considered irresponsible to self and peers. Observing negative behaviors and attitudes and failing to act on these observations is considered condoning them. The basic assumption underlying peer–community accountability is that the recovery of each individual is related to the recovery of all peers. Thus, each resident is accountable for the health and safety of the community.

Peers as siblings ("big brothers and sisters")

TCs universally characterize themselves as families or family surrogate programs, with the main informal roles defined in family terms. The sibling role is a particularly important one in understanding peer–peer and peer–community interactions within the TC. Big brothers and sisters relate similarly to any resident in the community whether the same or opposite sex. The primary goal of the sibling role is to teach residents concern and caring as in good families. This teaching is most evident when residents use the role of big brother or sister to facilitate each other in the recovery process.

The fostering of sibling roles also effectively inhibits sexual relating among peers due to the understood cultural taboo on sexuality among siblings. Furthermore, sexual restraint in the sibling role helps peers to relate to each other as people rather than sexual objects. Also, in their sibling roles, individuals often recreate the role they played in their primary or biological families. They may become "attention-getters," victims or perpetrators of abuse, the overindulged baby, or the over-responsible "parentified" sibling attempting to substitute for the absent or dysfunctional adult parent. These family roles, behaviors, attitudes, and emotions can thus be expressed, addressed, and changed as part of the socialization and therapeutic process.

Peers as role models

The role model is the generic, community member role for peers, in which each resident is expected to display the behavior, attitudes, and expectations of the community. The strength of the community as a context for social learning corresponds to the number and quality of its role models. In the TC, all members must be trainers, tutors, and examples of personal change in order to effect 24-hour, multidimensional training for large numbers of individuals.

Having multiple role models in a TC also minimizes the need for and influence of any one individual's leadership. Charismatic figures among residents and staff emerge, but their program-wide impact is diffused by the presence of many other peers who also function as role models. Thus, multiple role models assure the spread of social learning, they minimize potential abuses of power by individual peers, and they maintain the integrity of the community.

Role modeling refers to both a concept and a fundamental learning and training activity of the TC. The role model is the idealized peer who embodies the features of the other peer roles described above. However, three broad attributes which typify residents who are learning to be role models are *act as if, responsible concern,* and *seek and assume.*

Role models act as if when they behave as the person they should be, rather than as the person they have been. Despite inner resistance and views or feelings to the contrary, role models engage in the expected behaviors of the community and consistently maintain positive attitudes and values. Resident role models display self-motivation, commitment to work and other goals, positive regard for staff as authority, and an optimistic outlook toward the future. In the TC view, acting as if is not just an exercise in conformity, but an essential tool for complete psychological change. Feelings, insights, and altered self-perceptions often follow rather than precede behavior change.

Role models also exercise responsible concern. This concept, described in previous chapters, is closely akin to being "my brother's or my sister's keeper." Showing responsible concern requires a willingness to confront others whose behavior is not in keeping with the expectations and rules of the TC, the precepts of recovery, or the values of right living. Role models are obligated to be aware of the appearance, attitude, moods, and performance of their peers and to confront any negative signs in these. In particular, role models must remain aware of their own behavior and be engaged in the process prescribed for personal growth.

Role models seek and assume. They initiate rather than follow, volunteer for work rather than wait to be recruited, reach out to offer understanding and help without being asked, extend their efforts beyond expected limits or requirements, and take on responsibility without formal assignment. These examples of "seek and assume" counter attitudes of entitlement, foster self-empowerment, and push past personal limits to encourage continual work on oneself.

PEER ROLES IN THE SOCIAL LEARNING PROCESS

In learning, practicing, and modeling their various peer roles individuals change themselves and others. Early in treatment residents are viewed as just learning roles and so there is less demand on them for role performance. For example, they are learning how to *receive* pull-ups rather than *give* pull-ups. Conversely, senior residents are further along in all of their roles, so there is greater expectation on them from their own role performance and from mentoring the role development of junior residents. Thus, learning the various roles provides tangible evidence of affiliation and clinical progress.

Role training is primarily mediated by senior residents who teach by example and instruction. Senior peers show junior residents how to work, act as big brothers and sisters, pull-up others, reach out and pull-in, monitor, and not condone negative behaviors.

Peer role models, in particular, are potent change agents in the TC, providing the main incentive cues for others to change. In modeling the desired or expected behaviors and attitudes they show others *how* to change. In addition, the role model status itself represents a recognized position in the community that is socially reinforced.

Finally, "the role model as change agent" illustrates the fundamental concept of reciprocity underlying the mutual self-help process in the TC. In performing their roles, peers not only influence other residents but reinforce *self-learning*. Pulling-in others is keeping oneself in the process; pulling-up peers is a reminder to self-correct; and pushing up a peer is way of remotivating and reaffirming oneself. Performing a role for others is rehearsing it for oneself. Thus, peers practice what they teach and teach what they practice.

PEER SUBGROUPS WITHIN THE COMMUNITY

Although the TC fosters peer relating, it explicitly discourages permanent peer groupings because these potentially undermine the influence of the broader family or community. Thus, membership in specific peer groups must continually change such that no rigid subgroup alliances endure. Such change usually occurs for residents in their movement from junior to senior status and when they assume various work roles, rotate through different therapy and tutorial groups, sleep in different quarters, and participate in community-wide meetings and seminars.

To some extent, benign peer-group identities do emerge such as admission or graduation cohorts. However, these are broadly perceived identifications with others rather than specific organized groupings. Thus, all residents share membership in changing peer groups at one time or another. Individuals, in their functional and community member roles, transcend their position in or allegiance to any specific peer group. This fluid feature of peer composition neutralizes negative influences of discrete peer collectives and sustains a general perception of a single peer community.

Peer Cliques ("Tips") as a Community Issue

Peer formations do develop, but these are usually short-lived given the rotation dynamics of the TC. Smaller peer cliques ("tips" or recognizable segments of the community) can exhibit some of the familiar patterns of negative peer collectivities such as in-group exclusionary conversations, fixed seating arrangements in the dining or meeting rooms, condoning the negative behavior or attitudes of clique members etc. A particular problem is clique-like conduct during therapeutic groups such as encounters. "Tip members" may depend upon each other to deal with confrontations, indicating implicit or explicit mutual agreements ("contracts") to protect clique members from the probes of the larger group.

Not infrequently, the basis for peer cliques is shared involvement in negative or proscribed behaviors, which may include drug taking, sexual acting out, or other infractions of house or cardinal rules. However, the motivation of cliques may be less overtly destructive, providing a forum for shared gripes, negative attitudes, or threats to leave the program.

Some cliques emerge on the basis of common gender, age, or race–ethnicity. Such demographic or cultural groupings can foster affiliation with the program and engagement in the treatment process when *purposely* used for these ends. However, when these groupings emerge spontaneously and appear to be detached from the general membership, their clinical utility is diminished, and they present obvious integration problems for the community.

Other cliques derive from a shared sense of elitism. They consist of several members who view themselves as superior to others in their knowledge of and commitment to the program and in their self-assessment of their recoveries. Although they appear less flagrantly harmful to the program, these cliques are still divisive to the community in that they foster a "we–they" separation. Moreover, the elitist clique impedes the psychological growth of its members, reinforcing attitudes of entitlement and self-aggrandizement.

Cliques are particularly threatening to the general community because they resonate the negative influences of peers in the history of most residents. Thus, residents who observe clique behaviors are expected to report these to an expediter or other senior resident. Clique members will customarily be confronted in encounter groups to reveal the reasons for the cliques. The participants will suggest strategies for neutralizing these groups. Staff will break up cliques, for example, by changing rooms, facilities and job assignments, by imposing speaking bans on clique members, or—if the clique is suspected of serious negative behavior—through outright collective discharge.

Social and Cultural Subgroups

Residents in the TC represent the demographic and cultural diversity of the general population. Indeed, the TC may be viewed as the quintessential, pluralistic microsociety. Its model and methods encourage integration of age, gender, race–ethnicity, and social class. The social mix in the TC is viewed as necessary to teach the reality of social living in the macrosociety.[38]

Nevertheless, the problems and issues typically associated with diversity emerge in the community life of the TC: prejudice, stereotyping, cultural insensitivity, as well as peer cliques. In the present context, discussion is limited to diversity as it affects peer relations.

Race–ethnicity issues

Some peer cliques that form are racial or ethnic in composition, particularly where that group's membership represents a numerical minority in the program. Such groups are routinely disbanded in favor of maintaining a single peer community. But while race–ethnic cliques are not tolerated, the expression of racial or ethnic issues and concerns is encouraged for both management and clinical reasons. Special theme groups are held periodically not only to diffuse potentially divisive threats to the community, but also to expose personal and interpersonal strains that could interfere with individual growth. Resolution of race–ethnic conflict is often a first step toward exploration of personal issues. These kinds of race–ethnic groupings expose the overt and subtle forms of prejudice and stereotyping among residents and the feelings of isolation, anger, fear, and mistrust that can result.

In accordance with its fundamental approach, the TC *utilizes* diversity to enhance its messages of recovery, personal growth, and right living. Race–ethnic issues and problems are addressed in the TC teachings and through basic precepts of right living. Learning to accept those who are different is a means of learning to accept oneself. Dissolving stereotypical perceptions and attitudes concerning the self (images), as well as others (prejudices), is essential for achieving a more complete self-understanding.

The components of TC life that directly enhance tolerance for diversity are *communal interdependence*, *social proximity*, and *public disclosure*. Shared tasks and collective responsibility are essential requirements for both the daily operation of the facility and the furthering of mutual recovery. In the proximity of daily living, culturally diverse residents sleep, eat, work, and learn together, which blurs perceived differences and compels personal intimacy. Public disclosures about emotional pains surface the commonalties among residents, which fosters community acceptance of the individual regardless of cultural background.

---

[38] The general issue of cultural diversity in the TC is more fully discussed in De Leon et al. (1993); see also Deitch and Solit (1993a) and Stephens (1978).

Gender issues in TCs

Females are a numerical minority in most TCs, roughly reflecting the male–female ratio of hard-core drug abusers in the larger society (Coletti et al., 1992; De Leon & Jainchill, 1991; Jainchill, 1994; Jainchill et al., 1997; Stevens, Arbiter, & Glider, 1989; Winick & Evans, 1997). When comparing the social and psychological characteristics of female and male addicts, women's self-esteem is typically lower, their depression and anxiety greater, and their overall social potency in terms of work and marketable skills weaker (De Leon & Jainchill, 1991; Jainchill et al., 1997). Notably, females carry greater shame and guilt related to their past drug abuse lifestyle.

The generally worse psychological picture of female addicts reflects some of the pervasive negative effects of social role conditioning in the larger society, a point that has been termed the "self-stigma" hypothesis. Female addicts internalize the common view in society that they are more socially deviant than male addicts. Thus, they often present themselves as more disturbed and self-rejecting than do their male counterparts (De Leon & Jainchill, 1981-82; De Leon & Jainchill, 1991; Jainchill et al., 1997).

Another gender issue in the TC concerns female perceptions of safety, which reflect their history with males. Female addicts have often been introduced to drugs through males, and their relationships with males have often included physical abuse, rape, exploitation, and abandonment (Densen-Gerber, Weiner, & Hochstedler, 1972; Stevens & Glider, 1994). Thus, in the context of coed life in the community, the issues of physical and psychological safety and trust in relationships are paramount.

Generally the treatment approach for males and females is the same in the TC. However, some of the gender issues are addressed through changing the social roles of females within the structure. Females routinely hold positions in the upper levels of the resident hierarchy, and they become role models with elevated community status. Female residents facilitate groups, confront males (and females), and become staff members and directors of facilities. The opportunities for equal mobility in the social structure are in direct contrast to their experiences in the larger society and thereby help to challenge and modify stereotypical gender perceptions. These role changes also help to surface male-based prejudices, fears, and resentments to women in authority.

Additionally, in women's groups, participants share common concerns and experiences related to gender abuse and discrimination. Other mixed-gender groups explore and seek to correct role-conditioned negative patterns of male–female interaction, attitudes, and perceptions. Men's groups help men examine any abusive patterns in past and present relationships in which they were perpetrators or victims. Finally, special relationship groups focus on specific male–female relationships. In these, couples or dyads are assisted in learning new interpersonal skills, expressing fears and distrust, and clarifying mutual perceptions and misperceptions. In the TC view, if these gender issues are allowed to remain and fester, residents are vulnerable to dropout and relapse.

Not only does the TC approach seek to reveal how social-role conditioning has affected individuals, but also how the individuals can misuse these role factors to avoid personal growth and slow recovery. Peers may confront each other on "hiding" behind valid and invalid gender or race–ethnic injuries to avoid making personal changes. In the TC view, racial, ethnic, or gender prejudice notwithstanding, individual residents are ultimately responsible for their own selves. For example, in women's groups the focus remains on the individual female—how she may have contributed to her problems and how she can *empower herself* to change the circumstances of her life now.[39]

Thus, gender issues are addressed at the level of social organization by emphasizing social empowerment for females in a setting that is numerically dominated by males; at the group level by holding gender-specific and mixed-gender groups to explore and confront perceptions and attitudes; and at the individual level by helping specific people examine negative patterns of abuse in relationships as well as change their perceptions and attitudes.

CONCLUSION

A defining element of the TC model is the use of peer roles for social learning. This chapter has described how the various community and functional roles in the social organizations are utilized by peers to change themselves and others and how socially conditioned race–ethnic and

---

[39] Actual role training in theme groups is informal and unstructured. The reactions, perceptions, and expectations of peers (and staff) are the feedback residents need for clarification of their social and interpersonal role difficulties. Seminars and tutorial sessions in which information and training is often provided by staff and invited guests offer more structured training of social-interpersonal roles and relationships. Role-playing, as well as direct instruction in behavioral and attitudinal change, may be employed in tutorials and skills-training sessions on the subjects of friendship, parenting, citizenship, etc.

gender roles and issues are addressed. The following chapter describes how the community utilizes interpersonal relationships and roles within and outside of the program to foster social and psychological change in the individual.

Chapter 12

Relationships

Residents in the therapeutic community (TC) engage in a variety of *interpersonal* roles and relationships both within and outside of the program. Friendships and attachments, romantic or sexual, "naturally" emerge within the peer community and are profoundly affected by the insistent intimacy of the TC community life. The relationships that are maintained outside of the community are naturally affected by the treatment experience, and they can reveal much about the individual's recovery and personal growth. The present chapter examines how these interpersonal relationships are utilized to transmit community teachings on right living and recovery.

RELATIONSHIPS: THE PERSPECTIVE AND APPROACH

The poor quality of past friendships and romantic attachments has been implicated in the drug problems of substance abusers in general (Casey & Preble, 1969; Chi'en et al., 1964; Glynn & Haenlein, 1988; Khantzian, 1985; Oetting & Donnermeyer, 1998).

Among residents in TCs, the relationship problems that most commonly surface are related to sexuality, interpersonal fears, and lack of relationship skills and values. These mainly stem from their social and family histories. For example, the social relationships of residents in the TC have been marked by mistrust, repeated disappointments, unhealthy dependency, exploitation, abuse, and sometimes violence. Thus, residents often lack both the skills and the courage necessary to be authentic participants in their relationships with others.

Residents also present a variety of emotional, behavioral, and attitudinal problems related specifically to sexuality. These reflect histories of being victims or perpetrators of sexual abuse including rape and incest. Additionally many display inadequate sex education, and confusion concerning the place of sexuality in relationships. Sexuality is, therefore, a major treatment issue for substance abusers, especially within the context of a coed community.

In the TC perspective, the relationship problems of residents relate to their overall social and psychological adjustment as well as to their substance use. Problems that arise in friendships and romantic attachments as well as sexuality in the TC help reveal residents' fear of *trust* and lack of experience with real intimacy. Sometimes relationships within the TC reveal frankly negative relationship behaviors such as irresponsibility, manipulation, exploitation, and abuse of friends and romantic partners.

The past experience residents have had with relationships has usually been within the context of drug use and related criminal activities. These typically were negative or unconventional and involved getting high, sexual acting out, and engaging in crime ("ripping and running"). Although they may also have included conventional social activities such as listening to music, going to dances and movies, or simply spending time together, their main peer attachments were drug related, involving not only using drugs together but frequently dealing, prostitution, and pimping (De Leon, 1976).

The TC is a culture and context for peer relationships that is radically different from that of the past, encompassing what peers do together, what they say to each other, their common norms and values, and shared personal experiences. In a drug-free environment removed from the outside world, residents work and communicate about personal problems, personal change, and right living. Within this culture, relationship problems and issues can be used to promote recovery and personal growth.

First, relationship issues and problems are used to stimulate self-examination. Real and imagined injuries in friendships, romantic expectations, and the like often reveal problems residents have in maturity and socialization, such as maintaining illusions, having an exaggerated sense of entitlement, and being self-centered. Of special clinical significance is how relationship problems can precipitate resident acting in or acting out reactions. For example, disappointment and disillusionment may *invert* into personal withdrawal or *convert* into hostility and anger toward specific individuals and the program itself.

Second, relationships are utilized to experientially teach individuals social, interpersonal skills and relationship skills. Third and perhaps most critical to the TC, however, is that peer relationships can foster the therapeutic alliance between the individual and the community. Positive relationships mediate healing and social support experiences. These encourage the individual to immerse in the therapeutic and educational activities of the community that lead to individual change.

The general approach to relationships in the TC consists of four interrelated strategies: management (regulation), educational, therapeutic, and social training. *Management strategies* utilize rules, sanctions, and community regulation of conduct to maintain the physical and psychological safety for the community as well as the individuals. *Educational strategies* teach information and clarify values concerning relationships. This approach employs seminars to provide specific information and general education. *Therapeutic strategies* consist of general encounter groups, individual counseling, and special sessions that center on self-examination and interpersonal problem-solving concerning relationship issues. These are specifically designed to surface individual feelings, attitudes, and concerns in contrast to intellectual understanding.

Social training strategies prescribe the community expectations and procedures guiding relationships. Relationships in the TC are managed as specific aspects of social learning. In this approach individuals experientially learn how to conduct themselves in relationships. The liaison itself is used to train interpersonal skills and clarify values, to identify and modify relationship behaviors and attitudes that have been negative, and to surface broader psychological issues for the individual such as fears and mistrust.

The issues and problems that residents display are common to all varieties of relationships, and the general approach to these remains the same. Of special importance to the individual and the community, however, are three main types of relationships: sexual relationships, romantic relationships, and friendships.

SEXUALITY IN THE TC

Substance abusers display problems, issues, and confusion in their information, conduct, attitudes, and values concerning sexuality (Simpson, Knight, & Ray, 1993; Winick, 1981). For example, residents in TCs may have knowledge about drug use, sexuality, and HIV and AIDS, but they may not alter their conduct with respect to drug use or safe sex (De Leon, 1996b; Des Jarlais, Jainchill, & Friedman, 1988; Galea, Lewis, & Baker, 1988). Residents in TCs are often uninformed or misinformed about facts regarding normal psychological and biological sexuality (Stevens & Glider, 1994). This usually reflects deficiencies in formal education. Relatively little is understood concerning anatomy, physiology, abortion, contraception, menstruation, and even masturbation.

In addition, drug users typically have poor role models with respect to sexuality. Often, parents, siblings, and surrogates have been sexually abusive (or abused themselves) or have been overcontrolling and punitive. Personal histories of abuse, rape, and incest are common in the history of substance abusers (e.g., Young, 1995).

Some of the more common sexuality issues encountered in TCs are related to sexual feelings, sex roles, values, and attitudes. Both sexes must learn to manage strong sexual impulses, particularly among young adults whose level of physiological arousal affects their physical and psychological adjustment in residential or restrictive settings. Preoccupation with sexual thoughts and erotic feelings and fantasies can intrude upon attention and concentration and manifests itself in hyperactivity in some, withdrawal in others.

Inability to manage feelings associated with aberrant past sexual incidents or relationships often results in confusion concerning homosexuality, heterosexuality, and bisexuality. Difficulties in this area are compounded by jail experiences, which may involve circumstantial homosexual encounters, and the street lifestyle, which commonly involves prostitution or pimping or the exchange of sex for drugs.

Problems of self-perceived physical beauty, competition with peers, and the need to project an image of strength ("macho") that are familiar issues of sexuality are worsened for drug abusers, insofar as they struggle with a comparatively lower self-esteem than do non–drug abusing peers. Additionally, there are gender-specific variations on some of these problems. Females, for example, often see themselves as sex objects or have used sex for survival, approval, or acceptance. For males, the pressure to sustain a macho image has often compelled inordinate frequency of sexual activity, abusive or exploitative behavior, and demeaning attitudes toward females. Males often do not distinguish between sexuality and sensuality, such as affection, feeling, and expression. Many males experience pressures from performance and expectation demands. For males and females, sexual activity initiated too early in life has often resulted in a sexual jadedness characterized by loss of feelings and cynical attitudes.

Finally, specific negative consequences to healthy sexual adjustment arise from the history of drug use itself. These primarily relate to the psychopharmacological effects of chronic drug use as well as the distortions in attitude, values, and self-perception arising from the socially negative lifestyle. Chronic use of heroin, for example, is known to lower or suppress libido (e.g., De Leon & Wexler, 1973; Jaffe & Martin, 1975) and though less well documented, sexuality experienced under the influences of speed, cocaine, depressants, and alcohol is notably distorted. In general, then, chronic substance use produces unreal attitudes and sensations that, in short, falsify the experience of sexuality (Khantzian et al., 1990; Washton, 1989).

The General Approach to Sexuality

Elements of the management, educational, therapeutic, and social training strategies are used to address the issues of sexuality. Male–female social interaction is unrestricted during all activities in the daily regimen. However, separate sleeping arrangements are strictly maintained. Infractions of the rules and regulations prohibiting sexual interactions and inappropriate conduct are met with community sanctions. There is a moratorium on the resident's sexual interactions until clinically appropriate. Privileges may then be granted for safe sex during furloughs and in the context of romantic relationships. Seminars are given on a periodic basis covering such matters as: basic anatomy and physiology of genitalia; abortion; contraception; masturbation; safe sex practices; and conceptual distinctions between sexuality, sensuality, affection, and lust.

Therapeutic groups and individual counseling are used to facilitate disclosure of traumatic and abusive sexual histories and vulnerabilities concerning physical image, sexual performance, beauty, and strength, and also to encourage expressions of fears, anxieties, and expectancies concerning the individual's sexual behavior. Residents are helped to understand how their sexual behavior and attitudes are used for social survival, personal acceptance, coping, and manipulating, and how drug taking masks non-drug-related feelings (often guilt, anger, self-hatred, boredom, insecurity, etc.) or, conversely, synthetically heightens (increases) feelings of potency or desire. In both gender-specific and gender-mixed groups, behaviors and attitudes concerning sexual stereotypes and trust are directly addressed and retrained.

Sexual relationships in the TC are managed as specific aspects of social learning. These liaisons are granted as privileges earned through displays of self- and social responsibilities that enhance individual growth and motivation. Focus is upon direct training of sexual conduct and modification of negative attitudes in particular respect for the sexual partner.

The general approach to sexual relationships varies somewhat for relationships within and outside the TC and for different subgroups of residents at particular stages in treatment. Sexual relationships within the program that develop among senior residents in the later stage of treatment are acknowledged by the community provided these are conducted in accordance with social expectations. With staff permission and clinical review, safe sexual liaisons among consenting adults can be consummated on an overnight pass or furloughs. The social, sexual features of these liaisons can provide data on treatment issues, such as social skills, maturity, and responsibility. Thus, residents are expected to disclose problems or issues of their sexual relationship in special group settings as they would any personal or social material.

The same expectations and general approach apply to resident sexual conduct with significant other sexual partners outside of the program. Residents must comply with the moratorium until they are better prepared to re-engage their outside relationships during brief furlough periods. Sexuality issues in these relationships are open matters for the community, and if needed, the residents' outside partner may participate in special groups in the program (see the last section of this chapter on relationships outside of the TC).

For residents without one consistent sexual partner, there is no change in the expectations or approach. However, particular emphasis is placed on the places, the people, and circumstances associated with residents' sexual liaisons on furlough. These factors, assessed by peers and staff, may be indicators of lapses in socialization and personal growth. In all cases, there is a singular focus upon safe sexual practices and breaking the historical association between drug use and sexual acting out, which is so common among substance abusers.

In most cases the sexual issues residents encounter on furlough are addressed through educational, therapeutic, and social training approaches. However, disciplinary sanctions may be invoked if residents display indicators of poor socialization in the behavior, attitudes, and values associated with their sexual episodes. These include, for example, unsafe practices, drinking or drug taking, coercion of others, violence, and obtaining money or gifts. Sanctions may also be applied for any form of sexual mistreatment of others that are viewed as lapses in the overall socialization process, such as manipulation, lying, and irresponsibility.

Homosexuality

In addition to precocious heterosexuality, a considerable number of residents in TCs have had homosexual and bisexual experiences. The prevalence of declared homosexuals among residents, however, is not remarkably different from the general population (De Leon, 1971, 1976).

The apparent discrepancy between stated homosexual experiences and homosexual orientation may reflect pressures toward nondisclosure. No individual is refused admission to or discharged from the TC because of sexual orientation. Until recently, however, resident disclosure of gay and lesbian histories and issues was discouraged and avoided, and explicit homosexual overtures could lead to immediate discharge (De Leon, 1971; Freudenberger, 1977). Also, there was little peer tolerance for homosexual relationships or liaisons outside of the program when residents were on furlough. These perceptions and reactions mirrored, in part, the stereotypes and the social stigma of the macrosociety toward homosexuality. They also may have reflected psychological issues of the male-dominated staff of the earlier TC programs concerning unresolved sexual roles and identity (see Freudenberger, 1974, 1976, 1977).

Contemporary TCs have changed their tolerance levels toward greater acceptance of homosexuality (although residents may still be disinclined to disclose a homosexual orientation). The management of sexual conduct in the TC is the same for homosexuality as it is for heterosexuality. The socialization and psychological growth issues for residents are viewed as universal, regardless of sexual preference. However, a special focus of education and therapy is upon teaching distinctions concerning sexual orientation and sexual behavior. Many residents have had same-gender sexual episodes in the context of their lifestyles and circumstances, e.g., childhood abuse, sexuality in prisons, and sexual liaisons in situations of drug use. These residents learn to distinguish between their homosexual or bisexual experiences and their primary sexual orientation or preference. The training of the interpersonal skills, attitudes, and values needed for healthy relationships also remains the same regardless of sexual preference.

ROMANTIC RELATIONSHIPS

In the TC perspective, romantic relationships include but are more complex than sexual conduct. They involve behaviors, attitudes, values, and skills for maintaining meaningful, constructive, and often stable interpersonal relationships. Thus, romantic relationships are essential to normal healthy living, but the approach to these within the program is defined by community and clinical considerations.

Certain relationships within the program present community issues. For example, romantic relationships between staff and residents as well as between senior and junior peers are strictly prohibited. Romantic attachments involving staff and peers not only disrupt the orderliness of community life but can subvert the credibility of the community itself. They replay scenarios of sexual abuse, exploitation, and past irresponsibility, resurfacing emotional trauma and reinforcing cynicism in the residents as well as in the staff. Romantic relationships among staff members are also strongly discouraged, and they are prohibited when involving senior with junior staff.

Likewise, romantic attachments involving senior and junior peers, while less disruptive, have all the same potential problems, violating as they do the sibling roles that are—by definition—asexual and nonromantic. Senior residents are expected to be role models who act as guides to "younger" residents rather than as romantic or sexual partners.

Romantic relationships among program peers, on the other hand, are viewed as more appropriate when the residents involved are at similar (and later) levels in the program and comparable stages in their recoveries. These guidelines minimize exploitation in relationships and create a safe basis for teaching residents the skills, attitudes, and values of healthy relationships.

While permitted to some degree, romantic relationships within the treatment program also contain significant clinical issues for the individuals. Romantic attachments between peers in the program can impede the socialization and psychological growth of the individual members in the relationship. Relationships can distract residents from their main focus of working on recovery and personal growth. Relationships can also "privatize" the participants, encouraging dyadic and secret communication in place of more general disclosure and in some cases fostering collusion to protect the relationship at the expense of individual growth. Self-examination can become limited as peer confrontation is deflected away from any probing or reality testing that may threaten the survival of the relationship. In other words, the relationship itself can become more important than the recovery of the individuals who are in the relationship.

For these reasons, TCs usually place a limited moratorium on romantic peer-relations within the program to maintain a psychologically safe environment and to better prepare residents to engage these relations constructively. To be prepared generally means that a resident is well affiliated with the peer community, stable in his or her various community roles, and committed to the change process. For a resident who is progressing in this way, a romantic attachment can facilitate continued individual growth and provide the basis for learning new relationship skills and values.

Residents who are interested in having a romantic relationship with a peer must convey their wishes to staff, who provide feedback as to the participants' readiness for a relationship. Usually permission is deferred until both residents are in the later stages of the program. If given the TC's "blessings" to proceed, the residents involved may then be accepted by the community as a couple. Staff may also permit the couple to have dates while on brief furloughs, which might include for example, going out to dinner, bowling, or seeing a movie.

Physical affection is allowed but the couple is expected to refrain from sexual intercourse for a period of time, and then only during furlough, off the program premises.[40] This delay provides the opportunity for participants to learn important relationship skills and values, particularly communication and responsible concern. It also assures that both members mutually agree to having sex and can engage in safe sex. Couples are expected to openly discuss their relationship with other peers, often using groups to resolve relationship conflicts and concerns. In all phases of the relationship, the focus of peer and staff guidance for the couple is on restraint, personal honesty, and responsible concern.

FRIENDSHIPS

In the TC, friendships can be distinguished from romantic, sexual, and other peer relationships. Friendships are special attachments or *bonds* to particular individuals. The bonding histories of substance abusers in TCs are varied and are a special aspect of their problems with relationships in general. For some there is little evidence of any meaningful or enduring attachment to other persons. As a result they are often personally isolated, socially distant, and are not directly influenced by others.

---

[40] In the past, some TCs maintained special "guest rooms" in the facility to permit overnight privacy to bona fide couples (e.g. those permitted by staff as well as residents who were married to each other). However, these rooms have been phased out, for the most part, in response to criticism from the macrocommunity, which sometimes misperceived the issue of sexuality in TCs. Moreover, the need for special rooms in relationship training has been seriously questioned by the programs themselves. It should also be noted that for adolescents in TCs, the sexual moratorium remains throughout their residential stay, although the other components of relationship training are provided.

Some residents have formed strong but unhealthy or self-destructive bonds with others. These may involve attachments to parents or relatives that have retarded the resident's overall maturation or bonds with drug using spouses, boyfriends, or girlfriends that have blocked developing positive relationships with others. Regardless of their negative bonding histories, all residents must have positive bonding experiences to facilitate their recovery. Negative bonds have to be replaced with positive bonds, or the ability to bond itself must be developed.

In the TC perspective, friendships in and outside of the program are critical elements of the problem as well as the solution. Friendships inevitably emerge in the life of the community. Whether formed during or prior to entry in the program, friendships exert positive or negative influences on residents in treatment. Negative friends may sustain drug-related thinking and attitudes, condone poor participation, facilitate non-compliance, encourage dropping out of treatment, or actually accompany a resident in leaving the program. Additionally, breakdowns in friendships and overt fights or covert antipathies between particular residents can undermine the moral and psychological safety of the community.

Conversely, positive friends show responsible concern for the individual and responsibility for the community. They can reinforce recovery and right living teachings, engage individuals early in the program and sustain their motivation throughout the process, and affirm progress and positive change. Thus, friendships formed or sustained by the shared experiences of positive personal change in the TC are powerful mediators of the change process itself.

In the TC approach, friendships are integral components of community as method. As noted above, positive bonds with specific individuals can facilitate affiliation with the general community. Specifically these relationships are utilized for teaching and therapeutic purposes. For example, positive friendships are necessary for creating drug-free social networks that sustain recovery. This involves learning how to identify and resist the influences of negative thinking and behaviors in others, particularly with respect to drug use. These skills are acquired in the everyday activities of the TC, which compel residents to challenge negative thinking and behaviors in peers and they are reinforced when the peer community assists individuals in identifying positive and negative friendships outside of the program.

Friendship issues are addressed in groups and informal peer aggregates. These may highlight the integrity elements of the friendships such as honesty, parity, and responsible concern. Or, they may surface individual issues of personal growth, e.g., immaturity, negative attitudes, and emotions. Conflict resolution sessions involving friends stress values, communication skills, and realistic expectations for both the target participants and the group membership.

Those friendships that persist in their negative elements may be managed like negative peer cliques ("tips"). For example, residents will be physically separated and placed in different housing, they may be banned from speaking to each other, or, in some cases, one or both friends may be discharged from the program. These strategies are supported by other peers, who stress the issues to be learned about positive friendships. Here, a resident—through the confrontation of a peer—explores what it means to be a friend:

> You were talking about smokin' dope, leaving this place and telling me to make it with you. To you a friend is someone who'll rip and run with you, give you money to get high, or maybe get down with you. What kind of a friend is that? Is that someone who really cares? You don't care about anyone; you don't even care about yourself.

RELATIONSHIPS AND ROLES OUTSIDE THE PROGRAM

Residents' relationships outside of the program eventually become known to staff and peers through conversations and groups. Emotional issues and practical problems surface concerning mates, children, and parents. These typically center on feelings of frustration, anger, guilt, and regrets that have often triggered drug use and other negative behavior. Themes commonly relate to past irresponsibility in meeting obligations, past manipulation of significant others, and past verbal and physical abuse. In the TC view, the resident's relationships and roles outside of the program must be addressed and changed to assure stable recovery.

Although outside relationships are considered critical, the TC approach is to place these "on hold" initially. Newer residents in particular are instructed by peers and staff to temporarily suspend active involvement in relationships outside of the program. This approach is grounded in several clinical assumptions that address outside relationship issues: the needs for emotional stabilization, a perspective, community affiliation, and skills training.

Distance from the circumstances and people in the resident's life is temporarily needed to facilitate *emotional stabilization* during the early days of treatment. New admissions to residential treatment are often experiencing considerable stress involving their outside relationships.

Those relationships are usually troubled, which may be a cause or consequence of residents' drug use prior to seeking treatment. Thus, new residents cannot effectively function in their outside roles as parents, children, spouses, or friends until they achieve emotional stability.

A related clinical assumption is that separation is necessary to gain *perspective* on outside relationships. Generally, the residents must have some understanding of themselves in order to examine, understand, and perhaps change their roles and relationships outside of the program. Thus, a period of self-examination and change is needed before an individual can profitably re-engage their other relationships and assess who they are as parents, children, friends, spouses, employees, or citizens.

This assumption concerning outside role relationships is illustrated in an example involving a female resident who cannot tolerate her guilt concerning her children in foster care. The peer group provides a perspective on her threats to leave treatment prematurely.

> You got here because of your drug use and its because of your drug use that you couldn't take care of your kids. First take care of yourself, then you'll be able to take care of your kids.[41]

Affiliation with the peer community is the foundation for initiating therapeutic change in the TC. Thus, a critical goal early in treatment is to rapidly assimilate the new resident into the community. This process of early affiliation can be hindered or subverted if the resident continues to be heavily involved or preoccupied with the people, problems, or obligations of his or her outside relationships. Thus, involvement in outside roles and relationships is minimal until the individual's affiliation with the community is established. However, when timely, outside relationships can be resumed and these can be constructively utilized to further growth and sustain the resident in the program.

Residents who are affiliated begin to learn *generic relationship skills* in their peer relations within the program, which can be transferred to their relationships outside the program. These include communication skills such as active listening and talking and conflict resolution skills, which are trained in the various community groups. Additionally the TC values of responsibility, honesty, responsible concern, and respect must be clarified for residents in their application to relationships.

---

[41] Even in recently implemented modified TCs for women and their children, the perspective remains valid. Although women have ready access to their children and additional child care is provided, the treatment of the mother in peer community remains primary (see Stevens, Arbiter, & McGrath, 1997, and Winick & Evans, 1997).

Peer and staff monitoring of residents' relationships conduct and skills outside of the program is ongoing. Following furloughs and overnight passes, debriefing sessions may center on issues and problems encountered with spouses, family, friends, employers, and children outside of the program.

Finally, residents must acquire *specific skills* in particular social roles outside of the program. For example, a notable development in recent years has been the incorporation of special initiatives for training skills in parenting or communication for family and significant others. The individual's use of these resources is an important indicator of how well he or she has learned responsibility and accountability. Thus, consistent with its method, the community utilizes these special activities to assess the participation and progress of the individual in the change process.

CONCLUSION

This chapter has described how relationships in the program, such as friendships, sexual and romantic partnerships, and roles and relationships outside of the program such as those with spouses, parents, and children are utilized in the recovery process. Relationships are used to teach authentic interpersonal skills and healthy values in a peer culture and context uncontaminated by drug use and other forms of alienation. The community approach to relationships is guided by the individual's clinical progress, reflected in their movement through the stages of the program. These program stages are the subject of the following chapter.

Chapter 13

Program Stages

In the therapeutic community (TC), program stages are prescribed points of expected change. Individual status can be described in terms of typical profiles at various points in the plan of the program. Residents, living in a peer community, are also "working the stages of the program."

The program stages do not directly reveal the process of change. Rather they convey the process in terms of individual movement within the organizational structure and planned activities of the model. This chapter provides a description of the program stages as the main structural component of the TC model, specifically designed to facilitate the change process. Later chapters describe the process itself in terms of changes in residents as they move through the stages of the program.

PROGRAM STAGES AND THE TC PERSPECTIVE

The stage format is grounded in the perspective and approach of the TC. Multidimensional change in the individual unfolds as a process of developmental learning which is viewed as stages of incremental change. Thus, stages and phases of the program mark the individual's passage in the learning process. The relevance of the stage format to the individual, the disorder, and recovery are illustrated in specific examples.

Residents in TCs have problems making and keeping of commitments, completing tasks, defining and pursuing social and personal goals. For new residents, in particular, lifestyle and identity changes are abstract, distant, and unachievable goals. Indeed, they struggle to get through days or hours without faltering in simple routines.

Program stages define concrete points of *goal attainment* based upon explicit community expectations. The end points of each stage are well marked in terms of expected behaviors and attitudes. Achieving the goal of each stage in itself constitutes an explicit social reinforcement for resident change. For example, attaining the status of senior resident, re-entry candidate, or graduate achieves public acknowledgement in addition to wider privileges and highly valued job functions.

Thus, the stage format reframes the long-term objectives of change into shorter-term goals that can be defined, perceived, and pursued. In providing a blueprint of step-by-step learning toward tangible and reachable goals the stages address the resident's key problems in delay of gratification and task completion. The sequential periods of stage-related expectations and demands, striving, and accomplishment counter the motivational fluctuations inherent in long-term residency in a relatively unchanging environment.

The stage format *distributes learning* and training in manageable increments. Information is transmitted in small bites and repeated in various ways to assure that it is correctly processed by the individual. It provides the structure for residents to practice what they are learning and allows them to falter and begin again.

The stage format facilitates staff and peer *assessment* of where individuals are in meeting program expectations for change. The person at admission is not the same as the community member three months later. A complete and accurate picture of residents emerges only gradually in their changing relationship with community. As residents experience understanding, acceptance, and trust in the community, they reveal and share who they are within the community. Conversely, the peer community eventually observes all of the dimensions of individuals revealed in their various social roles and interactions. Most relevantly, the stage format is the vehicle for resident self-assessment. Where the resident is in terms of the program stage also highlights what the resident is working on in terms of self-development.

THE PROGRAM STAGES: GENERAL DESCRIPTION

In traditional long-term residential TCs, there are three main program stages, induction, primary treatment, and re-entry, consisting of several phases or substages. These stages are described in terms of main goals, stage-specific activities, and typical outcomes. A stage prior to entry, the admissions evaluation, is included because it initiates the individual's orientation to the main stages of the program.

Admission Evaluation: A Pre–Program Stage

Traditional TCs maintain an "open-door" policy with respect to admission to residential treatment. This understandably results in a wide range of treatment candidates, not all of whom are equally motivated, ready, or suitable for the demands of the residential regimen. Relatively few are excluded because the TC policy is to accept individuals electing residential treatment regardless of the reasons influencing their choice.

The specific goal of the admissions stage is to identify those who are manifestly unsuitable for the TC and to prepare others for long-term residential treatment. The admission procedure is a structured interview conducted by trained paraprofessionals, usually program graduates. Initial interviews last 60 minutes and may be followed with a second interview, often including significant others. Additionally, records of previous legal, medical, psychiatric, and drug treatment histories are evaluated.

The major guideline for excluding clients is risk to the community—the extent to which clients present a management burden to the staff or pose a threat to the security and health of the community of others. Specific exclusionary criteria most often include histories of arson, suicide, and serious psychiatric disorder. Psychiatric exclusion is usually based on documented history of non-drug-related psychiatric hospitalizations or prima facie evidence of psychotic symptoms on interview (e.g., frank delusions, thought disorder, hallucinations, confused orientation, signs of serious affect disorder).

Generally, clients on regular psychotropic medications, including those on antidepressants, will be excluded because use of these usually correlates with chronic or severe psychiatric disorder. Also, the regular dispensing of medication, particularly in the larger TCs, presents a management and supervisory burden for the relatively few medical personnel in these facilities.[42]

Clients with medical conditions requiring medication are accepted to TCs, as are handicapped clients or those who require prosthetics, provided they can meet the participatory demands of the program. A full medical history is obtained during the admission evaluation, which includes questions on current medication regimens (e.g., asthma, diabetes, hypertension) and the necessity for prosthetics. Physical examinations and

---

[42] Modified TC programs for mentally ill substance abusers who require medication have been successfully implemented (see De Leon, 1997a; Nuttbrock, Rahav, Rivera, Ng-Mak, & Link, 1998; Sacks et al., 1997; Silberstein et al., 1997). Moreover, in several standard TCs a small proportion of the residents receive pharmacotherapy for mental or emotional conditions (e.g., Carroll & McGinley, 1998).

laboratory tests (blood and urine profiles) are obtained after admission to residency. Although test results occasionally require removal of a client from residency, such cases are relatively rare. Because of concern about communicable disease in a residential setting, some TCs require tests for conditions such as hepatitis prior to entering the facility or at least within the first weeks of admission.

Policy and practices concerning testing for HIV status and management of AIDS (acquired immune deficiency syndrome) or hepatitis C have been implemented by most TCs. These emphasize voluntary testing with counseling, special education seminars on health management and sexual practices, and special support groups for residents who are HIV positive or have a clinical diagnosis of AIDS (see Barton, 1994; De Leon, 1996b; McCusker & Sorensen, 1994).

In the TC perspective clients in the admission process are in a pre–residential stage of the program. The assessment-evaluation activities are viewed as interventions that can impact individuals to initiate a change process. These activities offer some orientation and preparation for the next stage of induction in the residential facility. They explore the individual's motivation to change and they provide information to the candidate on program policy and general approach, such as the planned length of stay, the requirements of participation in groups, fulfilling work assignments, and living with minimal privacy, usually under dormitory conditions in an open community. This orientation often clarifies applicants' perceived suitability for TC life or the degree to which they can or want to meet the demands of the TC regimen.

Stage 1: Induction

The induction stage is often defined as the first 30 days of entry. However, full induction into the program is usually not stable prior to 2–3 months of residency. Thus, though described separately, the main goal and activities of induction extend into the initial phase of primary treatment.

The primary *objective* of Stage 1 is to assimilate the individual into the community. Rapid assimilation is crucial in the early days when individuals are most ambivalent about the long tenure of residency and most vulnerable to premature dropout.

Typical activities that are carried out when new admissions enter the program facility illustrate basic elements of the TC approach. Individual needs for detoxification, medications, and health services are clarified.

Entitlements are processed and payroll checks are picked up by the program; cash and jewelry are turned over to admissions for safekeeping.

Shortly after entry into the residential facility, peers introduce themselves to the new admissions. Staff assesses that no drugs or other contraband are carried into the facility. The individual then gets his or her assigned sleeping quarters, takes a shower, and is provided with a meal in the dining room. Inductees engage in all of the activities of the daily regimen: work, meetings, seminars, groups, meals, recreation, and personal time. Although limited in their actual input, inductees are regarded as participants in the community. In contrast with later stages that focus upon therapeutic change, however, the community activities in Stage 1 focus upon encouraging affiliation through several specific strategies. These emphasize relative isolation, crisis intervention, focused orientation, and supportive counseling.

New residents require *relative isolation* in terms of minimal contact with family or others outside of the facility. Usually, they are permitted several phone calls to significant others. Written correspondence in and out of the facility is limited and is monitored by staff to detect negative content or contraband. Problems from the outside can distract the new resident from attending to, much less concentrating on, what must be learned in the new environment; active interactions with those on the outside can also undermine the development of new relationships in the program.

Clinical, administrative, and ancillary staff attend to the immediate and pressing needs of the new resident, including legal, medical, family, children, and financial matters. Initial *crisis intervention* is designed to reduce stress and concern associated with pressing situations and life circumstances. However, assistance is limited to the mitigation of immediate or acute problems that could potentially subvert the new residents' retention in the program. It is not intended to provide the new resident with longer-term solutions. Complete relief from outside pressures could paradoxically reduce the resident's perceived need for self-change through treatment. Eventually, longer-term solutions to their circumstantial problems must be the responsibility of the residents.

Focused orientation is informally conducted by peers, who escort the individual around the facility explaining rules, regulations, and procedures; introducing people; and talking about themselves. In their movement throughout the facility new residents are rarely alone; they are usually accompanied by more senior residents who continually clarify the norms and expected behaviors of the community, monitor the residents' behavior, and counter threats or comments about leaving the program.

Formal orientation sessions are initiated by senior peers and staff soon after entry into the facility. Orientation sessions include reading material, videos, and question and answer segments. Seminars are the main, formal orientation-activity. They focus on (a) cardinal rules (i.e., no use of drugs, no violence or threat of physical violence); (b) community or house regulations (expected conduct in the community, such as speaking, dressing, punctuality, attendance, manners); (c) program essentials (structure organization, personnel, basic procedures, program stages, philosophy, and perspective); and (d) TC tools (e.g., encounter and other groups, job functions, the privilege system). Later in Stage 1 the induction resident will assist senior residents and staff in orienting new admissions to the program. This limited use of role reversal is designed to help residents practice what they are learning in their own orientation and represents a status privilege that reinforces their own identification with the community.

In order to avoid elevating personal anxiety, all *therapeutic activities are moderated.* Group process during induction aims to facilitate involvement with peers, acceptance of the regimen, and training in the use of the groups. The intensity of personal confrontations is modest accompanied by concerned probe and inquiry.

Individual counseling by peers and staff is supportive in Stage 1. The aim of counseling is to reduce residents' characteristic anxiety and uncertainty about themselves, the treatment situation, and the future. A second aim of counseling is to reinforce role induction into the community. In these sessions, peers and staff emphasize what residents need to learn in orientation, what difficulties they are experiencing in adjusting to the environment, and how to effectively use their peers, groups, meetings, and job functions to help themselves. Table 13-1 summarizes the typical resident features at the end of the induction stage.

Stage 2: Primary Treatment

The primary *objective* of Stage 2 is to address the broad social and psychological goals of the TC. Throughout the ten months of primary treatment the main TC goals of socialization, personal growth, and psychological awareness are pursued through all of the therapeutic and community resources and activities.

TABLE 13-1. Resident Features: The Induction Stage

The orientation period resident
- Learned the policies and procedures of the TC, the program philosophy, and general stage plan
- Established some trusting relationships with staff and/or recovering peers
- Begins a personal assessment of self, circumstances, and needs
- Begins to understand the nature of the addictive disorder and the demands of recovery
- Makes a tentative commitment to the recovery process
- Has a firm commitment to remain through the first months of the program

Special stage issue:
The first 30 days of treatment are stressful for a number of individuals who have never been drug free for that period of time. Furthermore, the structure of the program is provocative, and exposure to the social and psychological demands of the TC often pushes individuals to confront realities and experiences that they have avoided through drugs. Thus the risk for dropout is greatest in this period.

Primary treatment generally consists of three phases, roughly correlating with time in the program (two to four months, five to eight months, and nine to twelve months). These phases are defined by the member's status in the peer hierarchy (junior, intermediate, and senior resident). The daily therapeutic–educational regimen of meetings, seminars, groups, job functions, and peer and staff counseling, remains the same throughout the months of primary treatment. In this stage, however, community expectations for the residents' full participation in all activities and roles markedly increases, as does the intensity of group process and peer and staff counseling. Job functions become more complex, privileges grant wider latitude, and seminar content expands to address a wide variety of themes relating to recovery and right living.

Stage-specific activities include vocational and educational services, which are gradually integrated into the daily regimen late in primary treatment commensurate with overall clinical progress and the resident's program commitment. Clinical interventions are designed by staff for unique problems or needs of the individual. These may include sessions with family members, special groups for psychosexual issues, and focused psychological counseling to deal with acute mental health problems. These interventions are limited, however, consistent with the community's peer, mutual self-help approach in the TC.

Formal counseling by staff in Stage 2 is also limited in order not to subvert the residents' use of the feedback from peers and in groups. Individual sessions with staff address issues of treatment planning, program adjustment or resident recalcitrance, psychological stress or personal crisis concerning outside affairs, or problems with public disclosure of especially sensitive information. These sessions are essentially problem solving, although therapeutic effects often occur. Table 13-2 summarizes typical resident features in the three phases of primary treatment.

TABLE 13-2. Resident Features: The Phases of Primary Treatment

The phase 1 resident
- Junior status in the TC system, limited freedom, and lower-level jobs
- Identifies oneself as a community member
- Conforms to the TC system
- "Acts as if"—understands and complies with the program, participating fully in daily activities: follows directions, adheres to the cardinal and house rules, and accepts disciplinary contracts
- Displays a general knowledge of the TC approach
- Accepts the seriousness of his or her drug use and other problems, and shows some separation from the drug culture, street code, and language
- Reveals decreases in the dysphoria
- Participation in groups increases, although communication and group skills are not fully acquired
- Displays limited personal disclosure in groups and in one-on-one sessions

The phase 2 resident
- "Sets an example" for other residents
- Elevated status in the social structure evident in privileges and job functions
- Greater personal freedom: can leave the facility without escort when going to prescribed places, for brief periods and for specific reasons
- Key attitudes reflect acceptance of the program, commitment to continue working on oneself in the program, and value for the role model attributes of honesty and responsibility
- Personal growth evident in adaptability to job changes, acceptance of staff as rational authorities, and ability to contain negative thoughts and emotions
- Reveals elevated self-esteem based on status and progress in previous eight months
- Self-awareness is manifest in identification of characteristic images
- Accepts full responsibility for his or her behavior, problems, and solutions
- Acquired group skills and is expected to assist facilitators in encounter group process

The phase 3 resident
- Established role model in the program; provides leadership in the community
- Increased personal autonomy evident in more privacy and bi-weekly furloughs
- Effectively runs the house as coordinator
- Eligible to be staff-in-training in executive management offices or special ancillary services
- Assists staff in monitoring the facility overnight and on weekends
- Involved with school or vocational training

Table continues

TABLE 13-2. Resident Features: The Phases of Primary Treatment

Table continued

The phase 3 resident *continued*

- Social interactions with staff are more spontaneous and relaxed, and socializes with a network of positive peers during recreation and furlough
- Reveals higher and more stable levels of self-esteem commensurate with senior status in the community
- Displays some insight into his/her drug problems and personalities; accepts responsibility for oneself and for other members in the community
- Fully trained participant in the group process and often serves as facilitators
- A high level of personal disclosure is evident in groups, in peer exchange, and in increased use of staff counseling

Special stage issues:

The concerns in primary treatment reflect the paradoxical effects of treatment improvement. An example is plateau in progress, where an improved level may lead to program completion but with limited growth and risk for relapse. A second example is the resident perception that he/she no longer needs treatment, possibly leading to increased risk of dropout prior to re-entry.

Stage 3: Re-Entry

The primary *objectives* of re-entry are to facilitate the individual's separation from the residential community and to complete his or her successful transition to the larger society. These are pursued in two distinct but continuous residential and nonresidential phases. In the early residential phase (approximately 13–18 months), the objective is preparation for a healthy separation from the residential community. In late re-entry (approximately 18–24 months), the objective is to complete a successful transition from residency and facilitate initial adjustment to the outside community.

The objectives of re-entry are fundamental to the TC's developmental view of recovery. Residents are expected to leave the community to live successfully on their own in the same way that young adults leave their parental homes. Physical detachment from the peer community represents a major landmark in the change process for the individual. What is learned during the period of residential living in the peer community is preparation for living in the world outside.

A critical distinction between re-entry and primary treatment as program stages is the use of the resident's increased exposure to the outside world to further his or her social and psychological goals. In preparing the resident for separation from the program, re-entry activities constellate around the theme of rehearsal and putting into practice what has been learned in the TC. Thus, how completely re-entry residents have changed along the major dimensions is evident in how they meet the increasing demands of the "real world."

In *early re-entry,* residents continue to live in the facility. They may be attending school or holding full-time jobs, either within or outside of the TC. The specific goals of early re-entry are to reduce the individual's dependency on the peer community as the primary source of learning and support and to increase the individual's involvement in the outside world. Thus, the stage-specific activities in the early re-entry phase are designed to strengthen the social and psychological skills needed for adjustment to the outside community. Emphasis on the rational authority of staff decreases under the assumption that the client has acquired a sufficient degree of self-management (autonomy). This is reflected in (a) increased personal privacy in living space and more privileges granting time away from the facility; (b) more individual decision-making regarding social plans and life design; (c) more shared decision making with peers in managing their re-entry quarters; and (d) more flexibility in the program demands made upon the re-entry candidate. Work and school schedules assume higher priority although these may interfere with attendance in meetings and other community activities.

Group process involves fewer leaders, fewer encounters, and more theme groups dealing with adjustment issues. Particular emphasis is placed on life-skills seminars, which provide didactic training in such matters as money management, job seeking, parenting, use of leisure time, use of alcohol, and issues of sexuality.

During the early re-entry phase, the making of individual plans is a collective task of the client, a key staff member, and peers. These plans are actually blueprints of educational and vocational programs, which include goal attainment schedules, methods of improving interpersonal and family relationships, and social and sexual behavior.

Unlike senior residents in primary residential treatment, re-entry candidates may live in a special facility or in a designated area of the main residential facility. The deliberate physical separation of re-entry candidates from other residents signifies their changed social status in the community and the need to facilitate their psychological separation from the community.

Although residents in early re-entry may be attending school or holding full-time jobs either within or outside of the TC, they are expected to participate in house activities when possible and to carry some community responsibilities. These typically include conducting special resident seminars, serving as experienced members ("strength") in encounter groups, assisting in marathons and retreats, and providing facility coverage at night.

Those in *late re-entry* are former residents who remain community members in a "live-out" status. They are involved in full-time jobs or education and maintain their own households with spouses, significant others, or often with other re-entry "live out" peers. They are expected to attend aftercare services such as Alcoholics Anonymous or Narcotics Anonymous or take part in family or individual therapy. The main objective of late re-entry is to complete a successful transition to the macrosociety. Although this phase marks the end of residency, program participation continues on a decreasing basis. Late re-entry places the individual in the real world to practice what they have learned outside of the controlled and protective setting of their residential community. Although sometimes oppressive, intrusive, and lacking in privacy, the 24-hour context of a controlled learning environment is also reassuring and protective. In contrast, late re-entry clients are "on their own" and their success in dealing with the real world depends upon the stability (i.e., internalization) of what they learned in the "controlled" world of the TC.

The specific goals of the late re-entry phase relate to transition and separation: (a) adjustment to prosocial living; (b) strengthening daily living skills; and (c) maintaining sobriety and right living outside of the facility. Adjustment to prosocial living involves learning to identify and address difficulties associated with work and relationships, developing a positive social network, and managing recreation and leisure time. Strengthening daily living skills involves education, training, or monitoring in matters such as budgeting, parenting, and health care. Maintaining sobriety outside of the facility involves training or monitoring the individual's coping with the social, circumstantial, and psychological triggers to drug and alcohol use

The training, educational, and therapeutic activities addressing these goals are conducted both at the program and elsewhere. Live-out candidates and those who have actually moved out do not attend facility seminars, groups, or meetings. They are expected to attend Alcoholics Anonymous or Narcotics Anonymous groups. They are also encouraged to engage in individual counseling with staff as needed, participate in evening "outpatient" groups at the program, and take part in family or individual therapy provided at the program or elsewhere. An additional program activity provides follow-up assistance in advocacy services such as initiating job development.

Late phase re-entry candidates informally relate to the main program. They are expected to "give back" to others as an element of their own recovery. Thus, they are invited to conduct seminars to serve as sponsors or big brothers and sisters for new residents. However, on a daily basis these individuals are not regularly seen in the peer community. They are viewed by staff and residents as siblings who have left the family to live on their own. This phase is viewed as the end of residency but not of program participation. Contact with program is frequent at first and gradually reduces to weekly phone calls, monthly visits with a primary staff counselor, and finally official termination. Table 13-3 summarizes typical resident features in phases of the re-entry stage.

TABLE 13-3. Resident Features: The Re-Entry Stage

The early re-entry phase resident
- Lives in special facility
- Attends school/training/and or paid job
- Assists in managing the facility
- Elevated self-esteem
- Displays insight into life problems
- Seeks and assumes new obligations without prodding
- Displays some anxiety about immediate future

The late re-entry phase resident
- Lives outside of the facility
- Engaged in full time work or part work and school
- Identification of the specific situations, views, experiences, and behavior that could be harmful to recovery;
- Discloses to peers and staff every element of doubt, concern, mistake, or fears that have been experienced and could be potentially harmful
- Seeks help where needed to further understand oneself and to strengthen appropriate coping skills, decision making, and problem solving

Special issue—re-entry as role conflict in the process:
The individual's progress in the transition to the outside world is complicated by the role aspect of his/her re-entry status in the program. Often re-entry candidates believe that they are "cured" or should be able to handle "real world" stress on their own. They tend to protect this image of recovered (vs. recovering) or making it on their own. Actually, the re-entry stage is the most demanding, as it presents explicit challenges to the recovering individual from which he/she has been protected during residential stay in primary treatment. The image of immunity common to the re-entry candidate appears to be self-developed and is not a treatment message of the community.

Program Completion

Individuals who complete all stages of the planned duration of treatment (e.g., 24 months) are candidates for program graduation. They present a typical profile reflecting the TC view of recovery. Program completers have been drug and alcohol free, have a job, are in school or in job training, and have resolved circumstantial impediments (e.g., housing, health, family, legal matters). Psychologically, they reveal significant declines in depression level and symptoms, and they display a positive outlook. Their commitment to the recovery process is firm; they accept the need to continue work on particular problem areas and on themselves in general. They may have formed linkages with individual therapists and self-help resources.

Finally, program completers are encouraged to maintain some relationship with the program as a member of an informal fellowship, taking on a sponsor role with new program clients. This also provides continuity for the former resident in terms of relationships, recovery, and right living teachings.

Completion marks the end of active program involvement. Graduation itself, however, is an annual event conducted in the facility usually a year beyond separation from residency. Although program stages have ended, what is learned in the treatment community is the set of tools to guide the individual along a steady path of continued change in the larger world. Completion or Graduation, therefore, represents a landmark in the recovery or change process, which signifies both an end and a beginning.

Aftercare

Actually, aftercare has not been a formal stage of the program in long-term residential TCs. However, a major but implicit goal of TC treatment is to initiate a continuing treatment or growth process well beyond graduation. Thus, aftercare plans are a special activity of the late re-entry phase of the program. These plans outline recommendations and steps for obtaining supportive and counseling services to address long-standing issues of the re-entry client. In the TC view of recovery, the lifestyle changes occurring in residential treatment are a prerequisite for effective use of aftercare plans.[43]

---

[43] The gradual shortening of the planned duration of residential treatment in recent years has compelled TCs to develop nonresidential components of the program. These offer "aftercare services" such as individual and family counseling, vocational and educational guidance, etc. Because of the shorter periods of residential treatment, however, these nonresidential components often must address primary treatment as well as aftercare issues.

PROGRAM STAGES AND THE TREATMENT PROCESS

The program stages are structural components of the TC model that are integral to the treatment process. From the first days of admission residents are aware that the stage-phase format is the structural guideline in the recovery process. In the plan of the program, individuals must meet the objective of each stage or phase, usually within general time frames. Movement across stages and phases is marked by explicit and formal procedures, which exemplify the self-help elements of the approach and change process. For example, residents themselves typically initiate the phase change through a written request to staff, often accompanied by a personal essay describing progress and reasons for the request. The request is reviewed by the primary staff person along with other staff and senior peers. The change is granted in private between the primary staff and the resident and then announced to the entire community in the next house meeting. In some cases, there are mini-stage-phase graduation ceremonies, which further affirm the importance of the progress of individuals.

The main criteria for stage-phase advances are time in program, completion of all stage-phase specific obligations and responsibilities to the community, and explicit changes in personal growth. However, distinctions in stage status, clinical status, and time in program are briefly discussed, illuminating the treatment process as well as issues of clinical and program policy.

Stage Status and Clinical Status

Junior, intermediate, and senior residents are at different positions in the peer hierarchy and generally at different stages of the program. Therefore, the program stages and the peer hierarchy converge to reinforce the individual's perception of self-change. At each stage, residents can see those ahead and behind them in the change process. However, some residents can learn to ascend the peer hierarchy and move through the stages without necessarily displaying significant, individual clinical changes. Thus, the actual clinical status of residents must be continually assessed as they move vertically in the structure and across the program stages.

Time and the Program Stages

Generally the longer individuals remain in treatment, the more likely their recovery and rehabilitative goals are achieved. Those who complete the planned duration of treatment reveal the best outcomes (e.g., Anglin & Hser, 1990b; De Leon, 1984b; De Leon, Jainchill, & Wexler, 1982; Hubbard et al., 1997; Simpson, 1979).

However, most admissions to long-term TCs do not complete the full 18–24 month planned duration of treatment. The majority of dropouts leave within the first 90 days of admission—that is, during induction and the initial phase of Stage 2, primary treatment (see De Leon, 1991). Despite individual differences in clinical progress, these early stage dropouts are generally not ready to engage the outside world effectively. Their relapse and recidivism rates posttreatment indicate the importance of completing the time correlated program stages.

The stage–time relations also bear upon program readmission policy. Approximately a third of dropouts (and a fractional proportion of graduates) from TC programs seek readmission to the same or another TC program (De Leon, 1991; Simpson, 1986). Readmissions are expected to complete all stages of the program, despite their time in program and their community status achieved in prior TC treatments. However, clinical progress from previous TC experiences may result in accelerated stage and phase changes.

These examples of dropout and readmission further underscore distinctions between time in treatment, program stages, and clinical progress. Positive outcomes following treatment relate to successfully completing the goals of the program stages, not simply meeting the planned duration of treatment (Coombs, 1981; Toumbourou, Hamilton, & Fallon, 1998).

The above distinctions also highlight policy issues with respect to individual differences. Not all residents require the same time to complete the phases and stages of the program. A flexible time–stage format based upon clinical needs and progress could accommodate individual differences although such a policy has been problematic for traditional TCs. Nevertheless, funding pressures and the increased diversity of clients have encouraged a number of programs to implement shorter planned durations of treatment (e.g. Karson & Gesumaria, 1997; Lewis et al., 1993). Although not firmly established, the effectiveness of these efforts appears promising for particular individuals (McCusker et al., 1995; Messina, Wish, & Nemes, 1999).

CONCLUSION

This chapter describes the major stages and phases of the TC program model: induction, primary treatment, and re-entry. Program stages and phases are structural elements of the TC model, which define where individuals are in the plan of the program. Each stage-phase marks the resident's acknowledged level or position in the social organization of the TC in terms of seniority of community status. It also signifies where individuals are in their socialization and psychological growth. How individuals change in their passage through the program stages depends upon their participation in the activities of community life. The following chapters in part IV organize and detail these activities or methods in the change process.

PART IV

Therapeutic Community Methods

In the therapeutic community (TC), all activities and interpersonal and social interactions facilitate recovery and right living. However, the daily regimen of structured activities are viewed as methods, designed to impact both individuals and the general community in specific ways. These methods can be organized in accordance with their primary purpose, *community and clinical management, community enhancement,* and *therapeutic–educational change.*

Community and clinical management activities (chapters 14 and 15) consist of privileges, disciplinary sanctions, security, and surveillance. These activities maintain the physical and psychological safety of the environment and ensure that resident life is orderly and productive.

Community enhancement activities (chapter 16) include the four main facility-wide meetings: the morning meeting, seminars, the house meeting held each day, and the general meeting, which is called when needed. These meetings strengthen the individual's positive perception of community and therefore its capability to teach and to heal.

Therapeutic–educational activities (chapters 17 and 18) consist of encounters, probes, marathons, and tutorials. The various forms of group process focus specifically upon changing the social and psychological characteristics of the individual as well as teaching work, communication, and interpersonal skills. Additional groups are scheduled as needed. These include, for example, relapse prevention, vocational and life skills training, and social and health education groups. Although not distinctive to the TC model, these groups enhance or supplement therapeutic and educational effects of the basic TC methods.

Chapter 14

Privileges and Sanctions

Privileges and sanctions constitute an interrelated system of community and clinical management through behavioral training. The management of the community is the responsibility of peers and staff. Indeed, the efficacy of the system itself depends directly upon peer involvement in its implementation. The norms and values of the TC challenge those of negative peer systems found in jails, the street, gangs, and the drug culture in general. Thus, staff remains the rational authority in the management system. However, the empowerment of peers as monitors and managers is central to assure community order and advance the socialization and psychological goals for the individual.

Privileges and sanctions are also distinctive components of community as method. Both are the community's explicit *responses* to how individuals meet its expectations. These responses reflect community approval or disapproval for individual behaviors and attitudes concerning the norms of daily living, recovery, and right living teachings of the TC. Social approval, in the form of positive peer support and verbal affirmation, and disapproval, in the form of negative criticism and correction, occur daily in the interaction of peers. Privileges and disciplinary sanctions, however, are the prescribed ways in which the community expresses approval and disapproval.

This chapter details the formal system of community privileges and sanctions prescribed by staff and the informal system of verbal affirmations and correctives implemented primarily by peers. Although separately described, privileges and sanctions are viewed as one interrelated system.

PRIVILEGES IN THE TC PERSPECTIVE AND APPROACH

Privileges are explicit rewards accorded by staff based upon changes in conduct and attitudes as well as overall clinical progress in the program. Although the privileges granted in the TC are quite ordinary, it is their social and psychological relevance to the individual that enhances their importance as clinical and community management methods.

The privilege system functions in *building the community*. It defines the explicit incentives and rewards for residents engaging and succeeding in the social system. Thus, privileges are the most explicit symbols of mobility and personal success in the microsociety of the TC. Privileges are important if the individual values the community that confers them. Thus, the individual's pursuit of privileges reflects his or her affiliation with the community. Reciprocally, privileges reinforce the credibility (i.e., integrity) of the TC, thereby encouraging affiliation.

Privileges are used to promote *individual socialization and personal growth*. For example, substance abusers often cannot distinguish between privilege and entitlement and resist social demands to earn through effort. The system of privileges in the TC teaches residents that productive participation in a community is based on earning, not entitlement. Privileges acquire their importance and value in the TC because they are earned, which requires investments of time, energy, self-modification, risk of failure, and disappointment. Self-esteem emerges from self-effort, not entitlement. In the argot of the TC, "You get back what you put into it." This stresses the relationship between self-investment and self-gain.

Conversely, substance abusers have difficulty with tolerance of discomfort, disappointment, and frustration, and with it, the delay of gratification. For these clients, the loss of mundane privileges is uncomfortable and therefore serves as an effective consequence and component of their learning process.

As explicit outcomes that are contingent upon individual change in behavior and attitudes, privileges facilitate *goal attainment*. This pragmatic element of privileges is particularly suitable for individuals with histories of performance failure or difficulty in achieving goals. Accorded for clinical progress, privileges are indicators of personal accomplishment in the program. Each level of privilege signifies a position or goal in the change process.

Though minor in material value, privileges are concrete *symbols* of community status and personal autonomy. Privileges such as job promotions, change in resident phase status (junior to senior), and private time through passes and furloughs represent changes in community status. The material privileges that can be earned in the TC are small amounts of money, semiprivate living quarters, and amenities such as additional cosmetics, jewelry, or radios. Residents view these symbols as objective evidence of *perceived change* in self-management and self-efficacy.

CLASSES OF PRIVILEGES

The classes of privileges reflect increasing levels of individual autonomy and community status. Successful movement through each stage of the program earns privileges that grant wider personal latitude and increased responsibility for self and others. At the same time, each level of privilege presents the individual with new challenges to self-management. Table 14-1 illustrates the range of privileges appropriate or available at the main program stages. The rationale for these classes is briefly discussed.

TABLE 14-1. Typical Privileges by Stage in Program

PROGRAM STAGE	PRIVILEGE
Early stage	WAM (walking around money)—to purchase sundries
	Personal property—permission to keep
	First request for a pass—must include an escort
	Letter writing—permission to write with review by counselor
	A job change from the service crew—all promotions are considered privileges
	Job training as a night person—a position of community responsibility
	Special assignments—escort for hospital/legal trips, etc.
	Staff assistant positions—all positions working for staff are privileges
Middle stage	All previous stage privileges
	Can leave facility without escort—prescribed places, specific reasons, limited time period
	Bi-weekly passes
	Phone use—outside calls, limited time, identified parties
	Phone desk responsibility
	Group leader—can facilitate floor or "slip" encounter groups
	Stipend positions are available—positions in management, administration, ancillary departments
	Sleeping space—bottom bunks are given according to time and status
	Separate rooms reflect signs of responsibility for self and others
	Pre-re-entry status granted—this allows for added hours upon personal request

Table continues

TABLE 14-1.   Typical Privileges by Stage in Program

Table continued

Late stage	All previous stage privileges
	Overnight passes—reviews purpose, people, and experience
	Excused from evening activities
	Assists as staff on the house—monitors facility activities overnight with staff
	Requests itineraries from staff—self-planned schedules, 24–48 hours
	Reduced house duties—a resident who receives a stipend job on the outside or employment while living in a treatment house is no longer responsible for floor cleanup in the mornings

Privileges confirm the resident's overall *personal autonomy* and ability for self-management. For example, the privilege of passes and furloughs indicate that individuals can be trusted to move within and outside the facility on their own. They do not need to be monitored and are not threats to abscond, use drugs, or act impulsively. The purpose of these types of privileges is to test residents in the macrosociety.

Increases in small allowances of money as earnings aim to provide symbolic rewards and to teach appropriate money management. The privilege of unlimited letter writing and telephone calls allows the resident increased contact with people outside of the program. This privilege assumes that the resident has achieved sufficient affiliation with the program to resist negative outside influences. Such influences could undermine his or her commitment to treatment or destabilize progress.

Other privileges confer the resident's *community status*. When granted the privilege of being escorts, residents can be trusted to assume responsibility for peers. Work-related rewards like job promotions are viewed as privileges because they provide opportunities for the individual to serve the community and indicate that the resident can assume greater responsibility for the general community.

The resident may be permitted to acquire and keep certain material goods as amenities, like books, radios, TV, clothing, and jewelry. These signify that the resident can be responsible for property, is not preoccupied with social images, will not be distracted from the focus on self-growth, and will not misuse or abuse conveniences. Meanwhile, the accordance of private or semiprivate sleeping quarters assumes the resident's significant level of self-management and community involvement. Residents must demonstrate that their increased privacy does not foster self-involvement and personal withdrawal from the peer community.

Money: An Example of the Privilege System

Money is a major problem in the lives of substance abusers. Drug use and dependency directly cause money difficulties. Drug habits and episodes of compulsive (binge) use of drugs compel uncontrolled squandering of legally obtained money. This urgent need for money often leads to exploitation of family and friends, eventual loss of jobs and legitimate income, and frequently, seeking illegal means of income.

However, money difficulties also reflect social and psychological problems among substance abusers in TCs. Generally, they reveal an inability to understand the value of money, to legally earn money, or to manage money appropriately. Characteristically, residents are irresponsible in their use of money, and holding on to it strains their limited capacity to delay gratification.

Therefore, the meaning of money in the TC is complex. Resident's use of money in the TC is carefully arranged and monitored to address primary social and psychological goals. How residents obtain money and how they use money represents tangible behavioral examples of the general goals of socialization, maturation, and psychological growth.

The program controls all resident money in the TC. Indigent residents sign their subsistence (welfare) checks over to the program as payment for residency and treatment in the TC, while other residents may pay personal fees directly to the program. Regardless of fiscal status, however, residents are not permitted to access their own money during their stay in the TC without special permission. Money is given to residents as part of the privilege system, the goal of which is training responsibility in the use of money. As with any privilege, the timing, amount, and reason for giving money to residents is directly related to their social and psychological progress.

The privilege system includes *walking around money* (WAM), stipends, and salaries. WAM is a small weekly allowance initially given to residents early in treatment as a small entitlement. It allows them to purchase simple personal "wants" such as cosmetics, toothpaste, or cigarettes, as all basic needs are provided by the program. (The use of cigarettes is now being discouraged in many programs). Although an entitlement, WAM is also used as a privilege, one which could be taken away as a consequence of negative behaviors.

Stipends are modest remuneration for designated job functions held during the primary treatment stage. The stipend-paying positions are usually awarded to role models and thus are status symbols in the community. Stipend allowances increase incrementally to a maximum well below any minimum wage levels, as they are privileges rather than salaries. Thus, as a management action, residents can lose their money or both their money and the stipend position.

The way residents handle their money conveys information about their overall maturity and personal growth. For example, early in treatment residents may use their WAM to indulge themselves in cosmetics at the expense of other needs. Re-entry candidates still living in the residence are expected to buy their own sheets and linen. Or, a re-entry candidate who has recently moved out of the residence may allocate too much money to TVs or walkmans relative to other house needs.

Salaries are bona fide payment for full-time jobs, beginning in the early re-entry stage of treatment. These are employed positions, usually outside the agency. Although salaries are not viewed as privileges, they are still indicators of the individual's socialization and personal growth e.g., how residents budget their incomes, save money, plan for the future, and meet obligations.

"Drinking Privileges"

In past years, permission to drink alcohol while still in treatment was granted as a privilege to certain residents and under special conditions. For residents in the re-entry stage of treatment who had no history of alcohol misuse, social drinking on furlough and off premises was acceptable. The rationale in those years assumed that some residents in re-entry were not at risk for alcohol problems. Moreover, drinking was a common social activity in the macrocommunity for which these re-entry candidates needed to be prepared. Thus the drinking privilege was viewed as social training and preparation for those individuals not considered at risk for alcohol problems.

Contemporary TCs now take a conservative view on this matter based upon several considerations (e.g., Zweben & Smith, 1986). Drinking problems have been observed among some proportion of TC graduates who had recovered from their abuse of other drugs. Inappropriate drinking and denial of alcohol problems have been evident among some TC agency personnel as well as staff members. Also, the TC's policy of limited acceptance of alcohol use tended to inhibit former TC participants from utilizing AA 12-step groups.

Today, for most TCs alcohol use is viewed as a risk behavior for *all residents* (and recovered staff) regardless of their history with this substance. Use of alcohol is prohibited at any time during program tenure for any resident. Clinical policy insists on lifetime abstinence from all nonprescribed substances for all residents, which for primary alcohol abusers includes abstinence from alcohol. For residents with no history of alcohol problems the policy on posttreatment alcohol use varies across programs, although lifetime abstinence from alcohol is strongly recommended (De Leon, 1989). Finally, AA and other 12-step groups may be incorporated in the re-entry stage of the program and are routinely recommended for use during aftercare.

Informal Privileges and Affirmations

The intrinsic value in all privileges is that they are earned symbols of community status or personal autonomy. Thus, any action that confers this symbol can be an informal privilege in the TC. Some examples of informal privileges are selecting particular residents to give a seminar, lead a workshop, act as peer leaders in groups, or serve as tour guides for visitors. These activities are expected of residents at certain stages of the program. However, they are also viewed as privileges, spontaneously offered opportunities for serving the community that acknowledge the resident's personal autonomy. Thus, informal privileges are neither prescribed nor contingent upon any specific behaviors or attitudes. They may be delivered or taken away for various clinical and management reasons.

The actions of *affirmation and support* also reflect approval and community acceptance. However, they are not prescribed actions, except as part of certain rituals (e.g., closing group sessions or meetings). They are not necessarily contingent upon any specific behavior but are spontaneously offered as positive "strokes" to the person.

Peers are constantly encouraged and instructed to deliver affirmations and support to each other in expressions such as "Yes, you can do it," "You're doing great," "You're my role model," and with expressions of affection or love. Thus, the function of affirmation is broad in order to positively acknowledge individuals for who they are and for their efforts to change. Affirmation, support, and affection provide the crucial balance to verbal correctives and sanctions and keep formal privileges in perspective.

Clinical and Management Considerations

Most privileges are explicitly associated with phase or stage changes. However staff decisions about privileges are always based upon clinical assessment concerning social learning and personal growth. Two issues in particular are observed: *vested and personal status*, and *autonomy and dependency*. These underscore the relationship between the management and clinical goals of privileges.

For many residents, the symbolic power of community status can be overvalued, reflecting long-term deficits in social and self-efficacy as well as self-esteem. For these residents the gains in self-esteem from privileges may be exclusively identified with community position. Their vested status is externally defined; it is given and taken away by others, hence, it represents a limited form of individual growth. On the other hand, personal status represents elevated self-esteem based on internalized clinical progress and individual growth. Thus, the extent to which privileges and community position are reinforcing vested and personal status must be assessed. This may be indicated in the stability of the resident's self-perceptions when receiving or losing privileges.

With respect to the second issue, increased privileges can reinforce community dependency rather than personal autonomy. Residents may reveal improved self-management and responsibility within the perimeter of the program. However, the extent to which their autonomy in the community is generalized to the outside world must be assessed. The latter usually requires debriefing residents after passes and furloughs, peers giving feedback to staff, and staff contacting significant others. How well residents manage themselves on their own without the familiarity, safety, and boundaries of the peer community or without any social status in the macrosociety is a significant clinical issue highlighted by the privilege system.

CLASSES OF SANCTIONS

The term sanctions encompasses all forms of disapproval for behaviors and attitudes that do not meet the expectations of the community. Sanctions may be grouped into verbal correctives and disciplinary actions. Verbal correctives consist of peer and staff reactions delivered as consequences of negative behaviors and attitudes that are not infractions of the rules, but which fail to meet the expectations of the community. Disciplinary actions consist of specifically prescribed negative consequences delivered by staff for behaviors and attitudes that are infractions or violations of explicit rules.

Verbal Correctives

In the TC perspective and approach, verbal correctives are the main way that peers engage in community management. In their daily interactions, peers address all forms of resident behavior and attitudes that are inconsistent with right living and recovery. As with all consequences, verbal correctives are intended to facilitate learning in those receiving the correctives. However, they also have pervasive effects on the general community. Observing, reminding, and correcting others are potent reinforcers for self-learning. Thus, verbal correctives are the primary examples of the principle of mutual self-help.

Correctives may be informal and spontaneously delivered, most usually by peers, "on the spot" of the behavioral occurrence. Formal correctives, on the other hand, are planned interactions to be delivered in special places and involving staff as well as peers. The differences in correctives reflect the severity and persistence of the behavior or attitude addressed and, particularly, the resident's time in program.

Instructions are usually one-to-one conversations with the resident based on observations of the resident's negative or unacceptable behavior or attitudes. Peers (or members of the staff) provide information in a positive frame about how individuals are expected to behave. Though earnest, this conversation is supportive and unemotional; it carefully details the incorrect and correct distinctions that the resident must understand.

Verbal pull-ups are statements from one or more peers to another peer. These statements are reminders of any lapse in awareness of expected behavior and attitudes. Awareness lapses include time (e.g., punctuality, attendance), obligations (e.g., tools and personal property out of place, used cups not removed), motivation (e.g., slouching in posture, slowness of movement, delay in assuming a task), and manners or etiquette (e.g., saying please, thank you, excuse me). Unlike the instruction, the pull-up assumes that the resident knows the appropriate behavior or attitude, and therefore, as a reminder, it is more corrective than instructive.

Although commonplace in the everyday affairs of the community, the pull-up is perhaps the most effective means of consequential teaching in the TC. Properly executed, pull-ups are the most frequent moments of mutual self-help training. Those receiving the pull-up are required to listen without comment, assume that it is valid, quickly display the corrected behavior, and express gratitude at receiving it (e.g., "Thank you for telling me"). Thus, in its narrow focus on the target behavior and frequent use, the pull-up has wide impact on the socialization of residents.

Delivering pull-ups is the responsibility of all residents and illustrates the extreme importance that the TC places on member accountability in the management of themselves and others in the community.

Bookings or written pull-ups are used under certain circumstances: (a) when verbal pull-ups have been repeated for the same behavior, (b) when the target behavior is viewed as serious, or (c) when it actually violates minor house rules. The written pull-up states the peer observations about a particular resident and is submitted through the communication chain to staff. Consequences may be designed for the pulled-up residents, and these are usually announced in the house meeting. The residents have the option of appealing, but they must comply with the final judgment of the staff.

Talking-tos are stern verbal correctives, generally occuring after previous pull-ups and bookings. Delivered by peers under staff supervision, this corrective addresses persistent negative behaviors and attitudes, particularly when these have impacted others in the community. Examples are repeated episodes of poor manners, lapses in awareness, interpersonal insensitivity, subtle intimidation, disrespect, or any conduct that fails to reach community expectations.

One or more peers inform the staff of the behavioral episodes through the communication chain, either verbally or in writing as in the above booking case. A meeting in the staff office or sometimes in the resident's room is then arranged in which peers speak to the resident in strong but supportive tones, pointing out the pattern of behavior, impact on others, and possible consequences if it continues. The fact of the talking-to may also be announced in the evening house meeting of the entire membership.

Reprimands (verbal "haircuts"), the most severe verbal correctives, are delivered by staff for repeated negative behavior or attitudes. Residents alone are prohibited from delivering reprimands as they have not acquired enough self-control and could exploit the reprimand to ventilate their own emotions regarding another individual.

Some key differences between the talking-to and the reprimand are the direct involvement of staff and peers in its delivery, its prescribed structure, its critical tone, and its punitive intent and possible disciplinary actions.[44]

---

[44] In former years, verbal reprimands were called "haircuts," which were occasionally followed by the shaving of the head for males or the wearing of stocking caps for females. These practices were usually last step measures prior to actual discharge. They have all but disappeared, although the term "haircut" for reprimand is still used in many programs.

The prescribed format of reprimands is the most formal or ritualized of the verbal correctives. A resident may be called into a staff office to be confronted by staff and peers. The resident would stand quietly in front of a staff member and several peers and for perhaps five minutes be spoken to, or sometimes yelled at, about his or her persistently negative behavior. The resident does not respond, listens in respectful silence, makes eye contact with others, and after the verbal reprimand, is quickly dismissed from the office. Reprimands are designed to focus a recalcitrant resident's attention on hearing what is being said and feeling the seriousness of the impact of his or her behaviors on others. In some cases disciplinary sanctions may follow reprimands (see following sections for explanations of these).

The presence of peers during the reprimand is a critical element in a properly delivered reprimand. It is designed to maximize the vicarious learning concerning community expectations and to discourage possible negative peer associations ("tips"). Most importantly, the credibility of the reprimand is enhanced because the confronted resident cannot easily disallow or ignore what was being said in the witness of peers.

Although sometimes harsh in tone and loud in volume, the contents of the reprimand should remain illuminating and instructive. Key points should include the following: identification of the behavior confronted and explanation of why it is negative, offensive, or unacceptable; clarification of how the behavior is self-defeating, how it impedes growth and recovery, and if unchanged, how it may lead to destructive outcomes; and illustration of positive alternative ways of behaving in similar situations.

DISCIPLINARY SANCTIONS IN THE PERSPECTIVE AND APPROACH

In the TC, disciplinary sanctions consist of a variety of negative consequences prescribed for behaviors and attitudes that violate explicit rules of the community or persistently fail to meet community expectations. As with all elements of the TC, sanctions have multiple functions for the community and the individual, reflecting the TC perspective and approach.

Community Learning

Sanctions promote community awareness and peer self-management and maintain social order through addressing individual and collective infractions. The entire facility is always made aware of who is being sanctioned, as well as the reasons sanctions are chosen. Thus, sanctions provide vicarious learning experiences by being deterrents to other residents violating the rules, subsequently serving as symbols of safety and integrity that strengthen community cohesiveness.

Peer self-management is a critical component of sanctions. The disciplinary system is managed directly by staff, although its integrity and efficacy is dependent upon involvement of the resident peers. Rules and sanctions provide opportunities for peers to manage each other. Peers are instructed and expected to detect infractions, confront these, and actively support the implementation of all forms of sanctions. Thus, peers as community monitors reinforce their own self-management.

There may be several residents who may be directly involved in *collective infractions*; others may be aware of these infractions but make no effort to expose them to staff. The latter, defined as condoning of negative behaviors or rule breaking in others, is an infraction itself that must be addressed through various forms of sanctions delivered to the individuals involved. However, collective infractions often signal more pervasive problems in the facility and may require a community-wide response. As described in chapter 16, general meetings are often called to mobilize the peer community to reaffirm its positive purposes by learning from the collective infractions of others.

Individual Learning

Disciplinary sanctions are critical in the socialization process in particular and in the treatment process in general. A defining element of socialization in the TC is learning to live in a community with prescribed rules, norms, and expectations. Adherence to rules is essential for social order but also indicates the individual's acceptance of the TC as a culture of change (Des Jarlais, Knott, Savarese, & Bersamin, 1976). However, residents in TCs are characteristically nonconformist, oppositional, and lack accountability for their actions and obligations. In particular, they do not readily learn from the consequences of their behaviors.

In the TC, the process of socialization occurs mainly through *consequential learning experiences*—changes based upon the social and personal impact of the individual's actions on others. Although negative behaviors are not encouraged, they are expected to appear. Indeed, sometimes their appearance is necessary in order for positive learning to occur. Unrevealed problem behaviors and thinking often remain uncorrected. These not only are potential threats to the community, but they inhibit authentic change for the individual. Thus, in the treatment process, sanctions are *clinical interventions*. They raise the individual's awareness of the personal and social consequences of sanctioned behavior and help him or her understand the conditions influencing this behavior.

Indeed, decreases in the frequency of infractions along with positive reactions to the sanctions themselves are an important sign of *clinical progress*. Each reoccurrence of a sanctioned behavior is assessed for any increase in awareness and self-understanding as well as the presence of alternative positive behaviors. Additionally, the residents' emotional and intellectual acceptance of the sanction is an important indicator of his or her commitment to change and overall maturity.

In the treatment process, the effects of sanctions in modifying behaviors are *incremental* over time. For example, a change sequence with respect to smoking marijuana may proceed as follows: (a) the individual is smoking marijuana on furlough but does not disclose this, (b) the individual is not smoking but does not reveal thoughts and longings about smoking, (c) the individual is not smoking but shares thoughts and longings about smoking with peers or staff, (d) the individual is not smoking and is not preoccupied with smoking.

In another example of change over time, threats of violence may incrementally change: (a) "I'm gonna punch you in the mouth," (b) "I feel like punching you in the mouth," (c) "I am angry and frustrated with you." Also, clinical change is indicated in the speed of self-disclosure of negative behaviors and thoughts to others. This change may be associated with increased trust in the community and in the change process itself.

In summary, individual social learning based on sanctions occurs routinely in the course of daily living in the TC. The social ecology of the TC—the intimacy of its community life, interpersonal pressures, work demands, and authority structure—provide cues for eliciting the socialization problems in the individual. These elements of the TC setting are particularly provocative for residents who display personality characteristics marked by immaturity and antisocial features. Thus the fundamental assumption underlying the use of sanctions in the TC is that rule breaking reflects the characteristics of the setting, the individual, and the nature of the change process.

The Organization of TC Rules

TCs maintain an explicit code of rules and regulations that define the behavioral boundaries of physical and psychological safety of the community. Violation and infractions of these lead to formal sanctions or disciplinary actions delivered by staff. The code of rules may be organized into three levels of strictness reflecting their importance to the safety and health of the community (see Table 14-2).

TABLE 14-2.   Cardinal, Major, and House Rules

Cardinal rules
> No physical violence, threats of physical violence, or intimidation against any person
> No drug, alcohol, or related paraphernalia
> No sexual acting out, including romantic or sexual physical contact

Major rules
> No stealing or other criminal activity
> No vandalizing or destroying property
> No contraband or weapons

House rules
> Acceptance of authority (listening and behaving)
> Punctuality (being on time)
> Appropriate appearance
> No impulsive behavior
> Proper manners
> No lending or borrowing
> No receiving gifts without staff permission

Cardinal rules address behaviors for which there is near zero tolerance in the community. Violence or threats of violence, and drug use (based upon self-disclosure, peer report, or urine testing) or sexual acting out in the facility are considered direct threats to the physical and psychological safety of the community. Moreover, residents who cannot restrain these behaviors while living in the facility represent a particularly difficult management burden for staff. Also criminal behavior on and off the premises, including parole and probation violation, are treated as transgressions of cardinal rules. There may be explicit criteria for disciplining infractions of cardinal rules, for example "three strikes and you're out." More often, there is automatic discharge although some flexibility may be exercised on a case by case basis.

Major rules address behaviors that can be tolerated only within narrow limits or not at all. This refers to destruction of property, stealing, and by extension, all other illegal (nonviolent) acts, including possession of contraband, weapons of any kind, and more recently gang representations.

These frankly antisocial behaviors are common indicators of the "disorder and the person" that are not expected to completely cease from day one in treatment. Nevertheless, their potential threat to the community results in severe disciplinary sanctions and only one episode may be tolerated.

House rules address the behaviors and attitudes that are viewed as typical socialization problems to be modified. The rules more closely represent the norms, values, and expectations of daily life in the community. Adherence to these is necessary to preserve safe, orderly living in the community and to structure recovery and personal growth. Infractions of the house rules are expected in the trial and error learning process.[45]

Disciplinary Actions for Minor Infractions

Unlike verbal sanctions, the main forms of disciplinary actions include a punitive, as well as a corrective component. Staff delivers specific as well as combined actions if clinically appropriate. For all infractions, a case by case guideline is invoked based on the mutual criteria of community tolerance and individual learning.

Learning experiences are actions employed to address less serious negative behaviors that usually include persistent noncompliance with community expectations. The teaching component of any disciplinary action is viewed as resulting in a learning experience. However, specific learning experiences are special assignments for particular residents to achieve a targeted behavioral or attitudinal outcome. These may include written essays to raise awareness of a particular behavior or close monitoring by a peer to highlight the resident's immaturity ("glue contracts"), community apologies and strenuous physical workouts.

Demotions in job functions such as from expediter to the service crew may be accompanied by transfer from a double room to a dorm. Demotions are usually applied for minor infractions and overall general negative attitude.

Signs may be worn by the resident, strung around the neck or pinned to the shirt. These display what the resident must remember concerning an

---

[45] The above rule classification is fairly uniform across a diversity of TCs. Program differences in rules may be specific to a setting such as prisons and hospitals, or for subpopulations such as homeless substance abusers in TC shelters, the mentally ill chemical abusers in community residences, adolescents, or individuals with AIDS.

infraction. Typically, the themes center on a social label (e.g., liar, thief, manipulator) and what they must do to change (e.g., speak respectfully, listen, stop reacting or threatening people).

Signs are usually implemented to heighten and sustain residents' awareness of their refractory behavior as a first step in learning. The sign is also a constant reminder to residents and a signal to the community as to what the residents are working on in order to change themselves. Thus, community members are expected to read signs and ask sanctioned residents to explain the contents. This interaction involves the community in implementing the disciplinary measure, facilitates the learning effect through verbal repetition of the theme, and supports the residents in their willingness to publicize their effort to change. Contemporary TCs use signs much less often than in the earlier days, but they retain the use of written assignments and peer discussion of these to achieve similar learning effects.

Speaking bans instruct one or more individuals to refrain from speaking to certain other residents in the facility for the disciplinary period. Speaking bans are implemented to interrupt negative communications among particular pairs or groups of residents. Typically such communications are invitations to drug use or sex; cynical judgments about the program; threats, suggestions, or plots to abscond; or hostile statements about staff or other residents. Residents are suggestible to any communication that offers escape from the demands of the program, and they are particularly vulnerable to these early in treatment or in periods of change. The explicit lesson of the ban is to discourage negativity by contamination. However, during the period of the ban, other peers may speak instructively to the banned resident in attempts to change the negative themes.

Bum squad or *spare parts* are actions that assign the resident or residents to various lower status chores including sanitation, cleanup after house meetings, and odd jobs in general for a limited period of time, typically 1–3 weeks. The chore obligation consists of short blocks of time between 5 p.m. and 9 p.m. in the evening and longer intervals on weekends and may be in addition to the resident's regular job function. On call and on command for any job that needs to be done, the resident can be inconvenienced with respect to sleep, recreation, and personal time. The disciplinary element in this action stresses meeting obligations with a good attitude, tolerating demands, and paying service to the community.

Loss of privileges is generally commensurate with the severity of the infraction and the stage in the program. Thus, some or all privileges could be taken away for the disciplinary period, which also may vary depending upon the infraction and the individual program stage. Removing privileges is the main action indicating loss of personal autonomy for the individual. Thus, the loss of privilege is a learning experience only if the resident feels an emotional reaction. For example, loss of all privileges is a serious consequence for senior residents who have more time invested in the program and personal investment in their autonomy. For more junior residents, the loss of the privilege to wear a personal assortment of clothes, for instance, may be a more appropriate consequence.

Experiencing the loss of privileges heightens the resident's awareness of the lesson to be learned. The training element in this action is that increments of positive change in the resident's attitude or behavior could gradually earn back privileges such as articles of clothing or jewelry, furloughs, and semiprivate sleeping quarters.

Disciplinary Actions for Major Infractions

Violation of cardinal rules or repeated infractions of other rules can lead to a variety of other punitive actions. These can be implemented for individuals as well as the entire community.

Loss of phase status, or "being shot down," involves regressing a resident back one or more levels in the peer hierarchy and encompasses loss of privileges as well as loss of program time. Less frequently used, this severe action is judiciously implemented to assure clinical benefits.

House changes involve transfering a resident or residents to other facilities in the agency. Staff implements a house change when infractions suggest that the resident's adjustment problem may be specific to the particular facility. Transfer is more a tactical step than a disciplinary action, although it may be accompanied by other disciplinary actions. It attempts to provide the particular resident with a new start in a new facility with different staff and residents. Sometimes the transfer is viewed as a last option before actual discharge from the program.

Administrative discharge involves expelling the resident from the program usually for violations of the cardinal rules or repeated infractions of other rules, other threats to the safety of the community (e.g., fire setting, drug possession, dealing). Staff members carefully explain the community and clinical reasons for the discharge and present various options to the individual. These include referral to a different TC or another treatment modality, or the option of returning to the program after a period of time, such as 30 days.

As with all sanctions, the intent of expulsion is to maintain the integrity, safety, and morale of the community and to facilitate learning for the individual. For example, expulsion may compel an individual to realistically consider status and options and seek readmission to the program. Readmission is generally contingent upon certain conditions, such as acceptance of a disciplinary contract on his or her return and the loss of previous time in program—that is, the resident's willingness to start over. Thus, expulsion, although a terminal action, contains a disciplinary or training element as it often highlights the individual's readiness for treatment in general or suitability for the TC in particular.

Other behaviors that are not rule governed but often result in discharge with referral are suicidal threats, chronic psychological symptoms and complaints, and delusional or hallucinatory behaviors. Although less directly related to community safety, these problems present a management burden to staff in terms of time and surveillance, tend to undermine peer morale, and require special settings and treatment services.

House bans are applied to all residents in the facility and consist of taking away all privileges for a period of time. Such bans are instituted to redress negative attitudes that appear to be pervasive in the facility. All recreational trips are canceled, as are all furloughs or passes. These actions are accompanied by more frequent encounter groups in efforts to bring the sources of negativity in the facility to the surface (these may be a specific person or cadre of people who display negative behavior and attitudes) or to expose any pervasive expression of negative attitudes.

Under the house ban, the entire facility suffers discomfort from the misbehavior of one or more residents. It stresses the TC expectation that all peers must be accountable for the misbehavior of some residents. Thus, the house ban is a disciplinary measure that reminds all residents of their collective, management responsibility to maintain the safety and health of the community.

Disciplinary Tools

Some staff actions are commonly utilized as a minor form of sanction in themselves, as tools to facilitate a regular disciplinary action or as preparation for a major sanction. Thus, the resident may be instructed to sit on a special bench, stay in a relating booth (the latter two are described in the chapter on the physical environment), or participate in special encounters.

The *bench* is a chair situated in a common area, where a resident can sit indefinitely until he or she decides whether or not to change behaviors or attitudes. Staff sends the resident to the bench for minor infractions or "acting-out" behaviors, such as negative attitudes, vague threats, excessive hostility, insubordination, noncompliance, and threats to drop out of the program. The bench also places the resident "on hold" until the staff decides on a course of action or has the time to "deal with" the individual.

The *relating booth* is a desk with two chairs placed in a common area where residents can conduct one-to-one conversations. Similar to the bench, it is also used as a tool in disciplinary actions. The resident with a major or minor infraction is assigned to sit all day in the booth, reviewing the behaviors and attitudes relating to his or her infractions with other residents. Peers "run the data" of the TC, that is they discuss, explain, and repeat concepts of recovery, community, and right living as these relate to the infractions.

Leaving treatment against clinical advice is considered an infraction that requires some disciplinary action for the resident who returns to the program. Readmissions may be placed in a relating booth so that they can share with peers their experiences while they were gone. This helps to raise the consciousness of other residents who may be thinking about leaving. The return of the dropout along with his or her relating of the painful and troubling experiences on the outside can reinforce the message that remaining in treatment is the key to recovery.

There are several teaching elements of the bench and relating booth: (a) They are places for "time out" where the resident can review his or her actions and decisions; (b) they permit peers to continually interact with the resident toward clarifying the resident's behavior and decisions; and (c) they help to train patience and self-control.

Contracts

Disciplinary actions are usually implemented as agreements or "contracts" between the individual and the community that prescribe *how* an infraction or violation of rules is to be redressed by the individual. Either verbal or written, contracts outline the specific conditions for modifying inappropriate or unacceptable behaviors and attitudes. Thus, contracts specify the particular behaviors to be changed, the possible consequences if these are not changed (e.g., discharge), the steps or actions the resident will take to prevent the behavior from reappearing (e.g., work with certain peer monitors), the positive or appropriate behavior to be practiced (e.g., alternatives), and the duration of the contract (e.g., 1–3 weeks), after which it will be reviewed by staff with peer input.

Contracts are designed to provide a positive learning experience. The period of the contract provides an opportunity for the resident to examine his or her negative behavior and to practice changing that behavior with staff and group support. Its one to three week duration teaches residents to stop and think about their decision (reflect, review, and recommit). The consistency in applying the contract and the explanation of its meaning strengthens respect for staff, whose authority is supported by peers.

DISCIPLINARY SANCTIONS: CLINICAL CONSIDERATIONS

The objective of all disciplinary actions is to employ the least severe sanction to achieve maximal learning. Inappropriate sanctions can be nonproductive either by engendering rebellion or through dilution of their effects. The selection of specific disciplinary actions is based upon considerations that assure a sound outcome for the individual and the community. Overall, implementing sanctions requires careful clinical decisions that review the nature of the infraction, the individual, and the method. Some of the specific considerations in these decisions are summarized in Table 14-3.

A general guideline in the use of disciplinary actions is that the individual and community goals of sanctions must be *balanced.* Tolerance for violations or infractions for the sake of individual trial and error learning must be weighed against these infractions' potentially erosive effects on the community. For example, modifying threats of violence may require several trials in the socialization process. However, allowance of these behaviors can also undermine the physical safety of the community and eventually erode psychological trust in general. The infractions, along with the disciplinary actions for individual learning, must be carefully assessed in the context of community life.

Discipline means to teach, stressing the distinction between learning and punishment. In most cases, the element of punishment in sanctions is less important than their "time out" and teaching features. Thus, though often perceived as punitive, the basic purpose of the disciplinary action is to provide a learning experience by compelling residents to attend to their own conduct, reflect on their own motivation, feel some consequence of their own behavior, and consider alternative forms of acting under similar situations.

TABLE 14-3. Some Specific Considerations in Disciplinary Actions

Nature
- Frequency and severity of the infraction (extent of regression vs. relapse)
- Type of drug use: licit vs. illicit, pot/alcohol vs. cocaine, or use vs. sales (reversion to primary drug)
- Alone or with others and use with or influencing others
- Type of criminal activity, violence to person/property or drug use, possession, sales

Circumstances
- Infraction off vs. on TC premises ("respect for the house")
- Social and psychological conditions associated with the infraction
- Individual disclosure vs. denial and detection by others
- Individual disclosure of other violators ("breaks the street code," affirms the community)

Stage in treatment (expected behavior, meaning of error)
- Adult/adolescent facility and age of individual
- New admission, junior or senior peer

Learning potential
- Individual acceptance of disciplinary contract; complies with loss of position and privileges
- Individual understanding of infraction and its implication for the community and recovery

Discharge options
- Discharge with readmission after minimum period out, e.g., 30 days
- Discharge with no readmission
- Referral to appropriate settings

SEXUALITY: PRIVILEGE AND SANCTION

Sexuality is approached differently from the other rule-governed behaviors in the TC. Unlike violence, drug use, and other antisocial or criminal behaviors that must be eliminated for stable socialization, sexuality must be managed, understood, and retrained as part of the socialization process itself. Chapter 12 discusses the educational and therapeutic approaches to sexuality; this section focuses upon the management approach.

A cardinal rule in the TC prohibits sexual acting out during residency in any of its forms—flirtation, seduction, manipulation, and any actual physical engagement, with or without mutual consent. This restrictive feature is based explicitly upon clinical and management rationales as well as a moral position. Sexual behaviors that are not intrusive on others are not formally regulated, for example, masturbation, pictures (but not pornography), scatological jokes, and banter when they occur at appropriate times and places. However, these behaviors and attitudes are informally assessed as indicators of social and personal growth.

Violations of the cardinal rule on sexual liaisons may not necessarily lead to expulsion but generally result in other disciplinary measures. These vary but are designed to provide learning experiences concerning issues of impulse control, sexual attitudes, conduct, and adherence to community expectations.

The community aim of this cardinal rule is to maintain the perception of safety in the coeducational intimacy of community life. Both genders, females in particular, must be in a social environment that provides complete protection from any form of sexual demand, intimidation, or abuse. For the individual, the primary aim of the cardinal rule is to teach the importance of restraint in the management of impulses. A long period of restraint permits clarification and development of new social and sexual perspectives by teaching impulse control and social relationship skills.

The management strategy imposes a moratorium on the social and sexual demands on residents. The message transmitted to the resident is that life during residency is devoted to gaining insight, expressing important feelings, and developing new social, communication, and practical skills. Moreover, this learning best unfolds without the distraction and pressures of serious relationships or sexual activity. In accepting the moratorium on sexuality, the resident effectively places self-growth as the highest priority. The sexual privileges granted after the moratorium are both rewards for growth and new opportunities for personal learning and change.

CONCLUSION

This chapter has described privileges and sanctions as an interrelated system of positive and negative consequences that maintains social order and facilitates socialization and personal growth based upon the individual's social impact on others. Privileges and sanctions are the community's response to how the individual meets its expectations. Thus, they are effective as consequences because of the individual's relationship to the community. Seeking privileges reflects the individual's affiliation with the community. Conversely, the individual's acceptance of and learning from disciplinary sanction reflects the underlying influence of community separateness, which in its ultimate implication is dropout or discharge.

Community and clinical management extend beyond privileges and sanctions. The safety and integrity of community life requires continual surveillance of the physical and psychological status of the facility. How this task is conducted is the subject of the following chapter.

Chapter 15

Surveillance and Security

In the therapeutic community (TC), surveillance means supervision and management of the orderliness and safety of the physical environment, as well as the health and conduct of the social environment. Although residents conduct the daily activities of the house, the staff is responsible for the supervision of all resident activities. Staff members are constantly observing and monitoring *how* residents manage themselves and their environment.

Although visibly present, staff members are not dominant in the facility. Supervising from the background rather than from center stage, much of their influence is vicarious or otherwise indirect. In the intimate confines of a TC, residents are always observing staff members, their schedule, and their habits, and particularly staff involvement in the program. Staff members spend time in their offices only to complete their clerical and report writing chores or engage in individual counseling. Mainly they are on the "floor" continually surveying the facility, not only to supervise but also to motivate residents. During these multiple walks throughout the facility, the staff readily compliment residents on the status of the facility and otherwise encourage positive work activity.

Thus, through modeling and feedback to residents, staff indirectly manage the facility and the program. They directly supervise and manage on a regular basis, however, through three facility-wide surveillance activities: *general inspection*, the *house run*, and *urine testing*.

GENERAL INSPECTION

A key value in the TC is the health, cleanliness, and attractiveness of the physical environment. Individual residents, roommates, and dormmates are responsible for the orderliness and cleanliness of their "private" living quarters. Resident service crews are responsible for the daily maintenance of the common spaces of the facility, the expected results of which are swept and washed floors; polished brass in entrance ways, stairwells, and elsewhere; sanitized bathrooms; scrubbed kitchens; tidy dining areas, lounges, and day rooms; clean external grounds, etc. Staff and senior residents will routinely inspect and assess whether the house is properly maintained through daily house runs (described below).

However, senior staff may order and review an organized community-wide effort to intensively clean and refurbish the entire facility. These general inspections, or *GIs* (adapted from the military usage), may be a weekly house activity. However, they are often motivated by special events such as annual graduations, special tours, guest visits, or holidays. Sometimes they are called for after a period of community instability or simply as interventions to energize the membership.

All residents will be recruited for one to several days in activities that go beyond daily maintenance to include repairs, painting, and decorating. The residents are organized into crews led by senior residents and supervised by staff. The results of the GI are reported to the entire community by staff, usually in a house meeting and often in a climate of affirmation and success.

The GI is a useful community and clinical management activity. It is a special form of collective participation that aims to enhance a sense of community. It reinforces affiliation by sustaining *community pride* in the "family," house, or program. It also provides data as to individual attitudes, efforts, and skills particularly with respect to how they work with others under special incentives and community pressures.

THE HOUSE RUN

The house run is the main system of surveillance in the TC. It provides a global "snapshot" or impression of the cleanliness, operational order, physical safety, and psychological tone of the facility. Several times a day, a team consisting of staff and senior residents walks through the entire facility from top to bottom, perimeter to perimeter, examining the health, cleanliness, and order of the physical residence: its floors, ceilings, bathrooms, furniture, residents' sleeping quarters, kitchen, etc. Each team member carries a pad in order to write down all observations on the spot, as several house runs a day would result in a cluttered memory and inaccurate data. The information is communicated to all staff and resident coordinators to assure that relevant personnel have the same picture concerning the status of the house. Though obvious in its concept and simple in procedure, the house run is profound in its implications for community and clinical management.

In terms of management goals, house runs permit early detection of potentially larger problems such as those related to fire, sanitation, and security. Additionally, they help staff determine whether the people in the facility (residents or other staff) are in the places that they should be.

The physical condition of any setting is often an indicator of its overall operational management. Clean, orderly, and well-maintained facilities suggest responsible and effective management. However, in the social learning context of the TC, the physical status of the facility also provides essential and immediate information concerning the social and psychological status of the community. Thus, in terms of clinical goals, the cleanliness, security, and order of the facility also generate instant "data" concerning the behaviors, attitudes, and emotions of the residents.

The House Run and the TC Perspective

In the TC perspective, physical and psychological space are related. How residents relate to their physical space reveals issues of *discipline and training, self-control,* and *commitment or affiliation.*

Many residents have little training or discipline in the care of self and environment. Some may have the skills to maintain an orderly living space. However, they may refuse to exercise these as expressions of oppositional and defiant attitudes. Thus, room disorder, disorder in personal effects, and neglect of property may be signs of lack of commitment to self-change, disaffiliation, or challenge to the community.

Learning to order the physical environment encourages residents to exercise self-control over their emotional behavior. Controlling impulses and exercising self-discipline is a primary problem for a large majority of substance abusers. House runs focus the resident on managing the external observable environment. Thus, strengthening the behavior needed to maintain an orderly environment helps clients acquire control over more difficult and subtle emotional behaviors.

Similarly, maintaining an ordered environment helps clients acquire orderly thinking. Many substance abusers reveal thinking that is false, contradictory, illogical, and in general, confused and lacking organization. Training them to order the physical environment also teaches by concrete example that they can order their cognitive environment. In the argot of the TC, "a clean bed" means "a clean head."

Method

The main components of the house run are team composition, schedule of the run, and the communication of information. These elements separately and in combination reflect the perspective of the TC and are essential in achieving the clinical and management goals of the house run.

The house run team

There is no single formula for the house run team, and it may vary with the size of the program. Small program teams generally include the director and junior staff and may include senior residents, such as coordinators and expediters. In larger programs, more responsibility falls on the senior residents who are frequently accompanied by junior staff. The team approach in the house run is especially important for management and for clinical reasons.

Thoroughness and reliability are more likely when different eyes see different things. The more people survey the house and the more often the house is surveyed, the more likely the "true" physical and psychosocial health of the environment can be assessed.

Teams provide coverage of the house and *training* opportunities. Senior staff on the house run team remain in close touch with the facility, obtaining immediate information as to the health of the facility; they can also monitor and train lower level staff and senior peers in the house run procedures.

The visual presence of the house run team, seen frequently walking through the entire facility, is a symbol of the program's commitment to provide support and maintain order and safety in the environment. In making its rounds, the team observes and criticizes, instructs and encourages—activities signifying a *concerned community*.

Gender issues are addressed in the team approach. The house run is conducted by both males and females. This provides residents with normative examples of nonsexual gender interaction and cooperation. Training good hygienic habits in the residents is facilitated when they are aware that they are being observed by members of both sexes. For example, the dorms and rooms of male and female residents are checked by staff of both sexes. This indicates to room residents that members of the house run team have overcome their anxieties, sensitivities, and social conditioning concerning sexual roles and differences.

All sleeping quarters and toilets are gender-separate. An explicit house rule prohibits entry of the opposite sex into these areas without appropriate announcement. For example, the house run team has authorized access to any area of the facility. However, they are mandated to knock loudly on all doors of rooms and dorms and audibly state their gender and intention to enter (e.g., "man on the floor"). This announcement may then be repeated by any female resident on the floor to appropriately alert other female residents. Any individual resident or staff member who violates the gender privacy rule (or any of the other rules) is subject to disciplinary action.

Schedule of house runs

Depending upon the size of the facility, a house run is conducted two or three times in a 24-hour day. These are scheduled at random to avoid anticipation by residents. For example, a daytime house run is conducted when residents are *not* expected to be in their rooms but in their proper place at the proper time. Without authorization for health or other reasons, residents are in violation if they are found undressed, asleep, or sitting in the dormitory or in their room. To avoid errors, prior to the house run the team must be prepared with an authorized list of residents who are on bed rest, floor watch, or otherwise out of the facility.

Communication

As house runs are conducted throughout the day, information is communicated across all staff shifts to assure consistency, accuracy, and appropriate responses to house run problems. For example, the night-shift house run team may discover food in a resident's room, which is an infraction of house rules. However, information from the day shift may indicate that there is insufficient food for meals in general, a cause for food hoarding among some residents. Thus, rather than lack of discipline or another reason, hunger may account for food in the resident's room.

This communication pattern also illustrates the important element of community *accountability* in the house run. A resident who does not dust his or her room properly reveals a negative attitude, and all residents and staff who fail to detect or correct this minor disarray amplify its negative effects. Moreover, senior staff who overlook a house run that is inadequately conducted by junior staff also reveal a lax attitude. Ignoring a small item of disarray can ultimately result in a larger erosive attitude in the house for both staff and residents.

Management of House Run Problems

The house run is conducted to assess the physical status of the facility, its cleanliness and compliance with regulatory codes of health and safety, and the overall health of the community. However, its fundamental clinical purpose is to assess the status of individuals in terms of self-care, self-management, and their relationship to the community. For example, the cleanliness and order of the *private living space* of residents are indicators of attitude and emotional status. Residents train and monitor each other in maintaining the shared and individual space of the dorms. Thus, in shared quarters, inadequately attended individual space points to self-centeredness, indifference to others, and peer group weakness. Similarly evidence of poor *facility* care suggests community disaffiliation, hostility, and indifference. Some typical clinical problems are noted in Table 15-1.

TABLE 15-1.   Some Clinical Signs in the House Run

Room care

Residents are required to have their rooms clean and in good order prior to breakfast. Beds must be correctly made, clothing put away, laundry assembled, toiletries neatly arranged, shoes arrayed under the bed. Not meeting these expectations suggests poor task completion, a negative attitude, or refusal to conform to house rules, poor self-control.

Reading material (educational literature) and pictures

The nature or lack of these materials reveals levels of overall maturity. Specific negative indicators are comic books and publications exclusively devoted to physique and beauty, entertainment, and sports. Photos of family, children, friends, or noted social and political figures are positive signs of personal growth. Age-expected accessories such as portraits of sports and musical heroes are acceptable, although nude or pornographic pictures are not.

Facility care

Neglect (e.g., dust or dirt in hidden places such as exit signs, picture frames, window sills) suggests poor work motivation or shallow awareness of house needs. Tools of violence (e.g., match sticks, weapons, knives, drugs) or jailhouse "shafts' (a melted down toothbrush with a razor stuck to it) telegraph disaffiliation and serious adjustment problems. Damage to the facility (e.g., deliberate destruction of property and the breaking of furniture or windows) can indicate disrespect for the community, low frustration tolerance, or poor control of others' negative reactions.

Table continues

TABLE 15-1. Some Clinical Signs in the House Run

Table continued

"Out of pocket"

Residents not in the appropriate places at the appropriate times often signals negative characteristics or problems. Alone, residents are prone to sleeping, fantasy, day dreaming, and preoccupation with negative thoughts as well as social isolation (being a loner). Several residents out of pocket suggest defiance and rebelliousness, disaffiliation, or poor adjustment to the community and its regimen.

Interpersonal problems

House runs detect incidents of resident abuse to each other. For example, several residents may be "setting up" a colleague by deliberately disordering his or her physical space.

Management of house run problems is essential for maintaining individual commitment to treatment as well as community stability. Social contamination refers to the spread of a negative attitude. A single resident, rooming with several others, whose space is in disarray can potentially contaminate others with an "I don't care" attitude. This is particularly important among new residents who are the most ambivalent about remaining in the program and are susceptible to negative influences. Moreover, the accumulation of negative attitudes across vertical levels of residents and staff inevitably leads to larger management problems. At this point, a major effort is needed to clean the house and dissipate generalized negative attitudes among residents and staff. The actions employed for house run problems are consistent with TC management and clinical goals. Actions vary depending upon factors considered for any infractions discussed in the chapter on privileges and sanctions. These include the circumstances, severity of the violation, number of people involved, and stage in treatment. Additionally, issues of training may influence how actions are taken. For example, for minor infractions, actions may be taken on the spot—to role-play the appropriate management approach for the junior members of the house run team. Typical actions for various levels of house run problems are briefly illustrated in Table 15-2.

TABLE 15-2.   Typical Actions for House Run Problems

Verbal pull-ups

Used mostly for the least severe infractions, often in conjunction with a positive affirmation. For example, the house run team may compliment the resident on the good order of the room, *except* for the shoes that are strewn about, reminding the resident about "clean bed, clean head."

Sharper correctives may be delivered on the spot. For example, pornographic pictures in the private space may bring a verbal reprimand. The team members focus on citing the infraction and the specific correction along with a terse rationale. Residents are expected to silently listen and respectfully make the correction.

Learning experience

May be implemented for residents who repeat minor infractions in house management or fail to understand the clinical value of the correction. Consists of an instruction from a staff person to complete a written assignment on the importance of maintaining an ordered space.

Floor bans

Directed to roommates of dormmates who have displayed poor management or infractions of floor rules. All residents involved (room, floor, or dorm) are on restriction of movement (e.g., recreation and passes) for a period of time during which they devote themselves to getting the designated space in order. This action stresses the concept of collective responsibility in the safety and health of the facility. Residents are expected to monitor each other in maintaining facility standards.

Encounters

May be implemented for persistent house infractions and associated negative attitudes. Initiated by peers the resident (or residents) may be confronted on poor self-management and attitudes towards the community, e.g., indifference to standards, disregard for peers, and defiance of authority.

Expulsion

May be invoked for serious violations of safety, health, and cardinal rules. For example, the presence of weapons, incendiary materials, and drugs and drug paraphernalia are viewed as clear dangers to the community and explicit signs of individual incorrigibility.

GI house ban

For facility-wide neglect; contains a punitive element as it interrupts many activities and restricts individual freedom until the house is in complete order. Moreover, concern about the punitive aspect of the GI house ban motivates the peer membership to monitor each other in maintaining an ordered house. Thus, the GI promotes collective *accountability* and strengthens self- and peer-management.

URINE TESTING IN THE TC PERSPECTIVE

TC residential facilities are drug-free environments. The presence of any chemical substance in a TC is not tolerated, as it is completely inconsistent with its perspective. Medications such as aspirin or insulin are secured in the medical offices and strictly managed by the medical staff. In most TCs there are no psychotropic medications, these being rarely prescribed for residents. Thus, only caffeine, cigarettes, and prescribed medications for medical conditions (when also supervised by medical staff) are permitted on the premises or in the environs of the TC agency.[47]

Urine testing is employed in the TC as an *adjunctive tool* to its community approach. It is implemented as unannounced random screening to assess prevalence of drug use on the premises or to detect or validate probable drug use off premises in suspected particular individuals.

The use of urine screens was not always routine and is still not universal across TCs. Regulatory, funding, and referring agencies such as the criminal justice system have mandated urine-testing protocols in TC programs. In the past, however, publicly funded TCs did not readily accept or implement testing mandates, challenging these as contradictory to the self-help perspective and subversive to the peer-management approach.

Urine testing was viewed as an external control of drug use, which substituted for, indeed impeded, the learning of self-control. Testing shifted the responsibility for surveillance and monitoring away from the peers to the toxicology laboratory. Hence, urine testing as a detection method undermined the profound utility of community as a management method. Moreover, the procedure of urinating in a bottle under observation was viewed as psychologically diminishing to individuals

---

[47] In past years American TC agencies have served alcohol to invitees on special occasions, such as fund-raising dinners or program anniversaries. These events were utilized for training the residents selected for the service staff. In their roles as waiters and waitresses, these residents could observe the appropriate use of alcohol (by invitees only) in a positive social context. However, in recent years North American TCs prohibit any resident exposure to alcohol use. Special program events convened on premises are alcohol free, or they are conducted off premises if alcohol is served.

There are cultural differences with respect to alcohol on premises. In some Latin countries, for example, TC staff may be served wine at lunch or dinner. In the USA no use of alcohol or nonprescribed drugs is permitted by anyone on premises. However, staff use of alcohol off premises is an issue that is still in debate among TCs.

engaged in a self-help recovery process grounded in honesty and collective trust. Finally, the utility and validity of urine tests, themselves, were seriously doubted as these time-limited sample methods are subject to false positive and false negative results.

Over the years, however, TCs have comfortably integrated urine testing (and in some instances hair assays) into their program regimen. Although this acceptance is consonant with regulatory mandates, it also reflects the overall maturation of TCs as human services agencies. Monitoring techniques are viewed as necessary to assist peers and staff in managing the wide diversity of clients and drugs used and in curbing high-risk health behaviors in the recent generation of admissions. More importantly, however, TCs have learned that *any* potentially useful technology relating to health, education, or therapy can be successfully incorporated into its perspective and approach.

Thus, urine testing has come to be endorsed by the TC as a tool to assist the community in maintaining a drug-free environment. Staff implements rather than imposes testing in a peer community that expects adherence to the rules of abstinence and to the code of individual honesty. Self-disclosure of drug use and agreement to be urine tested reflects the individual's acceptance of these norms and his or her affiliation with the community.

Refusal to be tested may be an indication of personal dishonesty or represent a challenge to community norms. Thus, urine testing is like any behavioral confrontation in that the peer community tests individual honesty and affiliation in matters that are critical to both the individual and the community. However, acquiring both abstinence and affiliation with the community is a trial and error learning process. Therefore drug use or failure to self-disclose use is not unexpected, particularly early in treatment. Urine testing provides a tool for assessing individual progress, particularly with respect to affiliation, as the sanction underlying testing is the potential loss of the community.

Monitoring the presence or use of substances remains the primary responsibility of the peer community. Peers reinforce the norms of a "clean environment" through direct instruction and role modeling. Moreover, peers are best able to detect drug use in each other based upon keen observation of physical, behavioral, attitudinal, and emotional signs. Peers who suspect or observe any sign of drug use in others, but do not immediately report these to staff, undermine community norms and expectations by condoning the negative behavior of others.

Thus, as with any activity in the TC, urine testing is utilized in accordance with the TC perspective and approach. Keeping the environment free of drugs reflects the pervasive influence of peer management. In their instruction, detection, and confrontation of drug use, peers replace the street code with the community norms.

Urine Test Procedures

The main urine test procedures used by most TCs are unannounced random urine screens and incident-related testing procedures. These procedures are implemented under different conditions and have somewhat different goals. However, the discretionary use of both procedures is not unusual.

Random urine screens consist of collecting urine samples from randomly selected residents, or sometimes from all residents in small facilities, on randomly selected days. Implemented routinely as part of the program management protocol, its primary goal is to assure a drug-free environment. Program-wide urine screens may also be unannounced but not randomly implemented. These are based on suspicion of a "dirty house," for example, drugs on the premises or multiple resident drug use.

Incident-related urine testing is more usually implemented based on an observation or probable cause. Peer or staff suspicion of a resident's drug use in the facility, or more likely, on his or her return from furlough could result in a urine test. The resident is asked about drug use and may be urged to provide a urine sample.

Residents who deny the use of drugs or refuse urine testing on request are rejecting a fundamental expectation in the TC, which is to trust staff and peers enough to disclose undesirable behavior. The voluntary admission of drug use initiates a learning experience that includes exploration of conditions precipitating the infraction. Denial of actual drug use, either before or after urine testing, can block the learning process and may lead to administrative discharge or voluntary dropout.

Urine testing is often an independent means of validating the resident's *denial* of any drug use. The test can validate the specific self-report and support the general credibility of the individual. Moreover, although actual drug use may be ruled out by test results, the suspected incident can facilitate supportive discussions concerning the resident's overall psychological status.

Thus, urine testing is viewed less as a deterrent to drug use than as a means of reinforcing the relationship between the individual and the community. The community expects the individual to self-disclose incidents of drug use; the individual trusts that peers and staff will react appropriately and helpfully in such disclosure.

Disciplinary Actions

When positive urines are detected, the action taken depends on the main clinical and community considerations for any rule violations. Typically these include the drug used, time and status in the program, previous history of drug and other infractions, and particularly, locus and condition of use. Actions may involve expulsion, loss of time, radical job demotions, or loss of privileges for specific periods. Of special relevance for the actions taken is the consideration of where and when drug use occured. Distinctions between drug use on and off premises have important clinical and community implications.

Drug use (or drug paraphernalia) in the facility is a violation of state and federal law, constitutes a threat to the peer community through contamination and demoralization, and is a striking clinical sign of resident disaffiliation. These problems are multiplied when incidents involve several residents. Drug use on premises usually results in administrative discharge.

Resident use of substances outside of the facility less directly threatens the community but underscores clinical implications for the individual and perhaps problems in the program. These incidents usually occur during a day pass or overnight furlough. They also occur during program hours when residents are out of the facility for various reasons, e.g., recreation, school, and work as escorts or drivers.

Review of the "triggers" or reasons for drug use is an essential part of the action taken. Understanding the social, circumstantial, and emotional influences in the reuse of drugs is critical to the learning process. In addition to the negative sanctions, peers invest considerable effort in focusing the individual on the conditions of drug use and the lessons learned. Thus, the drug use incident is exploited as a learning episode for the individual. In particular, the self-disclosure of infractions and the acceptance of urine testing are considered critical signs of the individual's relationship to the program and his or her commitment to work at change.

CONCLUSION

This chapter has described the main facility-wide surveillance activities of the GI, the house run, and urine testing, actions implemented in the management of the community. The management goals of surveillance are to maintain the safety and health of the facility. The facility is *home* and thus, must be physically clean from drugs and a source of community pride. However, the cleanliness, security, and order of the facility also generate "data" concerning the self-care, psychological safety, and self-management of the residents. A secure, well-managed environment is essential for the effectiveness of the main, community therapeutic and education activities to be described in the following chapters.

Chapter 16

Community Meetings

Community is the primary means of teaching and healing in the therapeutic community (TC). Thus, in the TC most activities are collective and are designed to strengthen the sense of community. These activities may be informal, spontaneous occurrences in any setting such as the dorms, the lounge, and the dining room, and they may be formal in that they are planned and regularly scheduled in prescribed places. This chapter presents an overview of the four main facility-wide community meetings as organized components of the daily regimen.

MEETINGS IN THE TC PERSPECTIVE AND APPROACH

The common purpose of the main meetings in the TC is to enhance the perception of community among the participants. However, each meeting has a distinctive format and specific goals. These differences reflect community and clinical management as well as psychological considerations.

Community and Clinical Management

Each meeting focuses on a specific component of community business and clinical transactions involving a large number of residents. Assembling the full house several times a day offers staff a ready means of monitoring resident location. This provides oversight of the physical security of the house and facilitates assessment of overall clinical status of the residents. Changes in individual or collective mood, attitude, and behavior can be quickly detected within a single day's observation. Staff and residents can spot potential problems early and later address them in groups, individual sessions, or special meetings.

Psychological Boundaries

The distinctive formats of the meetings assure residents that there is an appropriate time and forum for dealing with practical, personal, and community business. The specific guidelines for each meeting minimize uncertainty or surprise from unexpected interactions that could threaten residents' psychological safety. For example, personal confrontations, catharsis, or verbal correctives delivered out of context to individuals or the entire community carry the risk of physical or emotional injury and collective disorder (such as what occurs in jails, mental wards, schools, the streets, or in dysfunctional families). Thus, the goals, agenda, rules of participation, scheduled times, and fixed durations of each meeting strengthen the residents' perception of orderliness, coherence, and purpose to the program

Overall the various meetings are essential for efficient community as well as clinical management of the facility. Moreover, the use of different formats provides variation in the medium for delivering the same messages of recovery and right living. Changes in the mode of communication stimulate receptivity to the content of the communication.

Key Elements of the Main Community Meetings

Table 16-1 summarizes the key elements of the four main community-wide meetings. The morning meeting, seminar, and house meeting occur daily. The seminar, although its content is often educational, is discussed as a community meeting because it involves the entire house. The fourth, the general meeting, is assembled as needed. The rationale, method, and special clinical issues for each of these meetings are discussed separately in the following sections.[48]

---

[48] In addition to the four main meetings, however, a variety of other formal meetings, similar to those in business, educational, or human service settings, are convened in the TC. These are not community-wide, and their focus is specific to certain groups and issues. Although the conduct and procedures of these meetings are conventional, they are guided by the values, expectations, and teachings of the TC.

TABLE 16-1. Main Community-Wide Meetings

	MORNING	SEMINAR	HOUSE	GENERAL
Purpose	Initiate positive outlook Motivate participation	Teach concepts of the TC perspective Train conceptual and communication skills	Manage community business Disseminate information	Address community-wide problems Affirm community cohesion
Meeting Frequency	Daily	Daily	Daily	As needed
Duration	30–45 mins.	60–90 mins.	45–60 mins.	Open-ended
Composition	All peers and select staff	All peers and select staff	All peers and all staff	All peers and all staff
Staff Role	Preparation with peers Voluntary participation	Preparation Oversight Selective implementation	Preparation Oversight Selective implementation	Preparation Oversight Implementation
Peer Role	Preparation Implementation by peer teams	Preparation Implementation by select peers	Preparation Implementation Highest ranking peer	Senior peers assist staff

THE MORNING MEETING

Morning meetings convene every day following breakfast, assembling all the residents of the facility and the staff on premises. The meeting is brief (30–45 minutes) and is conducted by residents. The general purpose of the morning meeting is to initiate the activities of the day in a positive manner. However, the specific objectives of this meeting are to motivate individuals to accept the day's activities with a positive attitude, to alter negative social images in a playful way, and to strengthen awareness of the program as family or community. These objectives relate to, and reflect, the TC's view of the client and the role of community in the recovery process.

Although the morning meeting is an ordinary event, assembling people together to engage in cheery activities, it has special significance to the substance abuser for several reasons. Conventional people usually begin their day with some incentive or assistance, e.g., music, exercise, or jogging. Residents in TCs, on the other hand, have never learned or adapted to the routine of an ordinary day. They are characteristically described as night people, whose drug-involved lifestyle has resulted in a disrupted 24-hour sleeping and waking cycle. Even before serious drug involvement, many residents have had histories of truancy or have lived in homes that did not cultivate a regular morning routine. Waking up late reveals their boredom or lack of purpose in life and their cynical attitudes or apathy concerning schedules. For many, the only planned daily activities have usually revolved around drug seeking.

Psychologically, substance abusers tend to approach the day with various symptoms and negative emotions (e.g., fear or anxiety, frank depression, dysphoria, irritability, hostility), which may relate to drug effects and to the perceived and resented demands of routine life. If not dissipated early, these reactions tend to pervade behavior and attitudes throughout the reminder of the day. Thus, the morning meeting is a collective intervention designed to counter these characteristics. It provides a forum for teaching the entire community to *act as if* they are positive, motivated to engage the day, and optimistic about the future.

Method

The objectives of the morning meeting are achieved through a planned sequence of activities that are integrated into a single structured presentation, conceived and managed by the residents themselves. Most frequently these activities are the recitation of the treatment philosophy, brief discussion of a useful concept, a report on the weather, the reading of horoscopes, singing of songs, and presenting a word for the day. Skits, special awards, and poems are familiar but optional other activities. As with all meetings (and groups) effective implementation of the morning meeting involves three main steps: preparation, presentation, and follow-up.

Preparation is the most important ingredient in a successful morning meeting. The morning meeting is planned and conducted by resident teams assisted by staff. Staff (primary counselors) compiles a calendar or schedule of morning meetings in advance and designates which resident teams will run each morning meeting. Typically, these teams may be floor (dormitory) groups or departmental groups such as kitchen or service crews. Teams are given at least one week to develop the material to be presented.

The team identifies a coordinator who facilitates rehearsals, serves as emcee, and is the liaison with staff. There is always an activity that each resident on the team can present. Even if they cannot sing, deliver a poem, or report on the weather, they can read an item on current events or simply introduce another presenter. Thus, although residents are never pressured to participate, they are always encouraged to identify an activity that they can do. Finally, all materials needed for the meeting should be set up in advance.

Presenting a morning meeting

All residents and staff assemble in an appropriate area of the facility (usually the dining room or lounge) after breakfast at about 8:30 a.m. The meeting starts with everyone seated, with the exception of the resident coordinator, who serves as the master of ceremony and opens the proceedings with a loud "Good morning family." The house gives an ensemble response. Each of the main activities of the morning meeting is then presented by a different resident or residents of the team. A customary preplanned sequence of morning meeting activities may include the program philosophy, a concept and word for the day, a favorite color, a favorite person, a reading of the horoscope, the weather report, singing, and special productions. Table 16-2 summarizes typical elements of the morning meeting.

Generally, staff involvement in the morning meeting is limited to assisting in preparation and participating as an audience member. For example, staff review material such as jokes and poems as well as attend rehearsals in order to monitor taste and comic value. Staff may be a playful target of humor or they may be invited by the resident team to actively participate in a production. However, the morning meeting is an expression of the residents that should not be directly influenced by staff input or presence.

The staff team itself can conduct some morning meetings. They present these to the whole house for purposes of modeling, image breaking, and tutoring residents or inexperienced staff (as in a new program) on the implementation of morning meetings. Additionally, staff teams may present morning meetings during special retreats or training sessions to affirm the community method and their role model status in the TC.

TABLE 16-2. Elements of a Typical Morning Meeting

The program philosophy

Begins or ends the morning meeting. Recited by a resident leading the audience. Not interpreted but read or recited with feeling. Recitation of the philosophy in the morning meeting is viewed as a bonding mechanism, a means of reaffirming the value of the collective struggle toward recovery and life change.

A concept for the day

A well-known maxim or phrase (e.g., "honesty is the best policy"), written and presented with a brief explanation that reflects the residents' perception or personal understanding of it. Thus, individual differences in comprehension in the audience should not be inhibited by criticism, debate, or negation.

A word for the day

A single word or phrase drawn from any source (e.g., "resurrection"); a resident presents a formal definition and then underscores the word alone, or together with the concept, as the thought for the day. The use of the word and concept is to stimulate resident thinking particularly in relation to positive change as well as to enhance vocabulary.[a]

Horoscopes

From a book or a daily newspaper. A presenting resident calls out the birthdays of other residents, identifies and reads appropriate (and all) astrological signs, usually stimulating levity and spirited feeling, reaffirms the recovery process. The content of horoscopes is usually positive in tone, and often consists of simple wisdoms or encouraging indications that are readily accepted by these residents. This combination of playfulness and belief assists in creating a hopeful, positive outlook on the day.

The weather report

A briefly detailed report generally drawn from newspapers. The use is practical in that it dictates the appropriate dress for those who will leave the facility. It is also a simple, disarming reminder of the "reality" of outside living.

Singing songs

Presenting residents sing, sometimes accompanied by a musical instrument. The audience are free to join in singing, with rhythmic handclapping or fingersnapping.

Skits and productions

Also includes poems, jokes, impersonations, or humorous awards (e.g., worst dressed, biggest reactor, most positive resident). The theme of the various productions is mild, good-natured, fun, and free from serious or pointed criticism.

[a] Words and concepts may be collected in a book that serves as a source for future residents to access. Such books, like photo charts and letters from former residents and staff, are materials in the community's archives. These symbolize tradition and continuity with past participants in their successful struggle in the recovery process.

Follow-up of morning meeting

Every morning meeting is briefly assessed by staff either informally or, if needed, formally in staff sessions. The assessment is based upon observations and impressions of staff members who were present in the meeting, the resident coordinator, expediters, and the residents themselves. Some key points to review are the adherence to the basic format, level of preparation or planning, and the appropriateness of the material in relation to the goals of the meeting. Of clinical importance, however, are the overall energy, attitudes, and affect of presenters and audience. Individual differences in level of participation among presenters and audience reflect the extent of their affiliation with the community. Notably, improvement in the skill of presenting the meeting is a significant indicator of clinical progress. Thus, the follow-up information can identify incipient problems in the house and can guide treatment planning for individual residents.

Clinical Considerations of the Morning Meeting

The content and format of the morning meeting are completely positive and, notably, exclude all matters of a serious nature. These are reserved for other groups and meetings. The rationale for the strictly positive focus of the morning meeting involves several clinical considerations reflective of the TC perspective.

Criticism or negativity from others, problem solving, and "bad news" at the start of the day can destabilize anyone, particularly substance abusers who do not manage their emotions well. These unpleasant "realities" of daily life have predictably been escaped through *acting out* (e.g., drug use, crime, sexual abuse to self and others, violence) or *acting in* (e.g., apathy, *a*-motivation, emotional symptoms, sleeping excessively, physical complaints).

Although there are legitimate problems, interpersonal or community-wide, these usually do not have to be addressed immediately at the start of the day. Permitting the residents to ventilate negative or anxious feelings the first thing in the morning can reinforce their low tolerance for any form of discomfort. Conversely, teaching residents to wait for the right time and place to express feelings and solve problems increases their tolerance and keeps them stable and focused in their daily routine. Sometimes an obvious crisis may have to be addressed or processed in the morning (e.g., the illness or death of a resident or staff member).

However, this is generally rare and requires evaluation as to whether the issue can wait for discussion in other settings.

Problems and pains addressed in the morning can fragment motivation and performance, at work or in school, particularly for those who come from dysfunctional families where waking up to upset, chaos, and family abuse is common. Healthy families can delay addressing difficult matters until an appropriate time; they remain connected to each other and manage the day without destabilizing under tension. Thus, the positive morning meeting offers a corrective experience through role modeling positive family behavior.

The morning meeting also teaches residents moderation of excessive stimulation with the goal of developing consistency of responsible behavior. All people start the day with positive or negative feelings, which if unmanaged could disrupt the daily routine and fulfilling of obligations. Most learn to experience these contrasts of feeling without destabilizing the day's routine obligations. The positive emphasis of the morning meeting is designed to counter dysphoric feelings. However, the fun and excitement of morning meeting can stimulate affective intensity among residents, making it more difficult for some of them to go back to the ordinary business day. Among substance abusers the intensity of sensations has usually accelerated into the search for more stimulation and eventually to sensation seeking or binge-type behavior, drug use, or sexual abuse.

Thus, residents must learn how to handle swings in feelings without fragmenting or engaging in extreme behavior. How they manage their intensity from positive and negative feelings is an important clinical indicator of personal growth. Staying high from morning meeting versus feeling motivated to engage the day's obligations is clinical material for group and counseling sessions.

THE HOUSE MEETING

The house meeting is the primary vehicle for transacting the business of the TC. House meetings convene every night of the week, assembling all residents of the facility and staff on premises.

The main function of the house meeting is community management. This function must be conducted efficiently, as a considerable amount of information must be disseminated on all activities relevant to the residents, particularly assignment to encounters, job changes, and plans for the following day. This task is difficult considering the attention span of residents is generally relatively short, particularly when they are required to sit or stand quietly and listen rather than actively participate. Moreover, on the nights when house meetings precede encounter groups, the residents' anxiety levels are generally elevated, which further tends to distract their concentration.

House meetings also have a clinical purpose. They are a forum for positive and negative communications about residents' activities. For example, special achievements may be acknowledged. This not only rewards the individual who is recognized but provides incentive to others. Conversely, public announcement of mild individual and community pull-ups exerts social pressure, which could facilitate change.

Method

The house meeting is planned and conducted by a senior resident, usually a coordinator and sometimes an expediter, although staff presence (senior or junior) and supervision are essential. The coordinator develops the basic agenda and information to be transmitted. This involves a considerable effort in reviewing records and information concerned with daily traffic and client status. Senior and junior staff are responsible for identifying the resident job changes to be announced as well as encounter assignments, as these are important clinical decisions. The resident names for these activities are submitted to the coordinator for announcements.

Conducting the house meeting

All residents and staff assemble in the appropriate space in the facility, usually the dining room or the lounge after dinner. The meeting starts with everyone seated, with the exception of the resident coordinator who opens the meeting with a loud "good evening family," to which the house responds together. Casual discussion is discouraged in order to assure that each member of the community listens and obtains correct information, particularly with respect to group assignments and job changes. The coordinator then presents the basic business agenda in a customary sequence: taking attendance, introducing new residents (sometimes announcing the names of dropouts), announcing details of recreation and trips, identifying residents who are scheduled for special legal or medical appointments, announcing job changes, and assigning residents to particular encounters. This format does not vary, with the exception of special announcements and the scheduling of groups, which depends upon the night of the meeting. Encounter groups meet on three evenings every week immediately after the house meeting. On these evenings, residents assigned to encounters are announced. Other planned evening activities or leisure time may follow the house meeting on evenings in which encounters are not planned.

Clinical management in house meetings

The clinical items on the agenda are generally presented last. These are usually announcements of pull-ups or lists of contractees delivered by the coordinator or staff member. For example, the coordinator can read out the names of those individuals who are on contracts, i.e., disciplinary or learning experiences. These are recited quickly and in an emotionally neutral way only to identify contractees to the general community. This information is of special importance as the efficacy of the contract as a learning experience is enhanced when respected by the entire community. For example, the contractee has certain privileges taken away, such as eating with the rest of the house or with his roommates. If peers disregard this proscription, the power of the learning experience is weakened.

The coordinator may surface particular problems of a resident (e.g., "Would someone in Nancy's encounter group talk to her about her attitude") or enlist the community in deterring a particular resident from dropping out of treatment (e.g., "Johnny Jones wants to leave, please talk to him"). These suggestions can be immediately followed up in the subsequent encounter groups of peer conversations.

More formally, the coordinator may identify from a list of names those individuals who will receive verbal pull-ups. These residents are encouraged to modify improper conduct (e.g., cursing, poor room maintenance) or negative attitudes (e.g., toward work and meetings). The pull-up, delivered by the coordinator, is brief and the list of names short. These limits assure that the house meeting does not deteriorate into a general gripe ("dump") session. The content of the pull-up is mild and the emotional tone relatively light.

Provocative pull-ups can divert emotional reactions away from encounter groups, which usually follow the meeting and provide the better expressive outlet. Also, because the resident cannot respond in a house meeting, an overemotional pull-up can produce an excessive negative response later. Even properly delivered, the pull-up must be reserved for nights on which it can be followed up in the subsequent encounter group.

Residents may not direct a pull-up to another individual resident in the house meeting, although they are permitted to deliver *house pull-ups*. These can be directed to subgroups of other residents or the entire facility.

For example, a resident may exhort the community to display more motivation and openness; or conversely, another resident may deliver an affirmation to the community for its conduct and attitudes.

The house meeting can be an effective venue for enhancing clinical management. For example, residents on contract for serious infractions may be asked by the coordinator to *face the community* and briefly state the type and reasons for the corrective. The purpose of this activity is to strengthen the perception of an open community and, conversely, to avoid the corrosive effects of "secrets of the house." It also provides a vehicle for vicarious learning, and reinforcement of community values and expectations. These increase trust (i.e., safety in the community), minimize withdrawal by the resident who is sharing the experience, and inform the community to support the correction.

Clinical management in house meetings highlights a general issue in the TC approach concerning individual privacy and public disclosure. Public statements must not disclose personally sensitive material that may result in undesirable psychological effects on the resident. This issue is particularly compelling today in light of diverse client populations (e.g., adolescents, dually disordered, individuals with AIDS). A general guideline is to avoid public statements about personal matters and encourage the individual to eventually share such matters in groups and eventually, with the community. Preparation for such disclosure can be accomplished with staff and immediate peers.

THE SEMINAR

Seminars are both community enhancement and clinical management activities. They convene every afternoon, assembling all residents of the facility and selected staff on the premises. Thus, staff observation of the entire facility is regularized because the seminar meeting in the afternoon complements the daily morning meeting and the house meeting in the evening. Among the various groups and meetings, the educational format of the seminar is unique in its emphasis upon altering conceptual and communication skills.

The seminar is relevant to the TC perspective and critical to its approach. Many substance abusers in TCs have histories of educational deficit, learning difficulty, hyperactivity, and inability to listen or pay attention. Characteristically, they also display inferiorities concerning their intellectual capacity and anxiety related to verbal performance.

The seminar format attempts to train attention, listening, and speaking skills. The classroom setting, rules, and regulations require that residents intellectually perform "in normal ways." Thoughts, ideas, and verbal expression are validated and accepted with little or no criticism, permitting a relatively positive environment for training the intellectual domain of the individual. A direct self-esteem building activity, seminars are usually conducted by residents. Most importantly, seminars conceptually present the teachings of recovery and right living, which balances the resident's experiential learning in the TC.

The TC employs a wide variety of seminars in the pursuit of three main goals: intellectual stimulation, personal involvement, and social integration. *Intellectual stimulation seminars* encourage residents to think and react to ideas and information that are frequently new and unfamiliar to them. *Involvement seminars* aim to strengthen individuals' participation in TC activities. Often these seminars are employed as clinical tools to enhance the involvement of certain individuals who are observed to be withdrawn or detached. *Social integration seminars* expose the residents to mainstream people and issues. Thus, seminars vary in emphasis and format according to the goal they pursue. Table 16-3 briefly summarizes the most common types of seminars in TCs.

Method

The basics of all seminars include the adherence to certain procedures such as preparation, setting, rules, and feedback. *Preparation* involves identification of the seminar type, topic, and presenters. Selection of the seminar type and topic usually depends upon clinical recovery issues that are relevant to individual participants and to the entire community. Staff reviews the material for the seminar particularly for its clarity, feasibility (i.e., length), and relevance.

TABLE 16-3. Main Types of Seminars

Intellectual stimulation

- *The concept seminar* is the prototypical format and the one most usually employed. The concepts used relate to TC process and perspective. Concepts that are too abstract or removed from the resident are less likely to be attended to, understood or stimulating. On the other hand, concepts, ideas, great thoughts, and parables can be stimulating and forceful influences if they underscore the TC perspective, such as personal growth, self-reliance, and individual struggle.
- *The pro and con seminar* is an issue-oriented format that involves at least two resident speakers and a moderator (resident or staff) in a debate format. The topic selected should be relevant to the residents' experiences or deal with real world issues (drunk driving laws, abortion, decriminalization of drug).
- *The role induction seminar* is a didactic format used to orient residents to the TC perspective and approach including rules, procedures, social organization, program stages, etc. Additional topics are relevant to peer roles in the community such as big brothers and sisters, peers as managers, and monitors.

Personal involvement

- *Grab bag seminars* are various fun and game activities in which residents speak on topics of sense or nonsense that are randomly picked from a bag. The talk is extemporaneous, often in a light vein. This seminar is seen as an "image breaker" because it compels spontaneity in residents who cannot depend upon their usual speech or posture characteristics to deal with a certain situation (e.g., a resident may speak for ten minutes on being a fish).
- *Tell your story seminars* ask residents to talk to the house about the essentials of their lives, what they think went wrong, who they are, how they got to treatment, and what they want for themselves. The resident prepares the key points of talk in advance, which is designed to facilitate assimilation into the community. Variations on the theme of this seminar occur in small "get to know" groups.

Social integration

- *The guest speaker seminar* is given by an expert usually from outside the program. Topics include such matters as how to get a job, voting procedures; or, a chief librarian, or a member of the health department, will present their type of work. In addition to the educational value of this format, the lively discussion with such speakers tends to enhance the resident's sense of normalcy and their self-esteem.
- *House trip seminars* co-occur with the facility's visit to a museum, theater, botanical garden, national center, etc. The seminar may unfold either at the site or back at the facility, conducted by a staff person or occasionally by a guide at the visit site. In addition to exposure to the outside world, these events enhance camaraderie and social normalcy.

The *setting* of the seminar is a room arranged in classroom style. To accommodate the facility this space is usually the dining room, which must be restructured as a classroom. The materials to be included in the seminar—blackboard, flip chart, chalk, and any other required accessory (e.g., a projector, video system, stereo system)—are furnished in the room. At their option, residents may carry their own paper and pencils for taking notes.

The *rules* of the seminar are all of the cardinal and house rules, as well as those specific to the seminar format. Thus, cross talking, leaving the room without permission, or interruptions is restricted. Spontaneous expressions of laughter or other collective reaction, however, are not inhibited. Resident presenters must be permitted to conduct the seminar as they see fit, requesting feedback, discussion, and questioning at the appropriate time. Residents in the audience who wish to speak from the floor must raise their hands to be called upon. The floor speaker may choose to remain seated or stand at his or her place. During the floor speaker's comment, all other hands must be withdrawn.

These elements of the classroom participation situation are familiar in the schoolroom. However, they emphasize the importance of maintaining an orderly environment in which all participants can feel free to speak. Also, the rules and elements of the seminar facilitate training in patience, listening, and mutual respect for the opinions of others.

Generally the seminar should not exceed 60 minutes, although this period may be extended an additional 30 minutes depending on the topic, type, and speaker. Most seminar formats include audience *feedback* to the presenters concerning the conduct of the seminar itself. The audience provides hearty applause at the completion of seminars, following which the presenter (or presenters) or the moderator requests constructive criticism. Emphasis is on the positive strengths as well as the weaknesses in the presentation although the tone of feedback must be affirmative and helpful. Key points of criticism center upon adequacy of preparation, knowledge of material, and effectiveness of communication in terms of speaker energy, involvement, level of nervousness, and general demeanor. Suggestions are expected to be incorporated in later seminars by the same or other presenters.

Clinical Considerations

As with all activities, there are clinical considerations in the uses of the seminar. These involve selection of topics, the seminar as privilege, and the seminar as clinical information.

Generally, seminar *topics* should facilitate the residents' assimilation into the TC recovery process. However, the assimilation process is usually gradual and marked by resistance as well as healthy skepticism. The seminar is the main community forum for residents to intellectually challenge the perspective and the procedures of the TC openly and without fear of sanction. Therefore, the topics of some seminars should elicit doubts and provoke questioning and general discussion toward dissipating resistances and doubts.

Conversely, the topics or the presenter should not hold the potential for confusion, contradiction, or subversion of the resident's recovery experience in the TC. For example, seminars on specific political ideologies or religious sectarianism are considered not appropriate for residents in primary treatment, although these may be available in the re-entry phase of treatment. TCs subscribe to intellectual freedom, but they recognize the psychological fact that alternative perspectives and ideologies could impede the clients' progress, particularly early in treatment. Later, when clients obtain a certain degree of confidence based upon measurable change, they are more prepared to objectively evaluate various alternative views of treatment or recovery, as well as religious and political points of view.

Discussions of ideas, world events, and the daily news occur routinely in the TC, e.g., while watching the evening news on television, in tutorial groups, and informally among peers and staff. These sessions are "family talk"—brief exercises in world awareness, spontaneous thinking, and communicating. Although they do not contain the focused theme or single message of the seminar, family discussions of world events are encouraged to foster a general intellectual impact on the residents.

Most seminars are delivered by residents. However, there is an important clinical consideration in the selection of resident speakers. Speaking at a seminar is viewed as an *earned privilege*. It is a platform that affords the resident facility-wide visibility, commanding 60 minutes of important program time. Thus, resident speakers selected to give seminars should have sufficient role induction into the program and experience as seminar participants. This usually excludes residents of under 60 days, with the exception of those selected for personal and involvement and some role induction seminars.

The seminar also provides useful *clinical information* on the status of individuals as well as the community. Resident participation in seminars provides a basic observational source of data on the behavior and attitude of residents for staff and peers to address in other forums. In particular, the conduct of the constructive-criticism feedback phase provides useful clinical and community management information concerning individual presenters and the audience. For example, audience enthusiasm in providing feedback and the sophistication of its criticisms reflect overall attitude and involvement of the membership. Individual progress is revealed in the quality of the seminar itself and in the manner that criticisms are accepted and incorporated into later seminars by the same or other presenters.

THE GENERAL MEETING

The general meeting (GM) is called to address issues and correct problems that threaten the integrity of the community. Less frequently the GM is convened for positive reasons, for example, to congratulate the entire house on its progress or its efforts in a special project, or to provide important facility-wide information quickly, such as the movement of the program to another location, the opening of a new facility, etc. This section focuses upon the more usual use of the GM as a corrective intervention. The specific goals of the GM are to identify and correct problem people or conditions, reaffirm motivation, and reinforce positive behavior and attitudes. Thus, the broader purpose of the GM is to utilize problems to teach the TC perspective on recovery and right living and reaffirm the existing strength and support of the full community for its individual members.

Method

As with all formal meetings and groups, the method may be described in terms of preparation, conduct, and follow-up.

Preparation

The GM is the most demanding meeting to implement in the TC. Its long duration, the intensity of the participation, and its complex goals require considerable staff effort and clinical management skills. Preparation mainly involves problem identification, which is reviewed by senior staff, restriction of all facility activities in order to accommodate the meeting, and plans for actions to be taken, which may include individual and collective sanctions and follow-up resident group sessions.

Problems are usually *identified* by resident coordinators or staff and then reported to the facility director, who will actually issue the call for the meeting. These problems are detected from specific occurrences or incidents involving particular residents, or on rare occasions, staff members.

All of the problems that precipitate a GM are relevant to the entire community, although they may be classified as those that are community-

wide and those that are individual-specific. The latter problems involve
one or several residents, most often identified or implicated in repeated
infractions of house rules or violations of the cardinal rules. Community-
wide problems potentially can undermine the morale and the
psychological and social health of the community. These may also include
the frank infractions or violations of groups of residents, unexpected
increases in resident dropout, or negative behaviors and attitudes that
appear to pervade the residential facility. Individual and community-wide
problems are addressed publicly to contain the spread of negative effects,
serve as teaching examples, and foster re-affiliation of the errant
members. An illustrative problem is a resident or group of residents who
has committed an infraction of the major or cardinal rules, absconded
from treatment, acted irresponsibly while on the street, and then returned
to the program. The general meeting will deal with the facts of the event,
review the characteristic self-deceptions and manipulations that are
involved, and serve as a forum for expressions of feelings about the event.

Conducting a general meeting

The entire community, staff, and peers are utilized to achieve the goals of
the GM. At any time, all residents and staff (including those not on duty)
are assembled in the largest communal space for indefinite duration.

The rules of the GM are those of house meetings, centering upon
maintaining an orderly process in a safe environment. Particular emphasis
is upon sustaining a serious tone in the meeting and reflecting the urgency
of its purpose. Thus, humor and lightness are discouraged. In addition,
standard rules against violence or threats of violence are underscored,
leaving the room is prohibited, and seminar rules are invoked in order to
focus listening and attention.

Staff and the resident coordinator publicly call for the GM, citing
reports and observations of problem incidents and problem people. The
GM unfolds as three phases of activities that are not discretely planned
but are overlapping and continuous: problem clarification, community
expression, and community consolidation.

In the initial *problem clarification* phase of the meeting, the scope and
severity of the problems must be specified and those directly and
indirectly involved in the problem incidents, identified. This aim is
usually achieved prior to and during the GM through staff and resident
observations and disclosures, through confessions from the implicated
residents, and from others' spontaneous contributions at the meeting.

In the *community expression* phase, the problem residents are asked to face the community of peers and staff, state their infraction, and then listen without responding to the reactions from the community. Peers from the floor voluntarily stand up one at a time and speak to all or particular problem residents in any way they feel, with angry questions, affection, indignation, or disappointment, and then sit down when they are finished.

Essentially, this phase encourages collective ventilation of resident reactions to the problem people and incidents. These include anger, hurt, and disappointment at the errors of others, the disillusion concerning fallen role models, and the fear and anxiety concerning their own recovery (*vicarious relapse*). Balancing these reactions are expressions of concern and love, assertions of the value of friendships and the need for mutual support in the fragile process of recovery.

The third phase, *consolidation*, involves public re-affirmations of community teachings, application of specific disciplinary actions, and the convening of follow-up groups. A crucial step toward community consolidation is surfacing any covert problems within the general community.

Although particular residents and incidents precipitate the GM, these may be the "tip of the iceberg," signaling more widespread problems among other residents in the facility (e.g., drug use, sexuality, lying, stealing) but particularly, condoning the negative behaviors of others. The guilts in the membership usually associated with these hidden violations can be addressed in smaller peer groups that follow the phase of community expression. The process in these "pebble" groups is a gradual widening circle of individuals disclosing guilts, stimulated by the disclosures of others. This last phase of consolidation may continue beyond the period of the meeting itself as part of a general healing process.

Peer and staff roles

The activities and techniques employed to move the general meeting through the phases include therapeutic–educative elements of the TC, such as lecturing, confrontation, probe, and testimony. The peer functions in the GM include confrontation, disclosure and confession, affirmation, and recommitment.

However, the general meeting underscores the multiple roles and functions of staff members as managers, rational authorities, and role models. They manage the meeting, along with the resident coordinator, to guide it toward community consolidation. They are the rational authorities, designing and assigning appropriate disciplinary sanctions. Most essentially, they assertively role model the struggle of recovery through lecturing and personal testimony. Staff members may tell portions of their own recovery story, focusing on crises that precipitated relapse, self-defeating behavior, or actual separation from treatment. These stories offer hope to those who are in the midst of personal crisis, doubt, and confusion, or who are losing their way.

Staff may dispense a variety of actions emerging from the GM. There may be a clarification and reaffirmation of house rules. Evaluation of the overall management of the house not infrequently leads to a variety of specific disciplinary actions or learning experiences. These actions include prohibitions or loss of privileges either for subgroups or for the entire house, disciplinary sanctions for individuals or groups, discharge of certain residents and house bans.

Clinical and community issues

Community consolidation is evident in the wake of the GM in terms of individual and collective relief and positive outlook. However, effective GMs promote short- and long-term clinical effects on the individuals and enhancement effects on the peer community. In particular, follow-up groups and individual sessions are critical in dealing with the *aftermath effects* of the GM. This meeting will evoke unexpected feelings and reactions in many residents: guilt, loss of faith, disillusionment, anger at unfair sanctions, etc. Staff must be vigilant in observing the status of residents during and following the GM, providing assistance to residents directly or indirectly through other residents.

One such sanction that can create perceptions of injustice to the residential population is the *house ban*. Just as individual residents must accept a sanction as a learning experience, the entire facility must accept a house ban. The rationale for its use must be diligently explained as a key social and therapeutic message to all participants. Infractions of major or cardinal rules by a member or group of members is the responsibility of the entire community. As a consequence of the general meeting the house ban is used to foster community consolidation.

Thus, in the TC approach the GM—in its employment of community to address community problems—is a unique intervention. Though usually involving only a few problem residents, it provides the forum for all to learn vicariously. In this sense, it is essential that members experience it as a positive example of an entire community in the trial and error process of self-correction, recovery, and learning right living.

CONCLUSION

This chapter has described the main, formal facility-wide meetings. The morning meeting, seminar, and house meeting bring the entire community together on a daily basis, while the general meeting is convened when needed. Although each meeting has a specific purpose, all have the common objective of strengthening community cohesion. In the delicate balance between the needs of the community and the needs of the individual in the TC, the various meetings favor the community. In contrast, community groups, as described in the next two chapters, assemble specifically for the purpose of addressing the needs of the individual.

Chapter 17

Community Groups

In the therapeutic community (TC), the therapeutic and educational component that focuses specifically on the individual consists of the various forms of group process. The term group therapy is not commonly used in traditional TCs, signifying the fact that group process is a distinctive variation of its self-help approach. The first generation of residents evolved the encounter group as a unique form of group process. Over the years, the TC has developed and adapted various other forms and formats of group process. These address the different psychological and educational needs of the whole person and the wide variety of interpersonal and social interactional issues that emerge among individuals living in an intimate community.

The groups that are TC-oriented, such as encounters, probes, and marathons, retain distinctive self-help elements of the TC approach. The non-TC-oriented groups contain elements of conventional therapeutic and educational group formats. This chapter provides an overview of general elements and forms of group process in the TC. Focus is upon the TC-oriented groups although the use of non–TC groups is briefly summarized.

GROUPS IN THE TC PERSPECTIVE AND APPROACH

Conventional psychotherapy and group therapy have not been particularly effective with substance abusers entering TCs for various reasons. These reflect the person, the disorder, and fundamental elements of self-help recovery. Residents in TCs could not listen to or "behave" for others, whether they were parents, teachers, or mental health professionals. Indeed, in their history, many have manipulated therapists into enablers or have learned to use counseling "therapy" to hide from themselves. In part, this reflects the characteristics of rebellion and opposition to all forms of authority. However, it also reveals the unique and important element of mutual self-help in the recovery process.

The psychological and sometimes social status distance between the mental health therapist and the substance abuser often hinders the development of a constructive "therapeutic alliance." Individual acceptance of the "therapeutic authority" of the peer group is grounded in the credibility of a membership that is most unambiguously symbolized in recovered staff and recovering peers. Based upon common characteristics and experiences, residents "know each other" in ways that conventional "expert" therapists cannot know them; and, once residents are committed to personal and social change, they are the most credible and effective people to help each other pursue those changes.

There are distinctive elements inherent in the TC peer groups that strengthen the "therapeutic alliance" between the individual and the group. First, for most residents the peer group has been the main context for their negative socialization. Group process in the TC utilizes this context to positively *re*-socialize its members. Therapeutic authority resides in the peer role model or diffused across the many group members—that is, in the community.

Secondly, residents *trust* group process because they perceive similar others assuming the psychological risks needed to initiate change. As noted, they also listen to messages from peers, who can understand and accept the resident in ways that conventional therapists cannot. Thirdly, peer groups provide *continuity of relationships*. Residents live and work with many of the same people in the groups, a factor that increases trust and intimacy.

Groups and Community as Method

The community groups are critical but not exclusive program components in the TC. Groups in TCs are smaller units of the larger peer community. Thus, the groups' therapeutic and educational effects are enhanced by the myriad of community activities. As described in previous chapters, residents living and working 24 hours a day in TCs engage in a variety of social roles. The behaviors, attitudes, and emotions displayed in these roles provide the "data," or observations, for what residents address in groups. What residents learn about themselves in the groups is *practiced* in their various community roles. This accords with the objective and method of the TC approach—the use of the peer community and its context and expectations to change individuals.

Rationale for the Different Groups

As with community meetings, the different formats of the various groups in the TC underscore their common purpose of advancing the overall therapeutic and educational aims for the individual. However, the multidimensional nature of the resident's problems is more *efficiently* addressed through the use of different group formats. These minimize the disruption from crossover issues, feelings, and problems. Permeable boundaries across formats would impede the clarity of issues and the focus of the participants.

For the individual resident, the different formats signify *order and credibility* in the therapeutic protocol. This provides assurance that their various personal issues will eventually be addressed in a particular group. There is an appropriate time and place to reflect on concepts, learn practical skills, express feelings, resolve conflicts, or "get into" oneself.

The different formats also assure a certain degree of *psychological safety* for the individual participants. The somewhat different rules of interaction and expected outcomes help the resident to psychologically prepare for each type of group. When there are few deviations from the format, there are no emotional surprises. Residents are safer if there are no sharp confrontations in a sensitive probe group or harsh criticisms in a tutorial group. Thus, adhering to the distinctive formats of the different groups assures residents that there is an appropriate time and forum for dealing with practical, personal, and interpersonal issues, and it provides staff with clarity in following the range and course of the individual's therapeutic progress.

GROUP PROCESS: GENERAL ELEMENTS

Classifying group process into therapeutic and educational formats is somewhat artificial for various reasons. The activities of each are not necessarily exclusive to one type of group. Also, there are common outcomes that may occur in all groups. Regardless of the format, any group can be a setting for a particular individual to have intense emotions, gain insights, vicariously learn from others, or experience social relatedness and healing effects. There are general elements that extend across the main groups that clarify group process in the TC approach.

These include the roles of peers and staff, the group rules, and the tools of group process.

Peer and Staff Roles in the Main Groups

With the exception of the encounters and certain tutorials, peers do not have primary responsibility for the conduct of the groups. Senior residents may serve formally as assistant facilitators to staff. Informally, as experienced group players they are expected to role model the appropriate group behavior. Group leadership is discouraged, although peer leadership is desirable and emerges as a result of the process. The emphasis is upon developing cadres of peers whose experience provides the "strength" of the group. The concept of peer strength highlights the distinction between leaders and leadership; the former symbolizes a power role, while the latter reflects the influence of role modeling.

Particular groups emphasize different staff roles—as facilitators in encounters, as therapists or counselors in the probes and marathons, as teachers or guides in tutorials, and as managers and therapists in marathons. These staff roles are more flexible than fixed, often shifting within and across the different groups.

Nevertheless, all groups epitomize the mutual self-help element in the approach. In this forum, peers directly assist each other in the demanding process of self-change. Regardless of facilitator, whether staff or peer, the actual process involves peers interacting, sharing, suggesting, instructing, and confronting each other.

The General Rules of Group Process

Certain rules are uniform across all groups in the TC, while other guidelines vary depending upon the particular group or program. These rules and guidelines are spelled out in written material and orientation sessions, repeated by peers, and usually announced before each group. They address the necessity of maintaining the physical and psychological safety of the individual group participants.

An essential aim of all groups is to provide a forum for personal disclosure and free emotional expression, negative and positive, without the risk of social chaos or personal harm. Participants must feel physically and psychologically safe in the group setting in order to trust the process itself. Thus, the *main safety rules* of the program hold for all groups. These prohibit physical violence and verbal or gestural threats of violence and cultural pejoratives—that is, any form of stereotyping on the basis of race or ethnicity, age, or gender.

Participants must also be protected from the distortions of information that may occur through informal transmission outside the groups to the peer community. Thus members are cautioned against disclosing the contents of the group to any person outside of the immediate group. The *confidentiality rule* is not intended to shield the individual from the general community. Indeed, being open to, known, and accepted by the community is considered essential to the recovery process. However, the individual members, themselves (not others), are the ones who must choose to share authentic personal information with the larger community. For each individual, developing "community intimacy" is a gradual evolution associated with increased trust and affiliation. This emerges from continual and safe peer interactions in the daily regimen and his or her participation in the changing compositions of groups.

The Tools of the Group Process

Group tools are certain strategies of verbal and nonverbal interchange that are employed by participants to facilitate individual change in group process. These are designed to penetrate denial; raise awareness; stimulate reactions, particularly expressions of feelings or more generally acts of self-disclosure; and to promote a member's involvement in the group process. Although primarily used in the clinical groups, variants of these tools occur spontaneously in the other group formats.

There are two main classes of group process strategies: (a) *Provocative tools*—generally less supportive and more confrontational—are participant expressions that challenge the individual member to react or respond; and (b) *evocative tools*—more supportive and facilitative—are participant expressions that encourage the individual member to react or respond. Both types of tools are commonly used, although some are more prominent in certain groups or at certain points in group process (see Table 17-1).

Provocative tools, *hostility* or *anger*, *engrossment*, and *ridicule* or *humor*, are most pointedly used to penetrate denial and break down deviant coping strategies such as lying. However, their provocative elements risk personal injury. Hence, the main caveat in their use is that they focus on specific behaviors and attitudes, not address the unchangeable, nor attack the "inner" person. They are more often used in the encounter groups.

TABLE 17-1. The Tools of Group Process

PROVOCATIVE TOOLS

Hostility or anger

An emotional expression used by members specifically to communicate peer reactions to the individual. Words without feelings often fail to communicate a real message. Thus as a tool, the angry "feelings" expressed by members to another member aim to intensify the individual's awareness of his/her impact on others. They are also used to promote the expression or ventilation of feelings in the member who has lost connection with his or her own feelings.

Engrossment

A verbal strategy that aims to raise the individuals' awareness of their impact on themselves and others. It deliberately uses extreme exaggerations of their characteristic behavior or attitudes (or the consequences of these). The tool is generally humorous. It begins with an accurate observation, which one or more members weave into an overblown or distorted picture of the behaviors addressed. This tool is used to penetrate denial of a particular behavior or attitude.

Humor or ridicule

The use of all forms of humor such as banter, repartee, sarcasm, paradox, and comic imitation to penetrate denial and specifically to break false social images or masks. Humor promotes laughter at self and others and easier acceptance of individual weakness, and it can help to curb individuals' extreme views of their problems.

EVOCATIVE TOOLS

Identification

A gesture of understanding of another member's difficulty or pain based upon a similar life experience. Members speak to each other in terms of learning from shared similar experiences. Identification is used to erase perceived differences among participants in social status or in their recovery status. It also helps counter a sense of uniqueness or isolation and aims to facilitate self-disclosure, attitude change, and learning through role modeling while having therapeutic value for the user as well.

Compassion

A gesture of emotional understanding while still placing responsibility on recipients for their actions and for changing themselves. Members show compassion when they express understanding, sympathy, or sorrow for the other person's suffering as it is associated with a particular action, decision, or life event.

Empathy

A vicarious emotional understanding of the member's difficulty or pain. A gesture used to facilitate honest relating and to encourage behavior and attitude change. Empathy does not require identification with a similarly shared life experience. It is an expression of understanding based upon common pains in life, such as loss, disappointment, and despair.

Table continues

TABLE 17-1. The Tools of Group Process

Table continued

Affirmation

    Consists of various words and gestures that provide a signal to the individual of support, approval, encouragement, and validation. Affirmation extends beyond rewarding correct, good, or acceptable behavior to the broader theme of acknowledging that the individual is engaged in an honest struggle to learn and change. The group expresses affirmation for what members do but also for who they are in the struggle. Thus in all forms of group process, affirmation is particularly appropriate for balancing criticism.

PROVOCATIVE-EVOCATIVE TOOLS

Projection

    The members use of their own thoughts and feelings as the basis for their observations of another member. Projection does not invalidate the observation if the user is aware that the self is the source for seeing others. "You have been acting like you are going to split. I have similar feelings myself." Projection helps the projector to self-confront.

Gossip

    Two or more members of the group talk about a third member or several members as if the latter were not in the room. It is often used with humor to provide group feedback to the member(s) without the emotionality of the direct confrontation.

Carom shot

    An indirect and mild confrontation to avoid or weaken resistance from direct confrontation. The confronter speaks to another member whose problem is similar to a third member, the real target of the confrontation. For example, while speaking to Tony (who has not openly shared his threats to drop out of treatment), the confronter turns to a third member and asks "Jack, are you still thinking about leaving here?"

Lugs

    Indirect references to, pull-ups, or mild criticisms of others in order to raise awareness or reduce defensiveness. For example, the statement "Some people in this room have not been considerate of other people's feelings" illustrates this tool.

The evocative tools of *identification,   compassion, empathy,* and *affirmation* use various forms of emotional understanding primarily to facilitate self-disclosure and participation. Certain other tools, such as *projection, carom shots, lugs,* and *gossip,* are a mix of provocative and evocative elements. They use various forms of indirect communication to both challenge the individual and facilitate his or her participation, yet avoid the resistance and defense evoked by direct communication. These tools are generally used in encounters, though projection is common in other groups.

All group process tools are employed with *responsible concern*—that is, concern for the welfare of the other person. Literally, the phrase responsible concern refers to the expectation that all members of the community will respond to the behavior and attitudes of others who appear to be faltering in their recovery. The underlying message of responsible concern is that "Your recovery is important to my recovery" and that "I have a responsibility to help you by responding to your negative signs." Thus, the use of tools, particularly the provocative ones, must always reflect the element of concern for the individuals to whom these are directed.

THE MAIN CLINICAL GROUPS

The main clinical groups in the TC are encounters, probes, and marathons. Each differs in format, objectives, and method although their common purpose is to facilitate positive psychological change in the individual (Table 17-2).

TABLE 17-2.   The Main Therapeutic Community Clinical Groups

	BASIC ENCOUNTER	PROBES	MARATHONS
Stage	1–18 months	2–12 months	6–18 months
Frequency	3/week (min.); as needed after 12 months	3–4/client (min.); as needed after 12 months	2/client (min.); 1/client after 12 months
Duration	2 1/2 hours	4 hours	24–72 hours
Compo-sition	A senior or junior staff member or senior resident facilitates group process; 10-20 residents	A senior staff member with 1–2 junior members lead/facilitate group process; 12-20 residents	1–2 senior staff ± 2–3 junior staff ± senior residents assist, lead, direct, and facilitate group process; 20+ residents
Objectives	Raise awareness of specific behaviors/ attitudes	Obtain information on critical life events Preparation for marathons Surface emotional memories	Initiate resolution of critical life events through profound emotional reliving
Approach / Tech-niques	Verbal Confrontation of daily behavior and attitude	Verbal Supportive inquiry of sensitive life experiences	Varied–visual and auditory Planned activities, e.g., scenes, replaying of related sensitive life experiences Exercises Psychodrama and theater

Encounter Groups

Encounters are the cornerstone of group process in the TC. The term encounter is generic, describing a variety of forms that utilizes confrontational procedures as the main approach. The basic encounter is a peer-led group composed of 10 to 20 residents; it meets at least three times weekly, usually for two hours in the evening, and is followed by an additional 30 minutes for snacks and socializing. Although often intense and profoundly therapeutic, the basic objective of each encounter is modest and limited—to heighten individual awareness of specific attitudes or behavioral patterns that should be modified. As the encounter group is the most distinctive group format and the one most widely used in the TC, a full chapter (18) is exclusively devoted to describing the rational and method of this form of group process.

Probes

Probes are long group sessions conducted to obtain in-depth clinical information on residents in treatment. They go much beyond the here and now of the behavioral incident, which is the primary material of the encounter, to the events and experiences of the individual's history. Rather than confrontation, the probe mainly uses the evocative tools to facilitate individual disclosure. However, techniques may include role-playing, psychodrama, or some Gestalt elements. Mostly these are employed to artfully reduce defensiveness, resistance, and fear of strong emotional memories.

The *frequency* of probes varies with different programs. Optimally, however, a resident should experience at least three probes during their residential tenure in the TC. Initial probes are employed with the newer clients to facilitate their openness, trust, and identification with others and to increase the staff's understanding of important historical aspects of the person. The *duration* of these early probes can be limited to 2–4 hours each. Probes later in treatment are utilized either as extended therapeutic groups or as preparation for marathons (discussed below) and they run longer (6–12 hours). Probes may be conducted throughout the facility for a period of time to acclimate all residents for a marathon.

The *method* of probes involves considerable preparation. First, staff will identify the resident composition of the probe. Residents to be probed may be selected on the basis of certain recurrent problems in the community such as chronic hostility or rule breaking. These patterns may not be modified in the encounter groups and are approached from the nonconfrontational, in-depth perspective of the probe. Also, certain residents whose life history themes are similar may be selected to participate in a particular probe, e.g., those with histories of abortions, surrendering children for adoption, and incest. Generally, the number of members in a probe should not be less than 13 although they can be usefully conducted with groups as large as 20 if these consist of experienced membership.

Second, prior to the group, the staff examines the client's background and records and reviews clinical progress notes to determine sensitive areas or important life events, at least one of which will serve as the basic material for the probe. These events may be of a traumatic nature, such as abortions, giving up children for adoption, death of or abandonment by parents or significant others, incarceration or group home experiences, sexual abuse or violence that is committed against or by the resident, catastrophic incidents (e.g., fires, drownings, assault), or simply painful themes that may be in relation to chronic situations involving parents or siblings or have to do with intense personal guilt, etc.

Third, staff establishes a specific objective prior to the meeting for each resident to be probed. If the probe is designed to precede a marathon, its specific goal will be limited to facilitating disclosure, awareness, and perhaps some emotional release concerning a resident's theme. Although the probe may focus on several residents (sequentially), a secondary goal is to facilitate spontaneous disclosure in others as well as precipitate significant emotional experiences. Another goal of the probe is to increase intimacy and strength of a particular group. A common psychological outcome of a successful probe is to draw the members closer through mutual sharing of previously undisclosed material, which tends to reinforce group cohesiveness. Thus, probes are particularly effective in fostering experiences of healing and social relatedness.

The probe *format* is a small circle of participants. Informal accessories such as coffee and pillows are available, as the duration of the probe is considerably longer than the encounter. The basic approach is a group conversation guided by the staff leader who begins with the least-defended resident in order to obtain a successful effect within a reasonable short time. This strategy is employed to lower the resistance in others by creating a positive infectious effect. Thus, staff leaders generally know most about the clients with whom they will work. They subsequently direct the inquiry to others according to the specific theme of importance.

The minimal aim of the probe is to surface at least one important life experience. The probe is considered successful if the importance of a particular experience is acknowledged even without catharsis or an emotional processing ("working through"). Often a fuller therapeutic experience leading to resolution is reserved for either later probes or the intensity of the marathon or both.

The *get to know group* is a derivative of the probe and is usually the first group to be introduced to newer residents in the TC. It is generally conducted by a staff member and a senior resident. In the larger programs, the composition of this group is primarily a cadre of new admissions; in the smaller programs, the composition may be a mix of new and older residents. The explicit goal of this group is simply to introduce the new residents to others. Its implicit goals are to initiate affiliation and surface some biographical information for clinical purposes. Residents' personal stories center on the general questions of who they are and why they are in the TC.

The format of this group combines elements of the probe and a planned rap or conversation group. New residents may not be ready for personal disclosure or may be threatened by group process. Thus, no group pressure is exerted on the individual to relate to others or reveal any personal information. Group facilitators simply go around the room asking individual residents to say a few words about themselves.

Marathons and Retreats

Marathons and retreats are extended group sessions (e.g., 12–36 hours) utilizing elements and methods from all of the other groups. Thus, features of the encounter, probe, and tutorial (discussed in the next section) are integrated in specially programmed ways.

The primary objective of marathons is to initiate the process of resolving life experiences that have impeded the individual's growth or development. The marathon does not aim to cure but to encourage the individual to continue to address themes related to life-altering events. The general approach of the marathon is to dissipate defenses and resistances through the use of a variety of physical, psychological, and social techniques. Thus, deprivations (e.g., control of smoking, movement) and special stimulation in the environment (music, lights) may be employed. A prominent mode is to structure the marathon as theater, a series of many scenes replaying the significant life events of the membership. Thus, the marathon incorporates elements of psychodrama, primal therapy, and pure theater to produce its impact. Optimally, residents will experience at least two marathons during their treatment tenure.

Retreats differ from the marathon in several ways. The retreat is usually convened away from the main residential facility. It is organized around a particular theme, such as child abuse or gender issues, that defines the composition of the participants. It incorporates techniques and strategies from varied sources, such as physical exercises and spiritual readings. The schedule is balanced with work, recreation, and sleep rather than continuous participation used in the marathon to induce dissipation of defenses. Its explicit goal, to foster significant psychological experiences, is similar to the marathon, but its implicit goals are social, that is, to strengthen affiliation and bonding, renew commitment, and reaffirm the community.

THE MAIN GROUPS FOR TEACHING AND TRAINING

The educational and training objectives of the TC are pursued through tutorial groups and special workshops. The specific objectives of these groups are to teach personal growth concepts, to provide skills training for house jobs, and to provide clinical skills training. Each tutorial group has a somewhat different format specific to its objective.

Personal Growth Tutorials

Personal growth tutorials are distinctive in their clinical as well as educational significance for the resident. The program stresses the value of these sessions to enhance their overall impact. These groups are not routinely scheduled and effort is made to communicate to the participants that the tutorial is a *special event* signified by its staff stature, relaxed rules, and amenities. Coffee and fruit are available in the tutorial room, and cakes may be specially baked by the house or brought from the outside expressly for the tutorial. The event is planned for the late evening, and residents are assured that it will go on for many hours to permit spontaneous relaxed conversation. In particular, house rules are modified to allow the participants complete involvement in the tutorial. This may mean extending wake-up time to a later hour on the following morning or permitting absenteeism from an early morning job. The status of a senior staff person conducting the tutorial adds significantly to the special quality of the tutorial. These features of the personal growth tutorial are assumed to maximize learning because they communicate to the residents that they, and the event, are of special importance.

The *composition* of the personal growth tutorial consists of residents who generally have 6 and 12 months in primary treatment. There are some exceptions to this composition related to special issues. For example, a teenage tutorial would include any resident under 19 years of age and exclude the criteria of time in program. Depending upon the size of the facility, the optimal maximum number of residents in a tutorial group is 20. The personal growth tutorials may be programmed on an as-needed basis and the *duration* of any particular tutorial is from 4–6 hours.

Tutorials are conducted by junior and senior staff. The key criterion for selection of staff is whether the person is comfortable with the theme based upon objective information and personal experience. The staff member prepares a written outline of the tutorial involving several steps, the theme, method, and follow-up. The theme of the tutorial is thoughtfully considered in terms of its relevance to the treatment process and the composition and clinical needs of the group. Some tutorials, for example, are intensive intellectual sessions on ideas and concepts relevant to the TC perspective. Thus, a facility director or a senior resident with expertise may give a series of sessions on literary readings from Thoreau, Emerson, Ghandi, biblical and talmudic readings. Focus is upon intellectual processing of universal truths that illustrate right living and recovery.

Other themes may be TC-related concepts cast in discussions that are broader than personal recovery, such as making choices, freedom and responsibility, self-reliance, and healthy interdependence. The theme is presented mainly to initiate the freewheeling conversational process of the personal growth tutorial. It is not intended to resolve any intellectual matter but only to serve as a focused area of exploration to which the entire group returns periodically from the open discussion. Regardless of the theme, the implicit goal of the personal growth tutorial is to teach the residents how to explore an issue, concept, or question rather than to arrive at a specific conclusion or positions.

Unlike seminars, which are prescribed classroom style activities, the personal growth tutorial is more informal. Conducted in settings such as the lounge, it utilizes written materials (e.g., excerpts from poems, novels, newspapers, the dictionary, encyclopedias), novel approaches (e.g., introduction with a staff leader's personal experience), current events or newsworthy incidents (e.g., political election, drug-gang wars), or group exercises (e.g., special activities, games, or role-playing).

Participants are encouraged to question and free associate their ideas on the theme. They also are encouraged to discuss philosophies and the world, as matters that are of common concern to the others. However, they are steered away from emotional catharsis, personal problems, discussion of individual concerns about their external circumstance, or dissatisfactions with the program. Participants may ask any question of the staff leader. As an illustration, a staff person may be asked, "When you moved out of the program, did you go right back home after graduation?" Staff responds, "I couldn't be on my own right away, so I had to set a goal before that. Staying with my family for awhile, looking for an apartment, building up a nest egg…" This demonstrates how the staff leader emphasizes the principle of self-reliance, goal setting, and the common concern that many residents have about their own re-entry.

Follow-up is an informal process that aims to obtain feedback concerning the degree of the resident's involvement in the tutorial. A few days may lapse before the staff person samples several of the residents, usually those who were the most involved as well as the least involved, in a casual setting such as the dining room. Questions are designed to elicit some indication of what residents heard rather than what they specifically learned in the tutorial. Not infrequently clues as to the effects of the tutorial may appear weeks later in a quite different setting. For example, in a peer rap discussion or an encounter the resident may make a comment related to the theme of the tutorial such as "I think I'll live with my aunt after I leave the program. There's too much hassle at my house." In the TC approach the therapeutic or educational impact of any particular activity may be cultivated gradually over time through other such activities.

Clinical Skills Tutorial (The Mock Encounter)

The clinical skills tutorial is designed to teach new residents (and new staff) how to properly use the tools of group process. Its main method employs the "mock" or simulated encounter group consisting of an inner circle for the encounter participants and an observing audience to provide both didactic and experiential training. The critical training technique of the mock encounter is that of a *stop action*. The staff trainer is free to interrupt the proceedings of the mock encounter at any point to illustrate an activity that is characteristic of the encounter or, more importantly, the use of a particular group tool. This can be understood with the following illustration of *engrossment* as a tool:

Member #1: You're a funky person.

Member #2: I'm too f….. busy to take care of my room the way you want me to.

Member #1: Well, if you don't want to take care of your room, what we can also do is maybe just leave it and you don't ever have to clean it up and then we could just let the dust balls gather in the corner and then we could just sweep it up into a bag and make a pillow for you, and then you'd have a pillow. And then when it really gets bad, we can import some hogs from Arkansas...

Member #2: Okay, okay, I hear you...

Although it is a tutorial group, the mock encounter often has clinical effects on the participants and the audience. Those viewing the mock encounter frequently obtain insight or recognition of their own behavior in real encounters. The clinical impact of this form of experiential training is recognized in the common understanding of TC workers—"There is no such thing as a *mock* encounter."

The *follow-up* of the clinical tutorial is more formal than that of the personal growth tutorial. The staff person may ask residents to write up what they have learned about encounter tools. These write-ups may be graded by senior staff to provide feedback for the residents. Also, however, they permit the director of the facility to monitor the teaching and the clinical performance of the junior staff who are conducting real encounters. For example, if the write-ups indicate that residents still have a vague understanding of the objectives, duration, and conduct of the confrontation, then staff trainers of these encounters can be apprised of this matter.

Job Skills Tutorials

These groups involve, at one time or another, all residents of the house, as everyone at one time or another will engage in each job function in the facility. Thus, the themes of the job skills tutorials may be front desk management, phone and other communication skills, the expediter role, etc. The primary method of the job skills tutorial is usually role-playing, which occurs in the real setting of the job function. Senior residents, as well as clinical and facility support staff, are often the trainers and teachers of job skills tutorials involving TC work roles. The tutorials are offered to prepare the resident for on the job field training.

Workshops

Workshops differ from tutorials in that they involve selected residents, special themes or lessons, and special individual assignments. Workshops are generally more intensive than tutorials, often ongoing, and usually led by an expert frequently from outside of the TC. Their format is didactic and experiential.

Some workshops focus upon training or tutoring that prepares the resident for living in the larger society. For example, workshops in life skills, budgeting, parenting, or developing resumes are offered to residents in the re-entry stage, as preparation for their transition out of the TC. Workshops on other topics are available to all residents but in small group formats.

Interrelationships among the Main Groups

Although the main groups are distinctive in their specific purpose and method, they are viewed as interrelated clinical interventions with a common purpose of addressing the whole person. The group formats can be judiciously integrated to achieve significant psychological changes. The encounter may identify persistent behavior patterns that, as they change through confrontation, surface pains and memories of past injuries. The probe is particularly conducive to a more complete self-exploration of these emotions. The marathons provide a setting for a more intense re-experiencing of these past injuries, as well as eventuating their resolution through explicit exercises and strategies. For example, the encounter may identify behaviors associated with various guilts; the probe assists the individual in disclosing them; and marathons set the stage for initiating more dramatic resolution of issues related to these guilts.

Tutorial groups are primarily directed toward training specific skills or teaching verbal and nonverbal skills. These groups foster self-examination and understanding through ideas, contemplation, and conversation. Moreover, the process of skill development in these groups often surfaces emotional, attitudinal, and self esteem issues, which can be addressed in the clinical groups. Thus, the interrelationships across the various groups illustrate the importance of their *differences* in contributing to the process of changing the whole person.

OTHER GROUPS IN THE TC

In contemporary TCs, a variety of other groups meet as needed. These address special issues often related to particular cultural groups or subpopulations (gender, race–ethnicity, age, mental and physical illness).

Their focus is upon special issues (e.g., HIV, child abuse) or themes (e.g., women, self-esteem).

TC-oriented groups utilize the elements of the main group formats and clinical tools, although the content and specific goals differ. Special theme groups may focus on issues of gender, race, age, sexual abuse, cultural relevance, HIV/AIDS issues, or family alcoholism. Other thematic groups may be specific to program stages. For example, early stage induction groups address the issues of adjustment to treatment, and late stage re-entry groups focus upon issues of transition to the outside.

These special groups are generally conducted by primary and clinical support staff in the TC. The formats use elements from probes, tutorials, and sometimes retreats. Clinical criteria are considered for implementing these groups, such as relevance for the individual, stage in program, and resident readiness to explore these issues. Program management objectives may also be considered. Theme groups may be used for conflict resolution, social role education, and to facilitate engagement and enhance retention in treatment. For example, many TCs have incorporated 12-step groups into the primary treatment stage of residential treatment.

Other forms of group process that are *non-TC-oriented* follow more traditional educational and group therapy models. These are generally conducted by support staff (e.g., teachers, psychologists, and social workers in the program) or by invited experts from outside the agency. The most common examples are psychodrama, gestalt therapy, primal therapy, reality therapy, and more recently, relapse prevention and cognitive-behavioral groups, such as rational emotive therapy. Varieties of family groups include family alliance groups and, depending upon resources, family therapy and family systems groups.

There are considerations for effective use of the non-TC-oriented group formats. For example, they must be *appropriately timed.* Such interventions can undermine residents' affiliation with the community if introduced too early in treatment. Moreover, residents must be sufficiently along in their recovery to *appropriately utilize* these groups. Residents who have not acquired stable, socially acceptable attitudes and conduct are not likely to benefit from conventional therapeutic groups.

The professional therapists who facilitate these groups must be *appropriate leaders* in that they must have a thorough understanding of the TC approach. Specifically, they need to recognize and appreciate the specific purpose of the group, the nature of the client, the timing of the group in the context of community as method.

Tutorial groups that are non-TC-oriented center on parenting skills, child care, and health care, such as nutrition, physical self-care, sexually transmitted risks, and other health risk behavior. Educational and vocational groups include GED classes, trade skills, vocational counseling, and a variety of other life skills training, such as banking,' budgeting, seeking work, negotiating social systems, etc. The formats of these groups are generally conventional and are often conducted by support staff and others from outside the TC.

Thus, non-TC-oriented groups facilitate recovery when they are *judiciously integrated* into community as method. They enhance rather than substitute for the fundamental, mutual self-help group process in the TC.

CONCLUSION

This chapter has described the varieties of group process in the TC, which include the main clinical and educational groups—encounters, probes, marathons, tutorials, and workshops. These are supplemented by other more traditional, group process and teaching models. The various formats address the different psychological and educational needs of the whole person and the wide variety of interpersonal and social interactional issues that emerge among individuals living in an intimate community. However, the most widely used and distinct form of group process in the TC is the encounter, described in the following chapter.

Chapter 18

The Encounter Group

Perhaps the hallmark feature of the therapeutic community (TC) is the encounter group. This form of group process is a profoundly significant component of the TC model, illustrating by example some of the TC's basic teachings: compassion and responsible concern, the necessity for confronting reality, absolute honesty, and self-awareness as the essential first step in personal change. Although the focus is upon the individual, the encounter is also a unique community forum in which group process is utilized to resolve a variety of individual and collective issues.

Various "encounter groups" emerged outside of addiction treatment as a group form in the human potential movement. However, as it is practiced in the TC, the encounter or confrontation group was developed by people in recovery from chemical dependency quite independently of the human potential, traditional counseling, or therapy groups utilized in the mental health field. Alcoholics and drug addicts spontaneously evolved a purely self-help group process to address their disorder, their personalities, and their recovery.[49]

THE USES OF THE ENCOUNTER

Encounter describes forms of interpersonal exchange based upon the direct reactions of the participants to each other. These consist of personal feelings and thoughts about the other person, both positive and negative. Confrontation involves presenting concrete observations of behavior and

---

[49] The TC encounters should be distinguished from those encounter group forms practiced in T-groups or sensitivity training, particularly in their format and in the extent of confrontation (see Lieberman, Yalom, & Miles, 1973).

attitudes that elicit reactions or concerns in others. Sharing usually refers to an exchange of feelings or thoughts that does not require concrete observations and may not involve direct reactions of participants to each other. In the TC, encounter groups emphasize confrontational procedures in their approach. However, compassionate conversation, sharing, counseling, and other supportive interactions are essential to the efficacy of confrontational procedures.

As with all groups in the TC, the general purpose of the encounter is to change negative patterns of behavior, thinking, and feeling. However, the specific goal of each encounter is modest and limited—to heighten the individual's awareness of specific attitudes or behavior patterns that should be modified.

The simplicity of its goal should not be confused with the complexity of the encounter process. Individuals may undergo powerful experiences, which ultimately contribute significantly to personal change. However, *any* change in the right direction is an acceptable outcome in the encounter because it strengthens the likelihood that individuals will remain engaged in the process of change.

Encounters are also utilized to address a variety of interpersonal issues: resolution of member disputes or personality clashes, improving understanding and social relations between genders or between racial and ethnic groups, and solving interpersonal problems in the job function or member conflicts with the TC structure. Although the encounter format is adapted to accomplish particular aims, the specific *goal* remains the same—raising awareness of behaviors and attitudes as the initial step in the change process.

RULES AND ELEMENTS OF THE ENCOUNTER

Unlike the other TC groups, confrontation is a distinctive element of the encounter group. This involves prominent use of the provocative tools, more freewheeling member interaction, and more intense expression of emotions, both positive and negative. Thus, the general guidelines for assuring physical and psychological safety (e.g. the cardinal rules) and group confidentiality in all groups are amplified to address the special dynamics of the encounter groups (see Table 18-1).

The rationale for the rules and elements of the TC is briefly discussed in terms of the TC perspective and approach. Encounter groups in the TC are lively, emotionally charged sessions. Thus the rules to maintain order aim to minimize unnecessary movement or physical activity that may distract the focus of the encounter; they also discourage members from avoiding the intensity of the session.

TABLE 18-1. Rules and Elements of the Encounter

Rules maintaining safety and order—to prohibit or discourage the following:
- Explicit or implicit threats such as getting out of the chair during a confrontation
- Deliberate and collective verbal attacks on one member ("rat packing")
- Coming to the aid of a confronted member by interrupting the encounter; explaining, rationalizing, or otherwise defending the member ("red crossing")—in a proper encounter, the individual must engage the process without assistance in order to obtain the maximum benefits
- Name-calling; labeling; or stereotypic references to race, ethnicity, culture, gender, or family members
- Leaving the room without group permission, eating, drinking
- Walking around, except when seating is changed to maximize the number of face-to-face confrontations
- Irrelevant conversations
- Inappropriate dress such as clothing that projects a seductive or aggressive image
- Inadequate grooming such as being unclean or unshaven, which projects an image of disrespect or disregard for the community

Key elements enhancing the encounter
- *Natural language*
  All verbal expression is permitted, with those noted exceptions concerning safety and cultural pejoratives.
- *No authorities*
  Encounters are peer-conducted groups—facilitators, residents, or staff have no decision-making authority in the group process. Imposing such authority in the encounter forum impedes the spontaneity of the self-help process and disempowers the peers from confronting and resolving issues.
- *Total honesty and responsible concern*
  These are prerequisites for effective group process and for recovery in general. In reality these are ideal behaviors that must evolve over time; thus, rather than rules they are instructions, demanding repetition until they are routinely practiced.

The encounter group is pre-eminently a verbal forum employing everyday personal and social vernacular. Participants can verbalize in any way that allows honest personal disclosure and reaction, which often means the language of emotionality or sometimes the common idiom of the street.

Curse words may be permitted provided they are not incessantly repeated or deliberately pejorative. It is not uncommon to hear expletives such as "stupid," "asshole," "mother-f.... fool," or "sick." Although sounding offensive to the unfamiliar observer, these utterances are acceptable insofar as they stimulate emotional expression and otherwise further the group process toward its basic goal of raising awareness.

The choice of specific expletives, however, addresses only what is changeable about the individual, such as attitudes, faulty thinking, and negative behavior. The value of sharp language is to focus attention leading to awareness, not only through provocation, but through dramatization and humor. Beyond these objectives, however, such language is unproductive and sometimes harmful.

The raw vernacular of some encounter sessions has sometimes given rise to description of these groups as brutish or even dangerous. However, this is a misleading characterization of only one phase of the encounter, the confrontation. When a fully effective encounter unfolds through all of its phases, the language ranges widely, reflecting the rich variety of emotional change in individuals and in the group.

Cultural and gender *pejoratives* are not permitted. These are not only provocative but are fundamentally counter to the basic TC teachings concerning recovery and right living. Namely, regardless of cultural, demographic, and social background, the similarities among those struggling to change far outweigh their differences.

"Confront behaviors not people" is the overarching safety guideline of the encounter. Statements that denigrate the person are discouraged (e.g., "You're no good inside, you're evil"). In the TC view, the "inner" person must be treated with respect regardless of the negativity of his or her behavior and attitudes, in the past or present. This rule permits appropriate confrontation and criticism of observable behaviors and attitudes but still protects the individual's sense of self. It also reinforces a basic practice in the TC to foster positive self-regard. During the heat of the exchange in encounters, however, this distinction between behavior and the person could be blurred and must be re-clarified by facilitators and group members.

Breaking the rules of the encounter leads to the invoking of *sanctions*. These depend upon the type, frequency, and severity of the infraction. For example, threats of violence may result in immediate ejection from the group or if these have been frequent, expulsion from the program. Less severe departures from the guidelines are also addressed differently, particularly depending upon the stage in treatment of the participants. Actions may be mild, such as interruption by the facilitator or by the group followed by reminders or re-instruction as to the guidelines. Usually the peer strength of the group itself spontaneously invokes corrective actions. Indeed, a clear marker of the progress of members is the group's ability to keep itself safe and on track in the encounter process.

Infractions are expected to occur, as they usually reflect individual clinical issues. Thus, the action taken may be designed to clarify a problem to be addressed by the individual. Repeated infractions by individuals may lead to a later encounter for their noncompliant group behavior. Sometimes special encounters may be scheduled to deal specifically with pejorative attitudes of several individuals concerning gender or racial–ethnic prejudice, stereotyping, etc. Departures from the rules also reveal the TC-experience level among participants. Encounter experience generally improves with time in treatment, assisted by special tutorials on encounter skills.

THE ENCOUNTER FORMAT

All encounter groups in the TC are similar in their preparation, structure, and process. This and the next section detail them through the illustration of a prototypical group termed the "slip" or "floor" encounter. This group meets regularly at least three times weekly and represents the mainstay of group process in the TC.

The slip encounter is for all residents in primary treatment, but it is specifically directed to those of the junior and intermediate levels (1–9 months in treatment). However, the composition of the encounter groups includes senior residents (9–12 months) and re-entry candidates (13–24 months), who provide strength and experience to assist in facilitating the process. The residents themselves conduct the slip encounters. Junior staff and selected senior residents serve as group facilitators. The latter are viewed as "sophisticated" encounter players. Slip encounters are so termed because they require residents to write down on a slip of paper their need to talk to another resident in the group encounter setting.

The key to a successful encounter is *preparation.* In the slip encounter, staff meet with selected senior residents (encounter masters), who under staff supervision have the responsibility of preparing and coordinating each particular encounter. The steps in the preparation are as follows:

1. *Dropping a slip.* The content of an encounter is provided by the residents in the facility. In the slip encounter, residents complete a standard slip form consisting of their name, the person to whom they wish to speak at the encounter, and the main reason for speaking to that person. Typical reasons involve feelings or concerns about another resident's behavior or attitude. The reason is explained in

brief (less than ten words) and explicit terms. This is important, as the severity and clarity of the reason often determines its priority in being selected for the encounter. Any resident may complete a slip and drop it into the slip box to be scheduled for encounters on the same or another night, but all residents are encouraged to regularly drop slips.

2. *Planning.* Careful planning is critical to the success of encounter groups. In the slip encounter, staff together with encounter masters review the slips for interpersonal issues, range of issues, peer composition, and desired outcomes. To assure that slips will be honored within the time frame of the encounter they are consolidated by theme or similarities. Thus, multiple slips on one particular person can be stacked and reviewed for similarity. Additional criteria in slip selection are those of severity and clarity.

3. *Group assignment.* In the slip encounter, staff and associates assign 10–13 people to a particular encounter group (in small facilities, the group may consist of all residents). The chosen group reflects slip themes as well as membership, balanced by age, gender, race–ethnicity, and time in program. Careful selection and balance represent guiding considerations in the formation of encounter groups.

4. *The circle.* Participants in the encounter sit in a circle of chairs. Chairs should not be so comfortable that individuals become relaxed or lax in their body positions. A successful encounter depends upon a certain amount of tension, which is weakened or prevented by seating that is too comfortable. The actual circle may consist of a prearranged seating plan that can facilitate the clinical group process. For example, staff and associates will place themselves in a triangular formation in the circle. This permits continued surveillance of the participation of every member, whose cross-interactions can occur and be facilitated at the same time.

5. *Confrontation positions.* Confronters should essentially be opposite to those who will be confronted. Physical proximity tends to inhibit the flow and intensity of the confrontation. Additionally, in the slip encounter groups, two individuals who have slips with similar issues could be placed together and across from the resident to increase the impact of the confrontation. Those of the same race or ethnic backgrounds are placed opposite one another to both reduce tendencies toward mutual support and increase the visual field for observing one another's reactions. Often members of the same ethnic subgroups can readily detect each other's defenses through culturally conditioned gestures and postures. The basic composition of 13

participants includes 5 residents to be confronted, 2 senior and 5 other residents from the community, and a facilitator.

6. *Rotating the groups.* The participant composition of all encounters is continually changed primarily to assure that all residents of the facility have the opportunity to confront each other in these settings. By changing the composition, the larger community is strengthened as no single group or subgroup can become exclusive. Changes in the composition of participants, thus, counter tendencies for residents to mutually protect themselves through covert or overt agreements ("contracts"). Such dyadic relationships tend to soften confrontation between the members of these relationships. Also a consensus of observations across different groups about the behavior of a resident tends to increase acceptance of the validity of these observations by the resident.

THE ENCOUNTER PROCESS

An encounter unfolds as a process characterized in terms of four phases: the confrontation, the conversation, the closure, and the socializing phase. The first three overlap and reflect a continuous interchange between the individual and the group toward the goal of awareness and change. The last is a continuation of the closure phase but in an informal format.[50]

Confrontation Phase

The facilitator briefly reviews the rules of the encounter. The confrontation may then commence spontaneously or the facilitator may encourage particular members to speak referring to the contents of a slip. However, self-starting by the members is viewed as clinically sound in terms of empowering the peer groups.

Any resident may be confronted on any aspect of behavior or attitude. The confrontation ("indictment") is often presented by the resident dropping the slip, but others are expected to contribute their observations, expressions, and reactions toward marshalling the evidence for the

---

[50] The presentation of the encounter as a phased process is the author's attempt to provide a practical basis for training in this group form. It is particularly relevant for larger TCs serving many clients. Pragmatically, there is a need to widen the impact on more residents by shortening the encounter time for each resident. A phased format can increase the efficient use of the encounter.

validity of the confrontation.[51] The objective of the initial phase of the encounter is to have the encountered member hear and understand the confrontation. Thus, this phase focuses upon the presentation of the material or "data" to a particular member.

The *material* of the confrontation consists of the peers' observations and experiences of the confronted member's attitudes or behaviors toward himself or herself, the environment, or other people. In accordance with the rules of group process, unchangeable characteristics (e.g., age, race, gender, body features, or disabilities) are not subject to encounter. Focus is upon current or recent behavior and attitudes and how these affect others. References to past history of negative behaviors or resentments are limited. These may be acceptable only if they usefully highlight current patterns that must be changed. Some encounters are planned to address interpersonal conflicts that require resolution of past resentments. In these, as in all encounters, however, the confrontation may review the observations and issues of the past to address the conflict in the present.

The "data" are presented by one key member who is quickly joined by several peers addressing the same characteristic of the individual. A theme or pattern generally emerges that is elaborated upon by the group. Typical themes are sloppiness in habits, constant negative attitudes about treatment, keeping to oneself, and abusive or insensitive treatment of others. Thus, collective peer reactions form the basis of an effective confrontation and draw a picture of the confronted person's behavior and attitudes, which must be attended to by that individual.

The group urges the resident to hear the confrontation before responding. Thereafter, however, the resident is expected to *defend* himself or herself in any possible way within the rules of the encounter. Resistance is more likely early in the confrontation phase, reflecting the individual's reluctance to hear, much less accept the material presented. Highly emotional reactions, such as anger and hurt, or others like humor, indifference, or submissiveness are not unusual as defenses. Rationalizations as rejoinders to specific statements of the confrontation are common, but the group limits these until the confrontation is fully understood. The resident's fixation on a specific incident or observation may be a defense in that it prevents the resident from hearing or

---

[51] Historically, the term "indictment" was employed to describe the confrontation and is still used in some TCs. It is not adapted here since it clearly connotes a trial, wrongdoing, or guilt and does not reflect all varieties of behavior addressed in the confrontation. However, indictment may aptly describe some confrontations involving behaviors that injure individuals and threaten the integrity of the community, such as dishonesty or violation of cardinal rules and house rules (violence, drug use, sexual acting out, stealing, subgroup collusion).

acknowledging the main theme of the confrontation. The individual may also resist the confrontation through silence and withdrawal.

The confrontation makes use of *mixed tools,* e.g., humor, engrossment, and carom shots, which reduce resistance to listening and hearing the confrontation, while *provocative tools,* e.g., anger and hostility, may be elicited for defiant or persistent resistance (for tool definitions see chapter 17). In the initial phase of the encounter, these tools focus the attention of all participants on the confrontation; they energize the verbal exchange and induce general emotionality toward evoking expression of particular feelings. The use of all tools, especially the provocative ones, must always be accompanied by a demonstration of responsible concern.

Resistances and defenses, however, may not necessarily represent avoidance or rejection of what the group is saying. Rather, these could be genuine attempts to make sense of the confrontation. They may also reflect the individual's level of comprehension in understanding the communication, his or her honest belief in not grasping what the group is talking about, or simply the need for the member to assert himself or herself against group pressure. Thus, the individual asserting legitimate defenses weakens tendencies toward passivity. For group process these defenses make for more cogent confrontations. For example, a resident who assertively argues against the validity of certain observations compels the group to further clarify its charge through more data or more clearly expressed concerns. Such exchanges maintain the fidelity of the encounter process, the goal of which is to teach individuals to hear, acknowledge, and accept the group's valid reactions to their behavior and attitudes.

Conversation Phase

The confrontation phase is essentially passed when the member has heard and understands the data presented. Thus, the energy and interaction of the initial phase subsides once the group has achieved clarity in presenting the material and the member ceases to defend or resist hearing the confrontation. Nevertheless, the exchange continues because the member may not accept the validity of the confrontation. Understanding the confrontation is not equivalent to acceptance of the confrontation.

Cued by the member's understanding of the confrontation, there is usually a change in emphasis from presenting the specific data toward facilitating a genuine acceptance of the confrontation by the member. This involves weakening the intellectual resistance to honestly deal with the presented data and lessening the emotional defenses toward full personal disclosure. Thus, the conversation phase involves more quiet give-and-take, centered on the group's efforts to elicit personal disclosure from the member. Toward this objective the group encourages the member to (a) *focus* on the behavior and attitudes of the confrontation and not on other issues or problems; and (b) *relate honestly* by talking about his or her own true thoughts and experiences. The emphasis is upon the self, in first person, away from emotional detachment or intellectual abstraction and on expressing feelings as well as thoughts associated with the confrontation.

Generally, the depth of the conversational level is related not only to the validity of the encounter content but to the member's time in program. More experienced members will relate honestly to the confrontation more readily and disclose more feelings and insight.

The typical *defense* in the conversation phase against acceptance of the confrontational problem is rationalization, or making excuses for behavior. Of special note is a paradoxical defense, that of immediate submission to the validity of the confrontation (i.e., "quick cop"). This protects the member from fully feeling the impact of the confrontation, which impedes authentic acceptance and change. Silence may also appear late in the conversation phase as resistance or defense against experiencing painful feelings associated with the confrontational problem.

The main *tools* in the conversation phase are evocative, although persistent defenses may stimulate mixed tools (e.g., carom shots, gossip). However, to move the individual toward acceptance of the validity of the confrontation, the evocative tools are most effective (e.g., identification, compassion, empathy). Reconfrontation, that is, re-presenting the same observations and reactions of the group, is irrelevant in the conversation phase, and it may paradoxically strengthen the member's resistance and defenses of the earlier phase. Once accepted the conversation deepens to explore the individual's view of the issues and the reasons for his or her rationales and defenses. The group encourages the individual's expression of feelings concerning past or present.

Closure

The third phase of the encounter is evident when the member displays some level of acceptance and understanding of the confrontation and asks for help concerning personal change. Thus, the main objective of the closure is to provide the member with *feedback,* suggestions, and support for making a specific change in the confronted behavior and attitudes. Even in cases where the member remains essentially unmoved as to the confrontation, the group makes suggestions as to how the member can think about what was said and what aspects of the confrontation can be accepted.

The characteristics and specific suggestions of the closure phase emphasize the supportive assistance of the group. The member is encouraged to *make a commitment* to change: to state his or her honest intention to try to change the behavior or attitudes discussed. Toward this end, the member asks for and receives helpful suggestions as to how to change. This feedback emerges from similar experiences of the individual group members, who refer to their own efforts to change as encouraging examples of trial and error learning. To illustrate the importance of responsible concern, the key member who initiated the confrontation offers personal assistance and specific suggestions. Group sharing in the closure phase balances the impact of the confrontational phase of the encounter by highlighting the parity of all members in the group.

The suggestions offered are concrete actions or *specific assignments* (e.g., "talk to three people each day for a week about how you are feeling," "identify someone to monitor your room care"). Acceptance of these suggestions from peers indicates a positive attitude and commitment toward change. Assignments are not disciplinary contracts ("learning experiences") because peers have no formal management authority; more importantly, the encounter group process cannot be undermined by any perception of retributive or punitive outcomes.[52]

The *tools* of the closure phase are supportive words and actions such as affirmation, social warmth, and corrective perceptions. The effective peer encounter group is one that balances its confrontational and supportive elements.

Finally, in closure, the encounter process itself gets reaffirmed regardless of its difficulty and intensity. Peers give the message to confronted members that they are respected for engaging in the process. This is usually expressed in words of reassurance. Nonverbal forms of reaching out, such as hugging, are encouraged to heal or neutralize any painful feelings. These physical expressions of contact can occur after each individual encounter or at the end of the entire encounter session. As a collective ritual they symbolize the group's acceptance of the individual and remind all members that they are in a common struggle to change.

---

[52] The necessity for balance between responsible concern and confrontation to produce positive therapeutic effects has been emphasized since the first generation of TCs (e.g., Casriel, 1966; Casriel & Amen, 1971; Glasser, 1965; Ottenberg, 1978; Rogers 1970; Sugarman, 1974; Yablonsky, 1989).

The Social Phase

Immediately following closure, a thirty to forty-five minute period is allocated for socializing with coffee and snacks in a common lounge area involving all of the participants of the encounter. As in all activities in the TC, residents have the responsibility for setting up the social hour and for cleaning up afterwards, an assignment given to junior peers.

The importance of this social phase cannot be overemphasized, for it utilizes community to continue the closure phase of the encounter process beyond the formal group. In a relaxed and informal environment, conversations about the group may continue in softer tones, often leading to further resolution. Rather than issues, however, it is the people who are attended to in various ways. Although brief, this period offers specific benefits for the community and the individual.

The warmth and friendliness of these social conversations often correct any misperceived unfriendliness of the encounter through mutual clarification of points and contrasting attitudes. This "patching up" is done through expressions of support, consolation, humor, and affection, particularly toward residents who might have experienced hurt or discomfort during the confrontation. Mutual congratulations are offered either for staying in the process, giving feedback, or simply participating. Shared expressions such as "I've been through it like you" validate the encounter experiences. The individual can appreciate the benefits of the encounter when the discomforts are minimized through the communal and friendly interactions that follow. Finally, the social hour is also a ritual that reinforces the perception of community. It reunites all the participants after a period of group struggle.

Facilitators and staff may attempt further resolution and offer encouragement and support to encountered residents if necessary. Assessing how these residents "handle" the encounter is essential for planning counseling and later encounters.

Facilitators and staff also use the social hour to *assess* the clinical status of the participants even among those not encountered. Emotional expressions, energy level, and participation in the social hour itself are typical status indicators.

Evaluating the Encounter: Outcomes and Follow-Up

When is a particular encounter over? When does the group move on to the next person? Ideally, each encounter accomplishes its general purpose of strengthening group cohesion and its goals for specific individuals. In reality, outcomes vary depending upon a number of factors, e.g., the specific issues addressed, the proper use of the encounter, and the experience of the facilitators and participants in the encounter process.

Optimal outcomes reflect the degree to which the goal of each phase is achieved. For example, the member understands and accepts the validity of the confrontation, talks about the issues in self-disclosing terms, makes a commitment to change through concrete motions, and asks for the group's assistance in how to change.

Nonoptimal outcomes may include the resident's rejection of the confrontation or failure to achieve insight or disclose emotions. Moreover, individuals may display feelings but no insight, or obtain intellectual understanding but reveal no expression of feelings.

Although the immediate outcome of an encounter may not be optimal, it can still be acceptable. The minimal aim of the encounter is to *raise awareness*. Insight and emotional expression are desirable but secondary aims of the particular encounter. Thus, the group can agree to end an encounter if at the least the individual will consider the validity of the encounter (i.e., "gives it the barest"). Or, the group can affirm that an outcome is not optimal and defer the individual's issues to the next group. Ignoring such affirmation lowers credibility of the group process itself.

The expectation of obtaining a maximally favorable outcome in a particular encounter must be tempered by an understanding of the broader clinical process. The general guideline in these matters is *one encounter at a time*—each group can facilitate a small change in the individual. These changes mirror the phase objectives of the encounter itself: listening, hearing, awareness, acceptance, exploration (feelings), understanding (insight), and commitment to change. Thus each encounter should be viewed as an opportunity for members to learn these changes in small increments, both directly and vicariously. It is the continual process of change through many encounters that is important rather than the outcome of any specific encounter.

The above point stresses the importance of *follow-up* in evaluating the encounter. As with all interventions the steps taken after the actual encounter are critical to its successful application in the TC community. Staff and residents have the responsibility to monitor the status of the confronted residents in both formal and informal ways. For example, the "resident strength" of the encounter may write up the encounter after the session and then give it to staff for inclusion in the client's folder. The write-up highlights the three phases, focusing on the main theme and criteria for slips, typical resident defenses, outcomes, and any special issues or client's reactions that need to be followed up.

The write-up is discussed in a debriefing session with staff, usually the morning after the encounter. In addition to clinical considerations concerning individuals, group process is reviewed in terms of the quality of the slips, group impasses, and the overall participation level of all members. These assessments are essential to treatment planning for individuals and preparation for later encounters.

THE GENERIC ROLE OF FACILITATORS IN THE ENCOUNTERS

The encounter is fundamentally a *peer-conducted* group, which means the participants themselves manage all phases of the encounter process. However, successful encounters depend on experienced facilitators of group process. Facilitators can be senior peers, staff in training, or junior or senior staff members. Regardless of who facilitates the encounter, however, the primary role of facilitator remains the same—to assure the integrity of the peer-led process. Thus, facilitators encourage the peer leadership qualities that usually emerge in particular members.

Facilitators assist the group process to complete its agenda before, during, and after the encounter session. For example, facilitators help in the preparation of each session, monitor the participants' reactions including all of the members, and ensure that all of the planned encounters are carried out. In the slip encounter, for example, attempts should be made to honor all of the slips. If not, members should be assured that they will have their opportunity in the next session.

Staff Roles in the Encounter

The importance of staff members as facilitators in peer encounters varies with program tradition. For example, in some programs the facilitator is always a staff person; in others, staff only supervises senior resident facilitators while remaining out of the group process itself. In still other programs, staff will elect to facilitate certain encounters for various management or clinical reasons.

When staff persons facilitate peer encounters, however, there are particular considerations concerning their role and function. Senior staff especially are inherently perceived as both a management and clinical authority. Such perceptions could inhibit the spontaneity of the mutual self-help group process. Clinically, for example, staff conclusions or interpretations may be heard as immutable truths that could alter, or influence, the individual process of self-discovery.

Overall, in the peer encounter group, staff adheres to the role of the generic facilitator. As staff, however, they supervise the preparation of the encounter and selection of residents for the group composition and clinical follow-up. Well-trained staff members who are facilitators remain vigilant concerning the potential impact of their role on residents and the group process. They primarily serve as tutors of the encounter, observers of the clinical changes, and facilitators of the peer process.

"Resident Strength" Role in the Encounter

Certain members are selected by staff to serve as *resident strength* (experienced participants) in the encounters. In this role, they model correct encounter behavior. To be selected for resident strength is a significant privilege in the TC; it confers status on these residents and acknowledges their own progress in the program. Their skills in encounter modeling, facilitating the group process, developing write-ups, and participating in debriefing sessions all provide important data as to their own clinical progress. Their roles as peers, however, maintains their position as equal members in the group and thus, they can be confronted by others.

Facilitating the Encounter Process

During the encounter process, facilitators attempt to remain neutral. Although members can confront facilitators during an encounter, facilitators generally do not directly confront any member. Conversely, they avoid giving too much help to those being confronted by peers. Such help tends to disempower the individual member from fully experiencing the intensity of the encounter process. However, facilitators can and should protect the group from abuse, disorder and particularly inefficiency through managing impasses.

The encounter can falter or reach *impasses* for different reasons. Most often these reflect a combination of problems with group behaviors and certain resistant individuals. Ideally, the peer group itself can exercise its own limits and manage the encounter process. However, facilitation is needed when group self-management requires guidance.

Some reasons for impasses usually reflect problems in the preparation of the encounter by the staff, inexperience in encounter skills of the group members or resident strength, and the lack of facilitative skills in the group facilitator. Additionally, however, there are factors relating to the individuals confronted and to the substance of the issues themselves that contribute to impasses in the process.

For example, individuals may differ in their receptivity to engage the encounter. Even experienced members may not be ready to deal with certain sensitive issues against which they resist or persistently defend themselves. Individuals may also differ in their suitability to participate in certain encounters in terms of psychological factors, e.g., tolerance for group pressure, verbal capacity, or psychiatric vulnerability. The group's inability to adjust to these individual differences could lead to collective frustration and eventual impasse.

Impasses in the encounter phase process are evident in the behaviors of the group and individuals confronted. Typically the group displays collective and individual confusion as to the issues, boredom, poor participation, persistent frustration, or excessive use of provocative tools (e.g., hostility, overventilation of emotions, or even verbal abuse). Individuals display intractable resistance, overdefended confrontations, nonengagement, or withdrawal from the encounter. The common indicators of problematic encounters will usually be manifested as unclear and unsatisfactory outcomes.

Facilitators use various strategies to break impasses and keep encounters on course. These actions and words are directed to individuals or the entire group. For example, they *interrupt* or limit excesses in group behaviors. These typically involve overconfrontation, reconfrontation, overindulgence of ventilation, catharsis directed to individuals, and unnecessary ganging-up ("rat packing") on those confronted. They *redirect* groups to address explicit behavior and attitudes that are in the here and now, and they make clear the material or observations of the confrontation. Facilitators also speak to individuals who contribute to impasses, *assisting* them in moving honestly though the phases of the encounter. For example, they address overcompliance, or conversely, persistent resistance or defenses.

Encounters in which members have unrealistic or ambitious expectations of individual change often result in group frustration or individual discouragement. Thus, facilitators maintain a balance between the group pressure and the individual's status throughout the three-phase process. In this effort, they distinguish between group- and content-induced resistance and assess the resident's encounter experience and optimal level of self-awareness.

Experienced facilitators *maintain the integrity* of the encounter format. Keeping the encounter distinct from other formats in the TC assures its effectiveness. The potential for encounters to drift into other modes such as rap sessions, group therapy, or individual counseling can dilute the effects of encounters. For example, an effective encounter that is focused on currently observed behavior and attitudes often leads to spontaneous expression of feelings and insights concerning past experiences. However, exploration into past history should be limited and reserved for probes, marathons, or individual counseling instead.

Finally, facilitators keep encounters on course by *managing the time.* Groups that extend much beyond the planned limits may reflect inadequate preparation or inexperience among the members and facilitator. Often however, it reflects the natural, positive dynamics of the group. In contrast with group impasses, these dynamics reveal the vitality of the encounter process and should not be artificially inhibited. Remaining close to time limits, however, the facilitator can guide the group to comfortable closure, explaining that there will be many more groups to come, that patience is the rule, and that change is step-by-step.

VARIETIES OF ENCOUNTERS

The basic encounter can be adapted for a variety of purposes (see Table 18-2). Depending upon its purpose or group composition, the encounter can be modified in intensity (light to heavy confrontation) and format (no slip or formal confrontation) and the extent of staff involvement as facilitators (less or more). The goal and method is the same for all varieties of encounter groups. In all varieties, the aims of the encounter are to raise awareness toward changing behavior and to elevate self-understanding.

TABLE 18-2.   Varieties of Encounters in the TC

Inner and outer circles ("fishbowls" or "double O's")
> To accommodate a large membership, a gallery of outer circle residents silently observes the inner circle encounter as theater; they may or may not change roles to become participants. Within the active circle, however, the basic rules and guidelines apply.

Department encounters
> Geared to co-workers in the same departments or crews to resolve job performance and interpersonal problems related to work. Facilitated by department heads they may occur regularly, but for short durations.

Table continues

TABLE 18-2. Varieties of Encounters in the TC

Table continued

Walk-in encounters

Simultaneous encounters designed to maximize interactions in the entire facility. These allow residents to talk to people in several encounters by walking from one encounter to another. In these encounters, dialogues can be interchangeable across several groups. Facilitated by a staff (senior/junior), these groups vary in frequency and duration.

Room encounters

Geared to residents who sleep in the same room; meant to resolve performance and interpersonal problems associated with living space. Facilitated by the residents themselves, these encounters vary in frequency and duration.

Peer-level encounters

Geared to residents on the same level (e.g., age or treatment stage); addresses common level-related problems using identification to encourage disclosure and sharing; facilitated by a junior staff member or a senior resident, they occur as needed.

Mock encounters

Simulated encounters used for training staff or new residents in the encounter format. Details of this are provided in the chapter on overview of groups.

Hats-off encounters

Compositions are mixed staff–resident or senior–junior staff. Used for conflict resolution and represent the quintessential democratic forum, in that all formal status and authority in the community are set aside to foster a pure interpersonal encounter without repercussions. Facilitated by the membership itself, these groups meet as needed.

"Trap" encounters

These focus upon uncovering covert negative peer relationships. They are "surprise groups" called without notification to prevent preparation by targeted participants. Issues addressed are sexual acting out, use of drugs, mutual condoning. Facilitated by senior staff, they meet as needed.

Issues encounters

Focus upon specific behavior–attitudes and conflict resolution with respect to race–ethnic or gender issues. They consist of selected residents or the entire facility who discuss interpersonal data concerning these issues as well as instruction as to expected behaviors and attitudes. Facilitated by senior staff selected for the issue, these groups meet as needed.

Special encounters

Geared for unexpected situations that have to be addressed immediately, such as dealing with a person who is thinking of leaving the program. Residents can request this group and choose some of the participants. These are usually intensified encounters that display urgent concern for particular members, compelling them to examine their thinking and behaviors. Facilitated by a junior/senior staff person, these encounters are called as needed.

CONCLUSION

This chapter has detailed the main elements of the prototypical encounter group. The fundamental goal of the encounter is to facilitate behavioral and attitudinal change in the individual. This goal is achieved through a judicious balance of confrontation, support, and instructional feedback. Indeed, how individuals progress as participants in the encounter groups during their tenure in the TC reflects the change process itself. This process is the subject of the chapters in part V.

PART V

The Process of Change

During their stay in the therapeutic community (TC), residents live orderly lives and remain sober and socialized. Many leave and continue to lead drug-free, prosocial lives. What happens in the TC that influences individuals to change their lives? What are these changes and how do they come about? These questions are the subject of the six chapters in this section, which detail the process of change in the TC. Chapters 19–21 partition the whole person into the behavioral and subjective dimensions of individual change. Chapters 22 and 23 depict how individuals change through their interaction with the community. Lifestyle and identity changes are gradually internalized as individuals participate in the roles and activities of the program and immerse themselves in the life of the community. Chapter 24 provides an integrative social and psychological framework of the TC treatment process, reformulated from its perspective, approach, and model.

The volume concludes with chapter 25, which addresses issues of evolutionary change in the TC. It briefly outlines how the basic theory, method, and model can be adapted to retain the unique identity of contemporary TCs—as they move further into the mainstream of human services.

Chapter 19

Individual Change: Behaviors, Cognitions, and Emotions

In the therapeutic community (TC) perspective, changing the whole person unfolds in the continual interaction between the individual and the community. To capture the complexity of the whole person, however, requires a multidimensional description of the same individual over time. The social and psychological characteristics of the individual profiled earlier in the views of the person and disorder provide a snapshot, or static portrait, of the individual in the TC. These same characteristics can be reorganized into dimensions (global descriptors) and domains (related collections of behaviors and attitudes) to draw a dynamic picture of the changing individual.[53]

The present chapter provides this multidimensional picture of social and psychological change in terms of behaviors, cognitions, and emotions. The following two chapters focus upon the experiences and perceptions that are essential to the change process.

Four major dimensions reflect the community's objective view of individual change. The dimensions of *community member* and *socialization* refer to the social development of the individual specifically as a member of the TC community and generally as a prosocial participant in the larger society. The *developmental* and *psychological* dimensions refer to the evolution of the individual as a unique person, in terms of personal growth, personality, and psychological function.

---

[53] The relationship between dimensions, domains, and indicators can also be illustrated in research terms. Indicators are the basic observable behavioral data; domains are particular sets or collections of variables measuring these observations; dimensions are broader scales or metrics. Examples of such scales for measuring progress in TCs are currently available; see Appendix C.

The four dimensions and domains can be assessed qualitatively by staff and peer impression (e.g., the resident shows overall improvement in community status) and quantitatively with ratings along a scale (e.g., resident scores increases in affiliation and role model attributes). The bedrock indicators of these assessments are the specific behaviors and attitudes of individuals observed by others in the daily life of the community.

A multidimensional view is a strategy for describing different aspects of the whole person. In the change process the four dimensions are interrelated, the domains overlap, and some behavioral indicators are common to all. For purposes of clarity, however, the dimensions are separately discussed and accompanied by tables that summarize sample indicators of each domain.

COMMUNITY MEMBER DIMENSION

This dimension refers to the evolution of the individual as a member in the TC community and can be described by the two related domains of *affiliation* and *role model*. Affiliation defines the individual's perceived attachment to the peer community indicated in behaviors and attitudes that reflect ownership. Affiliation and ownership are proprietary terms, referring not to material possessions or property, but concern for and pride in the program and the peer community, often expressed as "my program, my family, my community."

The domain of role model defines the individual member as an example of one who consistently meets the behavioral and attitudinal expectations of the community. Role models literally "walk the walk and talk the talk" of the community's teachings and values.

The two domains, affiliation and role model, are closely related. Those who are affiliated understand the TC perspective and the philosophy of the program, and as role models they transmit and illustrate their understanding by direct example. Table 19-1 illustrates typical indicators under each domain of the community member dimension.

Change in the community member dimension unfolds as individuals become totally immersed, or full participants, in the activities and roles of community life. Thus, evolving as a community member is essential for change in the other dimensions.

TABLE 19-1. Community Member Dimension: Domains and Indicators

DOMAIN 1. AFFILIATION

The individual's attachment to the peer community

Typical indicators:

Understands *community as method*

- Knows the philosophy and perspective of the TC
- Knows how to use the environment
- Uses tools
- Adheres to all rules
- Knows TC language and concepts
- Adheres to TC dress code (no jewelry, simple garments, personal cleanliness)

Expresses ownership (pride in the program)

- Maintains cleanliness and cares for property, furnishings, and program image both interior and exterior
- Volunteers for speaking engagements; conducts tours

DOMAIN 2. ROLE MODEL

The individual member is an example of one who meets the behavioral expectations of the community

Typical indicators:

- Gives "pull-ups" to individuals and to the community
- Uses "acting as if" as a mode of learning
- Displays personal vs. vested status
- Displays responsible concern
- Gives positive feedback to peers
- Seeks and assumes: self-initiates new tasks and areas of responsibility
- Works on self: shows awareness of behavior/attitudes that should change and names a personal strategy for addressing these changes
- Responsible to peers: orientation, buddy, big brother/sister; confronts others behavior
- Engages others in formal and informal settings
- Displays a high energy level in community activities

SOCIALIZATION DIMENSION

For most admissions to TCs a prosocial lifestyle has been rejected, never acquired, or eroded with continued drug use. Thus, the socialization or resocialization of the individual is fundamental to the TC goal of changing lifestyles.

The socialization dimension refers to the evolution of the individual as a prosocial member of the larger society and can be described by three related domains: *social deviancy, habilitation,* and *values of right living.*

Social deviancy describes the extent to which the individual is embedded in, or oriented to, an antisocial lifestyle in his or her conduct, language, values, and social affiliations. Deviancy is most explicit in a history of recent and past criminality (drug and non-drug-related), violence, negative peer (gang) associates, and personal relationships. Deviancy is also implicit in coping strategies such as manipulation, deceptions, and in negative or rebellious attitudes to systems, authority, and conventional lifestyles.

Change in social deviancy through the stages of the program involves a cessation of overt antisocial behaviors, renunciation of antisocial attitudes and values, and dropping of all forms of criminal, drug addict, or street images. These are replaced with prosocial opposites, grounded in absolute honesty.

The domain of habilitation describes the individual as socially potent in terms of educational and marketable skills and as socially effective in terms of social conduct and skills. Many residents in TCs do not possess the literacy, educational, and work skills to earn incomes or effectively negotiate the social system. They also lack the basic behavioral habits and attitudes associated with work readiness, the attitudes and values associated with a willingness to work.

A change in habilitation involves acquisition of prosocial work and study skills particularly in the elements of work readiness. In the TC view, the focus of change is learning or relearning *how* to be workers and students. Habits, attitudes, and values of work are essential for acquiring and maintaining work skills.

Habilitation also refers to effective social conduct, the behaviors and attitudes of civility and manners. Increasing numbers of admissions to TCs lack these basic elements of social intercourse. These skills are not only aesthetically pleasing but provide behavioral signs of order, safety, and predictability in social settings.

The third domain of socialization consists of the TC's values and teachings concerning right living. Changes in this domain are reflected in the extent to which the individual understands, accepts, and practices these values and teachings. The latter are essential in the socialization of the individual into the TC community and to the larger society. Thus, the domain of right living values is viewed as a critical component of "living right," which describes the totality of change in the individual in all dimensions.

Overall, the three domains of socialization describe the individual's repertoire of mainstream social and work skills, attitudes, values, and social conduct. Table 19-2 summarizes the typical indicators under each domain of the socialization dimension.

TABLE 19-2. Socialization Dimension: Domains and Indicators

DOMAIN 1. SOCIAL DEVIANCY

The extent to which the individual is embedded in or oriented to an antisocial lifestyle in their conduct, values, and social affiliations

Typical indicators:

- Cessation of all forms of antisocial behavior particularly violence and intimidation
- Renunciation of attitudes that are rebellious, cynical, or nihilistic
- Cessation of antisocial thinking and deviant coping skills, e.g., exploitation, manipulation, lying, "getting over" ("dope fiend" behavior)
- Dropping negative social "images" (e.g., macho, criminal mask) that convey invulnerability or indifference
- Shows respect for authority, people, and property
- Reveals distance from drug-involved lifestyle, friends, neighborhoods, language, attitudes

DOMAIN 2. HABILITATION

The extent to which the individual is socially potent in terms of educational and marketable skills and is socially effective in terms of social conduct and interpersonal skills

Typical indicators:

Social potency

- Displays positive job and study habits (e.g., punctuality, attendance, dress)
- Reverses poor attitudes to tasks (e.g., negative, cynical); to authority (e.g., rebellious, does not accept criticism); to subordinates (e.g., noncooperative)
- Displays work/study standards (diligence, 100% effort, striving for excellence)
- Work/study readiness and skills

Social effectiveness

- Displays manners (e.g., politeness and respectful speech and tone in all social situations) while dining, greeting peers, staff and visitors (on tours), answering the phones, and talking during seminars; doesn't scream in the lounge; plays radios softly

DOMAIN 3. VALUES

The extent to which the individual understands, accepts, and practices the TC teachings of right living

Typical indicators:

- Honesty
- Self-reliance
- Responsible concern
- Community responsibility
- Work ethic

DEVELOPMENTAL DIMENSION

The developmental dimension refers to the evolution of the individual in terms of personal growth, which can be described in two closely related domains, *maturity* and *responsibility.*

A psychological construct, the developmental dimension remains distinctive in the TC perspective. Immaturity and lack of responsibility are hallmark characteristics that substance abusers themselves view as basic to their other social and emotional problems. Treatment is often described as teaching individuals to "grow up and become responsible"—that is, fostering normative development. Thus, personal growth is an explicit and defining element of recovery and lifestyle and identity change.

The domain of maturity describes the individual in terms of social and emotional behaviors that are age and socially appropriate. The behavioral indicators of maturity are examples of the substance abuser's problems with self-regulation (e.g., controlling impulses, delaying gratification) and social management (e.g., displaying appropriate conduct in relation to staff and authorities, peers and the community).

The domain of responsibility describes individuals in terms of meeting obligations to self and the expectations of others. Responsibility means being responsive to the welfare and concerns of self, peers, and the program. From a developmental perspective, responsibility is a domain of personal growth—that is, learning to be responsible in terms of self-care (e.g., attending to health and cosmetic needs), social care (e.g., maintaining clean room, appropriate dress) and interpersonal care and obligations (e.g., keeping promises to others).

The domain of responsibility also includes the theme of taking responsibility for one's actions, thinking, and emotions. Personal growth is evident when individuals accept their *own* contribution to problems and assume the commitment to change themselves as part of the solution—more generally, when they "own" what they say and do.

Consistency and accountability are related aspects of responsibility. Changes in these are mainly described in terms of obligations in job functions and assuming and completing all chores. Table 19-3 summarizes the domains and typical indicators of the developmental dimension.

TABLE 19-3. Developmental Dimension: Domains and Indicators

DOMAIN 1. MATURITY

The developmental process in the TC involves incremental changes through the stages of treatment, reflecting personal growth—this refers primarily to maturity, that is, growing up

Typical indicators:

- Copes with desires/impulses with judgment and moderation
- Relinquishes the baby and lessens "acting out" conduct
- Handles authority and criticism in positive ways (hearing the concern behind the authority and criticism)
- Conforms to social expectation: relinquishing rebellion, utilizes socially acceptable conduct as a way of asserting individuality, identity, and obtaining satisfaction of one's needs
- Sets short- and long-term goals that are realistic; has patience to carry out each needed step; can understand the time effort and skills needed
- Shows increased tolerance for all varieties of discomfort (frustration, delay of gratification, anger, etc.)
- Displays emotional self-control (can manage impulses and disturbing feelings that could intrude on planned steps)

DOMAIN 2. RESPONSIBILITY

The extent to which the individual displays consistency and accountability concerning obligations and promises in tasks and interpersonal relations

Typical indicators:

- Attends to health and cosmetic needs
- Maintains clean room, appropriate dress
- Keeps promises to others
- Admits faults, minimizes blame on others or external circumstances, and seeks to personally rectify mistakes
- Surrenders patterns of manipulation to avoid the demands in procedure
- Sustains efforts in tasks despite setbacks, interruptions, and distractions
- Provides honest reckoning of how one carries out their obligations
- Monitors the behaviors and attitudes of others and the community

PSYCHOLOGICAL DIMENSION

The psychological dimension views the individual in terms of general mental and emotional functions that are basic to all learning and change. This dimension is comprised of three domains: *cognitive skills, emotional skills,* and *psychological well-being.*

The cognitive skills domain refers to the characteristic patterns of thinking of the substance abuser in terms of awareness, problem solving, and decision making. The indicators of changes in the cognitive domain center on the theme of recognition and modification of faulty patterns of thinking that lead to negative behaviors. These include individuals' general awareness of themselves in the social and physical environment, dropping their characteristic defenses toward seeing themselves, and acquiring insight—an understanding of the internal and external conditions that influence their behaviors.

Cognitive skills also include (a) reality assessment, the accurate appraisal of self, others, and circumstances in terms of "how they really are;" (b) judgment and consequential thinking in terms of recognizing and assessing outcomes of actions before they are taken; and (c) problem solving and decision making, which includes means-ends thinking and identifying alternatives or making choices in courses of action.

The emotional skills domain refers to common characteristics of communication and management of feeling states. Changes in the emotional domain center on the theme of managing affective states. These include tolerance, the allowance of feeling states without acting out in self-defeating or destructive ways, and control, the restraint or interruption of impulsive emotional expression.

Emotional skills also include identification or the recognition and accurate naming of feeling states; communication, which is the appropriate verbal and nonverbal expression of feelings to self and others; and understanding how one's feelings, behavior, and thinking are interrelated.

The third psychological domain of well-being refers to the overall mental and emotional health of the individual. Residents are troubled when they enter treatment, evident in a variety of physical, emotional, and mental complaints. These typically consist of symptoms of anxiety and depression, somatic aches and pains, which can be real or imagined, and mood-related disturbance, particularly dysphoria and anhedonia. These signs and symptoms may reflect psychopharmacological effects of drug use, the persistent disorder of residents' lifestyle, or chronic long-standing psychological disturbance. Regardless of their sources, however, they are expected to decrease or improve as an integral part of change in the whole person. Table 19-4 summarizes typical indicators of the three domains of the psychological dimension.

TABLE 19-4. Psychological Dimension: Domains and Indicators

DOMAIN 1. COGNITIVE SKILLS
The individual in terms of his/her learning how to be aware, think realistically, problem solve, and use judgment
Typical indicators:
Awareness
- Can assess the impact of other people's behavior on self
- Can assess the impact of self-behavior and attitudes on others
- Can assess the status of the physical environment

Insight
- Identifies external triggers to negative thinking, acting out, and drug use
- Identifies internal triggers to negative thinking, feelings, etc., acting out, and drug use
- Understands current feelings/behaviors/thinking in relation to past conditions, event, relationships

Defenses
- Reduction in use of excuses and typical defenses of denial, rationalization, projection, externalization, and somatization
- Dropping of images

Reality
- Sees events, people, and self as they actually are and has a willingness to confront these rather than avoid or escape
- Shows reality by checking with others to distinguish between
  -feelings and facts
  -thoughts and deeds
  -wishes, wants, and needs
  -illusion, disillusion, and disappointment
- Displays accurate self-appraisal in terms of resources and aspirations
- Puts private thoughts into words to test their reality

Judgment
- Considers information and the long- and short-term consequences of various actions
- Reviews alternatives in making decisions
- Checks personal judgment with others
- Separates emotions from thinking in decision making

Receptivity
- Reacts to confrontations, messages, and feedback without bolting or withdrawal
- Displays attention, listening behavior, and hearing of messages
- Considers message; as evident in questions and debate

Table continues

TABLE 19-4. Psychological Dimension: Domains and Indicators

Table continued

DOMAIN 2. EMOTIONAL SKILLS
This domain describes the individual in terms of his/her learning to identify, manage, and appropriately communicate emotions
Typical indicators:
  Emotional display and understanding
  - Reveals a range of emotional states
  - Changes from low levels of display, e.g. indifference, denial, withdrawal, to higher intensity levels (e.g., catharsis, ventilation)
  - Properly labels their own and others' feelings/experiences
  - Displays appropriate behavioral expressions of emotions that are acceptable, relieving, and effective (e.g., sharing, confronting)
  - Can identify triggers or determinants of affective experiences, and eventually can trace the situational, cognitive-emotional relations
  Communication
  - Renunciation of violence—"putting it into words rather than deeds"
  - For the high verbal—"putting into deeds rather than words"
  - Displays affective expression—uses emotional words and nonverbal gestures, reflecting honestly felt experience
  - Interpersonal—speaks to others directly and provides honest reactions rather than interpretations or false dialogue
  - Display guilts: disclosure, confession, and making amends
  - Receives the affective expressions of others openly

DOMAIN 3. PSYCHOLOGICAL WELL-BEING
This domain consists of the familiar signs, symptoms, and complaints associated with mental health
Typical indicators (reductions in the following):
  - Dysphoria
  - Anhedonia
  - Anxiety
  - Depression
  - Hostility/anger
  - Somatic aches and pains

INTERRELATED DIMENSIONAL CHANGE

Rather than discrete, bounded descriptions of the individual, dimensions, domains, and indicators are interrelated and interactive in several ways. Behavioral indicators may be *common* to several dimensions. For example, speaking disrespectfully to staff may be a behavioral indicator of the socialization and developmental dimensions. However, it is the collection of behavioral indicators in related domains that captures change in particular dimension. For example, behavioral changes in both the role model and affiliation domains reflect an overall improvement in the dimension of community member.

Changes in one dimension may be *associated* with changes in other dimensions. For example, cessation of rebelliousness and respect for authority are behavioral indicators of socialization. These may be correlated with improved tolerance levels or delay of gratification, which are indicators of maturity. Changes in civility and manners in the domain of habilitation (socialization dimension) may also be associated with increases in affiliation (community member dimension) indicating that the individual is conforming—that is, behaving as expected in order to sustain peer acceptance.

Dimensions may also be *interactive*, mutually influential, in that changes in the domain of one dimension may directly facilitate or accelerate change in the domains of other dimensions. For example, role models (in the community member dimension) are expected to display personal growth, exemplified by managing impulses (developmental dimension). Thus, in striving to be role models, residents must actively work on their maturity.

Similarly, skills such as consequential thinking or problem solving (cognitive domain) require some degree of self-regulation, such as impulse control and delay of gratification (maturity domain). General awareness, meanwhile, which is a basic skill in the psychological dimension, is also a prerequisite for changes in virtually all of the other dimensions.

INDIVIDUAL DIFFERENCES AND DIMENSIONAL CHANGE

Not all residents start at the same place on a dimension, nor do they progress in a uniform way. Although members are expected to arrive at certain points in the treatment process, individual rates of change vary.

A dimensional view of change that is broader than the concrete behavioral indicators is important for understanding individual differences. For example, two residents fail to carry out a staff instruction. For one, the behavior illustrates a pattern of insubordination and rebellion. For the other, it is a sign of cognitive deficit or fear of failure. In this case, the same "negative behavior" could lead to the same community response, such as a disciplinary sanction, but yield different and unintended results, such as premature dropout.

A dimensional view of change, therefore, clarifies differences across individuals particularly in their potential for change and in their rates of change. It assists in the assessment of individual limits in behavioral resources, identifies small signs of progress (e.g., positive change may occur on some but not all indicators of a domain), and permits some flexibility in intervention strategies.

However, individual differences do not necessarily call for special preference, unique treatment strategies, or even extra attention. Rather, they underscore the need for program flexibility to make the messages of recovery relevant for individuals at different points in the change process. Individual differences can be accommodated when programs focus upon the *fact* of change rather than the rate of change and particularly upon the individual's willingness to continue in the process.

CONCLUSION

This chapter presented a multidimensional view of the whole person to describe the individual in the change process. The social and psychological profile of the resident is reformulated into four interrelated dimensions, community member, socialization, developmental, and psychological. Each illustrates typical indicators of individual change in terms of objective behaviors, cognitions, and emotions. Changing the "whole person," however, includes how individuals perceive and experience the program, the treatment, and themselves in the process. These subjective areas of individual change are explored in the next two chapters.

Chapter 20

Individual Change: Essential Experiences

In the recovery perspective of the therapeutic community (TC), lifestyle and identity changes reflect an integration of behaviors, experiences, and perceptions. Indeed, enduring change in the individual depends upon this integration. Individuals must actively engage in the behaviors to be changed, they must feel the feelings associated with this engagement, and they must understand the meaning or value of the change in order to see themselves, others, and the world differently.

In the community milieu of the TC, individuals continually display observable behaviors or actions, words, and gestures that indirectly reflect their "inner" life to others. However, the change process is directly understood by the participants through their experiences and perceptions, primarily revealed by what they think and say to themselves and others. These experiences and perceptions are described separately in this and the following chapter for purposes of illuminating their distinctive significance in the change process.

CLASSIFICATION OF ESSENTIAL EXPERIENCES

Obviously, experiences can occur on a moment to moment basis leading to an endless and not useful listing of such events. The qualifier term essential underscores those particular experiences that staff, residents, and observers agree are necessary for the individual to remain in and benefit from the treatment process. These essential experiences can be conceptualized under three broad themes: *emotional healing, social relatedness and caring,* and *subjective learning* (see Table 20-1). Though interrelated, each of these themes is separately discussed.[54]

TABLE 20-1. Essential Experiences in the TC Process

EMOTIONAL HEALING

Emotional healing refers to moderating the various physical, psychological, and social pains that residents experience in their lives directly or indirectly relating to their substance use.

Nurturance-sustenance

These assure the basic provisions of daily maintenance: three meals, housing, clothing, cosmetic accessories, as well as medical, dental, and various social and legal advocacy services. Nurturant experiences provide relief from the circumstantial pressures, distress, and uncertainties that can pull individuals out of treatment.

Physical safety

Maintaining the safety of the social environment is essential for sustaining psychological safety in the change process. The code of the TC is collective security, managed by the community itself and providing relief from common fears and anxieties associated with physical safety.

Psychological safety

For most residents in the TC, such experiences relieve covert, but long-standing intrapersonal and interpersonal fears. The essential experiences reflecting psychological safety are blind faith, trust, being understood, and being accepted by others.

SOCIAL RELATEDNESS AND CARING

The past social relationships of residents in TCs are characterized by personal isolation or attachments with others that are unhealthy or frankly self-destructive. The social relatedness experiences that are essential to recovery include identification, empathy, and bonding.

SUBJECTIVE LEARNING

These are experiences associated with various positive and negative consequences during the social learning process. These center on the theme of self-efficacy and self-esteem.

This table is an adaptation of material from "Therapeutic Communities for Addictions: A Theoretical Framework," by G. De Leon, 1995, *International Journal of the Addictions, 30* (12), p. 1623. Copyright 1995 by Marcel Dekker, Inc. Reprinted with permission.

---

[54] Several of the essential experiences in the present formulation are similar to concepts in the literature. These include "bonding" (Kooyman, 1993) and "self-efficacy" (Bandura, 1977; DiClemente, 1986). Bell emphasizes the concept of "connectedness" and its relationship to trust in the change process (see Bell, 1994).

EMOTIONAL HEALING EXPERIENCES

Healing in the TC refers to palliating or lessening feelings of emotional pain and discomfort in its various forms. Fears, anger, guilts, hurt, confusion, and aloneness are examples of the emotional pains common to residents in TCs. These are associated with specific circumstantial stresses, pressures, threats, and longer-term psychological injuries and with personal and social isolation. For many residents in the TC use of drugs has been the main, if not the only, means of reducing their emotional pains. Thus, without the relief from emotional pains or learning to tolerate these feelings the extent or stability of overall individual change remains limited.

The emotional healing experiences can be further organized into three classes, *nurturance, physical safety,* and *psychological safety.* Although not exhaustive, these summarize the common sources and types of healing that must occur in the TC if individuals are to affiliate with the program, engage, and remain in the change process.

Nurturance–Sustenance

The nurturance experiences are primarily those of relief from the worries, preoccupations, and anxieties associated with circumstantial pressures, distress, and uncertainties concerning immediate day-to-day living. Such relief is found in the meals, housing, as well as medical, dental, various social and legal, and advocacy services provided by the TC. Rather than privileges, these provisions are entitlements, which ask nothing of the individual except participation in the program activities. The basic nurturance experiences are essential for new residents to remain through the first weeks of treatment.

Physical Safety

Being physically safe is an elemental but essential healing experience for those who have characteristically lived with fears and anxieties associated with their drug abuse lifestyle, street life, domestic violence, and sexual and interpersonal abuse. The TC maintains strict adherence to cardinal rules against violence, threats of violence, stealing, sexual abuse and harassment, and drug or alcohol use. The security of the facility itself with respect to daily traffic and unauthorized intrusion is steadfastly maintained. Moreover, enforcing the rules governing personal security is the responsibility of the residents themselves as well as the staff. Thus, the code of the TC, collective security, is managed by the community itself and provides relief from specific fears and anxieties associated with physical safety. The experience of physical safety is essential for developing and maintaining psychological safety in the social environment of the TC.

Psychological Safety

Although many individuals in TCs have lived precariously, rebelliously, or antisocially, they are fearful of facing themselves, other people, the demands of ordinary living, and of change itself. To face these fears, individuals must feel psychologically safe in a community of others that supports and affirms personal risk taking. The essential experiences reflecting psychological safety are *blind faith and trust,* and *understanding and acceptance.* These profound healing experiences relieve covert but long-standing intrapersonal and interpersonal frustration and fears and sustain the individual in the change process itself.

Blind faith and trust

Recovery from addiction (and perhaps from any disorder) often includes an element of faith—personal belief in an eventual positive outcome without necessarily having verified evidence supporting that belief. Blind faith, however, is indicated when individuals "act as if" they have faith, without a clear or firm personal belief in the eventual outcome. Residents in TCs are exhorted by others to "have blind faith," that is, to comply with the demands of the program without question, even if they cannot see, do not understand, or even believe in the benefits in doing so. Emotional risk taking, particularly in the form of personal disclosure, staying with the program, and "acting as if" are constant demands in the process of recovery and continued personal growth.

In the earlier phases of the process, individuals take risks based upon their blind faith in what others say and display. Later in the process individuals take risks based upon their *own* past blind faith experiences that have resulted in no harm and positive personal change—that is, they learn to have blind faith—a self-instruction encouraging them to engage in new behaviors and thinking. Thus, as an initial experience relating to others and later as a learned mode of thinking and acting, blind faith reflects the change process itself.

Trust problems are prominent in the lifestyles of substance abusers. They characteristically mistrust others and themselves. They have also failed to develop or have lost the trust of others. However, recovery in the TC cannot occur without full disclosure of the private self. Thus, residents must have trust, an experience of complete physical and psychological safety, in order to completely reveal themselves to others. Indeed, trust is integral to all of the healing experiences. Individuals allow themselves to be seen, heard, understood, and accepted by others, and bond with them as well when they have some degree of trust.

Within the "fishbowl" environment of TC life, trust develops from repeated experiences of personal safety. Individuals continually reveal vulnerabilities to others and encounter their social, interpersonal fears without hurtful consequences. This requires risk taking, trying new behaviors, exposing basic skill deficits, and disclosing weaknesses, fears, and needs. Eventually residents learn to "trust the process" itself—that is, they feel safe to continue engaging in risks and relying on others, the program regimen, and the course of change even if there is uncertainty concerning outcomes.

As with blind faith, trust becomes a mode of thinking and learned behavior associated with past safe experiences. For example, individuals learn to openly engage new people and situations by instructing themselves to trust their feelings, others, or the process.

Understanding and acceptance

Substance abusers have long-term difficulties with being understood and accepted by others and even more importantly, with understanding and accepting themselves. Frustration and anger most often define their experience of being misunderstood by family, teachers, employees, within relationships, and by authorities. Typically, these experiences serve as cues, excuses, and rationalizations for their drug use and other oppositional or negative behaviors. The individual denies or fails to perceive his or her own contribution to being misunderstood and not accepted by others. The chronic social, financial, family, legal, and health problems associated with their drug use bewilder, exasperate, and eventually wear out the understanding of interested others, confirming the resident's frustration and anger.

Although the experiences of understanding and acceptance are interwoven, the distinctions between the two have clinical significance in the change process. Understanding does not necessarily imply acceptance, and being understood and accepted by others differs from self-understanding and self-acceptance.

Others display understanding when they validate the logic or reasons for the individual's behavior, thinking, or feelings. The experience of being understood by others is one of relief, a decrease in frustration arising from not being attended to, heard, or regarded. The unique feature of the peer community is its capacity to understand the individual member. Based upon their shared characteristics and common life experiences as substance abusers, peers know each other, how they think, and what they feel (e.g., their rationalizations, images, deceptions, and typical defenses of underlying feelings, such as weaknesses, fears, loneliness). They also know how each other reacts to the treatment process, e.g., their skepticism, resistance, and fears about change itself.

Understanding in the peer community is conveyed through paraphrase, reclarification, elaboration, reframing, or identification (telling their own similar story). An example follows:

Group: "Why did you shoot dope when you went out?"

Member: "I thought I could test myself, been here six months and figured that this was my third pass and thought I didn't have to run away from my old friends, that I couldn't stay away forever."

Group: "So you hung out, listened to some music, said you could have one taste, and on and on. That's what we all go through a lot. You're always going to be tested; but you can't risk tests now, its too early, you haven't changed enough."

Behaviors, or misbehaviors, can be understood but still not accepted. Understanding by others does not necessarily imply condoning the negative behavior and false images of the individual. Rather it reveals peer understanding of the function of these behaviors as defenses and images for the individual.

In the TC, acceptance distinguishes between the person and their behavior. Actions and attitudes may be understood, criticized, restrained, and rejected. However, the individual is accepted as a person who is a fallible, suffering, and struggling equal. These are existential features that are shared by all members of the community. Thus, acceptance emphasizes the fundamental differences between what people do and who people are. The community indicates its acceptance of the individual in different ways: (a) inclusion of the individual into all activities, groups, and relationships; (b) equal treatment of members regardless of the individual's social class, race or ethnicity, religion, psychological problems, personal vulnerabilities, or history of past actions; (c) its continual affirmation of support and concern for the individual's struggle to change; and (d) its demonstrative expressions of affection and love. In their own words, residents often define the experience of acceptance in the TC as the first time that others understood and cared for them for who they really are and did not reject them for who they were or what they have done in the past.

Hallmark characteristics of substance abusers in general are their lack of *self-understanding* and *self-acceptance*. Their rationalizations cloud honest examination or expression of their true feelings and thoughts; their history of misbehavior and guilts, both real and imagined, make it difficult for substance abusers to gain a clear perspective of who they are and virtually impossible for them to accept themselves.

Unable to understand or contain their reactions to setbacks in meeting performance expectations invariably leads to total self-rejection. For example, the guilt arising from a lapse to drug use, failed expectations, or broken promises can precipitate a full-blown binge episode of drug use and other negative behaviors, which cascades into total self-rejection. Indeed, their inability to separate their negative thoughts and actions from their true "inner self" defines their poor identity.

The paramount importance of self-understanding and self-acceptance as a goal of recovery is reflected in the words of the residents themselves. Examples of these are underscored in various testimonials and program philosophies: "Coming out of the darkness to face myself," "I avoided confronting myself and am beginning to face reality," "Only by being honest with myself and others...will I begin to grow," "By facing myself and others, I will change my life."

Thus, acquiring self-acceptance is a profound healing experience in the TC. It ameliorates long-standing emotional pains associated with failure, discouragement, and disappointment, and it provides the subjective basis for coping constructively with setbacks and for eventual identity change.

Self-acceptance experiences involve an individual's rejection of the defended self, the false thoughts, feelings, actions, and attitudes associated with various personal and social images (e.g., tough guy, clown, criminal mask), and revealing the authentic self, the honest thoughts and "true" or "real feelings" of the individual without self-criticism, judgment, or castigation. Authentic feelings and thoughts shift the individual's self-perceptions and judgments from "who I have been" to "who I really am."

In the peer community, self-acceptance is facilitated by acceptance from others. The requirements for acceptance by the community are individuals' willingness to confront themselves in terms of how they have behaved, to honestly reveal themselves in terms of their private thoughts and feelings, and to commit themselves to working on personal change in terms of living right. Thus, the peer community rejects the defended and false individual and accepts the undefended, authentic individual who is honestly suffering and struggling to change.

THE SOCIAL RELATEDNESS AND CARING EXPERIENCES

Personal isolation or unhealthy attachments with others characterize the past social relationships of residents in TCs. Their loss of self-control and disordered lifestyles have alienated them from friends and significant others. For many, this alienation precedes their drug problems such that they have marginal identification with any family or community and no real friendships.

In the TC view of recovery, relating to and caring for others are essential for changing the antisocial patterns, social withdrawal, and interpersonal estrangement that characterize the individual's overall disorder. The key social relatedness and caring experiences are *identification, empathy,* and *bonding.* The common element across these experiences is that they all arise from social interaction and reflect the individual's intellectual and emotional relationships with others.

Identification

Residents in the TC experience identification when they perceive similarities between themselves and others in behaviors, feelings, and life experiences and events. The words, behaviors, and life stories of peers and staff have meaning because they give expression to the personal stories of the individual. As with other social relatedness experiences, identification also helps to counter a sense of problem uniqueness and personal and social isolation.

In any community setting, however, identification is limited by individual differences in age, gender, social class, and race–ethnicity or cultural characteristics. For example, adolescent abusers in TCs have difficulty identifying with older addicts. They see their drug use and related life experiences as different: They have not lost their resources; their drug use is still exciting; they are not "tired of the life;" or they do not see themselves as "drug addicts" because they don't use heroin, don't inject drugs, or believe they can stop whenever they really want to.

Nonidentification can also be illustrated in the lifestyle and race–ethnic or subcultural differences that can obscure the fundamental similarities across individual residents. For example, Hispanic or African American substance abusers may not readily relate to the life stories of each other. Some White drug abusers, particularly those who are socially advantaged, may not identify with addicts who are non-White and socially disadvantaged. They cannot easily share the view that their drug use is a disorder of the whole person; more importantly, they cannot see or accept the commonalties in the persons behind the drug use.

It is through the diversity of people living in community, however, that identification becomes a reliable mechanism for self-change. Individuals of different exteriors (such as age, gender, race, or social class) learn and change when they "relate to" their similar interiors—the common perceptions, feelings, and issues of their disorder—and their similar efforts at recovery.

Of the social relatedness experiences, identification is the least complex or difficult to produce. There are no interactive demands placed upon new residents other than paying attention to what other residents are doing or saying about themselves. Witnessing similar others tell their stories initiates a cognitive process of change in the individual. These stories stimulate reflections on their own story, but particularly they engender perceptions of the possibility and hope about personal change.

The self-reflections and perceptions stimulated by identification are key change elements in the change process. Generally, the closer the similarity in life story, the more impactive is the identification experience. But as residents continue in the change process, the basis of their identification broadens beyond those with concrete similarities in life stories to those who role model the work of personal change itself.

Empathy and Compassion

Meaningful change cannot occur without individuals experiencing feelings, their own as well as the feelings of others. Empathy and the related experiences of compassion and sympathy indicate that the individual is affected, or emotionally moved, by the feelings of others. For example, individuals experience empathy when they recognize, understand, affirm, and support peers who reveal their disappointments, hurts, sadness, or loneliness.

Empathy is a particularly important experience for substance abusers, who characteristically have been unaware of, or insensitive to, the effects of their behaviors on others. Their lack of empathy reflects their characteristic self-involvement, avoidance of discomfort, pursuit of gratification, general impulsivity, and poor tolerance for emotions in general and guilts in particular. Thus, they do not readily receive or accept the empathic and compassionate expressions of others, nor do they communicate these experiences to others.

Compassion and sympathy are also expressions of understanding for the suffering of others, usually in gestures of sorrow, pity, or concern. Sympathy is an expression of consolation, or comforting others to alleviate specific painful moments, such as their fear or grief. Sympathy or sorrow for the other person's suffering is also expressed by compassion, which, however, is associated with a particular action or decision. For example, reprimands by peers or disciplinary contracts by staff can be delivered with understanding of members' problems and struggle to learn. Thus, compassion is essential to moderate the confrontations and criticisms of behaviors.

The distinctions between identification, empathy, sympathy, and compassion are frequently evident during group process. For example, tears for the other person's story or feelings is empathic, while tears for the resident's own story heard through the other person is identification. Tears for the specific suffering of the other person is sympathetic. When group members express care and concern in understanding each other's past mistakes, they are showing compassion.[55]

The caring experiences are critical recovery goals for the individual. Empathy and compassion (as well as sympathy) are the emotional domains of social relatedness through which the individual gains deeper self-understanding and acceptance. The awareness of and sensitivity to the feelings of others stimulates the individual's awareness of his or her own feelings. The expression of caring *for* others facilitates caring feelings for oneself.

Although socially related, the caring experiences are profoundly healing for the individual, himself or herself. They dissolve addicts' characteristic objectification of or indifference to other people that has

---

[55] Precise definitions of empathy are lacking in the psychological literature. However, there is general agreement on the two aspects of empathy: affective, in that a person feels what another is feeling; and cognitive, in that a person understands what another person is feeling and why. Research in developmental psychology points to both genetic and social learning influences in the evolution of empathy (American Psychological Association, 1997).

immunized them from experiencing the social and interpersonal consequences of their behaviors. They correct or counter the long-term effects of historical injuries and early deprivations, and they provide felt evidence for and optimism about personal change.

The caring experiences are essential mechanisms in the change process itself. Learning to share feelings reduces personal isolation and reinforces affiliation with the peer community, which fosters continued engagement in the process. These experiences are also necessary elements of community as method. Resident's past stories are marked by negative themes, for example, hurting others and themselves or repeated performance failures. These negative themes must be confronted by peers, often in judgmental tones, for purposes of raising awareness, exposing guilts, or breaking down negative patterns of behavior and thinking. Thus, in the demanding interactions of the self-help process, the expressions of caring are moderating influences, which balance the elements of challenge, criticism, and confrontation.

Bonding

The bonding histories of substance abusers in TCs are varied and are a special aspect of their problems with relationships in general. For some, there is little evidence of any meaningful or enduring attachment to other persons. As a result they are personally isolated, socially distant, and not directly influenced by others. For others, bonding has primarily involved negative attachments.

TABLE 20-2.   Some Community Features that Promote Bonding

Dissolution of defenses and images

Results from community demands of "being oneself," which for many addicts involves dropping masks, e.g., masculine pride or criminality. These demands expose the individual to intense, emotional experiences that have not often been experienced in the past.

Emotional vulnerability

Occurs with the spontaneous experience of emotions and feelings, such as fear, hurt, weakness, despair. These evoke affection, reassurance, encouragement, and friendships.

Mutual risk taking

Produces bonding effects that are similar to those observed in adventure escapades or wilderness ventures. In experiencing risk with others, new powerful feelings are associated with challenge, self-discovery, and self-efficacy. These may occur in the everyday groups in the TC or on special occasions and settings such as retreats or marathons.

Within the TC community, residents may form special attachments to particular peers and staff members. These attachments may gradually evolve from the identifications and empathic and compassionate experiences that occur routinely in daily interactions. However, positive bonding is also facilitated by the intimacy, context, and expectations of the peer community. These features intensify the shared experiences of change and growth that promote strong attachments to others (e.g., Table 20-2). Indeed, former residents remember these experiences and remain connected to the peers with whom they "grew up in the TC."

Personal relationships in general and bonding in particular are profoundly important elements in the change process. The individual's affiliation with the community and their bonds with specific others can mutually foster change. For example, bonding with some peers early in the process can keep the individual in the program long enough to develop affiliation with the community. Or, conversely, initial affiliation with the "generalized other" (community) will gradually desensitize individual fears of forming personal attachments with particular others.[56]

In summary, the social relatedness and caring experiences are fundamental in the use of community as method to facilitate the process of change. They balance the confrontational, judgmental, and instructional elements needed to modify behavior and attitudes. Residents can hear the challenges, criticisms, and judgments of peers, and accept the sanctions, disciplinary, and corrective responses of the community only if they also feel the concern and compassion of the community and perceive themselves as understood and accepted by others.

Finally, the social relatedness and caring experiences are integral in establishing attachments with drug-free peers. Bonds are attachments to specific individuals, while affiliation is a collective attachment to the broader community. New individual and collective attachments counter the historically self-defeating influence of negative peer groups. They also reverse the disaffiliation and personal isolation that characterize many chemical abusers. Attachments teach those recovering how to positively use people to interrupt personal crisis or stress that could lead to relapse.

SUBJECTIVE LEARNING EXPERIENCES

In the TC, social learning unfolds as an interaction between the individual and the community. The individual engages in behaviors and attitudes that

---

[56] An excellent discussion of bonding in the TC process is contained in Kooyman (1993).

produce positive and negative responses from the community. These are objective consequences, such as rewards, privileges, and disciplinary actions, reflecting community expectations. However, there are also experiential or *subjective outcomes* associated with these consequences. For example, the positive learning effects of rewards, privileges, job promotions, and peer recognition occur only if residents experience these as positive events. Similarly, disciplines, demotions, or bans are effective teaching consequences if they are experienced in a negative way by the resident.

Typically the subjective outcome experiences involve self-evaluative perceptions, thoughts, and feelings. For example, when residents revert to undesirable behaviors leading to disciplinary actions or social disapproval, negative experiential consequences may occur on the theme of *self-rejection* (e.g., disappointment, worthlessness, failure, or guilt). When residents engage in new, effective behaviors and attitudes or positive thinking, they may experience subjective outcomes occuring on the theme of *self-efficacy* (e.g., confidence, mastery). Beliefs that the individual can do something well or succeed are associated with *self-esteem* (e.g., perceptions of self-value or worth).

The importance of the subjective learning experiences are underscored in the TC perspective and method. Self-efficacy and self-esteem are profoundly linked with the disorder and with recovery. Persistent episodes of relapse to drugs or alcohol invariably lead to loss of confidence in the ability to stop use, escalating difficulties in work and social relations, and often perceptions of hopelessness about the possibilities of self-change. Self-efficacy must be acquired or restored through repeated corrective experiences. These involve learning how to maintain sobriety in the variety of situations and circumstances that hitherto have been triggers or cues for leading to the reuse of substances.

Among many of the residents in TCs, however, self-efficacy and self-esteem problems extend much beyond the inability to control drug use to all areas of their daily living. For these residents, self-efficacy must be experienced in all domains of performance, work, social relations, emotional management, and self-control in general.[57]

Thus, the community context provides the multiple opportunities for obtaining the subjective outcomes that are critical in the change process.

---

[57] In the social and psychological literature, self-efficacy refers more specifically to cognitive factors, such as expectations and beliefs concerning the individual's ability to cope successfully with stress or triggers to drug use (e.g., Marlatt & Gorden, 1985). In the TC, self-efficacy is broadened into experiences that include these cognitive factors, as well as emotional responses and self-evaluative perceptions.

Self-efficacy and self-esteem experiences are associated not only with remaining abstinent but with the individual's successful performance in a variety of community roles.

Community and the Essential Experiences in the Change Process

Three characteristics of the essential experiences, their interrelatedness, public nature, and reciprocity, illuminate how individuals change in the context of community. All of the essential experiences have the common functional objective of sustaining the individual in the change process. Although there is no fixed sequence as to the occurrence of essential experiences, they are *interrelated.* For example, individuals must feel cared for and protected in the community in order to engage in the activities that lead to the essential psychological and social-relatedness experiences such as blind faith and trust. The latter, in turn, increase the individual's initial receptivity to engaging in the personal disclosures that lead to experiences of being understood and accepted. Similarly, identification, a primary social-relatedness experience, generally precedes the more complex experiences of empathy, compassion, and bonding. Finally, in the change process the healing and social-relatedness experiences encourage behavioral change that results in self-efficacy experiences leading to further behavioral and experiential changes.

Although experiences are private subjective changes in the individual, they are *public events* associated with observable social behaviors. Individual displays of empathy, compassion, understanding, and acceptance toward others are also observable indicators of residents' own subjective changes. Thus, these public displays provide some measures of how residents are changing internally.

Experiential changes in the individual can also *reciprocally* produce experiential changes in others. For example, when the community displays understanding and acceptance through words, actions, and gestures, individuals experience being understood and accepted. Conversely, when individuals display understanding and acceptance, they can facilitate these experiential changes in others. Moreover, healing and subjective learning are also reciprocal effects reflecting both receiving and giving in the community. For example, self-efficacy in communicating experiences results when individuals display nurturance, empathy, compassion, understanding, and acceptance to others.

CONCLUSION

This chapter described the experiences that are considered essential to the change process within the TC. These are conceptualized under three broad themes: emotional healing, social-relatedness and caring, and subjective learning. However the essential experiences are interrelated and interdependent in the process. Thus, the community is the social context for behavioral and experiential changes that lead to changes in how individuals live, how they see the world around them, and in particular, how they perceive themselves. The following chapter focuses upon these perceptions and their contribution to the change process.

Chapter 21

Individual Change: Essential Perceptions

The therapeutic community (TC) is a culture of change. All of the activities, social roles, interpersonal interactions, and community teachings focus upon the theme of individual change. Any change in the direction of right living and positive social and personal identities is considered progress.

The community's observations and affirmations of change provide external or objective validation of the individual's progress. However, the individual's recognition and acknowledgement of self-change provide subjective validation of progress. Both sources of validation facilitate the change process itself by reinforcing the individual's participation and involvement in the community.

The perceptions that are considered to be essential to recovery are interrelated, although they can be organized into classes to clarify their contribution to the process. These groupings, like those of the essential experiences, are analogous to the behavioral domains described in chapter 19. Perceptions related to treatment reflect the individual's motivation, readiness, and suitability to engage in the process of change in the TC. Perceptions of progress reflect how residents see themselves changing as individuals in the process, summarized as self- and identity change.

PERCEPTIONS RELATED TO TREATMENT

Although community life in the TC contains an omnipresent message to "stay the course," residents constantly struggle to remain in the treatment situation. How they perceive their problems, the need for change, the program environment, the demands of treatment, and the pushes and pulls from outside of the program compel contemplation and redecision to continue in the process on an almost daily basis. These perceptions may be grouped into four classes: *circumstances, motivation, readiness,* and *suitability.* These are described in Table 21-1.[58]

TABLE 21-1.   The Essential Treatment-Related Perceptions

Circumstances

A number of life situations and conditions drive people to seek treatment in TCs, including legal, fiscal, health, family, social, domestic, and employment problems. These various conditions differ across individuals and may change over time for the same individual. However, they are all perceived as some form of external pressure that compels the individual to seek admission to treatment, remain in treatment, and leave the treatment situation. Thus treatment itself must utilize these external perceptions to sustain the individual in the change process.

Motivation

Individuals are motivated when they are moved to seek and remain in treatment by various "inner reasons"—for personal change. These may be positive, such as desires for a new lifestyle, the "good things" in life, personal growth, or better social and family relationships, or negative, such as the need to abate or eliminate feelings of guilt, self-hatred, or personal despair based upon their hurting and failing themselves or others. Intrinsically motivated individuals come to perceive that they themselves are the problem rather than the drugs or their life circumstances, and they accept the fact that it is *they* who must change, rather than the world around them.

Readiness

Individuals may be motivated to change but many have not actually accepted the necessity for treatment. Motivated individuals who are not specifically ready to engage in the treatment process may perceive non-treatment alternatives as viable, such as managing their own problems through self-control; making situational changes in employment, relationships, or geographic location; or getting help and support from religion, family, or friends. Thus those who are ready for treatment have rejected all other options for change, that is, they perceive treatment as their only alternative.

Suitability

Residents in the TC may be motivated and ready for treatment, but do not necessarily perceive the TC as appropriate for their needs. Thus, suitability refers to the self-perceived match between the individual and the TC treatment. Suitability for treatment in the TC is indicated by the resident's acceptance of the TC approach: its goals, philosophy, and teachings; its social learning methods; and its emphasis upon making a long-term time commitment to treatment.

From "Therapeutic Communities for Addictions: A Theoretical Framework," by G. De Leon, 1995, *International Journal of the Addictions, 30* (12), p. 1620. Copyright 1995 by Marcel Dekker, Inc. Reprinted with permission.

---

[58] Scales measuring these treatment-related perceptions are currently available; see Appendix C.

The perceptions related to treatment are *interrelated* in various ways. Readiness to engage treatment cannot occur without sufficient internal motivation to change. Suitability for a particular treatment such as the TC is unlikely in an individual who is not ready for any treatment. Moreover, extrinsic circumstances or pressures often induce or clarify intrinsic motivation. For example, repeated problems with the law, health, employment, and social and family relationships eventually lead many individuals to acknowledge their problems with drugs and their need to change themselves. However, although extrinsic pressures bring the individual to treatment, it is intrinsic motivation that sustains continued participation in the process. Many graduates of TCs assert that they came to treatment through court referral or family pressure but remained in treatment because of their own motivation, which they strengthened through program participation.

Treatment-related perceptions are also *changeable.* Shifts in motivation, readiness, and suitability can occur daily such that residents continually make decisions concerning their reasons for treatment and their need for a long-term residential program. These shifts reflect the attractions and pressures from outside of the program, such as friends, family, and social and employment circumstances. But they also relate to the influences inherent in residential life such as positive and negative interactions with peers and staff, program demands, or boredom with the daily regimen.

Treatment progress itself can have unpredictable effects on motivation, readiness, and suitability. For example, rapid improvement in the early days of treatment could result in premature dropout. Paradoxically, a transient perception of well-being could lessen motivation or readiness to continue in treatment (i.e., "flight into health"). Residents who are no longer feeling bad may conclude that they can handle their problems on their own, and they no longer perceive the necessity for treatment. Conversely, delayed or slow improvement may lead to demoralization, weaken readiness to continue, and result in early dropout, particularly in individuals who cannot delay gratification.

Ironically, important changes in perceived suitability for the TC can occur *after* individuals actually encounter the demands of the community environment. For example, they may see themselves as different from others in terms of their drug use and their cultural and social background. They may view the program negatively, its structure and discipline as too harsh and its participation requirements too demanding or lacking in sufficient personal attention. Such perceptions of mismatch between the individual's needs and the program's approach can also lead to premature dropout.

Suitability also refers to perceptions of community or program *integrity*. These include the individual's perceptions of the consistency, credibility, and honesty of the program; staff behavior; and the TC system in terms of fairness and fidelity (delivering on what it promises). These perceptions could influence resident affiliation with the community, retention in the program, and continuation in the change process.

Much of the effort of the community is directly or indirectly aimed at monitoring and modifying these treatment-related perceptions, which shift continually throughout the resident' tenure in residence. Peers and staff attempt to sustain the individual's motivation to change and to reaffirm the suitability of the TC setting. Daily interactions help the individual to reassess and minimize the importance of outside influences and to remind the individual of the gains made and the problems that still need to be addressed in the TC. "You gotta be in it to win it" is a common TC colloquialism that captures the important interaction between motivation and retention in treatment. "This program is your family, it's what you need to change your life" paraphrases various expressions that address the individual's perceptions of suitability. Indeed, community emphasis upon peer monitoring of the integrity of the program underscores the necessity of maintaining perceptions of suitability.

PERCEPTIONS OF PROGRESS

Perceptions of progress or improvement are critical to the process of change itself. Residents remain in treatment if they see evidence of change in themselves. Even seeing the progress of other peers evokes hope and possibility about self-change. Such perceptions help to sustain the individual's motivation to continue in the process, particularly early in the treatment, the period of highest vulnerability to dropout. Thus, the process of change is facilitated when residents can acknowledge to themselves that they are different—that they have actually changed in reference to their past profile.

Perceptions of progress occur at different levels of complexity. Residents may simply see themselves as behaving differently or feeling differently. More complex contrasts are those in which residents perceive themselves changing as people, that is, self-change. The concepts of self and identity are wholly subjective terms that express how individuals perceive themselves as individuals. Both terms refer to complex self-perceptions, which are viewed as critical to the stability of recovery. Perceived changes in patterns of behaviors, attitudes, and emotions gradually expand or contribute to overarching perceptions of self- and identity change. The following sections describe in some detail the essential perceptions of progress traced in the concepts of self- and identity change.

The Concept and Levels of Self-Change

Self is a central concept in the TC perspective. The disorder and the person are inextricably bound such that self is the nexus of the whole person. TC teachings speak to the individual as taking responsibility for their own recovery; they emphasize that change itself involves mutual self-help leading to self-esteem. Thus, residents are not simply treating their addiction, or modifying their behaviors and attitudes, they are working on *changing themselves.*

These perceptions of self-change may evolve in terms of levels of complexity. Each level represents how individuals see their personal growth, and each level defines the particular problem they are "working on in treatment." Indeed, the residents' awareness and acceptance of what they are working on is a significant marker of their engagement in the process (see Table 21-2).

TABLE 21-2. Levels of Perceived Self-Change

Self-care

Individuals learn personal habits and attitudes that are physically healthy. Many residents have ignored or never learned healthy habits. More fundamentally, maintaining physical health and personal care is a positive sign of psychological health—the resident investing in himself or herself. An example of a perceived change in self-care is:

"I let myself go to hell, slept in the streets, teeth were rotted, didn't shower for days, didn't pay attention to what I ate, or who I had sex with. I see now that taking care of myself—staying clean, healthy, being groomed, eating right—is really caring about my life, myself."

Table continues

TABLE 21-2.   Levels of Perceived Self-Change

Table continued

Self-control

Individuals learn the restraint and modification of impulsive behaviors. Typical incidents involve reactions such as hostility, cursing, verbal threats, actual violence, threats to use or actual use of drugs, and sudden exits from treatment itself. Residents see these incidents primarily as provocations from the outside rather than from their characteristic impulsivity in coping with such incidents. Self-control is indicated when individuals perceive the problem as internal rather than external, as one of regulating their impulses. This involves working on modification of specific behaviors in particular situations to avoid harmful consequences. An example of perceived change in self-control is as follows:

"If somebody looked at me in the wrong way, I'd come off on him. I'm learning to hold my mud, deal with it, don't go crazy. Now when someone says something I don't like, I walk away, maybe deal with it in groups."

Self-management

Individuals learn to recognize and modify patterns of behaviors and attitudes across many different situations. Residents learn to organize various behavioral incidents that appear to be isolated and unrelated into a pattern or general problem. Thus, at the level of self-management, the individual is working on handling feelings and attitudes across many social and interpersonal situations. These include cravings, urges, and impulses, as well as feeling states such as anger, insecurity, and frustration. An example of perceived change in self-management is:

"I gotta big problem with handling feelings; gotta lot of anger in me, fear and hurt. I'm learning to stop acting off feelings. Now, if I feel hostile, angry, or afraid, I stop and think before I act. If I start thinking about drugs, I look at what I'm feeling, push it aside and keep working."

Self-understanding

Self-understanding involves conceptualizing beyond single behavioral incidents and patterns of behaviors. In the more advanced phase of this level, the resident is working on seeing connections between current patterns of behavior, attitudes, and feelings from a life history perspective, such as family background and earlier conditioning events. An example of perceived change in self-understanding is:

"I thought, in my family's eyes, I have always been a bad kid; so that's who I've been, a bad kid; but I wasn't really bad inside, just confused. A lot of my drug use and acting out was me being a bad kid. I don't see it that way any more."

Self-concept

Individuals learn to reframe a view of themselves in broader terms. Reframing is based upon changes in behaviors and self-perceptions in the other areas. The changes in self-concept are typically expressed as modifications of earlier negative self-evaluative statements:

"When I came in here I was out of control, irresponsible; wouldn't listen and couldn't deal with structure, authority. Now, I handle myself, I'm more realistic—and feel like a mature person."

Self-perceived change appears to be developmental, grounded in actual behavioral and experiential changes and is variable. These characteristics are briefly discussed.

The levels of perceived self-change are interrelated and overlapping, but for many they appear in a developmental sequence. Self-care is primary. Individuals who do not attend to their physical health or personal care do not perceive themselves as changing and make no further investment in the process of self-change. Perceptions of self-management of patterns of behaviors, attitudes, and feelings depend upon previously learned control of specific behaviors in various situations. Consistency in self-management is a prerequisite for self-understanding. Individuals must reliably perceive themselves as managing negative patterns of behaviors, attitudes, and feelings in order to explore and understand the early sources of these patterns. Also, a change in self-concept is contingent upon firm personal evidence that there has been a stable change in old patterns together with some new understanding of how these patterns have developed and shaped residents' self-definition.

Perceptions of self-change are obviously related to behavioral and experiential changes discussed in previous chapters. Stable perceptions of self-change must be grounded in actual changes in behaviors, thinking, attitudes, and emotions. Moreover, essential experiences are closely related to self-perceived change. For example, individuals accept themselves more readily when they understand themselves and when their self-concept improves.

Finally, the perceived levels of self-change vary within and across individuals. Not all are working on the same level, and for any individual, the stability of perceived change also varies. Some may have relatively good self-control and begin their work at self-management. Others may display good self-management and appear to have self-understanding. However, they reveal poor control or self-management in various moments and circumstances. For example, residents can display self-control in terms of reduced asocial behavioral episodes, or they may indicate some self-understanding of their problem as one of immaturity or irresponsibility. However, they may lack an understanding of the interpersonal and emotional cues for their drug use. They may not have the coping mechanisms for handling guilt (self-management).

Community and Self-Perceived Change

Assessing and affirming individual progress is a central activity in the TC. Staff evaluations formally assess the levels of self-change, while peers and staff assess them informally. Various strategies promote changes in perceptions at different levels of self-change. These may focus on specific behaviors and attitudes to teach self-control or self-management. Or, they are designed to teach individuals to see themselves conceptually. For example, in groups, rap sessions, and informal conversations, peers may provide the individual with different behavioral examples that illustrate patterns requiring change. These patterns may be labeled to underscore what the community is trying to teach the individual:

> You're a loner. You always arrive last at morning meetings, you speak last in the groups, you say little in seminars, sit in the back of the room during seminars, and eat by yourself. You're a loner.

Feedback strategies frequently affirm change in the whole person in order to raise individuals' awareness of their own progress. Moreover, the community encourages and instructs individuals to seek feedback from others as well as learn to give feedback to themselves on their own progress.

> You have changed—you're not the same person who came into this program. You're too hard on yourself. Tell yourself that you've changed. Ask anyone in this room whether you've changed.

Thus making individuals aware of their progress begins with specific behavioral situations but expands toward the whole person. The community regularly reminds its members that they are handling themselves, growing up, and showing maturity.

Recognition of individual differences guides the community's use of appropriate interventions for particular levels of self-change. Interventions for facilitating perceptions of self-control differ from those needed for self-understanding. For example, behavior modification strategies are more appropriate for the self-control and self-management. Counseling strategies that evoke self-disclosure are more appropriate for facilitating self-understanding.

All strategies aim to advance the individual to the next level of self-perceived change. Some residents may not comply with a behavior modification instruction unless they have some self-understanding. While others must modify their behaviors first, before they gain self-understanding.

Individual differences notwithstanding, recovery is unstable if perceived change is not based upon *actual* change. Thus, the individual needs to have moved through all of the levels to assure stable perceptions of self-change. Indeed, clinical experience indicates that relapse and return to treatment usually reflect missed steps in the process of self-change. Such missed steps often indicate perceptual changes that are not grounded in stable behavioral and experiential changes.

The Concept of Identity Change

Identity refers to an overarching self-perception that describes how residents see themselves as individuals, how they differ in respect to others and as social members in the world. Typical *personal* descriptives connoting identity change are "discovering who I am," "dropping my images," "getting to the person inside," and "becoming real." Typical *social* descriptives are being an ex-addict, "a recovering person," or "being a good parent." In some ways, identity labels capture how the individual sees himself or herself as a whole person.

Change in identity may be viewed as a summation of the self-changes described above. For example, residents gradually perceive themselves differently as they gain self-control and self-management; an altered self-concept is a key element of identity change. However, scope and depth are the critical distinctions between the interrelated perceptions of self and identity. Self-statements such as "I don't handle my feelings very well" refer to a characteristic way of behaving and thinking. These differ from identity statements such as "I am not the person I once was" which express perceived change in the total individual.

The *process* of identity change can be broadly described in terms of three phases: dissipation of old identity elements, restructuring elements of new social and personal identities during treatment, and continued identity development beyond treatment in the real world. During treatment, this process can be characterized in terms of changing self-recognitions that reflect the elements of social and personal identity.[59]

In the *dissipation* phase, individuals recognize their various negative and social images as a defended or inauthentic self and accept their true feelings and thoughts, or the " undefended self." These changes are reinforced or validated when individuals recognize that their undefended selves are understood and accepted by others.

In the *restructuring* phase of the process, new elements of identity are evident when residents recognize and accept a positive self-concept associated with their accomplishments in the program. This recognition reflects self-efficacy experiences in the various participant roles of the community in work and relationships with others. The initial changes of

---

[59] Similar phase formulations of the process of identity change in the TC are contained in Frankel (1989) and Casriel (1981).

identity are often reflected in residents' statements of self-efficacy such as "I am a person who can work, can have feelings, can complete things, can keep promises, can help others."

Continued *identity development*, however, depends upon changes in personal experiences and engaging multiple social roles outside of the treatment situation. There are inherent limits in the extent to which residents can change their identities while they are in treatment. Community as method facilitates the phases of dissipation and restructuring of identity change. Through confrontation, feedback, affirmation, and providing a context for acquiring new social roles, residents learn right living and develop positive self-perceptions. Achieving these goals prepares them to continue the process of identity change beyond treatment.

Residents must re-enter the real world and successfully assume new social roles as workers, parents, friends, and civilians in order to change their social identities. Through their real world experiences they must demonstrate to themselves that they also have changed their personal identities. This means that they live more authentically, are guided by values of right living, and have clarified some sense of purpose and meaning in their lives.

CONCLUSION

This chapter has organized the individual perceptions considered to be essential in the process of change in the TC: how individuals see their problems, their need for treatment, and the treatment approach itself. These perceptions are continuously in flux and influence whether residents remain in process. Perceptions of progress reflect how residents see themselves changing as individuals in the process, summarized as self- and identity change. Notably, the change in self-concept during treatment is the foundation for continuing the process of identity change in the real world.

Changing the whole person means integrating the behaviors, cognitions, emotions, experiences, and perceptions of the individual. Integration unfolds gradually as individuals become more deeply involved in the community. How this process of involvement occurs is characterized in the following chapter.

Chapter 22

The Individual in the Community: Participation in the Change Process

In the therapeutic community (TC) approach, it is the community that mediates the treatment. Indeed, a fundamental premise of the TC approach is that individuals change—*if* they fully participate in all the roles and activities of community life. The messages of recovery and right living are heard—if the resident is attentive and receptive. Emotional experiences and personal insights will occur—if the individual takes the personal risks of sharing, disclosing, and being vulnerable. Consistency in habits and performance develops—if the resident faithfully follows the daily routine; and accomplishment in work and completion of tasks are assured—if the resident devotes one hundred percent effort to his or her job functions and other communal obligations. Peer and staff counseling are useful for self-change—if the resident seeks these, listens, and applies what he or she hears. Thus, the therapeutic and educational impact of the community activities and relationships occur only if residents participate in these.

In the TC, however, participation signifies more than meeting community expectations. Individuals change when they are *totally involved* in the community. Indeed, the word "involvement" is not used casually by residents or staff. For example, the phrase "getting into it," used by peers, expresses their relation to the program, the people, and the process. Staff will routinely assess the clinical status of individuals in terms of their level of involvement.

Both participation and involvement are related to the program stages. As components of the TC treatment model, the stages define the program's plan for moving individuals toward the goals of social and psychological change. Individuals in the induction, primary treatment, and re-entry stages are at different points in the program plan. Participation and involvement, however, depict individuals in the treatment *process* as they move through the program stages.

In this chapter, the process of change in the TC is described in terms of participation and levels of involvement. In the initial sections, participation and community as method are tracked through the program stages. Some relations are outlined between the social and psychological dimensions of individual change and the community expectations for participation. In the last section, the process of multidimensional change through treatment is pictured in terms of levels of involvement in the community.

PARTICIPATION AND COMMUNITY AS METHOD

Participation and involvement link community as method to the individual in the change process. Participation is the key contribution the individual makes to the process. However, it is the community's continual assessment of and responses to the individual's participation and level of involvement that sustains him or her in the process.

As individuals move through the stages of the program, the context of community life is essentially unchanged. What does change, however, are the community's expectations for participation, assessment, and responses to the individual in each stage. As described in chapter 6, expectations are the explicit standards of participation in terms of performance, responsibility, self-examination, and autonomy. Assessments consist of the various community tests and challenges to evaluate whether residents are meeting these expectations, and responses are the community's reactions to its evaluations.

Generally, as individuals move through the program, tests and challenges are the main assessment strategies. However, community responses to the same behavior (e.g., affirmations, correctives, privileges, and disciplinary sanctions) will differ depending upon the changing community expectations.

During the induction stage of treatment, for example, residents are expected to learn and maintain behavioral standards of cleanliness and punctuality in their living space and personal appearance. An unkempt room, being unshaven, or being late for breakfast will evoke a community response that will vary over time. Community assessment assumes that the individual has not yet learned or accepted the expectation concerning these behaviors. Thus, the response is corrective, limited to the behavior itself, but also supportive to maximize its acceptance. Peers may repeat the expectation, its rationale, and provide explicit instructions to the individual. Sanctions to rule-breaking behaviors emphasize teaching the individual how to use the learning experience ("the contract") to understand the program expectations.

Early in primary treatment the response to the same behavior is more corrective and with a more critical tone. This reflects the assessment that the individual knows what the community expectations are and how to meet them,. "You should know better. You still may need somebody watching you for while. " In a later phase of primary treatment the community response to the same behavior is more complex, reflecting its assessment that the individual has *regressed* from meeting community expectations. Thus the response may be confrontational and critical but also include supportive exploration of the reasons for regression in behavior and attitudes: "You're room is messy. You don't talk to people. You're off by yourself. What's happening to you that you're not taking care of business."

In re-entry community reactions and actions also accord with expectations. What is acceptable in new residents may not be tolerated in senior residents. Community responses contain both confrontational and supportive elements that are designed to foster the learning process. The following is an example:

> A male re-entry resident displays negative behavior and attitudes such as flirting with a new female inductee. This may provoke a harsh community response, with relatively little instruction, plus intensive exploration of feelings behaviors and attitudes. 'You should know better. What kind of a role model are you, maybe you need another job function to remind you of who you are and what you're working on. Can you talk about why you hit on that girl?

Disciplinary sanctions for the cardinal rules remain fairly constant throughout the program stages. However, more flexibility may be exercised with respect to less serious infractions in accordance with community expectations. In the above example, the re-entry candidate may lose privileges or even community status for the social infraction.

COMMUNITY EXPECTATIONS AND THE DIMENSIONS OF INDIVIDUAL CHANGE

There is an intimate relationship between participation and the individual goals for self-change. *It is through striving to meet the community's expectations for participation that residents pursue their individual goals of socialization and psychological growth.* Meeting community expectations requires continual self-change in behaviors, attitudes, and emotional management. Moreover, the avoidance of or difficulties in meeting these expectations also results in individual growth through continual self-examination, re-motivation to engage in trial and error learning, and recommitment to the change process.

This relationship between community expectations and the dimensions of individual change can be briefly described. Changes in performance, responsibility, self-examination, and autonomy summarize individual progress from the perspective of the community's expectations. Changes in the community member, socialization, developmental, and psychological dimensions summarize progress from the perspective of the individual's treatment goals.

These two perspectives of individual change—the community and the individual—converge in the process. For example, when residents give a complete effort and consistently fulfill obligations, they are meeting community expectations in the areas of performance and responsibility. This involves characteristics related to being a community member (e.g., role modeling, affiliation) and to socialization (e.g., work habits and attitudes, positive social values).

Similarly, when residents disclose and confront their own attitudes and behaviors and initiate self-change without relying on prompting or approval from others, they are meeting community expectations in the areas of self-examination and autonomy. This involves individual changes in the developmental and psychological dimensions (e.g., maturity, emotional growth, judgment, decision making).

In both perspectives, however, change is viewed in terms of the whole person. Performance, responsibility, self-examination, and autonomy describe related characteristics of the same individual as do the social and psychological dimensions. Thus, meeting community expectations in the areas of participation may involve changes in all dimensions of the individual.

LEVELS OF INVOLVEMENT AND INDIVIDUAL CHANGE

Residents change because they are involved *with* the community and *in* the change process. They are viewed as involved when they are meeting expectations in all areas of participation. Their involvement is evident in the community roles, experiences, and perceptions that reflect their relationship to the community and in the social and psychological changes that unfold from this relationship.

The terms *engagement, immersion,* and *emergence* label the individual's level of involvement in the community. Engagement denotes tentative and limited involvement in the community. Immersion denotes a "totality of involvement" in the purpose and daily life of the community or program. Emergence denotes decreasing participation in the community associated with an increasing level of involvement in the world outside. However, emergence from the community assumes that individuals have been fully immersed in the community.

Engagement, immersion, and emergence are correlated with the stages of the program. Indeed, the set of typical resident features in the program stages contains many level of involvement indicators (see Tables 13-1, 13-2, and 13-3). However, where people are in the program stages may not necessarily reflect their actual level of involvement. Thus a more complete picture of the change process can be described in terms of levels of involvement.

This final section provides brief snapshots of individuals at each level of involvement. These are described behaviorally in terms of community roles, key experiences, and perceptions. Community roles (student, apprentice, mentor, leader) are employed here to summarize social and psychological changes in the individuals as they meet community expectations in all areas of participation. Thus, the process of multidimensional change can be depicted as a progression of community roles and associated experiences and perceptions as individuals deepen their level of community involvement.

Engagement

Early in treatment residents are relatively passive students learning about the community, its environment, purpose and procedures, and people, through exposure and specific instruction. In this early community role, however, individuals initiate social and psychological change. They must listen to others, follow instructions, understand the social organization of the TC and the philosophy of the program, begin to learn a variety of communication and group skills, comply with rules and regulation, display respect to staff and other peers, and carry out job functions.

The key experiences are physical and psychological safety, particularly trust. In this level individuals experience social-relatedness and caring experiences primarily as receivers from the community. Thus experiences such as safety, trust, and being understood and accepted help to facilitate affiliation with the community The main experiences of self-efficacy develop from remaining drug free, adhering to the rules, and simply staying in the program.

Perceptions of problems, the treatment environment, progress, and of the self are rudimentary. Motivation is limited and may reflect external pressures (e.g., legal, family) to changing the immediate problems and discomfort associated with drug use rather than achieving broader self-changes. However, seeing similar others engaged in recovery and right living is their first sustained exposure to the change process itself. Although such exposure continues throughout the TC, for new residents it establishes the fact of change in others and introduces the possibility of change in themselves.

By the end of engagement, residents view the community as safe and the program as useful. However, they may still be preoccupied with life outside of the program and maintain only a tentative commitment to continue in treatment. Perceptions related to self and identity are incremental through the levels of involvement. In engagement, perceptions reflect recognition of negative social images and awareness of "real feelings" and changes in self-care and self-control.

Immersion

During the phases of primary treatment, residents move through a series of community roles, apprentice, mentors, and leaders, as they gradually become immersed in the community. Each role reflects social and psychological changes associated with practicing how to use the community to learn about themselves, teaching and applying what they have learned to peers, and assuming responsibility for the conduct of the community.

Individuals experience healing, social relatedness, and caring both as transmitters and receivers. They begin to dissolve defenses to their vulnerability and increasingly identify with others in the struggle to change. They also display understanding, acceptance, and empathy for others. Self-efficacy experiences occur through sustaining as a role model and in maintaining the commitment to the recovery process itself.

Perceptions of problems, the program, and progress are grounded in treatment experiences. Motivation is intrinsic, reflecting an acceptance of long-standing psychological and personality problems in addition to their drug use. Perceptions of the credibility of the treatment environment are reinforced through the individual's own change experiences in adhering to the community expectations. Thus the program is perceived as the vehicle to change oneself.

Perceptions of self-change are confirmed through resident's effective use of the tools of the community. This perception is reinforced when the resident uses what he or she has learned to facilitate change in others. A critical marker is when the resident recognizes that behavioral consistency is necessary to sustain in any role commitment and acknowledges the accomplishment achieved in his or her various roles in the community. Thus changes in self-concept develop as simple but powerful recognitions associated with the levels of self-management and self-understanding described in chapter 21.

Elements of a changing social identity appear through experiences of self-efficacy occurring in residents' various community roles. Specifically a gradual restructuring of a social identity is defined by strong affiliation with the program, e.g., "I am a resident in Recovery House." Elements of personal identity also develop in the exposure of vulnerabilities and through absolute honesty in communication with others. Thus, fully immersed residents begin to "know who they really are." They recognize their true feelings, thoughts, capabilities, and limits. They also recognize that their undefended self is understood and accepted by others.

Emergence

Residents make a transition from their roles as mentors and leaders in the peer community to students and apprentices outside the community. Individual growth and change continue through meeting the tests and challenges in the world outside and particularly in experiences that confirm what they have learned about recovery and right living in the peer community.

The prominent *experiences* of healing and social relatedness are received from other re-entry candidates going through similar tests and challenges, and they are transmitted through helping others, both peers and more junior residents. The self-efficacy experiences derive primarily from meeting the direct challenges of new work and educational, social, recreational, and interpersonal situations outside of the program. In particular, individuals' self-efficacy increases as they deal with cues and conditions that threaten relapse and they meet the demands inherent in the multiple social roles in the "real world."

The *perceptions* reflecting motivation and readiness are related to the need to confront longer-standing personal and situational problems outside of the program. Perceptions of the credibility of the program and of the validity of the treatment process are confirmed through residents' increasing interaction with the outside world. They begin to apply what they have learned, which also affirms perceptions of progress and possibilities of continued change. However, perceptions of the future, its pitfalls, and possibilities, are often associated with anxiety and uncertainty about leaving the program.

In emergence, identity elements gradually and continually develop through the individual's interaction with the real world. Social identity elements may still reflect program affiliation: "I am a re-entry candidate of Recovery House." Other elements of social identity, however, are incorporated from the outside as individuals assume work and family roles in the larger community. The elements of personal identity reflect the internalization of right living teachings: "I am changed, more honest, real, and I have values." However, individuals continue to *identify* with the recovery or change process itself: "I am going through changes that I have to deal with...Who am I? A recovering person."

CONCLUSION

In this chapter, participation in the program and level of involvement in the community are viewed as the dynamic elements of the change process. Three levels of involvement, engagement, immersion, and emergence, depict the process of change as individuals move through the stages of the program. Meeting community expectations for participation at each stage deepens the individual's level of involvement in the community, which reinforces further participation and multidimensional change.

Individuals can reveal change and yet still not be "transformed." How stable are their behavioral and attitudinal changes? How well have they learned the teachings or how much have they experienced change? These questions are addressed in the following chapter, which outlines the concept of internalization in the change process.

Chapter 23

Internalization and Identity

At the core of the change process in the therapeutic community (TC) is the relationship between the individual and the community. Interrelated changes in behaviors, attitudes, experiences, and perceptions gradually evolve into lifestyle and identity change as individuals fully immerse themselves in the community and *internalize* its teachings.

For TCs the importance of internalization is especially salient considering that the power of community as method can readily produce change in observable behaviors and attitudes. However, these changes may not endure once the individual leaves or separates from the omnipresent influence of the peer community. Practically all residents in TCs display drug-free behavior during their residential stay. Many drop out, while others maintain the expected behaviors and attitudes that lead to completion or graduation from the program. That relapse occurs among a number of the dropouts and some of the graduates, however, underscores the relevance of internalization in the change process.

THE CONCEPT AND CHARACTERISTICS OF INTERNALIZATION

Internalization is a familiar psychodynamic concept connoting learning that involves "taking in" the behavior and teachings of others. In the TC, internalization is evident when new learning becomes a "natural" part of the individual's repertoire. For example, residents who become role models display changes in behaviors, attitudes, and values that reflect community expectations. However, internalization of these changes is viewed as more complete when role modeling shifts from meeting

355

community expectations to a personal mode of living based upon the individual's own experiences in this role.

Notably, internalization refers to how completely the individual accepts, practices, and applies what he or she has learned in the TC to new situations inside and outside of the program.

Characteristics of Internalization

The mark of internalization is the *transfer* of the influences on new learning from the external (objective) consequences to the internal (subjective) experiences of the individual. When learned changes have been internalized they appear more consistent and more self-initiated ("inner directed") than externally influenced learning. Thus the observable indicators of internalization are more difficult to measure than those of the behavioral and subjective dimensions.

In the TC internalization is inferred from patterns of behavioral, experiential, and perceptual change occurring over time. These may be described in terms of several broad characteristics: cognitive dissonance and behavioral conflict, generalization, learning to learn, and confirmatory experiences.

Cognitive dissonance and behavioral conflict

The TC teachings of right living and recovery are often in direct opposition to the residents' specific ways of thinking and general outlook about drug use, themselves, and the world (i.e., cognitive dissonance). Internalization is indicated when residents display decreasing skepticism and doubt concerning the validity of TC teachings and gradually replace old thinking with new thinking.

Similarly, TCs demand changes in conduct that are in direct conflict with characteristically socially deviant or socially disordered behaviors (i.e., behavioral conflict). Residents must adhere to formal rules and regulations and informal expectations. Internalization is indicated by decreases in the frequency and severity of behavioral infractions, frank rule-breaking, or passive participation in general.

Residents gradually meet the demands for change with less difficulty and view both the rules and the change positively. However, the signs of personal disruption frequently accompany the gradual dissolution of dissonance and conflict. Anxiety, anger, hostility, skepticism, resistance, defiance, and even threats to leave may signify the individual's struggle with relinquishing old patterns of conduct and thinking.

The element of struggle makes the important distinction between internalization and other forms of individual change such as *adaptation*. In the latter, individuals display situational learning—behavioral changes without necessarily undergoing the experiences that dissolve conflict and cognitive dissonance. For example, inmates can display the behaviors, thinking, and attitudes that are appropriate for safe survival in the prison community without eliminating old ways of thinking or behaving.

Thus, internalization requires that dissonance be dissolved by new learning based upon the resident's positive experiences associated with behavioral and cognitive change. Without experientially grounded change, old patterns are not replaced but can persist in parallel with new learning.

Generalization

Perhaps the most distinctive indicator of internalization is the resident's ability to apply TC recovery and right living teachings, concepts, and values to new situations both in and outside of the program. Within the program internalization is evident in the rate of change in which residents learn new behaviors and concepts. Their learning is more efficient and has fewer errors based upon the stability of their previous learning. For example, residents can be placed in community roles of greater responsibility, informal authority, and skill levels. Their effectiveness in these roles is acquired rapidly relative to learning earlier roles.

Outside of the program, new job functions and responsibilities pose the challenge of learning new concrete skills. Residents who have internalized their learning during treatment can transfer the values and attitudes associated with a work ethic; the skills of relating to others; the capabilities of assuming different roles; and the resiliency to deal with setback, success, and uncertainty.

Learning to learn

Not all of the individual's problems are addressed, much less solved, during tenure in the TC. Therefore a goal of the process is teaching individuals that learning is both a value and mode of coping in life. When individuals have experienced personal changes and perceive that these changes occurred through learning efforts, learning itself becomes a mode of solving problems, of coping with emotional and circumstantial difficulties.

Thus, learning to learn becomes internalized as a cognitive value, a guideline for meeting life's challenges. Adversity and stressful or demanding situations are perceived as opportunities to affirm personal change or personal growth. These perceptions maintain the individual's stability in the face of threat or pressure and permit them to assess, evaluate, and make sound decisions. Notably, these indicators of learning to learn reflect the community expectations of autonomy discussed in the stages of participation. Thus, learning to learn reflects the internalization of TC teachings.

Confirmatory experiences

Internalization, learning based upon subjective outcomes, also occurs through experiential learning *outside* of the peer community. On short furloughs and longer home visits or job searches, for example, newly acquired behaviors and attitudes within the program are tested in settings in the real world. Residents are presented with opportunities to engage in old and new situations with changed attitudes and levels of personal honesty, beliefs, values, and specific coping skills. Positive subjective outcomes from these trials in the world can reinforce the new learning, perceptions of self-change, and also perceptions of the program as a safe setting for valid learning. Even negative outcomes from these outside trials, if appropriately reviewed back in the program, will provide the references for continued learning and sustained affiliation with the program. Thus, various confirmatory experiences within and outside of the program facilitate internalization of the TC's teachings by strengthening trust in the people, procedures, and the process itself.

THE GRADIENT OF INTERNALIZATION

Treatment process in the TC refers to the interaction between client change and the myriad of community and individual interventions. In this interaction, the internalization of community teachings and new behaviors, attitudes, and values is gradual, variable, and not necessarily complete.

The course of internalization can be characterized as a gradient that depicts changing levels or stages of internalization. Four stages refer to changes during treatment, *compliance, conformity, commitment to program,* and *commitment to self.* Two additional stages, *continuance* and *integration*, illustrate the gradient of internalized change that extends beyond the treatment situation (see Table 23-1).

TABLE 23-1. Levels of Internalization in Treatment

Compliance

Individuals adhere to community norms and expectations primarily to avoid negative consequences. These may be the various disciplinary sanctions in the program or undesirable alternatives such as discharge to the street, return to jail, or home situation. Learning based upon avoidance of these external consequences is unstable, as the removal of the perceived external threat often results in noncompliance or dropping out of treatment.

Conformity

Individuals adhere to community expectations and norms primarily to maintain affiliation with the community, the friendships, bonding, or identification with the program. Affiliation is essential for maintaining the individual in treatment. However, it provides a limited basis for internalized learning in the change process. Learning primarily influenced by conformity can reverse when individuals are no longer under the afffiliative influences of the community.

Commitment to program

Individuals adhere to their own personal resolve or stated agreements with others to complete the treatment program. Commitment to program reflects some degree of conformity, since there is explicit community pressure to remain in treatment. However, this commitment is primarily based upon the individual's experiences and perceptions associated with the *possibilities* of self-changes, new life options, and particularly the need to have the experience of completion itself. Thus, commitment to program indicates that individuals have internalized the explicit TC goal of completion based upon their own subjective changes.

Commitment to self

Individuals resolve to remain in the change process as distinguished from completion of treatment. Commitment to self is primarily based upon significant experiences associated with actual self-change during treatment and recognition that personal change is a *continuing* process much beyond the TC treatment period. Thus, commitment to self reflects the highest level of internalization that can be achieved during the individual's tenure in treatment.

The gradient of internalization describes the gradual shift in the sources of influences on individuals in treatment. For example, compliance implies that factors external to the peer community are the main influences on the individual's behavior and attitudes. Typically these are fears of jail, family threats, street problems, circumstantial pressures, or lack of living arrangements. Conformity implies that factors internal to the peer community are the main influences on the individual's behavior and attitudes. These influences typically are social relationships and community status.

The levels of commitment imply behavioral and attitudinal changes that are based increasingly upon the individual's direct experience with self-change. These shifts along the gradient are illustrated in several examples: personal conduct, friendships, and role modeling. In each, the observed behaviors remain the same, while the sources of influence change (see Table 23-2).

TABLE 23-2.   The Gradient of Internalization: Three Illustrations

Personal conduct

In compliance, the resident initially keeps the room clean mainly to avoid trouble that could lead to discharge. In conformity, the resident keeps the room clean to maintain acceptance by the peers. At the level of commitment to the program, the resident keeps the room clean to be a role model in the community. In commitment to self, the resident maintains a clean room because he or she experiences the personal benefits of orderliness and cleanliness that feel good and make life easier.

Friendships

In the compliance and conformity stages, friendships are primarily based upon the nurturant experiences—the relief and comfort associated with reduced isolation. In the later stages of commitment, friendships reflect the personal benefits from the social relatedness experiences, such as identification and bonding.

Role model

Earlier in treatment, teaching new residents through personal disclosure ("giving it away") reflects the affiliative influences of conformity and commitment. Later, in the stage of commitment to self, giving it away reflects the personal benefit gained from reaffirming teachings for oneself. When someone "gave it you," it contributed to self-change. "Giving it away" to someone else reinforces self-change.

INTERNALIZATION AND THE LIMITS OF CHANGE IN THE TC

The concept and gradient of internalization capture how interrelated change occurs in individuals through their interaction with the community. However, for various reasons internalization may be incomplete: participation and affiliation may be superficial, learning may not occur in all behavioral dimensions, critical therapeutic experiences may not occur, and there may not be significant changes in self or identity. These limits of internalization in the change process result in profound clinical issues, which are illustrated in several examples.

Plateaus of Learning in the Change Process

During the course of change, the individual appears to be doing well, progress occurs on all dimensions, and learning is stabilized. Although this is a picture of improvement, it may also be indicative of plateaus in learning, the resident remaining too long at a particular point in the process. Time in program continues to accrue toward graduation although new learning has all but ceased. Thus, learning plateaus inherently limit the extent and course of internalized change.

The reasons for plateaus vary, relating both to the program and the client. The program may not clinically detect the frozen level of a stabilized resident who appears improved and who may also be useful to the program as a senior peer and worker. Thus, the community does not test or challenge the individual in the process. For example, senior residents often view themselves as having "arrived" at some end point—a view that may be inadvertently reinforced by junior residents and staff.

On the other hand, the individual may not move to the next level even if they are challenged, encouraged, or pressured. Sometimes this reflects deficits or limits in fundamental cognitive skills. More usually, individuals are not ready to move on because of emotional factors associated with anticipated demands of moving forward. These may include dealing with sensitive or deeper psychological issues, meeting increased performance expectations, or losing the stability of their hard-earned changes.

Arrested levels threaten stable recovery in different ways. Individuals may drop out because of boredom, failure to see a new learning opportunity, or incorrect conclusions that they are cured or ready to engage the outside world. Conversely, however, residents may remain until graduation with no further significant personal changes beyond the level achieved. This often reveals fears of the next step in the change process, for example, anxiety about separation from the program or the inability to see options in their lives outside of the program.

Plateaus are indicated in several ways: little or no changes in the domains after initial gains, the individual lacks willingness to take new risks in personal examination, and the individual fails to acquire the concept of learning to learn—that is, he or she does not accept learning as an important value for right living.

Readiness to engage the next level is evident when individuals volunteer for more responsibility in the community. They eagerly seek to participate in groups and particularly in special retreats and marathons offering high clinical impact, and they continue to self-examine and question the change process. Thus, readiness must be continually assessed by the individuals themselves, by peers, and by the staff to facilitate a movement through plateaus of learning.

Situational Internalization

Some residents can learn to walk and talk the expectations of the community yet still not achieve sufficient change to assure their recovery in the larger community. They may be excellent participants who reveal a high degree of conformity or situational internalization—that is, stable learning based only upon experiences within the confines of the residential community.

They perceive themselves as significantly changed individuals compared with their former lives. Indeed, they may be changed individuals while living within the microcommunity of the TC. However, as discussed above, without confirmatory experiences outside of the program they are not fully prepared to live successfully in the macrocommunity.

Situational internalization may also reflect plateaus of learning. Thus, for various reasons some individuals will not, or cannot, move beyond certain levels of change. Paradoxically, these individuals can live successfully while they are full-time residents in the program. Some move through the program stages and even achieve staff status. This in effect provides them the opportunity to be productive workers in the treatment agency. Although they may reside outside, their lives essentially remain in the program. For these individuals, situational internalization limits their identity change, which is defined largely by their permanent affiliation with the program.

Incomplete Identity Change ("Conversion Cures")

Sometimes TC successes are labeled "conversion cures" in the quasi-religious sense by observers and critics. In the TC, conversion is a shorthand term that can describe incomplete identity change. Conversion refers to both a phase and a role in the change process. The resident appears to undergo a distinctive shift from the negative past life to the positive TC lifestyle. The shift may be gradual and incremental but is often perceived by the individuals themselves and observers as a rather sudden "turn around." The resident displays the characteristics of the ideal role model as well as elements of early identity change.

Conversion can serve a positive function in the change process. During treatment, conversion is a desirable goal associated with full immersion into the program. The resident as convert is rehearsing and stabilizing the newly learned behavior, attitudes, and emotions of the sober, prosocial lifestyle. For some residents in re-entry, zealous adherence to the TC's recovery precepts and view of right living are necessary to sustain their immunity to negative influences in the macrocommunity. The reflex-like behaviors and attitudes that characterize the convert's role can reduce uncertainties about how to live or doubts about a newly forming identity.

Thus, the role of the convert can finalize individuals' separation from their past life and can assist them in coping with the uncertainties of a less familiar or unknown new lifestyle. However, remaining in the conversion phase or role can also impede the change process. For example, converts display inflexibility in their recovery thinking and in their use of program rhetoric. They can use the TC perspective to rationalize their not confronting new problems, doubts, and uncertainties. Paradoxically, these rationalizations reinforce personality characteristics of seeking relief rather than increasing tolerance for discomfort associated with new learning.

Rather than a more complete experiential learning, conversion can remain a dramatic example of conformity or program commitment. Identity changes are limited to the social roles and experiences in the program. Individuals must move past conversion to undergo the learning and experiences that gradually evolve into authentic identity change.

Internalization, Program Stages, and Retention in Treatment

Although internalized change is correlated with time in program, retention in treatment does not necessarily reflect the actual extent of internalization. Residents stay and complete treatment for various reasons that relate to the gradient of internalization. These may be external pressures (compliance), e.g., those from legal and family sources; the need for affiliation (conformity), e.g. avoiding aloneness and having social relationships; the desire to maintain their successful status as community member; or the intent to prove that they can complete the course (commitment to program).

Conversely, leaving treatment prematurely may not reveal the actual stage of internalization. For example, individuals may have critical therapeutic experiences at various points during their treatment tenure. These may result in significant changes in self-perceptions that move them into the levels of commitment to self on the internalization gradient. Nevertheless, they elect to drop out of treatment because they have learned all they could and need to move on in the change process in the outside world. While retention in treatment and program stages are correlated with individual changes, it is the extent of internalization that predicts the stability of these changes.

Thus, individuals differ in what they have internalized and in their stage of internalization whether they complete treatment or leave prematurely. Some graduates may be at early stages, while some dropouts may have achieved later stages of internalization. Clinical experience asserts that relapse and readmission to treatment reflects gaps or "missed steps"—incomplete internalization of critical changes during their initial treatment tenure. These gaps in the process must often be addressed in subsequent treatment admissions.

INTERNALIZATION IN THE CHANGE PROCESS BEYOND TREATMENT

The process of individual change is initiated rather than completed in treatment. During their stay in the TC, individuals learn to use the peer community to change themselves. When they leave, they must use what they have learned and experienced in the TC to sustain recovery and facilitate their personal growth.

Compliance, conformity, and commitment to program and to self describe internalization during the individual's tenure in community. However, internalized learning may continue among former residents who have been separated from TCs for several years. Not infrequently they report that a delayed or fuller appreciation of what they were taught in TCs did not occur until they had left the program and had opportunities to determine for themselves the validity of the lessons of treatment. Their *confirmatory experiences* result in a "retrospective internalization" of TC teachings, which guides continued right living not unlike the sustaining impact of good parental teaching. Indeed, these confirmatory experiences are critical elements in sustaining the individual in the change process beyond treatment.

Two additional stages depend upon confirmatory experiences to advance the change process beyond treatment, *continuance* and *integration*. Each illustrates the gradient of internalization as an interaction between the individual and the real world.

Continuance

In the stage of continuance, there is a personal resolve to maintain the behavior, attitudes, and values associated with a drug-free lifestyle. In addition, in this stage the individual addresses important psychological and social goals. He or she implements plans to improve life circumstances involving work, relationships, health, and meeting obligations and responsibilities. Therapy and other assistance strategies are utilized as support and guidance in the pursuit of these goals and for managing and learning from setbacks. The social network of the individual is exclusively composed of recovering peers and others who support the recovery process.

There are distinctive perceptual markers of the continuance stage concerning the meaning of drugs and of the change process. First, drugs are no longer seen as an option for coping with problems or experiencing life. Instead drugs are viewed as ineffective in providing relief, satisfaction, or escape, and drug use is seen as producing a worsening state. Drug-related thinking (e.g., anticipation of getting high, cynicism, rejection of social mores) is infrequent and does not compete with sobriety thinking (i.e., must deal with reality and self).

The second marker is continued commitment to the change process itself, which represents a stage on the gradient sustained by confirmatory experiences in the real world. The individual acknowledges the change process itself as a constant struggle and accepts this fact with enthusiasm, confidence, and humility.

Integration

Integration is a stage in the change process that emerges mainly after separation from treatment and a sustained period of sobriety in the larger community. It is an evolving stage with no obvious end point, in which continued individual change reflects influences merging from treatment teachings and everyday life experiences. The insights and coping strategies of treatment are validated through confirmatory experiences and are generalized to new social and personal situations. The individual gains perspective on his or her treatment experience, its benefits, limits, and uses in facilitating personal growth.

In this stage, sobriety is internalized. The individual does not consciously think about maintaining sobriety but accepts this as a prerequisite for living right. Affiliations are with mainstream circles and the "normal fraternity," including family, work, profession, religion, friends, and recovered peers. Life adjustment and self-actualization are the primary issues rather than recovery from chemical dependency. In their focus upon personal growth and psychological and existential issues, individuals may utilize professional assistance or guidance.

A change in identity is the distinctive marker of the integration stage. No single label describes how substance abusers see themselves, but several of the more frequently used social labels reflecting the effects of treatment are addict to recovering addict to nonaddict, social deviant to conventional person, baby to grown-up, and antisocial person to prosocial citizen. Individuals see themselves in positive terms, e.g., as recovering or formerly addicted, conventional, grown-up, or prosocial. They are no longer threatened by people associated with their past drug user identity. They can relate to active and recovering addicts in changed roles, e.g., as assistants or helpers, without requestioning their identity or where they are in recovery.

The shift in identity is gradual, as the elements of identity change are evident in the process during and following treatment. However, it is the conscious *perceptual contrast* marking the change in identity through which the individual reframes a retrospective self-perception: "Then is who I was" and "Now is who I am."

CONCLUSION

This chapter has detailed the concept, characteristics, and levels of internalization in the change process. Residents gradually incorporate the TC teachings and behavioral expectations through a process of experiential learning. Behavioral and cognitive changes are internalized when based upon positive subjective experiences. These changes foster new self-perceptions, eventually resulting in identity change. The concept of internalization unites the phenomenological and the behavioral features of the change process in the TC. However, a more complete picture of the *treatment process* is contained in the following chapter, which provides a conceptual framework of the TC as a unique social and psychological treatment approach.

Chapter 24

The Treatment Process: A Conceptual Framework

The fundamental premise of this volume is that the therapeutic community (TC) is a unique social and psychological approach for changing individuals. In this approach the continuing interaction between the individual and the community is viewed as the treatment process. However, the global psychosocial ecology of the TC, the wholistic nature of the disorder, the complexity of the individual, and the dynamic properties of recovery make describing, much less understanding, the process in the TC a formidable challenge.

In all approaches to substance abuse, the treatment process can be broadly conceptualized in terms of three main components: the treatment ingredients, which consist of the interventions or services delivered to produce changes; the ways in which the individual does change; and the mechanisms or principles that link individual changes to the treatment ingredients.[60] This chapter presents a conceptual framework of the treatment process in the TC. The essential elements of the perspective, model, and method are reformulated into the three broad components of the treatment process.

First, the *multiple interventions* (or treatment ingredients) in the process consist of the program structure, the people, daily regimen of

---

[60] In a pharmacological approach, for example, methadone is the active treatment ingredient linked to reductions in heroin use through a series of physiological events lessening craving and opioid-seeking behaviors. Analogous links are assumed in current nonmedical approaches. Particular interventions (e.g. supportive conversations, training, instructions, vouchers) are the active ingredients that presumably reduce drug-related behaviors through a series of interpersonal and psychological events (e.g., DiClemente & Prochaska, in press; Higgens & Budney, 1993; Miller & Rollnick, 1991; Stitzer, Iguchi, Kidorf, & Bigelow, 1993).

activities, and social interactions in the TC. Thus the community, its context and expectations for participation in these interventions, is the method for facilitating individual change.

Second, individual change is *multidimensional,* described in terms of objective social and psychological domains as well as subjective perceptions and experiences. Change unfolds as developmental learning through participation in the program and involvement in the community. Thus, the learning process is variable within individuals and across individuals. Third, *social and behavioral learning principles* and *subjective mechanisms* such as critical experiences, perceptions, and internalization are integral in the process itself. These link multidimensional changes with the multiple interventions in the community.

COMMUNITY AS MULTIPLE INTERVENTIONS

In the TC, all activities are designed to produce therapeutic–educational effects. In the change process, these activities, singly and in various combinations, constitute interventions that directly and indirectly impact the individual. Indeed, the term *global intervention* summarizes the use of all activities for teaching or healing and illustrates the meaning of community as method.

The present framework describes how these activities are implemented as interventions in the change process in terms of three broad characteristics. They are formal and informal, oriented to the community or the individual, and interactive in different ways that impact the individual.

Formal and Informal Interventions

Formal interventions are planned, routine, and they are usually regularly scheduled activities. They occur in designated or arbitrary settings and are mediated by staff or residents. Typical formal activities are the schedule of groups and meetings and one-to-one counseling sessions conducted by staff directly or by residents under staff supervision. Many activities are unplanned and informally mediated in the daily peer interactions. Residents are expected to monitor, correct, and instruct other residents in matters of security, rules, regulations, role model expectations, social manners, and civility. These personal disclosures, mutual sharing of thoughts and feelings, "rapping," and supportive affirmations are also interventional activities that spontaneously occur in peer dyads or in casually assembled groups in any setting.

Community Interventions

Although all activities are intended to change the individual, some may be delivered directly to the person and others indirectly to the community. The daily regimen of meetings, groups, seminars, job functions, community meals, and surveillance are directed to the general membership. As interventions, these activities are not contingent upon any specific event or problem in the community. Their impact on collective membership and the individual occurs through direct and indirect (i.e., vicarious) daily participation.

Specific interventions are not routinely scheduled but are dependent upon community needs. For example, the community pull-ups delivered by peers or staff (corrective reminders to the membership), house bans, general meetings, and special recreational events are implemented to address specific issues of the general membership. These may be problems to be solved or needs for inspiration or affirmation. The need for specific community interventions may be signaled by actual or anticipated events in the community, such as illness and deaths of residents or staff; local or national news events; or by perceived problems in the general community, such as unexpectedly high dropout, violence, drug use, poor participation, or low morale.

Individual Interventions

Certain interventions are specifically contingent upon the individual's behavior. These may be delivered by peers as pull-ups (corrective reminders to the individual), confrontations, affirmations, suggestions, and instructions occuring in and outside the clinical groups; or, they may be delivered by staff as privileges, job changes, phase changes, one-on-one brief or extended counseling conversations, verbal reprimands, and various disciplinary sanctions.

Although interventions may be targeted to specific individuals, they are also utilized to impact the general community. For example, as described in earlier chapters, disciplinary consequences for an individual devised and implemented by staff are informed by the observations of peers. Peer involvement elevates the incident and the corrective intervention to a community-wide teaching. In this way the individual, the peers, and the general membership are collectively *accountable* for the conduct of the community.

Interactive Interventions

The impact of particular interventions may be enhanced, delayed, or moderated in their interaction with each other. For example, the messages delivered in seminars may be clarified by informal peer conversations preceding and following the seminars. Or, an individual's acceptance of the observations made about him or her in the encounter group may not occur until he or she observes and confronts the same behavior in another member in a later encounter group. Thus, activities separately and in various combinations are required for some duration, intensity, and frequency to produce individual change.

MULTIDIMENSIONAL CHANGE IN THE PROCESS

Partitioning the "whole" individual into behaviors, experiences, and perceptions is a somewhat artificial device analogous to attempts at classification of the global milieu of the TC into separate interventions. As elaborated in the previous chapters, multidimensional change can be described objectively in terms of *interrelated* social and psychological behavioral domains and subjectively in terms of self-reported essential experiences and perceptions.

However, the idea of orderly or uniform change is idealized. Individuals differ in how much they share the same characteristics and particularly in their rates of change. Also, for specific individuals, change itself is notably variable. As individuals move through the program, they continually meet new demands and challenges. A stable level of change signals renewed efforts to continue to another level of self-learning and personal change, which reintroduces destabilization, new errors, uncertainty and then re-stabilized change. Although related in the process, the variability of behavioral and subjective changes is described separately.

Variability of Behavioral Change

Behavioral change is *uneven and erratic* in that it may occur on some but not all of the behavioral indicators. For example, in the domain of maturity, the resident may show reduction in certain behaviors (e.g., cussing on the floor) but not others (e.g., still talks back to staff). Within a domain, change may not be stable in that old and new behaviors and attitudes may appear, disappear, and reappear over time. For example, in the social deviancy domain, decreases in street jargon, antisocial attitudes, and drug talk are variable particularly in the initial months of the program.

Change across the behavioral domains and dimensions is *asymmetrical* in that it may not occur in a uniform way. Although domains and dimensions are interrelated, their rate of change is not necessarily correlated. For example, residents may show considerable improvement in socialization, but small or modest overall improvement in the psychological domains.

Variability of Subjective Change

Subjective changes are perhaps more variable than behavioral changes. Feelings and perceptions are continually in flux reflecting the interpersonal intensity of community life as well as the course of trial and error learning. For example, the experiences of being understood and accepted by others shift in daily interactions particularly during the therapeutic groups. Such experiences can affect changes in the individual's perceptions of the suitability of the TC itself. Perceptions of personal progress, all depend upon the stability of behavioral and attitudinal changes. Thus, how clearly individuals see themselves as different is in part associated with the variability in their behavioral changes.

Another source of variability in perceptions and experiences arises from influences outside of the community. Interactions with families and friends exert pressures on the individual to stay in or leave treatment. Revisiting old neighborhoods and coping with the real world during furlough continually test new learning and evoke experiences, which challenge the individual's perception of his or her progress and self-change.

Overall, the variability of the multidimensional change process reveals familiar elements of trial and error learning. Behavioral and subjective variability is greater early in treatment but gradually diminishes. For example, the experiences of physical and psychological safety are less stable in the first weeks or months of community life when individuals are learning to take the risks of personal disclosure. With time in the community, variability lessens reflecting incrementally stabilized behavioral and experiential change.

PRINCIPLES OF CHANGE

Thus far, the main elements of the treatment process in the TC have been described in terms of community interventions, behavioral dimensions, and the essential perceptions and experiences. How individual change occurs refers to the social and psychological principles and mechanisms linking the multidimensional changes with the interventions.

Social and Behavioral Learning Principles

All change in the TC is viewed from a behavioral orientation in terms of learning and training. Embedded in the community life of the TC are familiar behavioral training and social learning principles that explain how community teaches and trains individual change.

Social role training

Changing the social roles of individuals is an efficient way of facilitating learning across several domains of behaviors, attitudes, emotions, and values. The focus of role training is on constellations of related behaviors, skills, and attitudes that have social and psychological relevance to recovery. As described in earlier chapters the resident positions in the job hierarchy, such as expediter, departmental head, and coordinator, are all examples of work roles trained in the TC. Role model is a broader class of related behaviors and attitudes reflecting the values and expectations of the community. Typically these expectations are summed up in community roles, such as student, apprentice, teacher, and leader, which describe the changing relationship of the individual to the community. Thus, as individuals successfully learn their various social roles in the community, they undergo a wide range of social and psychological changes.

Vicarious learning

Vicarious learning is inherent in the context of community life, its rules, norms, daily regimen of activities, and informal interactions. Peers and staff role model the appropriate behaviors and attitudes as normative expectations of the community. Self-change is often initiated through observation of and identification with others in the day-to-day social and interpersonal interactions—hearing the different life stories and witnessing subtle and dramatic examples of changes in peers over time.

These features transmit powerful emotional and perceptual signals toward self-change. Also, indirect vicarious cues come from the information about others, e.g., the dispositions of dropouts and the successes of graduates and of staff.

Thus, the principle of vicarious learning is pervasive in community life. Residents imitate other people who are role models of change, and they identify with the stories of others, which facilitates self-change in thinking and perceptions as well as behavior. In general, the daily exposure to and perceptions of others in various stages of change foster self-change without specific instruction and provides incentives to engage in the trial and error learning process.

Efficacy training

All learning in TCs involves residents overcoming past failures concerning their performance in coping with drug use in particular and with life in general. Efficacy refers to performing the behavior that works. Efficacy and self-esteem refer to the individual's subjective outcomes associated with performing successfully the behavior that works. These involve perceptions and feelings expressed as increased confidence about performing in general, as well as the individual's changing beliefs and expectancies in his or her ability to deal with new situations in particular (e.g., Marlatt & Gordon, 1985). Meeting community expectations in performance, responsibility, self-examination, and autonomy involves increasing self-efficacy and self-esteem.

Underlying efficacy training, as well as the other learning principles in the TC, is the general concept of *trial and error.* The resident must engage in the new behaviors or attitudes in order to change. In the behavioral learning literature the phrase trial and error involves searching for the "right response." In the TC vicarious cues, social roles, and continuous feedback provide residents with clear instructions, suggestions, and examples that guide new learning. Thus, in the TC the term trial refers to trying or making valid attempts to follow these guides.

The community encourages and reinforces residents for trying to change—that is, for engaging in efforts to change. The term failure is rarely used except to describe not trying, or giving up rather than making errors. Trying also includes attempts to change attitudes as well as behaviors. Such efforts can also be experienced as change. Thus, in the TC trying *is* changing, and residents who see themselves as trying are often motivated to continue working at changing.

In the TC views of the person and recovery, errors or displays of the wrong behaviors and attitudes are essential for learning and individual change. For example, the entire system of privileges and disciplinary sanctions is based upon community expectations that social infractions, skill deficits, and negative attitudes will and should occur. These characteristics of the person and the disorder cannot be readily modified *unless* they appear. Negative behaviors and attitudes that are concealed to avoid community sanctions are not accessible to modification. Stable change involves learning the positive behaviors and elimination of the negative behaviors and attitudes.

Avoiding errors often signifies that residents are not taking the necessary risks for change to occur. They may stick with what they know best and take few chances in assuming new levels of role responsibility or in social interactions. Their avoidance of errors precludes their developing new tolerance for performance demands and reinforces their fears of criticism or failure. It also encourages tendencies to non-disclosure, secretiveness, and hiding of weaknesses, factors that contribute to poor self-esteem. Thus, the avoidance of errors limits the extent and stability of the individual's learning.

Finally, as was elaborated in the previous chapter, making errors is viewed as necessary to achieve internalization of new learning. Without experiential outcomes such as self-efficacy, learning is less likely to become internalized. Trial and error attempts produce objective and subjective consequences such that the resident can easily and quickly experience the differences between new and old ways of behaving. Thus, trying and making errors provides a reliable experiential basis for learned changes to become internalized.

Community as trainer

Although behavioral and social learning principles are evident in the TC, these are *naturalistically mediated* as an inherent characteristic of community as method. An explicit instruction by the community to the community is that peers and staff are the observers, monitors, and mediators of the messages of recovery and right living. Indeed, the role of community member itself is trained and mutually monitored. Residents are expected to be attentive to the physical and social environment of the facility, to offer specific instruction and feedback in support of individual efforts to change, and to express their concerns or affirmation concerning the status of the community itself. Staff, as community members, guide the residents to be role models and peer trainers and monitor the fidelity and impact of the daily activities as interventions for individuals and the community.

PERCEPTUAL AND EXPERIENTIAL MECHANISMS IN THE PROCESS

In the TC perspective, changing the whole person involves not only observable behaviors but subjective perceptions and experiences. This section discusses perceptions and experiences as *integral mechanisms* in the change process.[61]

Perceptual Contrast

Perceptual contrast occurs when residents acknowledge to themselves that they have changed in reference to their past profile. Contrast effects may simply be residents seeing themselves as behaving and feeling differently. More dramatic contrasts may be expressed as self- or identity change. Thus, perceptions of change and progress are outcomes in the process, but as contrasts they are also *contributors* to the process of change.

Perceptual contrasts of change or progress may occur as distinct events at particular moments, as in encounter groups or marathons. They may arise in other special circumstances away from the program such as in day trips or weekend furloughs. These situations provide the individual with explicit opportunities for making comparative observations and confirming personal changes with respect to how they experience the old neighborhood, the proximity of drugs and users, or how they relate to friends, the family, children, etc.

More often, however, the cues for contrasts are ordinary and emerge in the various roles and everyday activities of the community, e.g., seeing younger or newer residents who are earlier in the process, listening to a seminar, handling a stressful or provocative situation with peers or staff in a new constructive way, managing feelings differently, or simply noting the absence or reduced frequency of old thinking about drugs and related matters.

Although perceptual contrasts are private events, they illustrate how community life contributes to the change process. For example, residents are constantly interacting with others in various stages of recovery. Senior residents have the opportunity to objectively view the behaviors and attitudes of junior residents. They perceive the difference between their own behavior at an earlier time and their current behavior as role models. This perceived contrast of the personal past and present encourages

---

[61] The formulation of perceptions and experiences as mechanisms in the change process does not derive directly from the psychological literature. Rather it represents the author's attempt to integrate behavioral and phenomenological concepts in the change process.

forward looking perceptions ("where I am" to "where I want to be") that are further reinforced by peers, staff, and family.

Perceptual Kindling

Perceptual contrasts are kindled during treatment—that is, they usually represent the summation of smaller changes in behaviors, thinking, and feelings. When these changes reach a threshold of consistency or regularity, they culminate in the individual's clear recognition of a difference in themselves. Such perceptual contrast can facilitate larger or more rapid behavioral and attitude changes that lead to more pronounced perceptions.

Perception of a changing self is a higher order perceptual contrast in the change process that is kindled from smaller behavioral and experiential changes. For example, "I am growing up" is a self-perception that evolves from changes across many domains (e.g., maturity, responsibility, values, habilitation). Large perceptions such as self-change significantly reinforce the commitment to the change process itself. Thus, major perceptual contrasts (kindled in the process) are both critical goals as well as facilitators of the process itself.

TABLE 24-1. Perceptual Kindling in the Process: Several Clinical Examples

---

"Dry drunk"

A common expression among substance abusers that illustrates a negative example of kindling in the recovery process. Not infrequently individuals may display behaviors, attitudes, and feelings associated with active drinking prior to actually reusing alcohol or drugs. Uninterrupted, however, these small changes lead to perceptions of faltering ("I may as well drink"), which can precipitate full episodes of behavioral relapse.

"Act as if"

A key instructional concept in the TC that is a positive illustration of the mechanism of kindling. "Act as if" enjoins individuals to engage in positive behaviors and attitudes regardless of how they usually behave or actually perceive themselves. Continued "acting as if" gradually leads to perceptions of real change, which in turn sustains individuals in the change process.

Early engagement

A critical stage in treatment is induction, when individuals are at high risk to drop out of the program. Thus, perceptual kindling that initiates early engagement can sustain retention in treatment. For example, individual changes from listening to *hearing* others tell their story may lead to the individual's moving from the back to the front of the room. This change may be associated with perceptions of possibilities which are then followed by self-initiating their own story. These incremental changes leading to early engagement summate to perceptions of initial affiliation, which may then activate fuller behavioral participation in the program.

The concept of kindling underscores the "silent features" of the change process. Small unobserved changes in behaviors and cognitions eventually result in larger changes, which then become perceptible to the individual and to others. Table 24-1 illustrates the positive and negative elements of kindling in several clinical examples.

Therapeutic Events

In the change process, learning is erratic, gradual, and incremental. However, the course is punctuated by distinctive moments of personal change involving a "total" experience (i.e., related relevant thoughts–perceptions, feelings, and understanding). These moments mark critical experiences, which when associated with explicit circumstances, (e.g., in marathons) are viewed as therapeutic events. These special experiences singularly facilitate major changes, which may be behavioral (e.g., new effective ways of coping and responding), special insights (e.g., new understanding of the self in relation to outside influences), and commitments to change (e.g., re-decisions to continue in the process).

Therapeutic events appear to be "sudden," but they usually represent the individual's development in the program up to the point of occurrence. Occasionally, however, they are isolated incidents of "personal breakthroughs," sharp incremental changes in self-learning. These are viewed as critical junctures of change, which sustain the individual in the process and accelerate the overall rate of individual learning. Thus, the program attempts to induce therapeutic events at appropriate points in the process utilizing such activities as a special marathon or retreats.

From a process perspective, therapeutic events or moments, enhance the change process—that is, they link previous learning with current learning, which in turn mediates new learning. For example, individuals' reorganizing or reframing of his or her history, problems, and life options may foster a changing perspective of himself or herself. Although often involving painful feelings, therapeutic events are experiences that are essentially positive: They motivate the individual to continue actively engaging in the treatment and recovery process.

Overall, experiences and perceptions are critical dimensions of the whole person. These subjective elements also function as mechanisms in the change process. Either as consequences of interventions or correlates of behavioral change, they encourage participation, reinforce learning, and sustain individuals in the process itself.

Integrating the Elements of the Treatment Process

The treatment process in the TC can be framed as the dynamic relationship between the community as a context of planned and unplanned multiple interventions and multidimensional change in the individual. Dynamic means that the change process itself is variable and incremental (evolving in steps). Thus, interrelated changes in behaviors, attitudes, experiences, and perceptions gradually evolve into lifestyle and identity change as individuals fully immerse themselves in the community and internalize its teachings (see Figure 24-1).

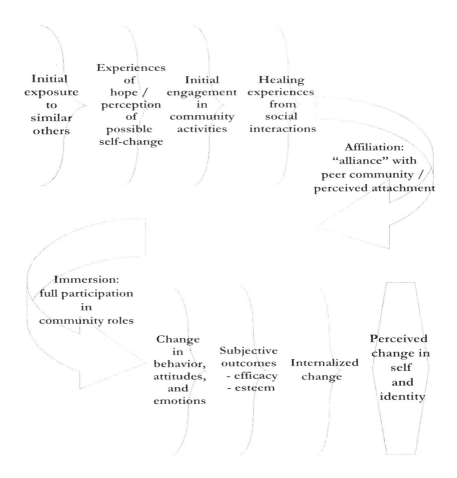

FIGURE 24-1.

The Treatment Process in the TC: Main Elements

Social and psychological principles, naturalistically mediated in the context of community life, explain how individuals learn in the TC and essential perceptions and experiences function as integral mechanisms in the process itself. However, community as a method stresses that individuals change socially and psychologically when they are fully immersed in the life of the community. Meeting expectations for participation in all community activities and roles leads to individual change that deepens involvement, continued participation, and further change. This ongoing interaction between the individual and the community captures the essence of the treatment process in the TC.

CONCLUSION

A conceptual framework of the TC treatment process as a unique social and psychological approach to changing individuals reformulates, but does not substitute for, the TC perspective and method. In the TC, recovery and lifestyle and identity change occur through "living right," which means the full participation in all of the activities and roles of the community and internalizing its values and recovery teachings. Full participation results in changes in lifestyle, which may be described as the integration of new behaviors, cognitions, emotions, attitudes, and values. Thus, changes in living guided by community eventually result in how individuals experience and perceive themselves—that is, identity change.

Chapter 25

Therapeutic Communities: The Challenge of Evolution

As the therapeutic community (TC) continues to evolve into the mainstream of human services, it is changing, reshaping its staffing composition, modifying its approach and to some extent resetting its goals. These changes are expected and consistent with the TC's own teaching which stresses that the *only certainty in life is change itself.* But in this evolutionary transition, there is a significant risk that the original model and method will mutate beyond recognition and—more importantly—lose its effectiveness. This is a risk that compels the TC to retain what is unique about its identity and its efficacy.

An explicit rationale for this volume is that a theoretical framework of the TC grounded in clinical and research experience can maintain its unique identity and the fidelity of its wider applications. This assumption is illustrated in several broad initiatives that are either underway or urgently needed to be launched: (a) the specification of the essential components of a *generic TC model*; (b) general guidelines for adapting and modifying the TC for special settings, special populations, and funding limits; (c) the codification of principles and practices of the TC into explicit *standards* to maintain the integrity of the program model and method; (d) the dissemination of TC *training and technical assistance* grounded in theory and method to sustain the fidelity of TC practices; and (e) the formulation of a relevant *research agenda* to refine TC theory and to improve the treatment approach.

In this final chapter these initiatives are briefly discussed. Though interrelated, each represents a strategy for retaining the essentials of the TC as it continually adapts its approach for the diversity of problems, people, and settings.

A GENERIC TC MODEL

Not all residential drug treatment programs are TCs, not all TCs are in residential settings, and not all programs that call themselves TCs employ the same models of treatment. Unfortunately, the label TC is often misused to represent programs in almost any setting. One effect of this labeling has been to cloud understanding of the TC as a drug treatment approach, how well it works, where it works best, and for which client it is most appropriate. The theory, model, and method of the TC formulated in this volume provide the basis for defining the essential components of a generic TC program model contained in Table 25-1.

TABLE 25-1. Components of a Generic TC Program Model

Community separateness

TC-oriented programs have their own names, often innovated by the clients and housed in a space or locale that is separated from other agency or institutional programs, units, or generally from the drug-related environment. In the residential settings, clients remain away from outside influences 24 hours a day for several months before earning short-term day-out privileges. In the nonresidential "day treatment" settings, the individual is in the TC environment for 4–8 hours, and then monitored by peers and family. Even in the least restrictive outpatient settings, TC-oriented programs and components are in place. Members gradually detach from old networks and relate to the drug-free peers in the program.

A community environment

The inner environment of a TC facility contains communal space to promote a sense of commonalty and collective activities, e.g., groups, meetings. The walls display signs stating in simple terms the philosophy of the program, the messages of right living and recovery. Cork boards and black boards identify all participants by name, seniority level, and job function in the program; daily schedules are posted as well. These visuals display an organizational picture of the program that the individual can relate to and comprehend, factors promoting affiliation.

Community activities

To be effectively utilized, treatment or educational services must be provided within a context of the peer community. Thus, with the exception of individual counseling, all activities are programmed in collective formats. These include at least one daily meal prepared, served, and shared by all members; a daily schedule of groups, meetings, and seminars; team job functions; and organized recreational/leisure time; ceremonies and rituals (e.g., birthdays, phase/progress graduations, etc.).

Table continues

TABLE 25-1. Components of a Generic TC Program Model

Table continued

Staff roles and functions

The staff are a mix of self-help recovered professionals and other traditional professionals (e.g., medical, legal, mental health, and educational) who must be integrated through cross-training grounded in the basic concepts of the TC perspective and community approach. Professional skills define the function of staff (e.g., nurse, physician, lawyer, teacher, administrator, case worker, clinical counselor). Regardless of professional discipline or function, however, the generic *role* of all staff is that of community member who, rather than providers and treaters, are rational authorities, facilitators, and guides in the self-help community method.

Peers as role models

Members who demonstrate the expected behaviors and reflect the values and teachings of the community are viewed as role models. Indeed, the strength of the community as a context for social learning relates to the number and quality of its role models. All members of the community are expected to be role models—roommates; older and younger residents; junior, senior, and directorial staff. TCs require these multiple role models to maintain the integrity of the community and assure the spread of social learning effects.

A structured day

The structure of the program relates to the TC perspective, particularly the view of the client and recovery. Ordered routine activities counter the characteristically disordered lives of these clients and distract from negative thinking and boredom, factors that predispose drug use. And, structured activities of the community facilitate learning self-structure for the individual, in time management, planning, setting and meeting goals, and in general accountability. Thus, regardless of its length, the day has a formal schedule of varied therapeutic and educational activities with prescribed formats, fixed times, and routine procedures.

Work as therapy and education

Consistent with the TC's self-help approach, all clients are responsible for the daily management of the facility (e.g., cleaning, activities, meal preparation and service, maintenance, purchasing, security, coordinating schedules, preparatory chores for groups, meetings, seminars activities, etc.). In the TC, the various work roles mediate essential educational and therapeutic effects. Job functions strengthen affiliation with the program through participation, provide opportunities for skill development, and foster self-examination and personal growth through performance challenge and program responsibility. The scope and depth of client work functions depend upon the program setting (e.g., institutional vs. free-standing facilities) and client resources (levels of psychological function, social and life skills).

Phase format

The treatment protocol, or plan of therapeutic and educational activities, is organized into phases that reflect a developmental view of the change process. Emphasis is on incremental learning at each phase, which moves the individual to the next stage of recovery.

Table continues

TABLE 25-1. Components of a Generic TC Program Model

Table continued

TC concepts

There is a formal and informal curriculum focused on teaching the TC perspective, particularly its self-help recovery concepts and view of right living. The concepts, messages, and lessons of the curriculum are repeated in the various groups, meetings, seminars, and peer conversations, as well as in readings, signs, and personal writings.

Peer encounter groups

The main community or therapeutic group is the encounter, although other forms of therapeutic, educational, and support groups are utilized as needed. The minimal objective of the peer encounter is similar in TC-oriented programs—to heighten individual awareness of specific attitudes or behavioral patterns that should be modified. However, the encounter process may differ in degree of staff direction and intensity, depending on the client subgroups (e.g., adolescents, prison inmates, the dually disordered)

Awareness training

All therapeutic and educational interventions involve raising the individual's consciousness of the impact of their conduct/attitudes on themselves and the social environment; and conversely the impact of the behaviors and attitudes of others on themselves and the social environment.

Emotional growth training

Achieving the goals of personal growth and socialization involves teaching individuals how to identify feelings, express feelings appropriately, and manage feelings constructively through the interpersonal and social demands of communal life.

Planned duration of treatment

The optimal length of time for full program involvement must be consistent with TC goals of recovery and its developmental view of the change process. How long the individual must be program-involved depends on their phase of recovery, although a minimum period of intensive involvement is required to assure internalization of the TC teachings.

Continuity of care

Completion of primary treatment is a stage in the recovery process. Aftercare services are an essential component in the TC model. Whether implemented within the boundaries of the main program or separately as in residential or nonresidential halfway houses or ambulatory settings, the perspective and approach guiding aftercare programming must be *continuous* with that of primary treatment in the TC. Thus, the views of right living and self-help recovery and the use of a peer network are essential to enhance the appropriate use of vocational, educational, mental health, social, and other typical aftercare or re-entry services.

From "Therapeutic Communities for Addictions: A Theoretical Framework," by G. De Leon, 1995, *International Journal of the Addictions, 30* (12), pp. 1603-1645. Copyright 1995 by Marcel Dekker, Inc. Reprinted with permission.

GENERAL GUIDELINES FOR ADAPTATIONS AND MODIFICATIONS OF THE TC

It is much beyond the purview of the present chapter to detail the current diversity of TC-oriented programs. Various examples of successful adaptations of the generic model are described in the literature (e.g., De Leon, 1997a). Table 25-2 summarizes general guidelines for modifying and adapting TC-oriented programs organized in terms of special populations, settings, and services.

Typically modifications and adaptations overlap and are interrelated. For example, mentally ill substance abusers may be treated in shelters, community residences, day treatment clinics, partial hospital settings, or on hospital wards. TC programs for criminal offender substance abusers are usually housed in correctional settings. Special services address the specific needs of particular populations, although some of these services may be offered to all populations in all settings.

TABLE 25-2. General Guidelines for Modifications and Adaptations of the TC for Special Populations, Settings, and Services

---

SPECIAL POPULATIONS
Adolescent substance abusers, adolescents with emotional problems, criminal offenders with substance abuse, HIV positive and AIDS clients, homeless men and women, mothers with children, mentally ill chemical abusers (MICAs), mentally ill chemical abusers in prisons, methadone clients

General guidelines
Appropriate staff are needed to treat various populations of substance abusers. Effective adaptation of the TC model and method for these special populations requires that all staff, regardless of professional training or treatment orientation, are committed to the implementation of the TC approach model and method. Additionally, treatment goals, duration, and intensity must be appropriate to the client.

Some key points
- *Cross training:* Staff with TC experience and traditional professional staff with TC or recovery experience must be trained together in the essential elements of the TC approach and in the problems, needs, and services of the special population.

- *Treatment goals:* Sobriety, socialization, and right living remain the primary goals of TC treatment for all substance abusers. However, additional treatment goals must be emphasized for the populations served; for example, for adolescents, normalizing their developmental trajectory; for mentally ill chemical abusers, fostering efficient use of mental health and social services; for the criminal offender, changing criminal thinking; for the homeless, maintaining permanent housing and securing employment.

Table continues

TABLE 25-2.   General Guidelines for Modifications and Adaptations of the TC
for Special Populations, Settings, and Services

Table continued

[SPECIAL POPULATIONS] **Key points** *continued*

- *Planned duration of treatment:* Not all residents need the same time to achieve the TC goals of treatment. Rather than a fixed planned duration of treatment, the critical criteria for movement through the program are clinical status and stage of recovery. Similarly, strategies should match clients with planned duration of treatment. For example, shorter TC-oriented residential treatments are appropriate for clients who are more socialized and habilitated, less psychologically impaired, and more capable of sustaining abstinence.

- *Intensity of treatment:* The demand characteristics of the traditional TC may not be appropriate for certain populations. TC clinical and management practices can be moderated depending upon the population in terms of disciplinary sanctions, peer interactions, and confrontation groups; and there is greater use of various group therapy formats. The basic TC program of peer groups, meetings, and communal interaction remains unchanged, although the daily regimen of activities is relaxed to permit more time and services outside of the primary program.

- *Flexibility:* The primary treatment in the TC is mediated by the peer community. However, there is greater focus upon individual differences with respect to needs and services. For example, the phase format is more variable and family involvement, mental health counseling, pharmacotherapy, and special education services are individually assessed and provided. There is greater use of psychoeducational strategies to teach clients the TC perspective and approach and the basic information about special problems and needs, e.g., fundamentals of mental illness, criminogenic thinking, family health, and dynamics.

SPECIAL SETTINGS

Ambulatory outpatient clinics, alternative schools, community residences for MICAs, community-based shelters, day treatment clinics, hospital-affiliated shelters, methadone clinics, jails, prisons, short-term community residences

General guidelines

The effectiveness of TC models in various prisons, hospitals, shelters, and clinics depends upon their successful integration into these settings. TC programs accommodate the goals, procedures, personnel, general practices, and restrictions of the settings in which they are implemented. Thus there is a general understanding and acceptance of how the TC operates within the host system or in linkages with other systems.

Some key points

- Orientation and training in the TC approach is provided to all relevant personnel in the system or setting to foster an understanding of the TC. Conversely, TC personnel must be oriented to the special features and requirements of the setting.

- Professional and working relationships between TC and non–TC personnel in the setting must be cultivated. Communication, sharing information, and mutual problem solving are ongoing activities among relevant personnel.

Table continues

TABLE 25-2. General Guidelines for Modifications and Adaptations of the TC for Special Populations, Settings, and Services

Table continued

[SPECIAL SETTINGS] Key points *continued*

- Commitment to support the TC is sustained through demonstrating that the program has a positive impact on the host system or setting, e.g., improved management of clients, elevated moral among staff and clients.

SPECIAL SERVICES

Child care/parenting, family therapies, mental health counseling, pharmacotherapy, special education, vocational counseling, relapse prevention training (RPT), rational emotive therapy (RET), other cognitive/behavioral therapies (CBT)

General guidelines

Various techniques, services, and interventions should amplify and enhance the effectiveness of the TC approach rather than modify or replace basic TC practices.

Some key points

- *Timing:* Services are introduced when individuals have a stable affiliation with the peer community and a full understanding of the TC approach.

- *Personnel:* The staff providing these services are oriented to and supportive of the TC approach.

- *Integration:* Special services are consistent with the TC perspective and approach and are judiciously integrated into the daily regimen of TC activities.

Table 25-3 illustrates examples of the above guidelines. It highlights some key modifications and applications of the TC treatment approach for three different populations in various settings: adolescents (e.g., De Leon & Deitch, 1985; Jainchill et al., 1995, 1997, 1999; Pompi, 1994); inmates in correctional settings (e.g., Lipton, 1999; Lockwood, Inciardi, Butzin, & Hooper, 1997; Wexler, De Leon, Thomas, Kressel, & Peters, 1999; Wexler & Williams, 1986); and mentally ill chemical abusers in institutional and community-based settings (e.g., De Leon, 1993b; Galanter, Egelko, Rohrs, & De Leon, 1993; Sacks et al., 1997; Silberstein et al., 1997).

In summary, successful adaptations of the TC adhere to the perspective on recovery and right living and to the fundamental approach—community as method. They retain basic components of the generic model including its social organization, work structure, daily schedule of meetings, groups, seminars, recreational activities, and program phases. The variety of staff needed in these adaptations are integrated conceptually in the TC perspective and approach through intensive and continuous cross training.

TABLE 25-3. Adaptations of the TC Approach: Three Examples

TCS FOR ADOLESCENTS

Clinical issues

Compared with adults, more adolescents enter TC programs under external/legal or family pressures; and most have social, vocational, and educational deficits along with psychological problems. They generally lack strong intrinsic motivation for personal change; they remain unemancipated from family support and are vulnerable to the social and sexual pressures of developmental change even after treatment.

Treatment goals

The traditional TC goals of recovery, to facilitate life style and identity change, may be too ambitious when applied to adolescent substance abusers. For adolescents, an overarching objective of treatment in TCs is to facilitate normative development. Normative development presumes that a young person has acquired a certain degree of immunity against re-engaging in serious drug abuse and/or related antisocial behavior. It also implies that the young person has sufficient maturity to engage "risk behaviors" including sexuality, social intercourse, and even the occasional recreational use of marijuana and alcohol without necessarily resulting in harmful consequences.

Adaptation and modifications

These include age-segregated facilities with considerable emphasis on management and supervision, fully deployed educational programs, greater family involvement and individual counseling.

TCS FOR INCARCERATED SUBSTANCE ABUSERS

Clinical issues

The special needs of substance abusers in correctional settings center on various themes, their social deviance and criminal "masks," their lower intrinsic motivation for change and conversely the influences of their nonrecovery reasons for seeking treatment in prison, their needs for postrelease treatment and aftercare services to reintegrate into the larger society.

Treatment goals

The basic goals of lifestyle and identity change remain the same. However there is increased focus upon changing criminal thinking, strengthening intrinsic motivational reasons for personal change, and sustaining their commitment to continue treatment after release from prison.

Adaptation and modifications

These are also shaped by the unique features of the correctional setting, e.g., its focus on security, its goal of early release, its limited physical and social space, and the prison/jail culture itself. Programs remain segregated from general prison population. Correctional officers and prison administrators, mental health and TC treatment paraprofessionals are cross-trained in the implementation of the program. For inmates who leave these prison TCs, models for *continuance of recovery* are established outside the walls in TC-oriented halfway houses.

Table continues

TABLE 25-3. Adaptations of the TC Approach: Three Examples

Table continued

TCs FOR MENTALLY ILL CHEMICAL ABUSERS (MICAs)

Clinical issues

The special needs of severely mentally ill chemical abusers center on the themes of the mental illness' symptoms, their fragility to intense social interactions, overall level of social dysfunction, their lower tolerance of structured regimens, their proneness toward social withdrawal, and their need for appropriate utilization of mental health services.

Treatment goals

The basic goals of lifestyle and identity change are viewed as long-term objectives that can be realized dependent upon the functional level of the individual. Realistic goals are the individuals' acceptance of the mutual effects of their substance abuse and mental illness problems, engagement into the change process, learning to use and be effective in the peer community, strengthening daily living skills, commitment to continue drug abuse and mental health treatment beyond the program, and preparation for vocational and educational training. Homelessness is a third major problem for many of these MICA clients. Thus an additional treatment goal is training clients to seek and secure permanent housing to minimize risk of relapse.

Adaptation and modifications

The clinical issues of the MICA clients shape the key modifications. There is greater focus on individual differences evident in more use of individual psychotherapy, case management, and skills training activities, more flexibility in the daily regimen of activities and in the phase format, a less demanding work structure, use of standard psychotropic medications, moderated intensity of group process, more focus on mental health issues, and greater use of psychoeducational formats. Adaptations in host settings such as hospitals and shelters require intensive cross training of personnel and accommodation to institutional features.

Modifications in practices and in program elements for special populations and settings center upon the treatment goals and planned duration of treatment, flexibility of the program structure to accommodate individual differences and in the intensity of peer interactions. Special services and interventions are integrated into the program as supplemental to the primary TC treatment. Successful implementation of TC program models within special settings requires accommodation to the goals, procedures, personnel, general practices, and restrictions of these settings.

PROGRAM STANDARDS

The theoretical framework outlines what the TC should be, and the generic components specify the essentials of the treatment model. How the TC approach is *practiced,* however, underscores the need for codified standards. Standards grounded in the TC perspective and method can guide implementation, management, and accountability of TC-oriented programs in all settings. As criteria for accreditation and licensure for programs and personnel, standards can assure the quality of TC practices.

Standards also provide a certain "immunity" to influences that potentially can mutate the basics of the TC approach. Contemporary TC agencies have established linkages with other human services and systems to serve special populations (e.g., criminal justice, mental health, child care, juvenile justice, and homeless shelters). The standards or regulatory requirements that govern services to these populations can neutralize or dilute, or alter the practices and principles of the TC (see for example, De Leon, 1997b).

A recent example of the "immunity" offered by the TC's *own* standards is illustrated in the correctional system. Standards for prison-based TCs have been developed by Therapeutic Communities of America (TCA).[62] Based upon the components of the generic TC, these standards provide a prototype for other populations and special settings.

THEORY, PRACTICE, AND TRAINING

Staffing compositions have changed to reflect a mix of traditional professionals; correctional, mental health, medical, educational, family, and child care specialists; social workers; and case managers to serve along with the experientially trained TC professionals. These compositional changes have introduced profound issues of staff integration (see De Leon, 1997b; Deitch & Solit, 1993b). Staffing issues reflect differences in vernacular, academic education, experience with addiction; and particularly in staff roles and functions within the unique context of a peer community model.

Achieving staff integration and assuring fidelity in implementing the TC model requires an organized training and technical assistance capability comprised of several key features: a *uniform curriculum* grounded in TC theory and practice and reflecting its codified standards; *an expert faculty of TC trainers* who possess the practical experience and

---

[62] These standards for TC programs in correctional settings have been published by The White House Office of National Drug Control Policy (ONDCP) (Therapeutic Communities of America Criminal Justice Committee, 1999, December). Additionally, standards for community-based residential TCs have been recently developed for CARF...The Rehabilitation Accreditation Commission (CARF, 2000).

conceptual understanding of the TC; a relevant *training format* that stresses staff integration through cross training of personnel from all disciplines; a training program with *university affiliation* to fully establish the credibility of the approach and its practitioners.

Several of these features are provided in current but diverse training efforts (e.g., Carroll & Sobel, 1986; Deitch & Solit, 1993a; Sacks, et al., 1996; Talboy, 1998). However, a large scale initiative (e.g., a national TC academy) is needed that incorporates and coordinates all of the above staff training components. An organized, cohesive training initiative represents a visible, compelling symbol of the maturity and distinction of the TC approach.

THEORY AND A NEW RESEARCH AGENDA

Three decades of evaluation research support the TCs theoretical perspective concerning the need for long-term treatment to change the "whole person" (e.g., Anglin & Hser, 1990b; Condelli & Hubbard, 1994; De Leon, 1984b; 1985; Gerstein & Harwood, 1990; Hubbard et al., 1989, 1997; Hubbard, Valley Rachal, Craddock, & Cavanaugh, 1984; Simpson et al., 1997; Simpson & Sells, 1982; Tims, De Leon & Jainchill, 1994; Tims & Ludford, 1984).

However, contemporary TCs are treating more diverse and difficult clients in shorter periods of time and with decreasing resources. This development defines the need for a *new research agenda* that addresses the validity of the TC perspective and approach for the current diversity of clients and settings. Several lines of inquiry in this agenda are illustrated in Table 25-4.

Overall, a new research agenda for the TC must be grounded in its theoretical framework and relevant to its current adaptations and modifications. Research should guide in what ways the TC model and method can be modified, for whom it works best, and how to improve the treatment process and to prove the validity of framework itself.

TABLE 25-4. Theory and a New Research Agenda: Three Lines of Inquiry

Planned duration of treatment and internalized recovery

TC theory asserts that duration of treatment is critically correlated with *internalized* learning. If individual changes are not internalized, recovery is incomplete. Premature dropout from treatment and relapse and recidivism are more likely. However, TCs have reacted to funding pressures by reducing the planned duration of residential treatment. Many TC agencies have added short-term (3–6 months) community-based residential programs. And, with few exceptions, the planned duration of treatment for modified TC programs in prisons, hospitals, and homeless shelters is typically 6–12 months.

Clarifying the effectiveness of different durations of and settings for TC treatment will depend on appropriate *client–treatment matching strategies.* Thus, research is needed to develop and evaluate assessment tools that illuminate which individuals belong in residential settings and how much treatment they need.

Economics and treatment

The discrepancies between the clinical realities and funding demands can be further reconciled in part through theoretically grounded econometric research. Studies are needed that illuminate the *actual* cost savings associated with treatment intensity (planned duration) and treatment setting (residential, institutional, nonresidential). TC theory suggests that increased cost benefit will be associated with *longer* treatment involvement reflecting greater internalized positive change. Thus, research must establish the high cost of *mismatching* clients to the wrong setting or of weakening the intensity/duration of treatment.

Treatment process and treatment improvement

Illuminating the process of change is essential to improve the TC treatment itself. If links cannot be explicitly established between program interventions, the course of client change and eventual outcomes, the effectiveness of any TC-oriented model remains unclear, much less proven.

The conceptual framework of the process presented in this volume provides a basis for operational definitions of the elements as well as appropriate measures, particularly the concept of internalization. Feasible methods of data collection are needed, as are analytic models for capturing the effects of global interventions in dynamic interaction with a changing client. Some recently developed instruments for assessing progress and process are contained in Appendix C.

BEYOND ADDICTION: A POST SCRIPT

The evolution of the contemporary TC for addictions over the past 30 years may be characterized as a movement from the marginal to the mainstream of substance abuse treatment and human services. The current stage of this evolution is perhaps the most exciting, risky, and challenging.

As outlined in this chapter the success, acceptance, and modification of the TC approach contain a paradoxical *threat*—the loss of its unique self-help identity as it assumes the characteristics of a mainstream public health entity. The current *challenge* is to retain its identity through a theoretically grounded generic TC model, codified standards for practice, an organized training initiative, and a research agenda that can refine its theory and improve practice.

Meeting the present challenge, however, is also the promise of the *future* of the therapeutic community. As a successful treatment for substance abuse, the TC offers a cutting edge approach for other social and psychological problems, a conclusion supported in the developing research on special populations and special settings (see for example, De Leon, 1997a).

While the current applications of the TC have targeted the substance abuse problem, they also have demonstrated how community as method can modify certain institutional settings and human services. The environments of jails, prisons, shelters, hospital wards, or schools can become *change-oriented communities*. The message of change is especially relevant for the disaffiliated and those struggling to acquire a personal and social stake in life.

Beyond the addictions and related disorders, however, the essential elements of the TC resonate the ideals of the good society—the humanistic concept of the whole person, the values of right living, the obligation to be role models, the power of self-help and mutual self-help, and the use of community as a method to facilitate individual growth. In a contemporary society marked by encultured drug use as well as a pervasive sense of loss of community, making these elements essential can revitalize the social climate itself.

References

Agnew, R. (1991). The interactive effect of peer variables on delinquency. *Criminology, 29,* 47-72.

American Psychological Association. (1997). *APA Monitor, 28* (11).

Anglin, M. D., & Hser, Y. I. (1990a). Legal coercion and drug abuse treatment: Research findings and social policy implications. In J. A. Inciardi & J. R. Biden, Jr. (Eds.), *Handbook of drug control in the United States* (pp. 151-176). New York: Greenwood Publishing Group, Inc.

Anglin, M. D., & Hser, Y. I. (1990b). Treatment of drug abuse. In M. Tonry & J. Q. Wilson (Eds.), *Crime and justice: An annual review of research, Vol. 13* (pp. 393-460). Chicago: University of Chicago Press.

Anglin, S. W., Nugent, J. F., & Ng, L. K. Y. (1976). Synanon and Alcoholics Anonymous: Is there really a difference? *Addiction Therapist, 1*(4), 6-9.

Archives of General Psychiatry. (Nov. 1998). Volume 55, No. 11.

Aron, W. S. (1975). Family background and personal trauma among drug addicts in the USA implications for treatment. *British Journal of Addiction, 7,* 295-305.

Bandura, A. J. (1977). *Social learning theory.* Englewood Cliffs, NJ: Prentice Hall.

Barr, H. (1986). Outcome of drug abuse treatment on two modalities. In G. De Leon & J.. T. Ziegenfuss (Eds.), *Therapeutic communities for addictions* (pp. 97-108). Springfield, IL: Charles C. Thomas.

Barton, E. (1994). The adaptation of the therapeutic community to HIV/AIDS. In *Proceedings of the Therapeutic Communities of America, 1992 Planning Conference: Paradigms: Past, present and future,* December 6-9, Chantilly, Virginia (pp. 66-70). Providence, RI: Manisses Communications Group.

Bassin, A. (1975, Autumn). Go help your brother! Triad theory and reality therapy for drug addicts part 1: Some theoretical tidbits. *The Addiction Therapist, 1*(3), 34-41.

Bell, D. C. (1994). Connection in therapeutic communities. *International Journal of the Addictions, 29,* 525-543.

Biase, D. V. (1971) Adolescent heroin abusers in a therapeutic community: Use of the MAACL to assess emotional traits and splitting from treatment. *Journal of Psychedelic Drugs, 4*(2), 145-147.

Biase, D. V. (1974). Who comes for drug rehabilitation?: A comparison of two groups of adult drug addict/abusers. In G. De Leon (Ed.), *Phoenix House: Studies in a therapeutic community (1968-1973)* (pp. 113-118). New York: MSS Information Corporation.

Biase, D. V., & De Leon, G. (1974). The encounter group: Measurement of some affect changes. In G. De Leon (Ed.), *Phoenix House: Studies in a therapeutic community (1968-1973)* (pp. 85-89). New York: MSS Information Corporation.

Biase, D. V., & Sullivan, A. P. (1984) Successful development of the self-concept with therapeutic community residents. In *Proceedings of the 8th World Conference of Therapeutic Communities* (pp. 2,175-184). Rome: Centro Italiano di Solidarieta.

Biase, D. V., Sullivan, A. P., & Wheeler, B. (1986). Daytop Miniversity-Phase 2 college training in a therapeutic community: Development of self-concept among drug free addict/abusers. In G. De Leon & J. T. Ziegenfuss (Eds.), *Therapeutic communities for addictions* (pp. 121-130). Springfield, IL: Charles C. Thomas.

Biernacki, P. (1986). *Pathways from heroin addiction: Recovery without treatment.* Philadelphia, PA: Temple University Press.

Blieland, C., Geralamino, A., & Smock, Trncila (Eds.). (1990). *World Proceedings of the Second World Institute of Therapeutic Communities: Back to Basics, Nov. 6-8, 1989,* New York: Promethean Institute & Division of Daytop Village.

Bratter, B. I., Bratter, T. E., Bratter, C. J., Maxym, C., & Steiner, K. M. (1997). The John Dewey Academy: A moral caring community (an amalgamation of the professional model and self-help concept of the therapeutic community). In G. De Leon (Ed.), *Community as method: Therapeutic communities for special populations and special settings* (pp. 170-198). Westport, CT: Greenwood Publishing Group, Inc.

Bratter, T. E. (1974). Helping affluent families help their acting-out, alienated, drug abusing adolescent. *Journal of Family Counseling, 2,* 23-31.

Bratter, T. E., Bratter, B.I., & Radda, H.T. (1986). The John Dewey Academy: A residential therapeutic high school. *Journal of Substance Abuse, 3,* 53-58.

Bratter, T. E., Bratter, E. P., & Heimberg, J. F. (1986). Uses and abuses of power and authority within the American self-help residential therapeutic community: A perversion or a necessity? In G. De Leon & J. T. Ziegenfuss (Eds.), *Therapeutic communities for addictions: Readings in theory, research and practice* (pp. 191-208). Springfield, IL: Charles C. Thomas.

Brehm, N. M., & Khantzian, E. J. (1992). The psychology of substance abuse: A psychodynamic perspective. In J. H. Lowinson, P. Ruiz, & R. B. Millman (Eds.), *Substance abuse: A comprehensive textbook* (2nd ed., pp. 106-117). Baltimore: Williams & Wilkins.

Bridgeland, M. (1971). *Pioneer work with maladjusted children: a study of the development of therapeutic education.* London: Staples Press.

Brill, L., & Lieberman, L. (1969). *Authority and addiction.* Boston: Little Brown.

Broekaert, E, Wanderplasschen, W., Temmerman, I., Ottenberg, D. J., & Kaplan, C. (1998). *Retrospective study of similarities and relations between the American drug-free and the European therapeutic communities for children and adults.* Manuscript submitted for publication. Department of Orthopedagogics, University of Ghent, Belgium.

Brook R. C., & Whitehead, I. C. (1980). *Drug-free therapeutic community.* New York: Human Sciences Press.

Brown, B. S. (1998). Towards the year 2000. Drug use—Chronic and relapsing or a treatable condition. *Substance Use and Misuse, 33*(12), 2515-2520.

Brown, S. (1985). *Treating the alcoholic: A developmental model of recovery.* New York: Wiley.

California Department of Corrections. (1998). *TC substance abuse programs for inmates.* Request for Proposal #C98.243.

Cancrini, L. Constantini, D., Mazzoni, S., Cingolani, S., & Compagnoni, F. (1985). Juvenile drug addiction: A study on typology of addicts and their families. In *Proceedings of the 9th World Conference of Therapeutic Communities* (pp. 59-68). San Francisco, CA: Walden House.

Carroll, J. F. X., & McGinley, J. J. (1998). Managing MICA clients in a modified therapeutic community with enhanced staffing. *Journal of Substance Abuse Treatment, 15* (6), 565-577.

Carroll, J. F. X., & Sobel, B. S. (1986). Integrating mental health personnel and practices into a therapeutic community. In G. De Leon & J. T. Ziegenfuss (Eds.), *Therapeutic communities for addictions: Readings in theory, research and practice* (pp. 209-226). Springfield, IL: Charles C. Thomas.

CARF...The Rehabilitation Accreditation Commission. (2000). *The 2000 behavioral health standards manual.* CARF, 4891 East Grant Rd. Tucson, AZ 85712.

Casey, J., & Preble, E. (1969). Taking care of business—The heroin user's life on the street. *International Journal of the Addictions, 4,* 1-24.

Casriel, D. H. (1966). *So fair a house: The story of Synanon.* New York City: Prentice Hall.

Casriel, D. H. (1981). The new identity process. In R. J. Corsini (Ed.), *Handbook of innovative psychotherapies* (pp. 569-583). New York: John Wiley & Sons.

Casriel, D. H., & Amen, G. (1971). *Three addicts and their cure.* New York: Hill and Wang.

Catalano, R. F., Hawkins, J. D., & Hall, J. A. (1983). *Preventing relapse among former substance abusers.* Seattle, WA: University of Washington, Center for Social Welfare and Research.

Chi'en, J., Gerard, D., Lee, R., & Rosenfeld, E. (1964). *The road to H: Narcotics, delinquency, and social policy.* New York: Basic.

Childress, A. R., Ehrman, R., Rohsenow, D. R., Robbins, S. J., & O'Brien, C. P. (1992). Classically conditioned factors in drug dependence, In J. H. Lowinson, P. Ruiz, & R. B. Millman (Eds.), *Substance abuse: A comprehensive textbook* (2nd ed., pp. 56-69). Baltimore: Williams & Wilkins.

Cole, S. G., & James, L. R. (1975). A revised treatment typology based on the DARP. *American Journal of Drug and Alcohol Abuse, 2,* 37-49.

Coletti, D. S., Hughes, P. H., Landress, H. J., Neri, R. L., Sicilian, D. M., Williams, K. M., Urmann, C. F., & Anthony, J. C. (1992). PAR village: Specialized intervention for cocaine abusing women and their children. *Journal of the Florida Medical Association, 79,* 701-705.

Condelli, W. S. (1986). Client evaluations of therapeutic communities and retention. In G. De Leon & J. T. Ziegenfuss (Eds.). *Therapeutic communities for addictions: Readings in theory, research and practice* (pp. 131-139). Springfield, IL: Charles C. Thomas.

Condelli, W. S., & Hubbard, R. L. (1994). Client outcomes from therapeutic communities. In F. M. Tims, G. De Leon, & N. Jainchill (Eds.), *Therapeutic community: Advances in research and application, NIDA Research Monograph 144* (National Institute on Drug Abuse, NIH Publication No. 94-3633, pp. 80-98). Rockville, MD: National Institute on Drug Abuse.

Coombs, R. H. (1981). Back on the streets: TCs impact upon drug abusers. *American Journal of Drug and Alcohol Abuse, 8,* 185-201.

De Leon, G. (1971). *Phoenix House: Who comes for treatment: Selected socio-demographic characteristics of 1,151 residents in the Phoenix House therapeutic community.* (Grant Foundation project). New York City: Author.

De Leon, G. (1974, September). Phoenix House: Psychopathological signs among male and female drug free residents. *Journal of Addictive Diseases, 1*(2), 135-51.

De Leon, G. (1976). *Psychologic and socio-demographic profiles of addicts in the therapeutic community.* (National Institute of Drug Abuse Grant No. DA-00831), New York City: Author.

De Leon, G. (1980). *Therapeutic communities: Training self evaluation* (National Institute of Drug Abuse Grant No. 1H81-DAO, 1976). New York City: Author.

De Leon, G. (1984a). Program based evaluation research in therapeutic communities. *Drug abuse treatment evaluation: Strategies, progress and prospects; Research, analysis and utilization system, National Institute on Drug Abuse Research Monograph 51* (pp. 69-87). Rockville, MD: National Institute on Drug Abuse.

De Leon, G. (1984b). The therapeutic community: Study of effectiveness. *National Institute on Drug Abuse Treatment Research Monograph Series* (ADM 84-1286). Washington, DC: Superintendent of Documents, U.S. Government Printing Office.

De Leon, G. (1985). The therapeutic community: Status and evolution. *International Journal of Addictions, 20*(6-7), 823-844.

De Leon, G. (1988). Legal pressure in therapeutic communities. In C. G. Leukefeld & F. M. Tims (Eds.), *Compulsory treatment of drug abuse: Research and clinical practice, NIDA Research Monograph 86* (DHHS Publication No. (Adm) 88-1578, pp. 160-177). Rockville, MD: National Institute on Drug Abuse.

De Leon, G. (1989). Psychopathology and substance abuse: What we are learning from research in therapeutic communities. *Journal of Psychoactive Drugs, 21* (2), 177-188.

De Leon, G. (1990-91). Aftercare in therapeutic communities. *International Journal of Addictions, 25*, 1229-1241.

De Leon, G. (1991). Retention in drug free therapeutic communities. In R. W. Pickens, C. G. Leukefeld & C. R. Schuster (Eds.), *Improving drug abuse treatment, NIDA Research Monograph 106* (pp. 218-244). Rockville, MD: National Institute on Drug Abuse.

De Leon, G. (1993a) Cocaine abusers in therapeutic community treatment. In F. M. Tims & C. G. Leukefeld (Eds.), *Cocaine treatment: Research and clinical perspectives, NIDA Research Monograph 135* (NIH Publication No. 93-3639, pp. 163-189). Washington, DC: Superintendent of Documents, US Government Printing Office.

De Leon, G. (1993b) Modified therapeutic communities for dual disorder. In J. Solomon, S. Zimberg & E. Shollar (Eds.), *Dual diagnosis: Evaluation, treatment, training, and program development* (pp. 147-170). New York: Plenum Press.

De Leon, G. (1995). Residential therapeutic communities in the mainstream: Diversity and issues. *Journal of Psychoactive Drugs, 27* (1), Jan-Mar, 3-15.

De Leon, G. (1996a). Integrative recovery: A stage paradigm. *Substance Abuse, 17* (1), 51-63

De Leon, G. (1996b). Therapeutic communities: AIDS/HIV risk and harm reduction. *Journal of Substance Abuse Treatment, 13* (5), 411-420.

De Leon, G. (Ed.). (1997a). *Community as method: Therapeutic communities for special populations and special settings.* Westport, CT: Greenwood Publishing Group, Inc.

De Leon, G. (1997b). Modified therapeutic communities: Emerging issues. In G. De Leon (Ed.), *Community as method: Therapeutic communities for special populations and special settings* (pp. 261-270). Westport, CT: Greenwood Publishing Group, Inc.

De Leon, G., & Beschner, G. (Eds.). (1977). *The therapeutic community: Proceedings of the Therapeutic Communities of America Planning Conference*, January 29-30, 1976. Rockville, MD: National Institute on Drug Abuse.

De Leon, G., & Deitch, D. (1985). Treatment of the adolescent substance abuser in a therapeutic community. In A. Friedman & G. Beschner (Eds.), *Treatment services for adolescent substance abusers* (DHHS Publication No. [ADM] 85-1342, pp. 216-230). Rockville MD: National Institute of Drug Abuse.

De Leon, G., & Jainchill, N. (1981-82). Male and female drug abusers: Social and psychological status 2 years after treatment in a therapeutic community. *American Journal of Drug and Alcohol Abuse, 8*(4), 465-497.

De Leon, G., & Jainchill, N. (1991). Residential therapeutic communities for female substance abusers. *Bulletin of the New York Academy of Medicine* (Vol. 67, No. 3, May/June, 277-290.

De Leon, G., Jainchill, N., & Wexler, H. (1982). Success and improvement rates 5 years after treatment in a therapeutic community. *International Journal of Addictions, 17*(4), 703-747.

De Leon, G., Melnick, G., & Hawke, J. (in press). The motivation-readiness factor in drug treatment: Implications for research and policy. *Advances in Medical Sociology.*

De Leon, G., Melnick, G, Kressel, D., & Jainchill, N. (1994). Circumstances, motivation, readiness and suitability (the CMRS scales): Predicting retention in therapeutic community treatment. *American Journal of Drug and Alcohol Abuse, 20*(4), 495-515.

De Leon, G., Melnick, G., Schoket, D., & Jainchill, N. (1993, Jan-Mar). Is the therapeutic community culturally relevant? Findings on race/ethnic differences in retention in treatment. *Journal of Psychoactive Drugs, 25*(1), 77-86.

De Leon, G., & Rosenthal, M. S. (1979). Therapeutic communities. In R. DuPont, A. Goldstein, & J. O'Donnell (Eds.), *Handbook on drug abuse* (pp. 39-48). Rockville, MD: National Institute on Drug Abuse.

De Leon, G., & Schwartz, S. (1984). The therapeutic community: What are the retention rates? *American Journal of Drug and Alcohol Abuse, 10*(2), 267-284.

De Leon, G., Skodol, A., & Rosenthal, M. S. (1973). The Phoenix House therapeutic community for drug addicts: Changes in psychopathological signs. *Archives of General Psychiatry, 28*, 131-135.

De Leon, G., Staines, G. L., Sacks, S., Brady, R., & Melchionda, R. (1997). Passages: A modified therapeutic community model for methadone-maintained clients. In G. De Leon (Ed.), *Community as method: Therapeutic communities for special populations and special settings* (pp. 225-246). Westport, CT: Greenwood Publishing Group, Inc.

De Leon, G., & Wexler, H. (1973, February). Heroin addiction: Its relation to sexual experience. *Journal of Abnormal Psychology, 81*(1), 36-38.

De Leon, G. & Ziegenfuss, J. T. (Eds.). (1986). *Therapeutic communities for addictions: Readings in theory, research and practice.* Springfield, IL: Charles C. Thomas.

Deissler, K. (1970). Synanon: Its concepts and methods. *Drug Dependence.* Washington, DC: National Clearing House for Mental Health Information.

Deitch, D. A. (1973). The treatment of drug abuse in the therapeutic community: Historical influences, current considerations, future outlook. *Drug use in America* (Vol. 4, pp. 158-175). Rockville, MD: National Commission on Marijuana and Drug Abuse.

Deitch, D. A., & Solit, R. (1993a). International training for drug abuse treatment and the issue of cultural relevance. *Journal of Psychoactive Drugs: A Multidisciplinary Forum, 25*(1), 87-96.

Deitch, D. A., & Solit, R. (1993b). Training drug abuse workers in a therapeutic community. *Psychotherapy: Theory, Research and Practice, 30*(12), 305-316.

Deitch, D. A., & Zweben, J. E. (1980). Synanon: A pioneering response to drug abuse treatment and a signal for caution. In Halpern & Levine (Eds.), *Proceedings of the 4th International Conference on Therapeutic Communities (pp. 57-70).* New York, NY: Daytop Village Press.

Densen-Gerber, J. (1973). *We mainline dreams: The story of Odyssey House.* Garden City, New York: Doubleday Press.

Densen-Gerber, J., Weiner, M., & Hochstedler, R. (1972). Sexual behavior, abortion, and birth control in heroin addicts: Legal and psychiatric considerations. *Contemporary Drug Problems 1,*783-793.

Des Jarlais, D., Jainchill, N., & Friedman, S. (1988). AIDS among IV drug users: Epidemiology, natural history, and therapeutic community experiences. In R. P. Galea, B. F. Lewis, & L. A. Baker (Eds.), *AIDS and IV drug abusers: Current perspectives* (pp. 51-59). Owings Mills, MD: Rynd Communications.

Des Jarlais, D. C., Knott, A., Savarese J., & Bersamin, J. (1976). Rules and rule breaking in a therapeutic community. *Addictive Diseases: An International Journal,* 2, 627-641.

DiClemente, C. C. (1986). Self-efficacy and the addictive behaviors. *Journal of Social and Clinical Psychology, 4(3),* 302-315.

DiClemente, C. C., & Prochaska, J. O. (in press). Toward a comprehensive, transtheoretical model of change: Stages of change and addictive behaviors. In W. R. Miller & H. Heather (Eds.), *Treatment Addictive Behaviors.* New York: Plenum.

Elliott, D., Huizinga, D., & Ageton, S. (1985). *Explaining delinquency and drug use.* Newbury Park: Sage.

Emrick, C. D. (1985). Alcoholics Anonymous. In B. T. Karasu (Ed.), *Treatments of psychiatric disorder: A task force report of the American Psychiatric Association* (pp. 1151-1162). Washington, DC: American Psychiatric Association.

Emrick, C. D. (1989). Alcoholics Anonymous: Emerging concepts: Overview. In M. Galanter (Ed.), *Recent developments in alcoholism, vol 7: Treatment research* (pp. 3-10). New York: Plenum.

Emrick, C. D. (1999). Alcoholics Anonymous and other 12-step groups. In M. Galanter & H. D. Kleber (Eds.), *The American Psychiatric Press textbook of substance abuse treatment (2nd ed.)* (pp. 403-412). Washington, D.C.: American Psychiatric Press, Inc.

Endore, G. (1968). *Synanon.* Garden City, NY: Doubleday.

Erickson, J. R., Stevens, S., McKnight, P., & Figuerdo, A. J. (1995). Willingness for treatment as a predictor of retention and outcomes. *Journal of Addictive Diseases, 14,* 135-150.

Fairweather, G. W., Sanders, D. H., Maynard, H., & Cressler, D. L. (1969). *Community life for the mentally ill.* Chicago: Aldine.

Frankel, B. (1989). *Transforming identities, context, power and ideology in a therapeutic community.* New York City: Peter Lang.

Freudenberger, H. J. (1974). How we can right what's wrong with our therapeutic communities. *Journal of Drug Issues, 4,* 251-259.

Freudenberger, H. J. (1976). Proceedings: The therapeutic community revisited. *American Journal of Drug and Alcohol Abuse, 3,* 33-49.

Freudenberger, H. J. (1977). The gay addict in a drug and alcohol abuse therapeutic community. *Addiction Therapist 2*(2), 23-30.

Freudenberger, H. J. (1980). *Bum out: The high costs of high achievement.* New York, NY: Anchor Press/Doubleday.

Furuholmen, D., & Andresen, A. S. (1998). *Felles-skapet som metode: Miljoterapi og evaluering i behandling av stoffmisbrukere.* Oslo, Norway: Cappelen Akademisk Forlag.

Galanter, M. (1990). Cults and zealous self-help movements: A psychiatric perspective. *American Journal of Psychiatry, 147,* 543-551.

Galanter, M., Egelko, S., De Leon, G., & Rohrs, C. (1993). A general hospital day program combining peer-led and professional treatment of cocaine abusers. *Hospital and Community Psychiatry, 44*(7), 644-649.

Galanter, M., & Kleber, H. (Eds.). (1999). *Textbook of substance abuse treatment (2ⁿᵈ Ed.).* Washington, D. C.: American Psychiatric Press, Inc.

Galea, R. P., Lewis, B. F., & Baker, L. A. (Eds.). (1988). *AIDS and IV drug abusers: Current perspectives.* Owings Mills, MD: Rynd Communications.

Gartner, A., & Riessman, F. (1999). Making the case for positive peer pressure. *Dialogue, Vol. 8,* 1-4.

Gerstein, D. R., & Harwood, H. J. (Eds.) (Institute of Medicine) (1990). *Treating drug problems Vol. 1. A study of the evaluation, effectiveness, and financing of public and private drug treatment systems.* Washington, DC: National Academy Press.

Glaser, F. B. (1974). Some historical and theoretical background of a self-help addiction treatment program. *American Journal of Drug and Alcohol Abuse, 1,* 37-52.

Glasser, W. (1965). *Reality therapy: A new approach to psychiatry.* New York: Harper & Row.

Glasser, W. (1969). *Schools without failure.* New York: Harper & Row.

Glynn, T., & Haenlein, M. (1988). Family theory and research on adolescent drug use: A review. In R. Coombs (Ed.), *The family context of adolescent drug use.* New York: Haworth.

Gorski, T. T. (1989). *Passages through recovery: An action plan for preventing relapse.* San Francisco: Harper & Rowe.

Goti, M. E. (1990). *La comunidad terapéutica: Un desafío a la droga.* Buenos Aires, Argentina: Ediciones Nueva Vision.

Gralnick, A. (1969). *The psychiatric hospital as a therapeutic instrument.* New York: Brunner/Mazel.

Guydish, J., Werdegar, D., Chan, M., Nebelkopf, E., & Acampora, A. (1994). Challenges in developing a drug abuse day treatment program. In B. Fletcher, J. Inciardi, & A. M. Horton (Eds.), *Drug abuse treatment: The implementation of innovative approaches* (pp. 195-207). Westport, CT: Greenwood Press.

Hawke, J., Jainchill, N., & De Leon, G. (in press). The prevalence of sexual abuse and its impact on the onset of drug use among adolescents in therapeutic community drug treatment. *Journal of Child and Adolescent Substance Abuse.*

Hawke, J., Jainchill, N., & De Leon, G. (1999). Gender differences in the relationship of suicidal behavior and violent crime among high risk adolescents in residential drug treatment. Manuscript submitted for publication.

Hawkins, J. D., Arthur, M. W., & Catalano, R. F. (1995). Preventing substance abuse. In M. Tonry & D. P. Farrington (Eds.), *Building a safer society: Strategic approaches to crime prevention* (pp. 343-427). Chicago: University of Chicago Press.

Hawkins, J. D., Lishner, D. M., Catalano, R. F., & Howard, M. O. (1986). Childhood predictors of adolescent substance abuse: Toward an empirically grounded theory. *Journal of Childhood Contemporary Sociology* [Special Issue: Childhood and Chemical abuse: Prevention and Intervention] 18 (2), 11-48.

Hawkins, J. D., & Wacker, N. (1986). Side bets and secondary adjustments in therapeutic communities. In G. De Leon & J. T. Ziegenfuss, Jr. (Eds.), *Therapeutic communities for addictions: Readings in theory, research and practice* (pp. 141-156). Springfield, IL: Charles C. Thomas.

Hendriks, V. M. (1990). *Addiction and psychopathology: A multidimensional approach to clinical practice.* Rotterdam, The Netherlands: Universiteits Drukkerij.

Higgens, S. T., & Budney, A. J. (1993). Treatment of cocaine dependence through the principles of behavior analysis and behavioral pharmacology. *Behavioral treatment for drug abuse and dependence, National Institute on Drug Abuse Research Monograph Series, 137* (NIDA NIH Publication No. 93-3684; pp. 97-122). Rockville, MD: National Institute on Drug Abuse.

Hiller, M. L., Knight, K., Broome, K. M., & Simpson, D. D. (1998). Legal pressure and retention in a national sample of long-term residential programs. *Criminal Justice and Behavior 25* (4), 463-481.

Hird, S., Khuri, E. T., Dusenbury, L., & Millman, R. (1997). Adolescents. In J. H. Lowinson, R. Ruiz, R. B. Millman, & J. G. Langrod (Eds.), *Substance abuse: A comprehensive textbook, 3rd ed.* (pp. 683-692). Baltimore: Williams & Wilkins.

Holland, S. (1982). *Residential drug free programs for substance abusers: The effect of planned duration on treatment.* Chicago, IL: Gateway Foundation.

Holland, S. (1983). Evaluating community based treatment programs: A model for strengthening inferences about effectiveness. *International Journal of Therapeutic Communities, 4*(4), 285-306.

Holland, S. (1986a). Measuring process in drug abuse treatment research. In G. De Leon & J. T. Ziegenfuss (Eds.), *Therapeutic communities for addictions: Readings in theory, research and practice* (pp. 169-181). Springfield, IL: Charles C. Thomas.

Holland, S. (1986b). Psychiatric severity in the TC. In A. Acampora & E. Nebelkopf (Eds.), *Bridging services: Drug abuse, human services and the therapeutic community-Proceedings of the 9th World Conference of Therapeutic Communities, September 1-6, 1985* (pp. 122-131). San Francisco, CA: Abacus Printing.

Hollidge, C. (1980). Psychodynamic aspects of the addicted personality and their treatment in the therapeutic community. In *Readings 'Congresboek 5e Werelfkonferentie van therapeutische gemeenschappen* (pp. 61-86),' Samsom Sijthoff, Alphen aan de Rijn.

Hubbard, R. L., Craddock. S. G., Flynn, P. M., Anderson, J., & Etheridge, R. M. (1997). Overview of 1-year follow-up outcomes in the drug abuse treatment outcome study (DATOS). *Psychology of Addictive Behaviors: Special Issue: Drug Abuse Treatment Outcome Study (DATOS)*, 11 (4), 261-278.

Hubbard, R. L, Marsden, M. E., Rachal, J. V., Harwood, H. J., Cavanaugh, E. R., & Ginzburg, H. M. (1989). *Drug abuse treatment: A national study of effectiveness.* Chapel Hill, NC: The University of North Carolina Press.

Hubbard, R. L., Valley Rachal, J., Craddock, S. G., & Cavanaugh, E. R. (1984). Treatment outcome prospective study (TOPS): Client characteristics and behaviors before, during, and after treatment. In F. M. Tims, & J. P. Ludford (Eds.) *Drug abuse treatment evaluation: Strategies, progress, and prospects. NIDA Research Monograph Number 51* (DHHS Publication No. [ADM] 84-1329; pp. 42-68). Rockville, MD: National Institute on Drug Abuse.

Jaffe, J. H. (1969). A review of the approaches to the problem of compulsive narcotic use. In J. R. Wittenborn, H. Brill, J. P. Smith, & S. A Wittenborn (Eds.), *Drugs and youth* (pp. 77-91). Springfield, Illinois: Charles C. Thomas.

Jaffe, J. H., & Martin, W. R. (1975). Narcotic analgesics and antagonists. In L. S. Goodman, & A. Gilman (Eds.), *The pharmacological bases of therapeutics, 5th Ed.* (pp. 245-324). New York: Macmillan.

Jainchill, N. (1994). Co-morbidity and therapeutic community treatment. In F. M. Tims, G. De Leon & N. Jainchill (Eds.), *Therapeutic community: Advances in research and application, NIDA Research Monograph 144* (NIH Publication Number 94-3633, pp. 209-231). Rockville, MD: National Institute on Drug Abuse.

Jainchill, N. (1997). Therapeutic communities for adolescents: The same and not the same. In G. De Leon, (Ed.), *Community as method: Therapeutic communities for special populations and special settings* (pp. 161-177). Westport, CT: Greenwood Publishing Group, Inc.

Jainchill, N., Battacharya, G., & Yagelka, J. (1995). Therapeutic communities for adolescents. In E. Rahdert & D. Czechowicz (Eds.), *Adolescent drug abuse: Clinical assessment and therapeutic interventions, NIDA Research Monograph 156* (pp. 190-217). Rockville, MD: National Institute on Drug Abuse.

Jainchill, N., De Leon, G., & Yagelka, J. (1997). Ethnic differences in psychiatric disorders among adolescent substance abusers in treatment. *Journal of Psychopathology and Behavioral Assessment, 19*(2), 133-147.

Jainchill, N., Hawke, J., Yagelka, J. & De Leon, G. (in press). Adolescents in TCs: One-year post-treatment outcomes. *Journal of Psychoactive Drugs.*

Jainchill, N., Yagelka, J. Hawke, J., & De Leon, G. (1999) Adolescent admissions to residential drug treatment: HIV risk behaviors pre- and post-treatment. *Psychology of Addictive Behaviors, 13*(3), 163-173

Jansen, E. (Ed.). (1980). *The therapeutic community: Outside the hospital.* London: Croom Helm.

Joe, G. W., Chastain, R. L., & Simpson, D. D. (1990). Reasons for addiction stages, In D. D. Simpson & S. B. Sells (Eds.). *Opioid addiction and treatment: A 12-year follow-up* (pp. 73-102). Malabar, FL: Krieger Publishing Company.

Joe, G. W., Simpson, D. D., & Broome, K. M. (1998). Effects of readiness for drug abuse treatment on client retention and assessment of process. *Addiction, 93*(8), 1177-1190.

Johnson, B. D., Goldstein, P., Preble, E., Schmeidler, J., Lipton, D. S., Spunt, B., & Miller, T. (1985). *Taking care of business: The economics of crime by heroin abusers.* Lexington, MA: Lexington Books.

Jones, M. (1953). *The therapeutic community: A new treatment method in psychiatry.* New York: Basic Books.

Kandel, D. B., & Logan J. A. (1984). Patterns of drug abuse from adolescents to young adulthood: Periods of risk for initiation, continued use, and discontinuation. *American Journal of Public Health, 74*, 660-66.

Kaplan, H. (1980). *Deviant behavior in defense of self.* New York: Academic.

Karson, S., & Gesumaria, R. V. (1997). Program description and outcome of an enhanced, six-month residential therapeutic community. In G. De Leon (Ed.), *Community as method: Therapeutic communities for special populations and special settings* (pp. 199-212). Westport, CT: Greenwood Publishing Group, Inc.

Kellog, S. (1993). Identity and recovery. In G. De Leon, H. Freudenberger, & H. Wexler (Guest Eds.), *Special Issue of Psychotherapy: Psychotherapy for the Addictions, 30*(2), 235-244.

Kennard, D. (1983). *An introduction to therapeutic communities.* London: Rutledge and Kegan Paul.

Kerr, D. H. (1986). The therapeutic community: A codified concept for training and upgrading staff members working in a residential setting. In G. De Leon & J. T. Ziegenfuss (Eds.), *Therapeutic communities for addictions* (pp. 55-63). Springfield, IL: Charles C. Thomas.

Khantzian, E. J. (1985). The self-medication hypothesis of addictive disorders: Focus on heroin and cocaine dependence. *American Journal of Psychiatry, 142,* 1259-1264.

Khantzian, E. J. (1997). The self-medication hypothesis of substance use disorders: A reconsideration and recent applications. *Harvard Review of Psychiatry, 4,* 231-244.

Khantzian, E. J., Halliday, K. S., & McAuliffe, W. E., (1990). *Addiction and the vulnerable self-modified dynamic group therapy for substance abusers.* New York: Guilford Press.

Kooyman, M. (1993). *The therapeutic community for addicts: Intimacy, parent involvement and treatment outcome.* Amsterdam, The Netherlands: Swets and Zeitlinger.

Krystal, H. (1988). *Integration and self-healing. Affect, trauma, alexithymia.* Hillsdale, NJ: The Analytic Press, L. Erlbaum Associates.

Lecker, S. (1974). *Family factors, interpersonal competence and drug addiction.* Unpublished report, Daytop Village, New York City.

Leshner, A. I. (Speaker). (1997). *Drug Abuse and addiction: Blending scientific and public interest psychology.* (Cassette Recording No. APA97-2276). Washington, DC: American Psychological Association.

Lettieri, D. (1989) Substance abuse etiology. In T. B. Karasu (Ed.) *Treatments of psychiatric disorders Vol. II* (pp. 1192-1202). Washington, DC: American Psychiatric Press.

Levy, E. S., Faltico, G. J., & Bratter, T. E. (1977). The development and structure of the drug free therapeutic community. *Addiction Therapist, 2*(2), 40-52.

Levy, M. (1987). A change in orientation: Therapeutic strategies for the treatment of alcoholism. *Psychotherapy, 24,* 786-793.

Lewis, B. F., McCusker, J., Hindin, R., Frost, R., & Garfield, F. (1993). Four residential drug treatment programs: Project IMPACT. In J. A. Inciardi, F. M. Tims, & B. W. Fletcher (Eds.), *Innovative approaches in the treatment of drug abuse: Program models and strategies* (pp. 45-60). Westport, CT: Greenwood Press.

Lewis, C. E., Rice, J. & Hetzer, J. E. (1983). Diagnostic interactions: Alcoholism and antisocial personality. *The Journal of Nervous and Mental Disease,* 171, 105-113.

Lewis, D. C. (1991). Comparison of alcoholism and other medical diseases: An internist's view. *Psychiatric Annals, 21,* 256-265.

Liberty, H. J., Johnson, B. D., Jainchill, N., Ryder, J., Messina, M., Reynolds, S., & Hossain, M. (1998). Dynamic Recovery: Comparative study of therapeutic communities in homeless shelters for men. *Journal of Substance Abuse Treatment, 15*(5), 401-423.

Lieberman, M. A., Yalom, I. D., & Miles, M. B. (1973). *Encounter groups: First facts.* New York City: Basic Books.

Lipton, D.S. (1999). Therapeutic community treatment programming in corrections. In C. R. Hollin (Ed.), *Handbook of offender assessment and treatment.* London: John Wiley & Sons, Ltd.

Lockwood, D., Inciardi, J. A., Butzin, C. A., & Hooper, R. M. (1997). The therapeutic community continuum in corrections. In G. De Leon (Ed.), *Community as method: Therapeutic communities for special populations and special settings* (pp. 87-96). Westport, CT: Greenwood Publishing Group, Inc.

Loeber, R., & Stouthamer-Loeber, M. (1986). Family factors as correlates and predictors of juvenile conduct problems and delinquency. In M. Tonry & N. Morris (Eds.), *Crime and justice: An annual review of research, Vol. 12.* Chicago: University of Chicago Press.

Main, T. (1946). The hospital as therapeutic institution. *Bulletin of the Meninger Clinic, Vol. 10,* 16-17.

Main, T. (1976). The concept of the therapeutic community: Variations and vicissitudes; lecture given at first S. H. Foulkes annual lecture, subsequently reprinted as a supplement to *'Group Analysis'*, *10*(2).

Malloy, J. P. (1992). *Self-run, self-supported houses for more effective recovery from alcohol and drug addiction*, Technical Assistance Publication Series Number 5 (DHHS Publication No. (ADM) 92-1678) Rockville, MD: Alcohol, Drug Abuse, and Mental Health Administration.

Margolis, R. D., & Zweben, J. E., (1998). *Treating patients with alcohol and other drug problems: An Integrated approach.* Washington, DC: American Psychological Association.

Marlatt, G. A. (1985). Relapse prevention: Theoretical rationale and overview of the model. In G. A. Marlatt & J. R. Gordon (Eds.), *Relapse prevention: Maintenance strategies in the treatment of addictive behaviors* (pp. 3-67). New York: Guilford Press.

Marlatt, G. A. & Gordon, J. R. (Eds.). (1985). *Relapse prevention: Maintenance strategies in the treatment of addictive behaviors.* New York: Guilford Press.

McLellan, A. T., Luborsky, L, Woody, G. E., & O'Brien, C. P. (1980). An improved diagnostic evaluation instrument for substance abuse patients: The Addiction Severity Index. *The Journal of Nervous and Mental Disease*, 168, 26-33.

McCusker, J., & Sorensen, J. L. (1994). HIV and therapeutic communities. In F. M. Tims, G. De Leon, & N. Jainchill (Eds.), *Therapeutic community: Advances in research and application, NIDA Research Monograph 144* (NIH publication No. 94-3633, pp. 232-258). Rockville, MD: National Institute on Drug Abuse.

McCusker, J., Vickers-Lahti, M., Stoddard, A., Hindin, R., Bigelow, C., Zorn, M., Garfield, F., Frost, R., Love, C., & Lewis, B. (1995). The effectiveness of alternative planned durations of residential drug abuse treatment. *American Journal of Public Health*, 85, 1426-1429.

Messina, N. R., Wish, E. D., & Nemes, S. (1999). Therapeutic community treatment for substance abusers with anti-social personality disorder. *Journal of Substance Abuse Treatment, 17*(1-2), 121-128.

Miller, W. R., & Rollnick, S. (Eds.). (1991). *Motivational interviewing: Preparing people to change addictive behavior.* New York: Guilford Press.

Millstein, R. (1994). TCs for the future –Views of national leaders. In *Proceedings of the Therapeutic Communities of America 1992 planning conference, Chantilly, VA: Paradigms: Past, present and future* (pp. 83, 84). Providence, RI: Manisses Communications Group.

Moberg, D. P., & Thaler, S. L. (1995). *An evaluation of Recovery High School: An alternative high school for adolescents in recovery from chemical dependency.* Madison, WI: University Medical School.

Mowrer, O. H. (1977). Therapeutic groups and communities in retrospect. In *Proceedings of the first World Conference of Therapeutic Communities*, Sept. 1976, Norkijping. Montreal: The Portage Press.

Nan Huat-Chin (1997). *Basic buddhism.* York Beach, ME: Samuel Weiser.

Nash, G. (1974). Community response to a narcotic addiction treatment facility: The case of Prospect Place. In G. De Leon (Ed.), *Phoenix House: Studies in a therapeutic community (1968-1973)* (pp. 25-41). New York, MSS Information Corporation.

National Center for Health Statistics (1993). *Advance Report of final mortality statistics, 1991* (DHHS Publication PHS 93-1120). Hyattsville, MD: Public Health Service.

National Institute on Alcohol Abuse and Alcoholism (NIAAA). (1993). *Alcohol and health: Eighth special report to the U.S. Congress* (DHHS Publication No. ADM-281-91-0003). Rockville, MD: Author.

National Treatment Improvement Evaluation Study (NTIES). (September 1996). *"Preliminary report: The persistent effects of substance abuse treatment—One year later"* Rockville, MD: U.S. Dept. of Health and Human Services, Substance Abuse and Mental Health Services Administration, Center for Substance Abuse Treatment (CSAT).

Nielsen, A., & Scarpitti, F. (1995). Argot use in the TC. *Deviant Behavior: An Interdisciplinary Journal, 16, 245-267.*

Nielsen, A., & Scarpitti, F. (1997). Changing the behavior of substance abusers: Factors influencing the effectiveness of therapeutic communities. *Journal of Drug Issues, 27*(2), 279-298.

The 1996-97 TCA Membership Annual Achievement Report. (1997, Fall). *TCA News: Therapeutic Communities of America,* 1 & 7.

Nurco, D. N., Hanlon, T. E., O'Grady, K. E., & Kinlock, T. W. (1997). The association of early risk factors to opiate addiction and psychological adjustment. *Criminal Behaviour and Mental Health, 7,* 213-228.

Nuttbrock, L. A., Rahav, M., Rivera, J. J., Ng-Mak, D. S., & Link, B. G. (1998). Outcomes of homeless mentally ill chemical abusers in community residences and a therapeutic community. *Psychiatric Services, 49*(1), 68-76.

Oetting, E. R., & Donnermeyer, J. F. (1998). Primary socialization theory: The etiology of drug use and deviance. I. *Substance Use & Misuse, 33* (4), 995-1026.

Ottenberg, D. J. (1978). Responsible concern. *The Addiction Therapist, 3* (1), 67-68.

Ottenberg, D. J. (1984). Therapeutic community and the danger of the cult phenomenon. In L. Bremberg (Ed.), *Third generation of therapeutic communities. Proceedings of the First European Conference on Milieutherapy, Sept. 1982,* Eskilstuna (pp. 218-238). Katrineholm, Sweden.

Pallone, N. J., & Hennessy, J. J. (1996). *Tinder-box criminal aggression.* New Brunswick, NJ: Transaction Publishers.

Platt, J. J. (1986). *Heroin addiction: Theory, research, and treatment. Volume 1. (2nd Ed.),* Malabar, FL: Krieger Publishing Company.

Platt, J. J. (1995). *Heroin addiction: Theory, research, and treatment. Volume 2: The addict, the treatment process, and social control.* Malabar, FL: Krieger Publishing Company.

Pompi, K. F. (1994). Adolescents in therapeutic communities: Retention and posttreatment outcome. In F. M. Tims, G. De Leon, & N. Jainchill (Eds.), *NIDA Research Monograph 144, Therapeutic community: Advances in research and application* (NIH Publication Number 94-3633, pp. 128-161). Rockville, MD: National Institute on Drug Abuse.

Powell, B. J., Penick, E. C., Othmer, E., Bingham, S. E., & Rice, A. S. (1982). Prevalence of additional psychiatric syndromes among male alcoholics. *Journal of Clinical Psychology, 43,* 404-407.

Preston, C. A., & Viney, L. L. (1984). Self- and ideal self-perception of drug addicts in therapeutic communities. *International Journal of the Addictions, 19*(7), 805-818.

Proceedings of the Therapeutic Communities of America 1992 planning conference, Chantilly, VA—Paradigms: Past, present and future (1994). Providence, RI: Manisses Communications Group.

Prochaska, J. O., DiClemente, C. C., & Norcross, J. C. (1992). In search of how people change: applications to addictive behaviors. *American Psychologist, 47,* 1102-1114.

Ramirez, E. (1984). Recent developments in the therapeutic community movement in Puerto Rico and Latin America. In L. Marsan, F. Angelucci, & M. Xella (Eds.), *Eighth World*

Conference of Therapeutic Communities (Vol. 1, pp. 177-205). Rome, Italy: Enzo Jacopino in collaboration with SEAT_SARIN.

Rapaport, R. N. (1960). *Community as doctor.* London: Tavistock Publications.

Ratner, M. (1973). Daytop: A therapeutic community with an open door at the end. *Drug Program Review.*

Ravndal, E. (1994). *Drug abuse, psychopathology and treatment in a hierarchical therapeutic community: A prospective study.* Unpublished doctoral dissertation, University of Oslo, Department of Behavioral Sciences in Medicine, Oslo, Norway.

Ravndal, E., & Vaglum, P. (1998). Psychotherapy, treatment completion and 5 years outcome: A prospective study of drug abusers. *Journal of Substance Abuse Treatment, 15*(2), 135-142.

Ray, R. (1999). *The Oxford connection* [On-line], Lynn's Recovery Site. Available: elite. net/~lcunning/oxfordconnnection.html.

Rogers, C. R. (1961). *On becoming a person.* New York: Houghton Mifflin, Co.

Rogers, C. R. (1969). *Freedom to learn.* Columbus, Ohio: Charles E. Merrill.

Rogers, C. R. (1970). *On encounter groups.* New York: Harper and Row.

Rounsaville, B. J., Rosenberger, P. H., Wilber, C. H., Weissman, M. M., & Kleber, H. (1980). A comparison of the SADS/RDC and the DSM-111: Diagnosing drug abusers. *The Journal of Nervous and Mental Disease, 168,* 90-97.

Rounsaville, B. J., Weissman, M. M., Kleber, H., & Wilber, C. (1982). Heterogeneity of Psychiatric Diagnosis in Mental Opiate Addicts. *Archives of General Psychiatry 39,* 161-166.

Sacks, S., De Leon, G., Bernhardt, A. I., & Sacks, J. Y. (©1996, revised 1998). *Modified therapeutic community for homeless MICA individuals: A treatment manual.* Center for Mental Health Services (CMHS)/Center for Substance Abuse Treatment (CSAT) Grant #1UD3 SM/TI51558-01. New York: NDRI/CTCR.

Sacks, S., De Leon, G., Bernhardt, A. I., & Sacks, J. Y. (1997). A modified therapeutic community for homeless mentally ill chemical abusers. In G. De Leon (Ed.), *Community as method: Therapeutic communities for special populations and special settings* (pp. 19-37). Westport, CT: Greenwood Publishing Group, Inc.

Salasnek, S., & Amini, F. (1971). The heroin addict in a therapeutic community for adolescents: A cultural rip-off. *Journal of Psychedelic Drugs, 4* (2), 138-144.

Seidel, R. W., Guzman, F. D., & Abueg, F. R. (1994). Theoretical and practical foundations of an inpatient post-traumatic stress disorder and alcoholism treatment program. *Psychotherapy, 31*(1), 67-78.

Sells, S. B., & Simpson, D. D. (Eds.). (1976). *Studies in the effectiveness of treatment of drug abuse.* Cambridge, MA: Ballinger.

Silberstein, C. H., Metzger, E. J., & Galanter, M. (1997). The Greenhouse: A modified therapeutic community for mentally ill homeless addicts at New York University. In G. De Leon (Ed.), *Community as method: Therapeutic communities for special populations and special settings* (pp. 53–65). Westport, CT: Greenwood Publishing Group, Inc.

Silbert, M. (1986). Delancey Street Foundation: An example of self-reliance. In A. Acampora & E. Nebelkopf (Eds.), *Bridging services: Drug abuse, human services and the therapeutic community-Proceedings of the 9th World Conference of Therapeutic Communities, September 1-6, 1985* (pp. 303-306). San Francisco, CA: Abacus Printing.

Simpson, D. D. (1979). The relation of time spent in drug abuse treatment to posttreatment outcome. *American Journal of Psychiatry, 136,* 1449-1453.

Simpson, D. D. (1986). 12-year Follow-up outcomes of opioid addicts treated in therapeutic communities. In G. De Leon & J. T. Ziegenfuss Jr. (Eds.), *Therapeutic communities for addictions: Readings in theory, research and practice* (pp. 109-120). Springfield, IL: Charles C. Thomas.

Simpson, D. D., & Friend, H. J. (1988). Legal status and long-term outcomes for addicts in the DARP followup project. In C. G. Leukefeld & F. M. Tims (Eds), *Compulsory treatment of drug abuse: Research and clinical practice NIDA Research Monograph 86* (ADM 88-1578; pp. 81-98). Rockville, MD: National Institute on Drug Abuse.

Simpson, D. D., Joe, G. W., & Brown, B. S. (1997). Treatment retention and follow-up outcomes in the Drug Abuse Treatment Outcome Study (DATOS). *Psychology of Addictive Behaviors, 11,* 294-307.

Simpson, D. D., Joe, G. W., Rowan-Szal, G. A., & Greener, J. M. (1997). Drug abuse treatment process components that improve retention. *Journal of Substance Abuse Treatment, 14,* 565-572.

Simpson, D. D., Knight, K., & Ray, S. (1993). Psychosocial correlates of AIDS-risk, drug use and sexual behaviors. *AIDS Education and Prevention, 5,* 121-130.

Simpson, D. D., & Lloyd, M. R. (1979). Client evaluations of drug abuse treatment in relation to follow-up outcomes. *American Journal of Drug and Alcohol Abuse, 6*(4), 397-411.

Simpson, D. D., & Sells, S. B. (1982). Effectiveness of treatment for drug abuse: An overview of the DARP research program. *Advances in Alcohol and Substance Abuse, 2,*7-29.

Slater, M. R. (1984). *An Historical Perspective of Therapeutic Communities,* Thesis Proposal to the M. S. S. program, University of Colorado at Denver.

Stephens, J. (1978). Conflicts of cultures in therapeutic communities. *Addiction Therapist, Special Edition, 2* (3 & 4), 106-108.

Stevens, S. J., Arbiter N, & Glider P. (1989). Female residents: Expanding their role to increase treatment effectiveness. *International Journal on the Addictions, 4,* 285-306.

Stevens, S. J., Arbiter, N. & McGrath, R. (1997). Women and children: Therapeutic community substance abuse treatment. In G. De Leon (Ed.), *Community as method: Therapeutic communities for special populations and special settings* (pp. 129-142). Westport, CT: Greenwood Publishing Group, Inc.

Stevens, S. J., & Glider, P. (1994). Therapeutic communities: Substance abuse treatment for women. In F. M. Tims, G. De Leon, & N. Jainchill (Eds.), *Therapeutic community: Advances in research and application, NIDA Research Monograph 144* (NIH Publication Number 94-3633, pp. 162-180). Rockville, MA: National Institute on Drug Abuse.

Stitzer, M. L., Iguchi, M. Y., Kidorf, M., & Bigelow, G. E. (1993). Contingency management in methadone treatment: The case for positive incentives. *Behavioral treatment for drug abuse and dependence, National Institute on Drug Abuse Research Monograph Series 137* (NIDA NIH Publication No. 93-3684, pp. 19-36). Rockville, MD: National Institute on Drug Abuse.

Sugarman, B. (1974). *Daytop Village: A therapeutic community.* New York: Holt, Winston and Rinehart.

Sugarman, B. (1986). Structure, variations, and context: A sociological view of the therapeutic community. In G. De Leon, & J. T. Ziegenfuss (Eds.), *Therapeutic communities for addictions: Readings in theory, research and practice* (pp. 65-82). Springfield, IL: Charles C. Thomas.

Talboy, E. S. (1998). *Therapeutic community experiential training: Facilitator guide.* Kansas City, MO: University of Missouri–Kansas City, Mid-America Addiction Technology Transfer Center (ATTC).

Therapeutic Communities of America Criminal Justice Committee (1999, December). *Therapeutic communities in correctional settings: The prison based TC standards development project, Final report of phase II* (Prepared for the Office of National Drug Control Policy [ONDCP]). Washington, DC: National Drug Clearinghouse, 1-800-666-3332 [NCJ179365].

Tims, F. M., De Leon, G., & Jainchill, N. (Eds.). (1994). *Therapeutic community: Advances in research and application: NIDA Monograph 144* (NIH Publication No. 94-3633). Washington, DC: Superintendent of Documents, US Government Printing Office.

Tims, F. M., & Ludford, J. P. (Eds.). (1984). *Drug abuse treatment evaluation: Strategies, progress and prospects. National Institute on Drug Abuse Research Monograph 51* (DHHS Publication No. [ADM] 84-1329). Rockville, MD: National Institute on Drug Abuse.

Toumbourou, J. W., Hamilton, M., & Fallon, B. (1998). Treatment level progress and time spent in treatment in the prediction of outcomes following drug-free therapeutic community treatment. *Addiction, 93*(7), 1051-1064.

Trimpey, J. (1988). *Rational recovery from alcoholism: The small book.* Lotus, CA: Lotus Press.

Vaillant, G. E. (1973). A 20-year follow-up of New York narcotic addicts. *Archives of General Psychiatry, 29,* 273-241.

Vaillant, G. E. (1981). Dangers of psychotherapy in the treatment of alcoholism. In M. H. Bean & N. E. Zinberg (Eds.), *Dynamic approaches to the understanding and treatment of alcoholism* (pp. 36-54). New York: Free Press.

Volkman, R., & Cressey, D. R. (1963). Differential association and the rehabilitation of drug addicts. *American Journal of Sociology, 69,* 129-42.

Waldorf, D. (1971). Social control in therapeutic communities for the treatment of drug addicts. *The International Journal of the Addictions, 6* (1), 28-43.

Waldorf, D. (1973). *Careers in dope.* Englewood Cliffs, NJ: Prentice Hall.

Washburne, N. (1977). *Dynamics of treatment in therapeutic communities.* (Technical Report No 5). Newark, NJ: Rutgers University.

Washton, A. M. (1989). Cocaine abuse and compulsive sexuality. *Medical Aspects of Human Sexuality,* 32-39.

Watterson, O., Simpson, D. D., & Sells, S. B. (1975). Death rates and causes of death among opioid addicts in community drug treatment programs during 1970-1973. *American Journal of Drug Alcohol Abuse, 2,* 99-111.

Wexler, H., De Leon, G., Thomas, G., Kressel, D., & Peters, J. (1999). The Amity prison TC evaluation: Reincarceration outcomes. *Criminal Justice and Behavior, 26* (2): 144-167.

Wexler, H., & Williams, R. (1986) The Stay'n Out therapeutic community: Prison treatment for substance abusers, *Journal of Psychoactive Drugs* 18, 221-230.

Wilmer, H. (1958). Toward a definition of the therapeutic community. *American Journal of Psychiatry, 114,* 824-837.

Wilson, B. (1957). *Alcoholics Anonymous comes of age: A brief history of AA.* New York: Alcoholics Anonymous World Services.

Winick, C. (1962). Maturing out of narcotic addiction. *United Nations Bulletin on Narcotics, 16,* 1-11.

Winick, C. (1980). An empirical assessment of therapeutic communities in New York City. In L. Brill & C. Winick (Eds.), *The yearbook of substance use and abuse, vol. II* (pp. 251-285). New York, NY: Human Sciences Press.

Winick, C. (1981). Substances of abuse and sexual behavior. In J. H. Lowinson & P. Ruiz (Eds.), *Substance abuse: Clinical problems and perspectives.* Baltimore, MD: Williams & Wilkens.

Winick, C. (1990-91). The counselor in drug abuse treatment. *International Journal of the Addictions 25* (12A), 1479-1502.

Winick, C., & Evans, J. T. (1997). A therapeutic community program for mothers and their children. In G. De Leon (Ed.), *Community as method: Therapeutic communities for special populations and special settings* (pp. 143-160). Westport, CT: Greenwood Publishing Group, Inc.

Wright, K. N., & Wright, K. E. (1994). *Family life, delinquency, and crime: A policymaker's guide.* Washington, DC: Office of Juvenile Justice and Delinquency Prevention.

Wurmser, L. (1974). Psychoanalytic considerations of the etiology of compulsive drug use. *Journal of the American Psychoanalytic Association, 22,* 820-843.

Yablonsky, L. (1965). *Synanon: The tunnel back.* New York: Macmillan.

Yablonsky, L. (1986). Some characteristics of the social structure & social organization of the TC. In A. Acampora & E. Nebelkopf (Eds.), *Bridging services: Drug abuse, human services and the therapeutic community—Proceedings of the 9th World Conference of Therapeutic Communities, September 1-6, 1985* (pp. 211-214). San Francisco, CA: Abacus Printing.

Yablonsky, L. (1989). *The therapeutic community.* New York City: Gardner Press.

Yalom, I. D. (1975). *The theory and practice of group psychotherapy.* New York: Basic Books.

Young, E. G. (1995). The role of incest issues in relapse and recovery. In A. M. Washton (Ed.), *Psychotherapy and substance abuse* (pp. 451-469). New York: Guilford.

Zackon, F., McAuliffe, W. E., & Chi'en, J. (1985). *Addict aftercare: Recovery training and self-help treatment, NIDA Treatment Research Monograph Series* (DHHS Publication (ADM) 85-1341). Rockville, MD: National Institute on Drug Abuse.

Zarcone, V. P., Jr. (1975). *Drug addicts in a therapeutic community: The Satori approach.* Baltimore, MD: York Press, Inc.

Zimmer-Hofler, D. & Meyer-Fehr, P. (1986). Motivational aspects of heroin addicts in therapeutic communities compared with those in other institutions. In G. De Leon & J. T. Ziegenfuss, Jr. (Eds.), *Therapeutic communities for addictions* (pp. 157-168). Springfield, IL: Charles C. Thomas.

Zuckerman, M. (1986). Sensation seeking and the endogenous deficit theory of drug abuse. In Szara (Ed.), *Neurology of viral control in drug abuse. NIDA Monograph Series 74* (pp. 59-70). Washington, DC: U.S. Gvt. Printing Office.

Zuckerman, M. (1994). *Behavioral expressions and biosocial bases of sensation seeking.* Cambridge, England: Cambridge University Press.

Zweben, J. E. (1993). Recovery-oriented psychotherapy: A model for addiction treatment. *Psychotherapy, 30,* 259-268.

Zweben, J. E., & Smith, D. E. (1986). Changing attitudes and policies toward alcohol use in the therapeutic community. *Journal of Psychoactive Drugs, 18* (3), 253-260.

APPENDIX A: GLOSSARY OF THERAPEUTIC COMMUNITY TERMS[*]

Acapulco gold - a type of marijuana.

Acid - LSD (lysergic acid diethylamide); a powerful hallucinogen.

AKA - also known as (police blotter usage).

Alky - alcoholic; a nearly obsolete term used mostly by persons of skid row or rural background.

Anywhere - used in the expression "Are you anywhere?" meaning, "Do you have any drugs?"

Awareness - special assignment given to a resident to heighten his or her awareness to a problem area.

Backbiting - belittling a person who is not present in the conversation.

Bad trick - a term from prostitute's argot, referring to a customer with some perversion demanding that the prostitute submit to unusual indignities, or to practices which injure or endanger her.

Bad trip - a frightening experience or psychotic break experienced while under the influence of a drug, most often a hallucinogen, but also other drugs such as amphetamines, to which the user may have an adverse reaction.

Bag - a packet of heroin, which is usually sold in small glassine envelopes or bags. A "nickel bag" was once the standard "fix," and actually sold for five dollars.

Ball - a verb meaning to have sexual intercourse. The term is used by both males and females to refer to their own activities.

Bandwagon - to go along with someone even though you disagree but will not say so (people pleasing).

Beans - amphetamine tablets.

Beat up on (someone) - to assault or commit violence against a person.

Behavioral contract - an agreement between the family, resident, and staff on changes that must be made for the resident to continue membership in the community (special usage).

Behind - a preposition used interchangeably with "after" or "following." It implies a causal connection between two events in a sequence: e.g., *"behind* all that went down, she split out of here."

Being aware - knowing what is going on around you at all times.

Belly - one's emotions; one is often said "to have a belly" when they are in control of their emotions.

Belly flip - a reaction to what another person says or does, caused by a sensitivity to a particular issue.

---

[*]This list has been compiled from various sources, including B. Frankel's *"Transforming Identities, Context, Power and Ideology in a Therapeutic Community"* (New York City: Peter Lang, 1989); V. P. Zarcone, Jr.'s *"Drug Addicts in a Therapeutic Community: The Satori Approach"* (Baltimore, MD: York Press, Inc., 1975); and resources from a number of TC agencies.

Bennies - nearly obsolete term for benzadrine, the earliest of the amphetamine drugs. These are central nervous system stimulants.

Big H - heroin.

Block - the action of one drug in preventing the patient from feeling the effects of another.

Bogus - phony, untrue.

Booking an incident - to report a rule violation.

Booking slips - written pull-ups.

Bottle story - a term used in Alcoholics Anonymous to refer to the personal testimony which is a regular feature of AA meetings. The speaker describes his addictive career, starting with his first drink and the stages of his gradual dissolution until he "hit bottom." Then he describes the stages of his recovery to the present moment.

Breakthrough - attainment of insight in therapy, usually through a sudden and dramatic catharsis, but the term may be used less precisely to refer to any highly charged emotional outburst during therapy.

Brick - a kilogram of marijuana.

Bring down - reduce the physiological and psychological effects of someone's "high" to a point at which he is no longer a menace to himself and others.

Bulldagger - this is a Black English term referring to a masculineappearing lesbian (see *dyke).*

Bummer - an unpleasant experience, especially one that was unexpected; often refers to experience of drug use.

Burn - swindle, especially by selling substandard drugs or some substance in place of the promised drug.

Busted - arrested, though not necessarily booked, by the police.

Cap - capsule.

Cardinal rules - laws of the community that protect the structure and safety of the program; an infraction of these rules may warrant expulsion from the program.

Caseworker - staff member offering social work services to residents.

C - cocaine.

Chick - street term for a woman.

Chip - take occasional single doses of heroin without becoming dependent on it; see "ride the horse."

Clean up - get free of drugs; adopt a way of life that does not involve dependence on drugs.

Clean - with no drugs in one's possession; physiologically free of drugs.

Coat-pulling - residents sometimes conduct impromptu get-togethers dubbed *coat-pulling* sessions, which are reminiscent of "self-criticism meetings;" during these sessions a group indulges in mutual monitoring of one another's conduct, punishing bad behavior by means of strong social disapproval (see *pulling coats).*

Cold turkey - abrupt withdrawal of drugs, with no attempt at tapering off the dose or alleviating the discomfort by means of other drugs.

Collar- a strip of paper used in filling a hypodermic needle with a narcotic.

Come down on - Crack down on, punish.

Come off - a verb phrase referring to the manner in which a person presents himself or herself to others, or the way (s)he appears to others—not necessarily authentic and not necessarily conscious.

Coming out sideways - to leak, to react—usually misplacing feeling or being sarcastic.

Con - (1) used as a verb, this word means to deceive others, or to manipulate others in a self-serving way; (2) as a noun, a *con* is either (a) a game of deception, or (b) the person who does the deceiving, also known as a *con man;* (3) an *ex-con,* on the other hand, is a former convict, a person who has spent time in prison. (This term has become part of standard American English.)

Connection - a dope peddler, especially one from whom one has bought before or who has been recommended by a friend.

Contract group - A group of residents, seldom more than three or four, who conspire secretly to violate a rule of the community. It often involves procuring and using drugs, but in one notable instance it involved violence and threats of violence instead.

Cook - dissolve a narcotic prior to injection.

Cool it - admonition to take it easy, or to stop doing something one is currently engaged in.

COP - (1) used as a noun to refer to a police officer; (2) used as a verb in two senses: (a) to buy or otherwise obtain an illegal substance, generally for one's own use (e.g., to cop drugs) and (b) to confess to some act of your own, usually reprehensible (e.g. "She *copped* to using pot").

Cop out - inform on, as in "I find it hard to cop out on a buddy."

Cop to - admit or confess to something.

Copman - a dealer in illicit drugs, usually the addict's regular source.

Cop-out - evasion or avoidance of the unpleasant, or of something one ought to do; an excuse made in order to run away from an obligation, either psychologically or physically.

Copping area - a place where illicit drugs can be obtained.

Creep - a person regarded as perverted or peculiar in an unpleasant way.

Crystal - methadrine.

Cutting dope - the process whereby heroin is mixed with various adulterants, most commonly dextrose and quinine on the east coast of the U.S. Since no one can know how much a drug purchased on the street has been cut or what substance has been used, addicts regularly run the risk of being cheated, of accidental overdose, or of adverse reactions up to and including death (see *hot bag*).

Dealing with - (a person or problem) term for an activity usually taking place within therapy hours, intended to allow or force a person to confront his or her problems in an honest and realistic fashion. Being *dealt with* is informally referred to by many residents as "being put on the hot seat," and is widely perceived as a painful and coercive experience, but also as a curative one.

Dealing - buying or selling illicit drugs.

Defocusing - talking about anything or anyone to avoid looking at your behavior and accepting responsibility for self (trying to take others in a trip elsewhere to avoid the issue at hand).

Demerit - a black mark on one's record for some minor rule infraction of a commitment.

Detoxify (or detox) - medically supervised withdrawal from drugs in such a way as to safeguard the patient's health and minimize the discomfort.

Dig - to like and understand, to appreciate something or someone.

Dime - a verb meaning to betray or inform, equivalent to the near obsolete terms "to rat" on someone, or "to squeal;" occasionally used in the elaborated form *drop a dime,* which points to its reputed origin in the street custom of taking revenge on an enemy by phoning the police.

Ding bat - a new resident who has not yet acquired TC tools or an older resident who does not apply what he does.

Do drugs - to use illegal or illegally obtained substance(s); *doing skag* is to use heroin, for example, whereas *doing pills* refers to using any one or more of a number of drugs in oral form. Habitual use is usually, but not always implied.

Doing your thing - when you are doing everything you should be doing in a therapeutic community.

Dope - (1) heroin (e.g., "he *shoots dope*") or (2) marijuana (e.g., "she *smokes dope*").

Down - depressed; sedated, especially by barbiturates.

Downers – barbiturates; sedatives; or other substances that have a soporific effect, usually in pill or capsule form. Most of these are in the barbiturate category, though some newer drugs have similar effects but different chemical composition and are classified as hypnotics rather than sedatives (e.g., Doriden, Quaalude). All are pharmacologically classified as central nervous system depressants (CNS's).

Dropping a lug - making indirect comments about someone, dropping hints with bits and pieces of what you really want to say.

Drop - take a drug, usually LSD, orally after first dropping it on some medium, such as a sugar cube; to take LSD (short for "*drop acid*").

Dry drunk - a state of feeling either *high* or low without the use of intoxicants, but with identical symptoms. Considered by Alcoholics Anonymous as part of an emotional withdrawal syndrome that occurs in the latter stages of physical withdrawal from alcohol, thus a normal part of recovery, though its severity varies.

Dude - term for a man or fellow; a male person.

Dump - to express strong negative feelings about someone, usually in the presence of others. The experience of the person *dumped on* is usually painful, and (s)he is not expected to tolerate it without protest, particularly if (s)he feels the criticism to be hostile or unjust.

Dyke - a female homosexual, usually the "masculine" or active partner in a lesbian relationship, whose appearance and behavior are deemed more mannish than womanly; also called a "*bull dyke*," or in Black American dialect a "*bulldagger*."

Encapsulated - someone that is spaced out and unaware of what's surrounding them.

Escort - a person assigned to accompany a resident at all times, usually a more senior and reliable resident who is not addicted to the same substance. The object is to prevent new and/or badly behaved residents from getting into trouble by providing them with continuous surveillance for a day or more.

Fay - a white person.

Feedback - response or reaction to something another person has done or said. The term is used most often in a context indicating that the response is constructive in intent. *Feedback* has acquired the status of a cliche, replacing ordinary terms such as "answering," "reaction," or "response."

Fink - an informer.

Fix - (noun) an intravenous injection of a drug (usually heroin); (verb) To inject a drug intravenously.

Flagging - when you are not concentrating on your job or on what you are doing.

Flip out - (1) a verb phrase meaning to go berserk or to lose one's reason; (2) also used jocularly to refer to being "crazy about" something.

Freak - a person addicted to or fixated upon a particular activity or interest.

Freak out - similar to *flip out* but stronger, usually referring to a true psychotic break resulting from the use of a drug, most commonly a hallucinogen or stimulant.

Fuck - (1) (noun) all-purpose expletive, freely used in street argot; (2) (verb) it refers initially to (a) the act of sexual intercourse, but also may be used as (b) a synonym for almost any sort of hostile activity; (3) *fucked-up behavior* is bad or antisocial; (4) to *fuck over* someone is to confuse them, or to get them into difficulty by exerting a bad influence; (5) *to fuck up* is to fail, lose control, or misbehave; (6) to be *fucked-up is* to be troubled or confused in mind or spirit, depressed, hopeless about one's present or future; (7) also used casually as an adjective or adverb, without any particularly forceful connotations (e.g., "Pass the *fuckin'* butter, please?").

G - a grain (of heroin or morphine).

Gas station - derogatory term applied by opiate addicts and others to methadone clinics that merely supply methadone without any attempt at therapy or rehabilitation.

Get behind - take (a drug).

Get down on - see "*come down on.*"

Get in touch with one's feelings - find out what one really wants or feels; be sincere with oneself and others; experience emotions, usually unpleasant, in strong fashion with behavioral signs.

Get it all out - to ventilate your inner feelings or share your troubles with someone. People are frequently admonished to *get it all out* when they appear troubled, angry, or depressed, in order to cure the condition.

Get one's head together - set one's thinking and, by inference, one's life in order, usually with some definite purpose in view.

Get sick - suffer involuntary withdrawal symptoms.

Getting it together - (1) the process of developing group solidarity, closeness, and cooperation, or, alternatively; (2) an individual's process of achieving improved personal integration. In sum, *getting it together* is both a group and an individual integrative process.

Getting off - experiencing a euphoric *high* when using a drug.

Getting on (someone) - riding or harassing another person; nagging.

Getting over on (someone) - taking advantage of another person's laxity, naivete, or kindness to put something over on them.

Getting/going straight - the process of rehabilitation, specifically with reference to straightening out emotional or cognitive disorder within the individual's mind or psyche.

Getting up - experiencing the high that accompanies drug use (synonymous with *getting off*).

Getting your rocks off - obtaining relief from sexual tension; this synonym for orgasm is used self-descriptively by both males and females from the street subculture.

Getting your shit together - solving one's problems—in this context those underlying one's addiction so that mental health is promoted through attaining insight into one's own weaknesses and failings.

Go down - in drug users' language, to take hard drugs, usually heroin; a term popularized by the Beatles' white album.

Going off - eventually "blowing your top" as a result of repressed feelings and resentments rather than dealing with them as they occur.

Going through changes - (1) being forced to make rapid adaptations to new circumstances that require reorienting one's thinking and/or previous definitions of the situation; (2) more generally, a disturbing or disruptive experience in which the old definitions break down.

Grass - marijuana.

H - heroin.

Habit - dependence on drugs; used to express the degree of such dependence, as in "I have a thirty-dollar-a-day habit."

Hang up - a problem someone is having difficulty solving.

Hang tough - to stay with it no matter what and not give up.

Hassle - trouble; problem; runaround.

Head - noun used to refer to habitual users of drugs in the hallucinogen family, many of which radically alter the user's perceptions of reality.

Head stuff - (1) substances that create radical change in perceptions and consciousness of oneself and the world, mostly hallucinogens such as mescaline, LSD, and others; also (2) a phrase used to refer to the kind of thought which comes from "intellectualizing" and "closing off feeling."

Heavy - grave or serious, not to be taken lightly, important, stirring, or dramatic. Thus a *heavy session* is a particularly dramatic therapy session, often extended in length without prior planning, and usually featuring catharsis for one or more group members. Therapists who conduct a great many *heavy sessions* tend to acquire a good deal of charisma in the community, and to have the reputation of being highly effective, even though follow-up statistics may not bear this out.

Heavy place - a state of mind in which one is prey to heavy feelings, as in "Joe said he was in a heavy place."

Hiding in the woodwork - not getting involved; trying to avoid being "a part of" through minimal participation in the community.

High - a noun referring to an intoxicated or drugged state, generally experienced or thought of as pleasant and desirable. Depending on the specific effects of the drug used, a *high* can consist of anything from somnolence to extreme excitement, hallucinations, and so forth.

Holding - in possession of illicit drugs.; original usage seems to have been to denote people with money, i.e. "loaded."

Hustle - obtain by illegal or underhanded methods; make one's living and/or feed one's habit by such methods.

Image - a mask or shield that one puts on to keep others from knowing you: a defense mechanism also referred to as a "jacket."

Incident - an occasion of serious rule violation involving one or more residents. Having an *incident* usually places one in danger of discharge for disciplinary reasons, though this is not mandatory in all circumstances. Use or possession of drugs on campus or any violent behavior are, however, *incidents* which bring automatic discharge.

Jacket - reputation of a person.

Jailing - someone giving the impression of "doing time;" holding on to your negative behavior patterns (street codes).

Jelly belly - to be extremely sensitive; generally someone who cannot handle ridicule or criticism.

Jitterbug - (1) an eager or overconscientious new resident; (2) a new staff member full of energy and enthusiasm about his job. Generally used by older blacks from the ghetto, but occasionally by others.

Jive - mislead someone in a cool, inwardly derisive fashion.

Jiving - (1) fooling around or "messing with" someone. This can have simply joking connotations (e.g., "I was just *jiving* you') or more serious connotations of misbehavior, especially of a sexual nature (e.g., "He's the guy that's been *jiving* that girl over there"); (2) an almost obsolete term used by older prostitutes, referring to the act of mimicking passion or orgasm.

Joint - (1) used with the definite article "the" this is a term for prison; (2) used with the indefinite article, a marijuana cigarette.

Jonesing - (1) undergoing withdrawal from heroin; a disposition of variable severity which strongly resembles intestinal flu plus a bad cold; (2) also used in noun form, e.g., "having a bad *jones.*"

Junk – heroin, or any opiate drug used intravenously.

Junkie - opiate addict with true physiological as well as psychological dependence.

Keep cool - remain unflustered in the face of provocation or insult; relax; suppress unwanted or potentially dangerous emotions.

Kick - (1) (noun) an emotional reaction, usually positive, "I got a *kick* out of the news"; (2) (verb) get rid of, especially a drug habit.

Kicking the habit/Kicking - refers to suffering withdrawal from opiates or other physiologically addicting drugs such as barbiturates, either voluntarily or involuntarily (e.g., in jail).

Lay a rap on (someone) - to "give someone the word" or advise them, to talk to them earnestly and persuasively.

Lay back (in the woodwork) - not getting involved; always in the background and never voicing opinions.

Lay on - give.

Lay something on someone - to place a charge or responsibility on a person, to advise them strongly to follow one's suggestion, to indicate definite expectations one has for someone.

Leaking - to express feelings indirectly and inappropriately.

Legal thing - a substance of addiction obtained from legal sources, as in the case of pills obtained by means of a doctor's prescription from a legitimate pharmacist, even if not used as prescribed.

Lid - about one ounce of marijuana.

Loaded - high; under the influence of a drug. Under some circumstances, this may refer explicitly to heroin, although its original meaning was "drunk."

Lose one's thing - become incapable of performing some activity central to one's sense of personal worth and identity.

Main line - inject a drug directly into a vein.

Mellow - comfortably high on some drug; compare "spaced out."

Mental masturbation - a pejorative term applied to the act of manipulating one's own consciousness to achieve a desired effect.

Meth - methadrine; one of the forms of *speed* (see below) or amphetamine, used either orally or intravenously, and quite dangerous in the latter form. It may cause cerebral hemorrhage through sudden and extreme elevation of blood pressure, or brain damage and a post-methadrine psychosis; see "crystal."

Mike - microgram, i.e., one-millionth of a gram.

Mind-fucking - Mixing up or confusing another person's mind, deliberately and with malice aforethought. Also phrased as "fucking over a person's head," generally by introducing bad thoughts in sly or surreptitious fashion.

Mr. TC - a person who works the therapeutic community program (walking the walk).

Nab - a police officer.

Narc or *Nark* - federal or state narcotics agent. *Narks* are feared as enforcers, officers of the laws penalizing possession and sale of illicit and/or dangerous drugs.

Needle story - "Narcotics Anonymous" equivalent to the Alcoholics Anonymous *bottle* story (see above), and used analogously as part of NA meeting ritual.

Negative contract - two or more people agree to have a secret contract not to disclose or confront one another; may be conscious or unconscious.

Negative feedback - criticism received from others.

Nod - semiconscious state induced by narcotics; to be in such a state.

Nodding off - also *nodding out* or *on the nod,* which are synonymous; refers to the stupor induced by the use of a narcotic following the initial rush or high. Nodding and scratching (in their literal meaning) are behavioral signs that a person has used an opiate very recently. This behavior is most marked in the novice user, who may or may not be addicted. It is less characteristic of old addicts well habituated to the drug.

Nose dive - the instant religious conversion feigned by skid row alcoholics when in urgent need of a meal and a bed in a mission house. The term comes from the fact that men meet the missionary's needs, as they conceive them, by falling to their knees and praying loudly for God's help in staying sober.

OD - (1) dangerous overdose of any drug. An *OD* is frequently cited as the cause of death on Coroners' records pertaining to addicts; (2) the term is also used jocularly to refer to overindulgence in anything pleasant, such as food or sweets.

Ofay - see "*fay.*"

Off and running - experiencing euphoria after taking drugs.

Off the wall - adjective phrase used to describe behavior that is highly agitated, irrational, or both.

Old addict - a person who has used heroin long enough to have established a high tolerance. This means that the addict can no longer rely on obtaining a rush (the ecstatic experience of early addiction). The *old addict* uses heroin primarily to avoid withdrawal sickness and to "feel normal" rather than to achieve a high, which s/he can seldom afford financially, and is often incapable of in any case.

Old lady - common law wife; steady girl friend; mother (old-fashioned usage). The usual function of this term is to rule out questions about the legal status of the relationship.

Old man - (1) one's steady boyfriend or lover, if the speaker is a woman; (2) one's father, if the speaker is a man.

Out front - frank, honest, open; in the open.

Out of it - inebriated or drugged to a point of unawareness of oneself, one's behavior, or events around oneself.

Outfit - the paraphernalia used for injecting narcotics: spoon, eye dropper, "collar," and needle.

Pad - a room, apartment, or other dwelling where one can take drugs; one's own room, especially when used for that purpose.

Panama red - a type of marijuana.

Paraphernalia - equipment for drug use, such as that needed to inject heroin.

Personalizing - taking something someone says in general about anything as a personal remark.

Pigeon - an informer.

Pigs - police.

Pill freak - a person who is addicted to drugs in pill or capsule form, usually ingesting a variety of substances, singly or in combination. Typically, *pill freaks* obtain most of their drugs "legally" (i.e., by prescription) and have never been part of the street subculture of heroin or methadrine addicts.

Pinned - adjective used to describe the appearance of an opiate addict's eyes shortly after use of the drug, when the pupils contract almost to the size of pinheads.

Pissed - angry or annoyed.

Play it safe/playing it close to the chest - doing just enough to get by.

Playing games - being dishonest with oneself and/or others; *conning* people or deceiving them, deliberately or unconsciously.

Points - hypodermic needles, as referred to by addicts.

Pop - take orally.

Pot - marijuana.

Processing - discussing the dynamics of what has occurred, in order to discover the how and why of unfolding events, with an implicit goal of improving the effectiveness of therapists and therapy. "Let's *process* what just went down" is often an invitation to attempt to understand what went wrong with the way things were handled.

Psyched-up - in a state of psychological preparedness or readiness. The term implies a state of tension or excitement, and may also imply persuading oneself of the necessity and/or rightness of what one is about to do.

Pulling a urine - to require a resident (or occasionally, an addicted staff member) to submit a urine sample for laboratory testing to determine whether or not drugs have been used.

Pulling your weight - taking responsibility for one's share of duties in the community.

Pusher - someone who deals aggressively in illicit drugs, usually with financial gain as prime motive.

Pushing buttons - to deliberately provoke or attack a person in a sensitive area to facilitate honest, unguarded reactions.

Rammies - a state of agitated depression characterized by feelings of boredom, restlessness, and unhappiness. Addicts often cite the *rammies* as the cause of their return to drug use after a period of good behavior.

Rap session - a group discussion led by community members with the purpose of increasing social awareness.

Rapping - conversing, usually in small groups, and usually at a level of discussion that is seen as serious and meaningful.

Rat - an informer.

Reacting - a verbal or nonverbal expression that reflects feelings indirectly.

Reds - barbiturates.

Rehash - summary; recapitulation.

Relate - (1) term used generally as a synonym for getting to know others more or less intimately, on a friendly basis. Thus "He won't relate to the group," is cause for concern; (2) identification with someone else's plight or state of mind, e.g., "I can really relate to what you're saying, 'cause I felt the same way when I first came here."

*Request form*s - a form to be used by residents who are requesting special privileges and/or asking to rise to the next phase.

Ride the horse - take heroin without becoming dependent on it.

Righteous junkie - a junkie who believes in taking junk as a superior way of life.

Rip-off - a theft or episode of stealing.

Run - (noun) a period of continual drug use during which a high is steadily maintained.

Run a game - manipulate; con; as in "I *ran a game* on him."

Running with - associating with, or hanging out with a person or group, e.g., "He been running with a motorcycle gang."

Rush - the intense pleasure experienced by opiate addicts during the early stages of their addiction, immediately after injecting the drug. Long-term addicts generally fail to experience this sensation, which is described as similar to orgasm but more intense, and located in the lower abdomen (see *old addict*).

Score - obtain illicit drugs, usually for money.

Selling wolf tickets - threatening someone.

Shades - dark glasses.

Shakedown - search, especially by police officers looking for drugs and drug paraphernalia.

Sharing yourself - revealing significant facts and feelings about one's life to others, usually within the therapy group. Reciprocity is implicit in the idea of sharing yourself, for others are then supposed to share themselves with you.

Shining - showing off in order to gain something in a manipulative way (i.e., doing your thing only in front of staff in order to get requests)

Shit - (1) one of the numerous terms for heroin; (2) all negative thoughts and feelings, which should be "gotten out" or dumped rather than "sat on." If retained, *shit* will obstruct a person's recovery and good relations with others.

Shooting a curve - going to someone else when you were already given a valid response by another.

Shooting gallery - an establishment for the purchase and use of illicit drugs, not only heroin but others as well. Both *junk* and *works* are available here for a price, and in some of these establishments addicts are permitted to remain until they have finished nodding.

Shooting up - injecting heroin or other drugs.

Shuck (or shucking)- manipulate; con; use a story to hide one's feelings or behavior.

Skag - heroine, especially the high-quality type.

Skin-popping - subcutaneous injection (as opposed to intravenous injection) usually of an opiate.

Slams - also (the) *slammer*, jail.

Sliding - when one is going through treatment without being challenged and therefore, not growing.

Slip - euphemism for an incident of drug or alcohol use; passing such events off as somehow accidental, or inadvertent, and to absolve the individual of responsibility for them.

Smack - heroin.

Smashed - intoxicated from drugs; implies a state of heavy intoxication, e.g., "He was *smashed* out of his mind."

Snitch - an informer; one who betrays a friend, especially to the police. Term carries strong moral opprobrium, both on the street and inside therapeutic community, where it is used to refer to street activities. It is thus distinguished from expressions of responsible concern such as *diming* or *coat-pulling;* (verb) - tell on, inform.

Snuff - kill.

Solid - an adjective expressing strong approval and appreciation.

Spaced out - under the influence of drugs; high.

Spade - a black person.

Speed - amphetamines or other drugs belonging to the class called central nervous system stimulants (CNS's). *Speeding* is (1) the sensation derived from using these drugs; or, (2) a description of the agitated behavior they produce.

Spike - a hypodermic needle.

Split - leave, usually from a group; from "split up."

Split to - absent oneself without leave, walking out of a facility impulsively; can be done covertly, merely by walking off the premises when nobody is looking, or openly by leaving officially against medical advice (AMA).

Spoon - a standard street measure of cocaine or a dose of heroin, so called because the drug is often dissolved for injection in a spoon; see "outfit."

Stabilize - build a patient up with successive doses of a drug to the point at which his system can tolerate it with few or no side effects. The dose necessary at this stage is called the "stabilizing dose," and varies with the individual.

Stash - a cache or store (e.g., of drugs).

Stoned - intoxicated on any chemical substance, including alcohol.

Straight - non-addicted, respectable, conventional; ignorant of and/or unaccustomed to the use of illicit drugs; a milieu in which nearly everyone is this way; *square* is a related term.

Strokes - verbal expressions of praise or approval, used generally as rewards for surmounting problems or temptations.

Strung out - in withdrawal and needing a "fix" but with no immediate prospect of obtaining the drug of choice, usually due to lack of funds and/or lack of strength to continue the quest; implies a state both sick and desperate.

Stuffing feelings - keeping feelings locked up inside and not venting them appropriately; tends to create resentments.

Stuffing - when one is wasting time and not doing their job.

Switch on - see "Turn on."

Tabbing - take a drug, usually a hallucinogen, in tablet form.

Taking a trip - evading a question; talking about anything and anyone instead of responding to the topics.

Taste - a single shot of heroin or another drug, not intended to lead to readdiction. It is an article of faith at therapeutic communities, however, that no addict can try a *taste* of any drug without becoming readdicted.

The man - can refer to either a dealer or a police officer.

Therapeutic cop-out - term applied to residents who use involvement in the problems of others to avoid dealing with their own (see cop).

Thing - one's drug of choice or substance of addiction; usually new residents are asked by older residents to identify their *thing* as part of getting acquainted.

Tip - two or more people who are always together, can be positive but more often acts as a negative contract.

To place a charge or responsibility on a person - to advise them strongly to follow one's suggestion, to indicate definite expectations one has for someone.

Trading - exchanging one kind of illicit drug for another, whether as a business transaction or a personal favor.

Tricked up - to encounter an obstacle or stumbling block; related to the term "tripped up."

Trip - (1) a drug episode, usually involving use of a hallucinogen; also, (2) a term used to refer to any experience which is amusing, enlightening, or exciting in a pleasurable sense.

Turn off - alienate, vex.

Turn on - begin taking a drug; to begin experiencing the high from the drug; traditionally used of marijuana.

Turning (someone's) *head around* - changing someone's personality or psychological set; this is the basis for changing addictive behavior.

Upper - central nervous system stimulants (CNS's), such as amphetamines, usually taken in pill or capsule form.

Uptight - tense, worried, or anxious.

Use/Using - the question "Is he using?" always refers to drugs.

Vibes - the impression given by a person, place, or event, as in, "I get good *vibes* from that cat." Short for "vibrations."

Went down - happened or took place; also used in the gerund form *going down.*

Where you're at - one's attitude or position concerning some issue, either implicitly or explicitly defined.

Where you're coming from - one's motives, or the reasons behind what one is doing or saying.

Whites - amphetamines; "uppers."

Works - equipment for injecting drugs, usually including a hypodermic syringe, needle, spoon, and matches (used to "cook" opiates); such equipment is not permitted on therapeutic community premises except for medical use, and possession of it is grounds for immediate discharge; synonym is *paraphernalia.*

Young addict - a novice to drug use, who still finds it easy to get high is not a matter of chronological age, but of length of addiction.

APPENDIX B: THERAPEUTIC COMMUNITY PHILOSOPHIES

The Daytop Philosophy

I am here because there is no refuge, finally from myself. Until I confront myself in the eyes and hearts of others, I am running. Until I suffer them to share my secrets, I have no safety from them. Afraid to be known I can know neither myself nor any other, I will be alone. Where else but in our common ground, can I find such a mirror? Here, together, I can at last appear clearly to myself not as a giant of my dreams nor the dwarf of my fears, but as a person, part of a whole, with my share in its purpose. In this ground, I can take root and grow not alone anymore as in death but alive to myself and to others.

[*Daytop is a traditional TC agency and a progenitor of TC programs around the world.*]

The Greenhouse Philosophy

Our philosophy starts by looking at ourselves, where we are coming from and where we are going. We are recovering addicts who have a mental or emotional difficulty. We were self-centered, angry, and critical people. We began to form bad habits and then those habits shaped us as lonely people looking for a way out.

Our symbol of *The Greenhouse* is a metaphor of the growth of a tree: A seed is planted and it grows only with the care it needs—water, sunshine, shade, and love. It will grow to be a tree and will take up space and air that, in time, will give protection and shade to others. With time, flowers will grow and will be the fruits of life.

As a self-help community, we support each other, we are responsible for our actions and our brother's. Thus, we will not see ourselves and them in dismay or isolation because now we have a home. We know how to relate and accept love. We are not alone. We are alive and an active part of society, like a beautiful tree in a forest fulfilling the cycle of life.

[The Greenhouse is a modified TC for homeless mentally ill chemical abusers (MICAs) in a hospital-affiliated shelter.]

Recovery Program Philosophy

We are here because we realize that drugs have made our lives unmanageable.

We have made a commitment to change for ourselves...for those we love...and for those who love us.

No matter how difficult we will succeed and take our rightful place in our community.

[The Recovery Program is a modified TC day treatment program in a hospital clinic setting.]

Stay'n Out Philosophy

Awareness is the key to one's mind's eye. This is the ability to create total comprehension within an indivdiual who seeks understanding and the beauty of self-existence.

We are committed to truth and the realization of oneself by setting forth on new directions, supplying materials, resources and the setting conducive to positive change.

As long as we are willing to learn the proper ways of becoming successful in this society of great turmoil, we will prosper.

Together we shall put forth all our work and efforts to the best of our ability, to gain a sense of achievement and satisfaction in ourselves.

We are here to benefit each other in growth and awareness, and to acquire a trust in oneself so that we may trust others in our lives.

We have come to the realization that we must stop running away all the time to avoid coming face to face with our real selves. Moreover, we have begun to attach the criminal mask and strip away our negative images, and live once again, not as people with character disorders, but as successful individuals.

[Stay'n Out is a modified TC for substance abusers in a prison setting and the prototype of such programs worldwide.]

APPENDIX C: ASSESSMENT INSTRUMENTS AVAILABLE FOR USE IN THERAPEUTIC COMMUNITIES

De Leon, G., & Melnick, G. (1993[c]) *Therapeutic Community Scale of Essential Elements Questionnaire (SEEQ)*. New York City: Community Studies Institute, 2 World Trade Center, 16th Floor 10048.

> The SEEQ assesses the extent to which a program has the generic characteristics of a therapeutic community (TC). The SEEQ measures the TC perspective, treatment approach and structure, community as therapeutic agent, education and work activities, formal therapeutic elements, and process.

Melnick, G., & De Leon, G. (1998). *The Client Matching Protocol (CMP)*. (Developed with funding from NIDA Grant #3 R01 DA08750, Rockville, MD). New York City: Center for Therapeutic Community Research at NDRI, Inc., 2 World Trade Center, 16th Floor 10048.

> The CMP objectively assesses the appropriateness of the match between client and three TC-oriented treatment settings: short-term residence, long-term residence, and ambulatory outpatient. The CMP criteria are based on patterns of drug use, previous long abstinence, criminal activity, and habilation.

Jainchill, N., Messina, M., & Yagelka, J. (1997). *Treatment Environmental Risk Index (TERI)*. (Developed with funding from NIDA Grant #R01 DA09896, Rockville, MD). New York City: Center for Therapeutic Community Research at NDRI, Inc., 2 World Trade Center, 16th Floor 10048.

> The TERI is a 100-item checklist that measures three different dimensions of the TC treatment environment. The physical dimension measures the physical aspects of the setting; the milieu dimension is concerned with the program's relationships with criminal justice, family, and the external community; and the program dimension assesses more specific aspects of the program, e.g., strictness of the rules and regulations.

Sacks, S. (1995). *Program Monitoring Form (PMF)*. (Developed with funding from Grant #1 UD3 SMTI51558-02, Center for Mental Health Services [CMHS]/Center for Substance Abuse Treatment [CSAT], Rockville, MD). New York City: Center for Therapeutic Community Research (CTCR) at NDRI, Inc., 2 World Trade Center, 16th Floor 10048.

> The PMF is a self-report instrument with demonstrated utility in measuring program fidelity. The client is asked to report whether or not each intervention occurred and, if so, whether or not the activity contained each of its defining components. The PMF assesses the fidelity between the intervention as designed, as outlined in the program description, and as delivered.

425

De Leon, G. (1992). *CTCR Baseline Interview Protocol.* New York City: Center for Therapeutic Community Research (CTCR) at NDRI, Inc., 2 World Trade Center, 16th Floor 10048.

The CTCR Baseline Interview Protocol is an instrument that provides a comprehensive description of new clients for reporting and comparison purposes. It measures demographic characteristics, psychosocial history, drug use, and medical, criminal, and legal history.

De Leon, G. (1993[c]). *Circumstances, Motivation, and Readiness (CMR) Scales for Substance Abuse Treatment.* New York City: Center for Therapeutic Community Research at NDRI, Inc., 2 World Trade Center, 16th Floor 10048.

The CMR Intake Version is a client self-report instrument that measures circumstances 1 (external pressure to enter treatment), circumstances 2 (external pressure to leave treatment), motivation (to change), and readiness (for treatment).

Melnick, G., & De Leon, G. (1996[c]). *Perception of Treatment Suitability Scales (PTSS).* (Developed with funding from NIDA Grant #R43 DA08972, Rockville, MD). New York City: Center for Therapeutic Community Research at NDRI, Inc., 2 World Trade Center, 16th Floor 10048.

The PTSS measures client subjective preference for treatment, including detoxification, drug-free outpatient treatment, methadone maintenance outpatient treatment, short-term residential treatment, and long-term residential treatment.

Jainchill, N., & De Leon, G. (1987). *The TC Client Progress Scales (TCCPS).* (Developed with funding from NIDA Grant #R01 DA 03617, Rockville, MD). New York City: Center for Therapeutic Community Research at NDRI, Inc., 2 World Trade Center, 16th Floor 10048.

The TCCPS instrument provides client and staff ratings of client participation in program activities. The TCCPS measures progress as a role model; attitude, motivation, and participation; performance on job functions; participation in therapeutic groups, and relations with others.

Kressel, D., & De Leon, G. (1998[c]). *The Client Assessment Inventory (CAI); The Client Assessment Summary (CAS); The Staff Assessment Summary (SAS).* (Developed with funding from NIDA Grant #5K21 DA00239, Rockville, MD). New York City: Center for Therapeutic Community Research at NDRI, Inc., 2 World Trade Center, 16th Floor 10048.

The CAI, CAS, and SAS instruments assess client progress along 14 clinically relevant domains under 4 broad dimensions: the developmental dimension, socialization dimension, psychological dimension, and community membership dimension.

Name Index

Note: Page numbers followed by letters *f, n,* and *t* indicate figures, notes, and tables, respectively.

Subject Index

Note: Page numbers followed by letters *f, n,* and *t* indicate figures, notes, and tables, respectively.